The Scots Overseas:
Emigrants and Adventurers from Aberdeen and North East Scotland, Fife, Moray and Banff, Angus and Perth, Southern Scotland, Glasgow and the West of Scotland, Orkney and Shetland, The Lothians and The Northern Highlands

I0126331

David Dobson

HERITAGE BOOKS
2008

HERITAGE BOOKS

AN IMPRINT OF HERITAGE BOOKS, INC.

Books, Cds, and more—Worldwide

For our listing of thousands of titles see our website
at
www.HeritageBooks.com

Published 2008 by
HERITAGE BOOKS, INC.
Publishing Division
100 Railroad Ave. #104
Westminster, Maryland 21157

Copyright © 2000 David Dobson

Other books by the author:

The Mariners of the Lothians, 1600-1800
Scottish Goldsmiths, 1600 - 1800
Scottish Soldiers in Continental Europe
Scottish Soldiers 1600-1800
A Directory of Scots in Australasia 1788-1900
Irish Wills and Testaments in Great Britain 1600-1700
The Mariners of the Clyde and Western Scotland 1600-1800
Scottish Schoolmasters of the Seventeenth Century
Scottish Seafarers 1800-1830
Mariners of Aberdeen and Northern Scotland, 1600-1800
Burgess Rolls of Fife 1700-1800 and St. Andrew's 1700-1750
Mariners of Angus, 1600-1800
Scottish Whalers
Mariners of Kirkcaldy, St. Andrews, and Fife, 1600-1800

All rights reserved. No part of this book may be reproduced or
transmitted in any form or by any means, electronic or mechanical,
including photocopying, recording or by any information storage
and retrieval system without written permission from the author,
except for the inclusion of brief quotations in a review.

International Standard Book Numbers
Paperbound: 978-01-58549-589-4
Clothbound: 978-0-7884-7039-4

EMIGRANTS AND ADVENTURERS
from
Aberdeen and North East Scotland

INTRODUCTION

Emigration has been for several centuries a feature of the demography of north eastern Scotland. The intensity and direction of this emigration has changed significantly from being relatively small scale and directed towards continental Europe in the early modern period to being substantial and channeled towards North America and Australasia from the mid-nineteenth century onwards. During the seventeenth century much of movement of people from north eastern Scotland was determined by economic opportunity, especially as soldiers of fortune or merchants, in Sweden, Poland, and the Netherlands but by the nineteenth century emigration was motivated by opportunities in the developing colonies and the United States as farmers, planters, merchants, administrators, physicians, teachers, clergymen and soldiers. The evidence which identifies those who left their native land to settle abroad, either permanently or temporarily, is far from complete but there is sufficient to establish the diverse destinations and range of social and vocational backgrounds of those involved.

David Dobson
St Andrews, 1993.

1

ARCHIVES

PRO Public Record Office, London

    AO Audit Office
    CO Colonial Ofice
    PCC Prerogative Court of Canterbury

SRO Scottish Record Office, Edinburgh

    CC Commissary Court
    CS Court of Session
    JC Justiciary Court
    RD Register of Deeds
    RS Register of Sasines
    SH Services of Heirs

USNA United States National Archives, Washington, D.C.

NEHGS New England Historical and Genealogical Society, Boston: Scots Charitable Society MS

PANS Public Archives of Nova Scotia, Halifax

PUBLICATIONS ETC.

ABR Aberdeen Burgess Register
AJObits Aberdeen Journal Obituaries
ANQ Aberdeen Notes and Queries
ANY Biographical Register of the St Andrews Society of New York, A. McBean (New York 1922)
APB Aberdeen Propinquity Books MS
AUR Aberdeen University Review
BA List of Officers of the Bengal Army, 1758- , V.C.P.Hodson, (London, 1945)
BBR Banff Burgess Register

2

Caribeanna, series (London 1910-)
CRA The Jacobite Cess Roll for the
County of Aberdeen in 1715,
A. & H. Tayler, (Aberdeen 1932)
EMA List of Emigrant Ministers to
America, 1696-1811),
G. Fothergill, (London, 1904)
ESG A List of the Early Settlers of
Georgia, E.M.Coulter & A.B.Saye,
(Baltimore, 1983)
F Fasti Ecclesiae Scoticanae, H.
Scott, (Edinburgh 1928)
FHR Florida Historical Review (series)
FPA Fulham Papers in the Lambeth
Palace Library, W.W.Manross,
(Oxford 1965)
GM Gentleman's Magazine (series)
IT Indian Traders of the
southeastern Spanish
borderlands, W.S.Coker &
T.D.Watson, (Florida 1986)
JAB Jacobites of Aberdeen and Banff,
A.M.Taylor, (Aberdeen 1934)
KCA Officers and Graduates of the
University and King's College,
Aberdeen, P.J.Anderson,
(Aberdeen, 1893)
MBR Montrose Burgess Roll
NS Northern Scotland, series
PSAS Proceedings of the Society of
Antiquaries of Scotland, series
RGS Register of the Great Seal of
Scotland, series
TOF Thanage of Fermartyn
(Aberdeen 1894)

ABBREVIATIONS   cnf confirmation
g/s gravestone
pro probate

3

EMIGRANTS AND ADVENTURERS FROM ABERDEEN AND NORTH EAST SCOTLAND, PART ONE.

ABERCROMBIE, William, born 1632, son of Rev. Andrew Abercrombie and Margaret Forbes in Fintray, Aberdeenshire, settled in Poland 1648, birth brief 1661. (APB)(F.6.56)

ABERNETHY, George, merchant in Aberdeen and Jamaica, 1751. (SRO.RD4.177.311)

ADAMS, Captain Henry, born in Aberdeen, Revenue Surveyor to the Rajah of Satara, died in Satara, East Indies, 4.6.1829. (A.J.Obits.)

ADDISON, Alexander, born in Keith, educated at Marischal College, Aberdeen, 1777, schoolmaster in Aberlour, married Jean Grant (born 1763) in 1786, judge of Washington County, America, died 24.11.1807. (F.6.394)

AIDY, Alexander, son of David Aidy, burgess of Aberdeen, and Catherine Burnet, emigrated from Aberdeen ca. 1637, settled in Danzig, birth brief 1670. (APB)

AIKEN, Roger, Episcopalian minister in Aberdeen and in Canada, M.A. King's College, Aberdeen, 1805. (KCA.2.398)

ALEXANDER, Thomas, born 1805 son of James Alexander and Margaret Crombie in Aberdeen, educated at King's College, Aberdeen, 1820 -1824, minister in Cobourg, Canada. (KCA.2.441)

ALLAN, Alexander, born 1798 in Morayshire, house-carpenter, naturalised in South Carolina 16.8.1847. (US.NA.M1183, roll 1)

ALLAN, Jean, prisoner in Aberdeen Tolbooth, sentenced to be transported beyond the seas 20.9.1800. (SRO.JC11.44)

ALLAN, Peter Duncan, mariner in Chewton, Victoria, Australia, son of William Allan, merchant in Aberdeen, who died 27.7.1848. (SRO.SH.1864)

ALLARDYCE, Frank, son of Rev. William Allardyce and Nancy Cruickshank in Rhynie, employee of the Honourable East India Company, died in Madras 6.6.1841. (F.6.330)

AMSLEY, Alexander, born 1776 Aberdeen, mariner, naturalised in South Carolina 24.7 .1804. (US.NA.M1183)

ANDERSON, Alexander, son of Alexander Anderson in Drumblade, educated at King's College, Aberdeen, 1825, surgeon in America. (KCA.2.456)

ANDERSON, Alexander, Aberdeenshire, estate manager, Carriacou, 1782. (PSAS.114.494)

ANDERSON, Andrew, Aberdeenshire, estate manager, Carriacou, Grenadines, 1782. (PSAS.114.494)

ANDERSON, Helen, wife of Alexander Stewart soldier in the McLeod Fencibles, prisoner in Aberdeen Tolbooth, banished from Scotland 25.4.1800. (SRO.JC11.44)

ANDERSON, John, from Boharm, Banffshire, surgeon in St Michael's parish, Barbados, pro 2.12.1714 Barbados, RB6/41/9

ANDERSON, Thomas Gordon, in Collendina, New South Wales, brother of William Torry Anderson in Aberdeen who died 15.10.1863. (SRO.SH.1865)

ANGUS, George, born 12.10.1794 son of Rev. Alexander Angus and Katherine Mair in Botriphnie, physician in the service of the Honourable East India Company, died in Aberdeen 7.4.1872. (F.6.302)

ANGUS, William, born 10.2.1771, son of William Angus and Elspeth Mortimer in Aberdeen, educated at King's College, Aberdeen, 1784-88, surgeon in Jamaica. (KCA.2.362)

ARBUTHNOTT, John, born 1762 son of Robert Arbuthnott and Mary Urquhart in Aberdeenshire, merchant in Rotterdam, died in Curacao 1785. (History of the Family of Urquhart, p207, Aberdeen 1946)

ARBUTHNOTT, William, born 1766, son of Robert Arbuthnott of Haddo-Rattray and Mary Urquhart, planter in Carriacou, Grenadines, 1783-, returned to Scotland before 1804. (PSAS.114.482)

ASHER, John Gordon, born 31.5.1837, son of Rev. William Asher and Katherine Forbes in Inveraven, surgeon major in Bombay. (F.6.345)

BAIN, John, educated at King's College, Aberdeen, 1820, minister and author in Galt, Ontario. (KCA.2.439)

BALNEAVES, Isabel, Links of Arduthy, Fetteresso, prisoner in Aberdeen Tolbooth, banished from Scotland 27.4.1799. (SRO.JC11.43)

BANNERMAN, Alexander, ba. 16.1.1786 in Aberdeen, son of Charles Bannerman and Margaret Wilson, soldier 1804-1825, Captain 20th Native Infantry, Bengal Army, married Penelope Smith in Cawnpore 1822, died Arakan 19.7.1825. (BA.1.88)

BARCLAY, James, born 1617, son of Rev. James Barclay and Bessie Duncan in Drumbled, settled in Memel, Prussia, 1635, birth brief 1661. (APB)

BARCLAY, William, born 1626, son of Rev. James Barclay and Bessie Duncan in Drumbled, settled in "Dutchylle", Prussia, 1643, birth brief 1661. (APB)

BARTHOLEMEW, John, from Aberdeen, married Catrijn Pieters from Antwerp in Gouda, Netherlands, 13.5.1590. (Gouda Marriage Register)

BARTLETT, Patrick, formerly in Banff then in Carriacou, by Grenada, later in London, executor of Joseph Cumming 1799. (SRO.CC8.8.131)

BAXTER, William, born in Aberdeen 1756, mariner, deserted from transport ship Pacific, master James Dunn, in New York 1777. (N.Y. Gazette and Mercury, 30.6.1777)

BEATTIE, James, servant at the Mains of Arbuthnott, prisoner in Aberdeen Tolbooth, banished from Scotland 28.5.1798. (SRO.JC11.43)

BELLENDEN, George, born in Aberdeen 1718, studied medicine, surgeon of the Swedish East India Company in 1740s, merchant in Gothenburg, Sweden, married Sarah Chambers 1747, burgess 1752, died in Gothenburg 5.2.1770. (AUR.42.40)(NS7.1.145)

BIRNIE, George, born in Aberdeen 1778, merchant in Charleston, naturalised in South Carolina 19.10.1818. (US.NA.M1183)

BIRNIE, John, born in Aberdeen 1787, millwright in Charleston, naturalised in South Carolina 11.10.1828. (US.NA.M1183)

BISSET, Samuel, born 1793 Aberdeenshire, saddler, wife Anne - born Banffshire 1793, naturalised New York 20.4.1821,

BLACK, Alexander, son of Gilbert Black, baillie of Aberdeen, and Isobel Duncan, emigrated from Aberdeen to Danzig in 168-, merchant in Posna, Poland, birth brief 1698. (APB)

BLACK, John, born 1762, merchant and member of HM Council at Halifax, Nova Scotia, died 9.1823 Summerhill, Aberdeen. (Newm ıchar g/s)

BLACK, George Watson, born 1796 son of Thomas Black and Margaret Innes in Aberdeen, educated at King's College, Aberdeen, 1809-1813, settled in America. (KCA.2.405)

BLACKHALL, William, in the University of "Bromyberrie", Prussia, son of Robert Blackhall, burgess of Aberdeen, and Elspeth Shand, birth brief 1647. (APB)

BLAIR, James, born 7.11.1792, son of James Blair, merchant in Stonehaven, and Elizabeth Taylor-Imrie, soldier 1809-1847, Lieutenant Colonel 5th Native Infantry, Bengal Army, married Charlotte Cecilia Van Renen 1827, died at sea 12.8.1847. (BA.1.159)

BOWIE, John H., born 1807 son of William Bowie in Aberdeen, to New York 1825, leather merchant in New York, married Mary Jane Busby, died 3.7.1859 Brooklyn. (ANY.II

BOYES, John, born 1651 son of Thomas Boyes, treasurer and councillor of Aberdeen, and Elspet Birnie, settled in Amsterdam, Holland, birth brief 1674. (APB)

BRAND, James, Aberdeen, house-carpenter in Carriacou, Grenadines, died 1776. (PSAS.114.494)

BRAND, Margaret, from Aberdeen, married George Mein, a soldier from St Andrews, in Geertruidenberg, Netherlands, 23.5.1638. (Geertruidenberg Marriage Register)

BREBNER, Archibald, born in Aberdeen 1770, merchant tailor, naturalised in South Carolina 16.5.1805.(US.NA.M1183)

BRODIE, Alexander, born 1738, son of Alexander Brodie of Windyhills, Morayshire, and Ann Dawson, merchant in Windyhills, St Mary's parish, Antigua, married Ann Kidder (1730-1801) in 1766, died in Antigua 1800. (Caribeanna 1.98)

BRODIE, Thomas, from Aberdeen, factor in Charleston, South Carolina, pro 27.7.1798 S.C.

BRUCE, Alexander, born 1789 in Aberdeen, grocer, emigrated from Grangemouth to New York, naturalised 18.4.1821 New York.

BOTHWELL, John, from Aberdeen, perukemaker in Charleston, South Carolina, pro 13.10.1777 S.C.

BRAN, Alexander, from Aberdeen, member of the Scots Charitable Society of Boston 1733. (NEHGS)

BROWN, Gordon, born 2.7.1784, son of Rev. Alexander Brown and Isabella Ord in Spynie, physician, died in Demerara 16.7.1813. (F.6.407)

BROWN, Louisa, born 22.6.1795, son of Rev. Alexander Brown and Isabella Ord in Spynie, married William Willox of the Ordnance Department, died in Sierra Leone 21.3.1826. (F.6.407)

BRUCE, James, in Australia, nephew of James Bruce of Inverquhomery who died 16.5.1862. (SRO.SH.1862)

BUCHAN, George, son of Robert Buchan of Portlethan and Marjorie Patrick, emigrated 1647, settled in Lublin, Poland, birth brief 1677. (APB)

BURGESS, James, in Demerara and Essequibo, son of William Burgess, tenementer in Rothes, who died 11.1831. (SRO.SH.1867)

BURNETT, James, merchant in Danzig, son of Thomas Burnett of Camphill and Margaret Keith, birth brief 1652. (APB)

CALDER, Archibald, Commisary of Stores in Antigua, burgess of Banff 1768. (BBR)

CAMPBELL, Alexander, merchant in Amsterdam, burgess of Aberdeen, 7.3.1682. (ABR)

CAMPBELL, Duncan, surgeon HEICS, Fort Marlborough, Sumatra, father of Margaret, cnf 1796 Aberdeen

CARMICHAEL, James, born 1754 Aberdeenshire, emigrated to America 1778, settled Pictou, Nova Scotia, 1783, buried New Glasgow, Nova Scotia. (PANS.MG100/224/30)

CARNEGIE, John William, b. 21.4.1814 in Aberdeen, son of David Carnegie, surgeon in Bombay, and Anne ..., soldier 1832-1862, Major of the Bengal Army, married Jane Scott in Calcutta 1838, died 6.1.1874 England. (BA.1.306)

CASSIE, James, prisoner in Aberdeen Tolbooth, banished from Scotland for 7 years 16.4.1796. (SRO.JC11.42)

CHALMER, Alexander, son of William Chalmer in Standingstones, Dyce, and Marjory Thomson, emigrated 1659, merchant in Varso, Poland, birth brief 1670. (APB)

CHALMER, Bartle, in Poland, son of William Chalmer and Agnes Kellie in Pitmeddan, birth brief 1648. (APB)

CHALMER, Sir James, in Silesia, Germany, son of Gilbert Chalmer, burgess of Aberdeen, and Christian Con, birth brief 1670. (APB)

CHALMER, Robert, merchant in Danzig, son of Gilbert Chalmers in Kintore and Elspet Reid, birth brief 1671. (APB)

CHEYNE, George, born 25.7.1802, son of William Cheyne, farmer in Auchterless, and Elizabeth Harper, educated at King's College, Aberdeen, 1818-18122, minister in Hamilton, Ontario. (KCA.2.434)

CHEYNE, John, burgess of Zakroczim in Masovia, Poland, son of William Cheyne of Baybush and Elisabeth Troup, birth brief 1637. (APB)

CHEYNE, John, in Pitercow, Poland, son of Thomas Cheyne of Pitfichie and Catherine Fraser, birth brief1646. (APB)

CHISHOLM, Adam, prisoner in Stonehaven Tolbooth, banished from Scotland 1799. (SRO.JC11.44)

CHISHOLM, Anne, prisoner in Stonehaven Tolbooth, banished from Scotland 1799. (SRO.JC11.44)

CHRISTIE, Alexander, son of Alexander Christie, merchant in Aberdeen, educated at King's College, Aberdeen, 1812, Hudson Bay Company employee. (KCA.2.415)

CHRISTIE, David, from Fraserburgh, member of the Scots Charitable Society of Boston 1743. (NEHGS)

CHRISTIE, George, born in Aberdeen 1735, indentured servant who ran away from his master George Burns, tavernkeeper, King's Head, New York City 20.2.1761. (New York Mercury, 2.3.1761)

CLARK, Alexander, son of Rev. George Clark and Isabel Fraser, emigrated from Aberdeen to Danzig 1693, merchant in Cracow, Poland, birth brief 1705. (APB)

CLAYTON, Captain James, died at Miramachi 18.5.1818, aged 27.(Banff g/s)

CLUB, Alexander, born 1767 in Fraserburgh, merchant, naturalised in South Carolina 25.9.1802. (US.NA.M1183)

COBBAN, James, son of James Cobban, merchant in Aberdeen, educated at King's College, Aberdeen, 1814, surgeon in Canada. (KCA.2.422)

COLLY, Francis, baptised 7.8.1748 son of John Colly in Mill of Kennarty, Peterculter, emigrated 1770, builder and architect, died 26.11.1781 in St John, Antigua. (ANQ.2.251)

COMBIE, James, died at Montreal 18.. (Banff g/s)

CONNON, Alexander Webster, in Cremore, County Wexford, Ireland, son of James Connon there once in Aberdeenshire who died 8.5.1865. (SRO.SH.1867)

COPLAND, Charles, born 9.6.1791, son of Patrick Copland and Elisabeth Ogilvie, educated at King's College, Aberdeen, 1805/09, settled in Jamaica. (KCA.2.396)

COUTTS, James, merchant in Crosna, Poland, then in Danzig, son of Robert Coutts of Auchtercoull and Jean Gordon, birth brief 1646. (APB)

COUTTS, James Cock, in Hong Kong formerly a wine merchant in Calcutta, son of John Couts, surgeon in Fraserburgh, who died 20.6.1843. (SRO.SH.1861)

CROMBIE, William, from Morayshire, member of the Scots Charitable Society of Boston 1745. (NEHGS)

CROOKSHANK, Benjamin, born in Aberdeen 1723, architect and cabinetmaker in New York, married Miss Beane 1758, died 14.8.1819, buried in St Paul's, New York. (ANY.I.201)

CRUDEN, Rev. Alexander, formerly in Farnham, Virginia, then in Aberdeen. pro 6.1792 PCC

CRUICKSHANKS, Alexander, from Banffshire, member of the Scots Charitable Society of Boston 1769. (NEHGS)

CRUICKSHANKS, Captain Charles, (American Loyalist?), from Haverford, Pennsylvania, settled in Elgin, cnf 13.8.1785 Moray.

CRUICKSHANKS, George, born 1796 in Rhynie, emigrated to Quebec 1817, settled in Laurens District, South Carolina, naturalised S.C. 1819. (S.C.Archives Mf.69)

CRUIKSHANK, James, indentured servant, to Carriacou, Grenadines, 1804. (PSAS.114.499)

CRUIKSHANK, William, born 6.1760 son of Theodore Cruikshank and Jane Allen in Boynsmill, Aberdeen, to Jamaica 1781, later a carpenter in New York, married Sarah Allen in New York 1795, died 9.1.1831. (ANY.I.390)

CRUICKSHANKS, William, born in Morayshire 1775, shoemaker, naturalised in South Carolina 15.8.1805. (US.NA.M1183)

CUMMING, Joseph, in Carriacou, by Grenada, cnf 3.7.1799 Edinburgh

DAVIDSON, Alexander, from Aberdeen, member of the Scots Charitable Society of Boston 1745. (NEHGS)

DAVIDSON, Charles, son of John Davidson of Tillychetly, educated at King's College, Aberdeen 1790/94, physician in Grenada, died 2.10.1804 in St George's, Grenada. (KCA.2.371)(A.J.Obits.)

DAVIDSON, John, Aberdeen, a former exile in Barbados, burgess of Aberdeen 14.11.1666. (ABR)

DAVIDSON, WILLIAM, Aberdeen, merchant in Riga, cnf 1782 Edinburgh

DINGWALL, Arthur Fordyce, ba. 26.8.1789 son of Rev. William Dingwall in Forgue, Aberdeenshire, soldier 1806-1830, Captain of 19th Native Infantry, Bengal Army, died Muttra 16.12.1830. (BA.2.64)

DINGWALL-FORDYCE, Arthur, ba. 12.7.1783, son of Arthur Dingwall-Fordyce of Culsh and Janet Morrison, soldier 1797-1812, Chief Engineer in Penang, died at sea 22.12.1812. (BA.2.204)

DONALDSON, John, prisoner in Aberdeen Tolbooth, banished from Scotland for 7 years 16.4.1796. (SRO.JC11.42)

DONALDSON, Robert, from Fyvie, planter in St Andrew's parish, Georgia, pro 10.10.1769 Georgia.

DOUGAL, Alexander, born 21.1.1782 son of Dr Hugh Dougal and Jean Seaton in Forres, soldier 1798-1802, Lieutenant of the 1st Native Infantry, Bengal Army, died Midnapore 18.12.1802. (BA.2.70)

DRUMMOND, John, merchant in Amsterdam, burgess of Aberdeen, 2.11.1698. (ABR)

DUFF, James, late of Madeira, died 1.4.1812, aged 71. (Banff ç/s)

DUFF, Patrick, born 28.3.1751, son of Patrick Duff of Whitehill and Crowie and Clementina Hay, soldier 1769(?)-1785, Captain of Bengal Army, died 1785 India. (BA.2.92)

DUFF, Patrick, born 1742, son of James Duff of Pitchaish, soldier 1760-1797, married (1) Anne Duff (2) Dorothea Hay, Major general of the Bengal Army, died in Edinburgh 2.2.1803. (BA.2.91)

DUFF, William, from Banffshire, member of the Scots Charitable Society of Boston 1760. (NEHGS)

DUFF, William, son of James Duff of Pitchaish, soldier 1777-1807, Lieutenant Colonel, 9th Native Infantry, Bengal Army, died Komona 18.11.1807. (BA.2.92)

DUFF, William, St George, Grenada, burgess of Banff 1797. (BBR)

DUFF, William Latimer, born 12.10.1822 son of Rev. William Duff and Mary Steinson in Grange, Strathbogie, U.S. Army General, died 27.6.1894. (F.6.315)

DUGAT, Robert, emigrated from Aberdeen ca 1639, settled in Poland, son of Robert Dugat, portioner of Ruthven, Aberdeenshire, and Marie Forbes, birth brief 1669. (APB)

DUGUID, William, born 31.10.1747 son of William Duguid in Old Meldrum, member of the Scots Charitable Society of Boston 1769. (NEHGS)

DUNBAR, James, Captain HEICS, son of James Dunbar of Kincorthy, cnf 1749 Aberdeen

DUNBAR, William, born 13.11.1740 son of Robert Dunbar in Dyke, Forres, member of the Scots Charitable Society of Boston 1766. (NEHGS)

DUNCAN, David, from Aberdeenshire, member of the Scots Charitable Society of Boston 1767. (NEHGS)

DUNCAN, James, from Elgin, settled in Charleston, naturalised in South Carolina 23.4.1839. (US.NA.M1183)
DUNN, William, from Aberdeen, member of the Scots Charitable Society of Boston 1741. (NEHGS)
DUTTART, Robert, from Aberdeen, workman in Amsterdam, married Anna Jansen in Delft, Netherlands, 9.3.1603. (Delft Marriage Register)
FAIRBAIRN, Francis, born 23.8.1770 son of James Fairbairn in Tarland and Migvie, Aberdeenshire, grocer in New York, married (1) Eliza Ten Eyck 1779 (2) Mrs Margaret Campbell, died 29.10.1830 Belleville, New York. (ANY.I.366)
FARQUHAR, Alexander, born 27.10.1761 son of Alexander Farquhar in Kintore, educated at King's College, Aberdeen, 1781, settled in Antigua. (KCA.2.357)
FARQUHAR, Allan, in Ban Ban, Queensland, son of Nathaniel Farquhar, advocate in Aberdeen, who died 19.7.1861. (SRO.SH.1864)
FARQUHAR, Robert, born 1635 son of Archibald Farquhar of Dillabe, Monymusk, and Margaret Ritchie, emigrated 1650, merchant in Lublin, Poland, birth brief 1687. (APB)
FARQUHAR, Robert, merchant in Poisnay, Poland, son of William Farquhar in Dillab and Jean Mercer, birth brief 1642. (APB)
FARQUHAR, Robert, son of John and Elizabeth Farquharson in Aberdeen, merchant in Charleston, South Carolina, pro 17.2.1784 Charleston
FARQUHAR, Robert, Lieutenant, Honourable East India Company Service, son of James Farquhar of Tullos, Aberdeenshire, 1832. (SRO.SH.1832)
FARQUHAR, William, born ca. 1627 son of Archibald Farquhar of Dillabe, Monymusk, and Margaret Ritchie, emigrated 1639, merchant in Lishna, Poland, birth brief 1687. (APB)
FARQUHARSON, John, physician in Charlestown, South Carolina, died in Aberdeen, pro 1.1791 PCC
FARQUHARSON, Robert Alexander, physician in Berlin, son of Donald Farquharson, postmaster in Ballater, who died 20.12.1852. (SRO.SH.1868)
FERGUSON, Charles, born 8.1708 son of Rev. Adam Ferguson and Mary Gordon in Crathie, died in Port Royal, Jamaica, 18.3.1747. (F4.189)
FERGUSON, JAMES, in Aberdeen, applied to settle in Canada 3.4.1827. (PRO.CO384.5.843)
FERGUSON, James, son of Andrew Ferguson, surgeon in Aberdeen, educated at King's College, Aberdeen, 1816-1820, Rector of Rutgers College, New Jersey, Superintendent of Public Schools in Lockport, New York. (KCA.2.427)

FERGUSON, William, ba. 27.5.1803 in St Nicholas, Aberdeen, son of John
    Ferguson and Sarah Mearns, educated at Marischal College, Aberdeen,
    1817-1821, catechist in Canada, Inspector of Schools in Dundas
    County, Ontario. (F.7.633)(KCA.2.430)
FERRIER, William, High Street, Banff, applied to settle in Canada 6.1827.
    (PRO.CO384.5.847)
FERRIS, John, born 1804, advocate in Aberdeen, wife Janet ..., born 1806 in
    Aberdeen, daughter Ellen, born 1828, settled by the Swan River,
    Australia, pre 1830. ("Bound for Australia" p.166, D.T.Hawkings,
    Chichester 1987)
FERRIS, Robert, born in Aberdeen 1810, servant, settled by the Swan River,
    Australia, by 1830. (ibid)
FINDLAY, Alexander, from Aberdeen, settled in St Stephen's parish, South
    Carolina, pro 17.1.1784 Charleston.
FORBES, Alexander, born 1628, son of Alexander Forbes of Drumlasie and
    Isobel Forbes, merchant in Poland 1644-, died 1664(?), birth brief
    1664. (APB)
FORBES, Alexander, born in Peterhead 1783, merchant, naturalised in
    South Carolina on 14.12.1807. (US.NA.M1183)
FORBES, Charles, Captain of the 60th Foot, died at Ticonderoga 1758.
    (Banff g/s)
FORBES, George, son of Captain I. Forbes in Glenconry, died in Bombay
    1804. (A.J.Obits.)
FORBES, James, Boyndlie, merchant in Bombay, 1839. (SRO.SH.1839)
FORBES, Janet, born 1735, daughter of Thomas Forbes of Waterton, and
    Margaret Montgomerie, died in Antigua 1775. (Family of Forbes of
    Waterton, Ped.II; Abdn 1857)
FORBES, Jean, born 1737, daughter of Thomas Forbes of Waterton and
    Margaret Montgomerie, maried Walter Thibou, physician in Antigua.
    (FFW.Ped.II)
FORBES, John, Captain under Major Robert Hog, who died in the Emperor's
    Service, son of Thomas Forbes, baillie in Aberdeen, and Marjory
    Menzies, birth brief 1648. (APB)
FORBES, John, of Alford, merchant in Amsterdam 1751. (SRO.RD4.177.6)
FORBES, John, son of George Forbes of Lockermick, Aberdeenshire, soldier
    1765-1803, Major General of the Bengal Army, married Mrs Isabella
    Hay Bradley in Cawnpore 1787, died Dunbar 2.10.1808. (BA.2.200)
FORBES, John, from Strathdon, educated at King's College, Abedeen, 1758,
    minister in St Augustine, Florida, 1764. (FPA.21.300)(EMA.28)
FORBES, John, born 20.12.1767 son of James Forbes and Sarah Gordon in
    Gamrie, Banffshire, merchant in Florida and the Bahamas, pro
    2.10.1820 Mobile. (Will Book 1)

FORBES, John, born 26.3.1788 in Aberdeen, son of John Forbes of Blackford and Anne Margaret Gregory, soldier 1804- 1805, cadet Bengal Army, died at sea 5.2.1805. (BA.2.201)

FORBES, John, of Skellatur, born 1732, Governor of Rio de Janeiro, died there 8.4.1808. (A.J.Obits.)

FORBES, Lewis Alexander, born 10.3.1823 son of Rev. Lewis Alexander Forbes and Penelope Cowie in Boharm, died in Geelong, New South Wales, 30.4.1852. (F.6.338)

FORBES, Patrick, son of Robert Forbes in Mowny and Margaret Farquhar, emigrated from Aberdeen 1650, settled in Creta, Poland, birth brief 1669. (APB)

FORBES, Roderick, Captain in the Honourable East India Company Service, son of Charles Forbes in Brux, died in Persia 4.1760. (A.J.Obits.)

FORBES, Walter, son of James Forbes in Round Lichnet, Aberdeenshire, and Margaret Black, emigrated from Aberdeen to Danzig 1696, merchant in Columne, Prussia, birth brief 1705. (APB)

FORBES, William, soldier from Aberdeen, married Jenneke Heyndricks in Sluis, Netherlands, 2.11.1626. (Sluis Marriage Register)

FORBES, William, born 1649, son of Alexander Forbes in Drumlasie and Isobel Forbes, settled in Poland 1661, birth brief 1664. (APB)

FORBES, William, son of Margaret Anderson in Aberdeen, vintner in St Michael's parish, Barbados, pro 24.10.1718 Barbados, RB6.4.388

FORBES, William Nairn, born 3.4.1796 in Auchterless, son of John Forbes of Blackford and Anne Margaret Gregory, soldier 1815-1855, Major General of the Bengal Army, married Sarah Greenlaw in Calcutta 1836, died at sea 1.5.1855. (BA.2.202)

FORBES-LEITH, Theodore George, born 7.10.1813, son of George Forbes-Leith of Knock, Aberdeenshire, soldier 1832-1839, Ensign of the Bengal Army, died Arakan 16.7.1839. (BA.3.42)

FORDYCE, Alexander, born 17.2.1786 son of Arthur Dingwall Fordyce and Janet Morrison in Aberdeen, educated at King's College, Aberdeen, 1798, merchant in Canada. (KCA.2.383)

FORDYCE, John, of Ardoe, "he went round the world with Anson", died 1793. (A.J.Obits.)

FORREST, James, born 25.10.1764 son of William Forrest in Cruden, bank accountant in USA, died 20.9.1831. (ANY.I.345)

FORSYTH, James, Lieutenant of the Indian Army, son of Elizabeth Brown (died 28.1.1854) and Rev. Dr James Forsyth in Aberdeen. (SRO.SH.1863)

FORSYTH, John Smith, born 1.1.1840, son of Rev. James Forsyth and Elizabeth Brown in St Nicholas parish, Aberdeen, died in Melbourne 20.11.1885. (F.6.40) { in China 1863: SRO.SH.1863}

FOTHERINGHAM, John, sutler from Aberdeen, admitted as a citizen of
    Leyden, Netherlands, 7.5.1607. (Leyden Citizenship book S.A.II, fo.26)
FOULERTON, Robert, son of Alexander Foulerton in Aberdeen, educated at
    King's College, Aberdeen, 1818, settled in Chicago. (KCA.2.432)
FRASER, Alexander, born 26.9.1811, son of Baillie Alexander Fraser,
    merchant in Forres, and Jane Warden, soldier 1827-1843, Brevet
    Captain, 45th Native Infantry, Bengal Army, died Benares 20.7.1843.
    (BA.2.215)
FRASER Donald, Aberlour, Banffshire, servant of Patrick Grant, emigrated
    from Inverness to Georgia on the Prince of Wales, arrived in
    Georgia 1.1736. (ESG74)
FRASER, Hugh, born in Morayshire 1769, Professor of Divinity in
    Georgetown, naturalised in South Carolina on 21.2.1817.
    (US.NA.M1183)
FRASER, John, born in Aberdeen 1678, to Darien, deserted to the Spanish,
    provided a deposition at Rancho Vieja Bay 28.3.1700. (Audiencia de
    Panama, Archives of the Indies, L.164, Seville)
FRASER, John, son of .... Fraser of Findrack, and grandson of .... Baird of
    Pitmeddan, died in Rome 30.7.1789. (A.J.Obits.)
FRASER, William, in Huntly formerly a farmer in Canada, brother of John
    Fraser, merchant in Huntly, who died 24.5.1863. (SRO.SH.1863)
GALE, Alexander, born 18.12.1800, son of John Gale, farmer in Coldstone,
    Aberdeen, and Jean Esson, educated at King's College, Aberdeen,
    1815-1819, minister in Hamilton, Canada. (KCA.2.423)
GARDYNE, Captain George, in Germany, son of Alexander Gardyne of
    Banchory and Janet Strachan, birth brief1639. (APB)
GARDYNE, Samuel, in Charleston, South Carolina, burgess of Banff 1785.
    (BBR)
GARWEIN, Janneken, born in Aberdeen, married Jacob Hill from Falkirk in
    Schiedam, Netherlands, 10.12.1639. (Schiedam Marriage Register)
GERARD, William, born in Aberdeen, married Christina Glass 17.5.1780,
    settled New York pre 1782, father of William. (ANY.II.16)
GIBBON, John, born 22.11.1784, son of Alexander Gibbon, mariner in
    Aberdeen, and Isabel Duncan, educated at King's College, Aberdeen,
    1798-1802, settled in Canada. (KCA.2.384)
GILLICE, John, son of John Gillice, lawyer in Keith, educated at King's
    College, Aberdeen, 1818-1822, physician in America. (KCA.2.434)
GORDON, A., North Lodge, Aberdeen, former Captain in the Aberdeen Militia,
    applied to emigrate to Canada 22.1.1827. (PRO.CO384.5.853)
GORDON, Adam, "principall and professor of the Greik tongue in the
    colledge of Mell in France", son of William Gordon, baillie of Banff,
    and Elizabeth Chalmer, birth brief 1648. (APB)

GORDON, Adam, born 11.10.1812 son of Rev. William Gordon and Catherine Brodie in Elgin, died Richmond Estate, St Vincent, 23.3.1832. (F.6.391)

GORDON, Alexander, son of Patrick Gordon of Harlaw and Rachel Leslie, emigrated from Aberdeen to Danzig 5.1688, merchant in Presneits, Poland, birth brief 1703. (APB)

GORDON, Alexander, Lieutenant in the Honourable East India Company Service, son of William Gordon of Nethermuir, died in the East Indies 23.8.1793. (A.J.Obits.)

GORDON, Alexander, born 29.5.1805 son of Rev. William Gordon and Catherine Brodie in Elgin, Sheriff Substitute of Sutherland, died in America. (F.6.391)

GORDON, Charles, son of Alexander Gordon, merchant in Aberdeen, and Jean Chalmer, emigrated from Aberdeen 4.1680 to Danzig, merchant in Warsaw, Poland, birth brief 1697. (APB)

GORDON, Lord Henry, son of the Earl of Huntly, in Polish service, burgess of Aberdeen 6.9.1664. (ABR)

GORDON, Hew, in Vangroba, Poland, son of George Gordon of Bray, Rhynnie, and Elspet Anderson, birth brief 1656. (APB)

GORDON, James, son of Patrick Gordon of Harlaw and Rachel Leslie, emigrated from Aberdeen to Danzig 1692, merchant in Culma, Prussia, birth brief 1703. (APB), merchant in Poland 1707. (CRA97)

GORDON, John, in Vangroba, Poland, son of George Gordon of Bray, Rhynnie, and Elspet Anderson, birth brief 1656. (APB)

GORDON, John, in Poland, son of John Gordon, burgess of Aberdeen, and Beatrix Leslie, birth brief 1646. (APB)

GORDON, John, Captain of the Swedish Army, died in Cracow, Poland, 1664, son of William Gordon of Cotton and Marion Gordon, birth brief 1668. (APB)

GORDON, John, son of Patrick Gordon and Marie Home in Aberdeen, minister of Wilmington, James City, Virginia, died 1705, birth brief 1705. (APB) (F.7.368)

GORDON, John, from Aberdeenshire, member of the Scots Charitable Society of Boston 1732. (NEHGS)

GORDON, John, born 24.3.1782 son of Thomas Gordon in Aboyne, educated at King's College, Aberdeen, 1795/99, settled in Jamaica. (KCA.2.379)

GORDON, John, born 19.5.1795 son of Rev. William Gordon and Catherine Brodie in Elgin, surgeon in the Honourable East India Company Service, died at Beni Boo Ali, Persian Gulf, 2.3.1821. (F.6.391)

GORDON, John David, wine-merchant in Xeres de la Frontera, Spain, son of Charles Gordon of Woodside, Aberdeenshire, 1834. (SRO.SH.1834)

GORDON, Marjory, daughter of Patrick Gordon yr of Kincraigie and Elizabeth Gordon, to Germany 1637, birth brief 1637. (APB)

GORDON, Maria de la Concepcion, in Madrid, Spain, sister of John Joseph Gordon of Wardhouse and Kildrummy who died 20.5.1866. (SRO.SH.1867)

GORDON, Nathaniel, born 1687, son of William Gordon of Goval, Aberdeenshire, to Poland 1701. (JAB.1.121)

GORDON, Patrick, in Poland, son of John Gordon, burgess of Aberdeen, and Beatrix Leslie, birth brief 1646. (APB)

GORDON, Patrick, possibly the son of Rev Patrick Gordon in Coull who was educated at Marischal College, Aberdeen, 1699, clergyman, to New York 1702. (EMA.30)

GORDON, Patrick, born 24.1.1770 son of Rev. George Gordon and Cecilia Reid, settled in U.S.A. (F.6.321)

GORDON, Robert, from Aberdeen, married Cecilia Crom from Amsterdam in Schiedam, Netherlands, 31.8.1602. (Schiedam Marriage Register)

GORDON, Robert, in Danzig, son of Alexander Gordon and Janet Maitland, birth brief 1649. (APB)

GORDON, Robert, from Aberdeen, member of the Scots Charitable Society of Boston 1757. (NEHGS)

GORDON, Thomas, born 1.7.1768 son of Rev. George Gordon and Cecilia Reid in Keith, settled in Overhall, Port Maria Bay, Jamaica, died 15.6.1807. (F.6.321)(A.J.Obits.)

GORDON, William, in Vangroba, Poland, son of John Gordon of Ardfork and Marjorie Seaton, birth brief 1655. (APB)

GORDON, William, born 1619, son of James Gordon and Jean Johnstone in Shithine, Tarves, settled in Poltuskie, Poland, birth brief 1655. (APB)

GORDON, William, from Aberdeen, member of the Scots Charitable Society of Aberdeen 1733. (NEHGS)

GRAHAM, James, prisoner in Aberdeen Tolbooth, sentenced to be transported beyond the seas 16.4.1796. (SRO.JC11.42)

GRANT, Anna, born 1.8.1762 daughter of Rev. John Grant and Anna Grant in Elgin, married James Brice, Collector of Revenue in Washington, Pennsylvania, later in Pittsburg. (F.6.394)

GRANT, Euphemia, wife of Rev. Louis A. Sery of the National Reformed Church of France, daughter of Lieutenant Edward Grant, Royal Navy, Rockhouse, Lossiemouth, who died 6.11.1857. (SRO.SH.1861)

GRANT, James, soldier from Elgin, married Ann Lindsay from Dundee in Schiedam, Netherlands, 19.12.1637. (Schiedam Marriage Register)

GRANT, James, prisoner in Aberdeen Tolbooth, banished from Scotland for 14 years, 16.4.1796. (SRO.JC11.42)

GRANT, James, in Hobart Town, Van Dieman's Land, son of James Grant, wheelwright in Nairn, 1836. (SRO.SH.1836)

GRANT, John, born 1718, servant to Patrick Grant, arrived in Georgia 1.1736. (ESG76)

GRANT, Ludovick, born 2.8.1786 in Duthil, Morayshire, son of Ludovick Grant, soldier 1800-1818, Captain of 16th Native Infantry, Bengal Army, died Calcutta 30.8.1818. (BA.2.318)

GRANT, Patrick, born 1712, farmer in Aberlour, Banffshire, arrived in Georgia 1.1736, received a land grant in Savannah, died 1740. (ESG.76)

GRANT, Thomas, Bance Island off the coast of Africa, son of Archibald Grant in Keith, cnf 1793 Edinburgh

GRAY, Mary, prisoner in Aberdeen Tolbooth, sentenced to transportation 14.9.1798. (SRO.JC11.43)

GREIG, Elizabeth, wife of John Manners, weaver in Aberdeen and a travelling chapman, banished from Scotland 25.4.1800. (SRO.JC11.44)

GREIG, William, from Aberdeen, member of the Scots Charitable Society of Boston 1731. (NEHGS)

HALL, Alexander Harvey, in Otago, New Zealand, formerly a Lieutenant in H.M. Indian Navy, grand-nephew of George Hall, housecarpenter in Aberdeen, who died 25.5.1835. (SRO.SH.1865)

HARDIE, James, born 1750 son of John Hardie in Aberdeen, educated at Marischal College, Aberdeen, 1779-1780, and at Columbia College in New York, settled in New York before 1787, teacher and author, died New York 1832. (ANY.I.236)

HAY, John, from Aberdeen, married Susanna Gray from Scotland in Rotterdam 13.2.1633. (Rotterdam Marriage Register)

HENDRIE, John, prisoner in Aberdeen Tolbooth, banished from Scotland 16.4.1796. (SRO.JC11.42)

HENRY, J., late of Aberdeen, died Halifax, Nova Scotia, 1813. (GM.83.670)

HITSEN, John, from Elgin, married Mayken Adriaens in Arnemuiden, Netherlands, 13.4.1630. (Arnemuiden Marriage Register)

HOSSACK, Alexander, probably born 1728 son of Alexander Hossack and Margaret Cook in Elgin, soldier in the French and Indian Wars 1756-1763, merchant in New York, married Jane Arden, father of David, William, Alexander, James and Jane, died 9.1.1826 Hackensack, New York. (ANY.I.206)

HUNTER, George, in Massourie, Upper India, son of Jane Barnes in Aberdeen who died 22.4.1868. (SRO.SH.1869)

INGRAM, George, smith in Banff, then in Trinidad, 1842. (SRO.SH.1842)

INNES, John, son of William Innes, baillie of Nigburgh, Foveran, and Helen Udny, merchant in Posna, Poland, birth brief 1688. (APB)

INNES, Robert, born 14.9.1745, son of Robert Innes, town clerk of Banff, and Margaret Gilchrist, merchant in Gothenburg, Sweden, by 1765, burgess of Montrose 1791, merchant in Newcastle 1795. (MBR)(NS7.1.146)

INNES, Thomas, in Poland, son of Rev. Jerome Innes and Margaret Seaton in Fyvie, birth brief 1652. (APB)

INNES, Thomas, from Banff, member of the Scots Charitable Society of Boston 1748. (NEHGS)

INNES, Walter, son of Alexander Innes of Kininvy, Banffshire, and Christian Young, emigrated from Aberdeen 1642, resident of Paris, France, servant to the Queen Mother of Great Britain, birth brief 1669. (APB)

INNES, William, born 1650 son of John Innes of Knockorth, Banffshire, and Elizabeth Bodie, emigrated 1668, merchant in "Wratslaffsco", Poland, birth brief 1685. (APB)

IRVINE, Charles, born 1693, son of James Irvine of Artamford, Aberdeenshire, and Margaret Sutherland, probably a Jacobite in 1715, merchant in Rouen, France, then a supercargo of the Swedish East India Company of Gothenburg in 1730s, died in Aberdeen 8.10.1771. (NS7.1.146)(AUR.42.43)

IRVINE, Francis, son of Sir Alexander Irvine of Drum, died in France, pro 1680 PCC

IRVINE, Francis, ba. 8.2.1786, son of Alexander Irvine of Drum and Jean Forbes, soldier 1804-1820, Captain of the Bengal Army, married Frances Sophia Harington in Calcutta 1815, died 16.12.1855 in Edinburgh. (BA.2.529)

IRVINE, Dr John, born in Aberdeen 1742, physician, died 15.10.1808 Savanna, Georgia. (Savanna Death Register)

IRVINE, Thomas, born 30.9.1685, son of James Irvine of Artamford, Aberdeenshire, and Margaret Sutherland, merchant in Gothenburg, enobled in Sweden 1757, married Margaret Irvine, died in Gothenburg 2.12.1765. (NS7.1.146)

JACKSON, Samuel, Aberdeen, servant, settled by the Swan River, Aberdeen, by 1830. ("Bound for Australia", p166, D.T.Hawkings, Chichester 1987)

JAMES, John, soldier from Aberdeen, married Elizabeth Steins from Scotland in Rotterdam 19.3.1595. (Rotterdam Marriage Register)

JOHNSTON, John, from Aberdeen, patroon in New Windsor, South Carolina, pro 23.7.1744 S.C.

JONES, Peter (?), "Pieter Jansz", widower from Aberdeen, married Jenneke Adriaens from Flanders, in Dordrecht, Netherlands, 4.12.1583. (Dordrecht Marriage Register)

JONES, Walter (?),"Wouter Jansse", soldier from Aberdeen, married Janetge Leen in Brielle, Netherlands, 8.9.1641. (Brielle Marriage Register)

KEITH, Alexander, from Aberdeen, minister in St Stephen's parish, South Carolina, pro 4.12.1772 S.C.

KEITH, James, from Aberdeen, member of the Scots Charitable Society of Boston 1743. (NEHGS)

KEITH, James, Aberdeen mariner, settled Newport, Rhode Island, pro 3.9.1781 Charleston, South Carolina.

KEITH, James, formerly in Charlestown, South Carolina, then in Blairshinnock, Banffshire, pro 11.1788 PCC

KEITH, John, son of Alexander Keith of Camculter, Rathen, and Margaret Fraser, emigrated 1658, settled in Danzig, birth brief 1672. (APB)

KENNEY, David, from Aberdeen, member of the Scots Charitable Society of Boston 1733. (NEHGS)

KERR, James, born 1797 son of William Kerr and Isobel Cuthill in Aberdeen, died in Mobile, USA, 1831. (Fordoun g/s)

LAURENCE, Andrew, born 3.4.1785 in Dunnottar, son of Andrew Laurence, blacksmith in Gallowton, and Catherine Beattie, died in Trinidad 10.8.1802. (Dunnottar g/s)

LAWRENCE, William, shipwright in Port Adelaide, Australia, son of William Lawrence, overseer at Tochineal, Banffshire, who died 19.9.1860. (SRO.SH.1869)

LEAL, Robert, farmer in Ireland, son of John Leal, farmer in Bogside of Brodie, 1854. (SRO.SH.1854)

LESLIE, Alexander, son of Rev. William Leslie in Rothes, merchant, died in Matanzas, Cuba, 1820. (F6.397)

LESLIE, Alexander James, in Christchurch, New Zealand, grand nephew of Elizabeth Leslie in Aberdeen, widow of William Lindsay. (SRO.SH.1867)

LESLIE, George, Adjutant General of His Imperial Majesty's Army, son of Andrew Leslie, portioner of Logiedurno, and Isabel Stewart, birth brief 1661. (APB)

LESLIE, George, born 1743, of Haddo, Jamaica, died in Old Aberdeen, 1793. (A.J.Obits.)

LESLIE, James, baker from Aberdeen, admitted as a citizen of Leyden, Netherlands, 10.5.1613. (Leyden Citizenship book, S.A.II.fo.70)

LESLIE, Sir James, of Pitcapple, Major General of the French Army, died in Thionville, Luxembourg, 1757. (A.J.Obits.)

LESLIE, James, son of James Leslie in Kair, Kincardineshire, educated at
King's College, Aberdeen, 1801-1802, merchant in Canada.
(KCA.2.389)
LESLIE, James, born 31.5.1797 in Elgin, son of Rev. William Leslie of
Balnageith and Margaret Sinclair, died in Bermuda 4.7.1819. (F.6.397)
LESLIE, John, born 13.10.1749 in Rothes son of Alexander Leslie of
Balnageith and Anna Duff, merchant in St Augustine 1786. (FHR.18.1)
LESLIE, John, born 1765, son of Professor John Leslie and Helen Ker in
Aberdeen, soldier 1782-1813, Major of the 5th Native Infantry,
Bengal Army, died at Rewah 2.12.1813. (BA.3.45)
LESLIE, Robert, born 3.2.1758 in Rothes son of Alexander Leslie of
Balnageith and Anna Duff, merchant in Florida 1792. (IT.19)
LEYS, John, ba. 17.6.1785 in Crathie son of Francis Leys in Inver and Janet
Michie, soldier 1800-1826, Lieutenant Colonel of 29th Native
Infantry, Bengal Army, died at Fatehgarh 14.12.1826. (BA.3.50)
LOGIE, William, born 10.8.1781 son of James Logie and Elizabeth Gordon at
Boat of Bog, Speymouth, Morayshire, soldier 1795-1828, Lieutenant
Colonel of the 34th Native Infantry, Bengal Army, married Elizabeth
Sophia Arnold in Cawnpore 29.8.1807, died at Saugor 13.1.1828.
(BA.3.74)
LOWE, Robert, in Cracow, Poland, son of Robert Lowe, merchant in Old
Aberdeen, who died 10.1707. (SRO.S.H.1715)
LUMSDEN, Thomas, born 12.6.1789 son of Harry Lumsden of Belhelvie and
Pitcaple and Catherine McVeagh, soldier 1807-1844, Colonel of the
Bengal Army, married Hay Burnett 1821, died 8.12.1874 Belhelvie.
(BA.3.96)
LYELL, George Simpson, in New South Wales, son of George Lyell in
Portobello once in Kinneff.   (SRO.SH.1861)
McBEAN, Archibald, born 1719 (?), farmer in Aberlour, wife Catherine
Cameron and son Alexander, emigrated from Inverness on the Prince
of Wales, Captain William Dunbar, to Georgia 20.10.1735, died in
Georgia 1740. (ESG83)
MACHRAY, William, prisoner in Aberdeen Tolbooth, banished from Scotland
23.4.1798. (SRO.JC11.43)
McDONALD, Alexander, in Aberdeen, former Captain of the Florida Rangers,
pro 4.1805 PCC
McHENRY, James, born 1788 in Forres, settled in America 1806, partner in
Andrew Low & Co. in Savanna, died 22.9.1826 Lexington, Oglethorpe
Co., Georgia. (Georgia Republican, 10.10.1826)
McLEAN, James Henderson, in Newry, Ireland, grandson of Robert McLean,
plasterer in Aberdeen, who died 16.2.1844. (SRO.SH.1861)

MacPETRIE, James, son of James MacPetrie in Aberdeen, educated at King's College, Aberdeen, 1815, surgeon in Tobago. (KCA.2.424)

MAIR, John, born 7.3.1798, son of George Mair and Carolina Stewart in Aberdeen, educated at King's College, Aberdeen, 1811-1815, physician and author in Canada. (KCA.2.411)

MAITLAND, William, son of William Maitland of Monletty and Jean Knox, emigrated from Aberdeen ca. 1654, merchant in Poland, birth brief 1670. (APB)

MARSHALL, William, in Australia, grandson of William Sinclair, feuar in Lossiemouth. (SRO.SH.1860)

MAXWELL, Mrs Marion, widow of John Menzies of Pitfoddels, died in Nancy, Lorraine, 25.5.1776. (A.J. Obits.)

MEARNS, Andrew, born in Aberdeen ca.1800, merchant in Savanna, Georgia, died 24.2.1820. (Colonial Museum and Savanna Advertiser, 25.2.1820)

MELDRUM, Thomas, Colonel in the service of the King of Denmark and Norway, burgess of Aberdeen 29.8.1681. (ABR)

MELVILL, Francis, born 12.12.1739 in Durris, son of Rev. Robert Melvill and Janet Greig, educated at Marischal College, Aberdeen, 1756, merchant in Amsterdam. (F.6.53)

MELVILL, John, born 25.2.1747 in Durris, son of Rev.Robert Melvill and Janet Greig, merchant in Amsterdam. (F.6.53)

MENZIES, PAUL, son of Sir Gilbert Menzies of Pitfoddels, a major in Russian service, burgess of Aberdeen 1671. (ABR)

MENZIES, Peter, soldier from Aberdeen, married "Aechtgen" Hay from Scotland in Rotterdam 3.12.1600. (Rotterdam Marriage Register)

MENZIES, Thomas, of Balgonie, Lieutenant Colonel of Russian Army, married Lady Marie Farserson in Riga, father of Thomas Alexander (died in Riga), John Ludovick, and William; died in Ukraine and buried in Szudna 1660, birth brief 1672. (APB)

MERCER, Laurence, merchant traveller in Poland 1649. (ASC.3.35)

MESTON, Rev. William, in Lille, France, brother of Thomas Meston, teacher in Aberdeen, 1851. (SRO.SH.1852)

MIDDLETON, Peter, son of George Middleton and Janet Gordon in Old Aberdeen, to Poland 29.6.1693

MILLEN, John, born in Aberdeen, settled in Savanna, Georgia, 1783, died 28.10.1811. (Savanna Republican, 29.10.1811)

MILNE, Alexander, born 1781, Lieutenant Colonel of the 19th Regiment, died in Demerara 5.11.1827. (Demerara g/s)

MILNE, Robert, born 22.4.1775 son of Rev. James Milne and Jean Milne in Rhynie, merchant in St Domingo, died 9.9.1814. (F.6.330)

MITCHELL, Alexander, from Aberdeen, member of the Scots Charitable Society of Boston 1694. (NEHGS)

MOIR, Gilbert, son of Dr William Moir of Scotstoun and Margaret Skene, emigrated from Aberdeen 1677, settled in Poland, birth brief 1695. (APB)

MOIR, John, from Aberdeen, M.D., member of the Scots Charitable Society of Boston 1703. (NEHGS)

MOIR, William, born 5.10.1777, son of George Moir in Cruden, Peterhead, educated at King's College, Aberdeen, 1792, writer in Edinburgh and Trinidad. (KCA.2.374)

MOLLISON, John, in Buenos Ayres 1851, grandson of John Rhind in Banff. (SRO.SH.1851)

MORDAN, Margaret, born in Turriff, married "Jan Domekenij" from Scotland, in Schiedam, Netherlands, 6.12.1636. (Schiedam Marriage Register)

MORRISON, William, surgeon in Banff, to Jamaica 1784. (PSAS.114.495)

MORRISON, William, son of Theodore Morrison and Catherine Maitland in Bognie, Fyvie, educated at King's College, Aberdeen, barrister in Quebec, married Catherine de Bronyac, settled in Grenada, Chief Justice of the Bahamas, died in Nassau. (TOF.156)

MORTIMER, Edward, born 5.3.1847 son of Edward and Margaret Mortimer in Banff, died in Ceylon 8.2.1871. (Banff g/s)

MORTIMER, William, born 2.1799 son of John Mortimer, fisherman in Aberdeen, and Jean Anderson, educated at King's College, Aberdeen, 1812-1816, merchant in Pictou, Nova Scotia. (KCA.2.414)

MURCHISON, Simon, wife and family in Nairn, applied to settle in Canada 12.3.1819. (PRO.CO.384.5.89)

MUIR, William, born 1575 in Aberdeen, soldier, married Jenneken Jeners, daughter of Alexander Jeners in Aberdeen, in Breda, Netherlands, 8.9.1596. (Breda Marriage Register)

MUNRO, Rev. James, born 1747 in Orbiston, Morayshire, educated at King's College, Aberdeen, 1772, minister in West Nottingham, Maryland, 1785-, in Antigonish, Nova Scotia, 1807-1819, died there 17.5.1819. (F.6.396)

MURDOCH, Alexander Ritchie, in Newcastle, New South Wales, grandson of Alexander Ritchie, sawyer in Forres, who died 17.7.1857. (SRO.SH.1868)

MURRAY, Alexander, born in New Deer, educated at King's College, Aberdeen, 1746, schoolmaster and clergyman in Aberdeenshire, emigrated to New York, missionary in Reading, Pennsylvania 1763, died in Philadelphia 14.9.1793. (F.6.342)

MURRAY, Alexander, born 10.6.1757 son of Rev. Alexander Murray and
Isabel Gordon in Duffus, Morayshire, soldier 1779-1796, Captain of
the Bengal Army, died 6.12.1796 Calcutta. (BA.3.357)
MURRAY, John, born 12.3.1781 son of Andrew Murray and Jean Grant in
Morayshire, soldier 1800-1802, Ensign of the 10th Native Infantry,
Bengal Army, died at Cawnpore 25.4.1802. (BA.3.361)
MURRAY, William, from Banff, member of the Scots Charitable Society of
Boston 1751. (NEHGS)
NICHOLSON, Jean, servant to William Forrest in the Mains of Ludquharn,
Longside, Aberdeenshire, prisoner in Aberdeen Tolbooth, banished
from Scotland 26.4.1799. (SRO.JC11.43)
OFFICER, John, son of George Officer, merchant in Fraserburgh, settled in
Australia pre 1859. (SRO.SH.1859)
OGILVIE, James, born 1747 son of William Ogilvie and Helen Baird in Banff,
died in Jamaica 6.6.1774. (Banff g/s)
OGILVIE, James T., born in Banffshire 1819, clerk in Charleston,
naturalised in South Carolina 27.7.1846. (US.NA.M1183)
OGILVIE, John, born 1753 son of William Ogilvie and Helen Baird in Banff,
died in Antigua 30.8.1770. (Banff g/s)
OGILVIE, Patrick, born 12.9.1774, son of John Ogilvie in Midmar, educated
at King's College, Aberdeen, 1787-1791, surgeon in St Domingo.
(KCA.2.368)
OGILVIE, William, born 1742 son of William Ogilvie and Helen Baird in
Banff, died in Bassora 9.5.1783. (Banff g/s)
OGSTON, William, born 1725 son of William Ogston and Elizabeth Ritchie,
farmer in Aberdour, to New York. (TOF.392)
ORCHARDTON, Sir John, son of Sir Andrew Orchardton of that Ilk,
Aberdeenshire, and Elizabeth Robertson, Captain of the Swedish
Guards 1663. (RGS.II.495)
PANTON, William, born 1740s son of John Panton and Barbara Wemyss in
Aberdour, Fraserburgh, merchant in South Carolina 1765-. (IT
PARK, Ernest Gordon, born in Aberdeen, carpenter, to USA 1842, settled in
Union District, South Carolina, 1842, naturalised S.C. 9.10.1849.
(LDS.Mf.R4646)
PARK, George, born 3.11.1777 in Dunnottar, son of William Park and
Rebecca Middleton, died in Guadaloupe 1807. (Fetteresso g/s)
PATTERSON, Robert, from Old Meldrum, member of the Scots Charitable
Society of Boston 1774. (NEHGS)

PATTILLO, Robert Alexander, born Huntly 17.1.1740, settled Nova Scotia 1780, married Mrs Elizabeth Roberts Bartlett in Liverpool, Nova Scotia, father of Elizabeth, Margaret, Alexander, Thomas, Margaret and James, died 31.12.1833 Chester, NS, buried at St Stephens cemetery. ("Patillo Families", Fort Worth, Texas, 1972)

PAUL, Alexander, born 3.5.1848 Banff, drowned in Lake Huron 7.1870. (Banff g/s)

PIRIE, George, born 9.4.1798 son of John Pirie and Christina Robertson in Cairnie, educated at King's College, Aberdeen, 1817, surgeon in USA. (KCA.2.429)

RAIT, Alexander, from Bervie, member of the Scots Charitable Society of Boston 1746. (NEHGS)

RAIT, Archibald, son of Archibald Rait of Lentush, Old Rayne, and Elizabeth Abercrombie, emigrated 1650, settled in Lisnae, Poland, birth brief 1676. (APB)

RAMSAY, William, in Florence, Italy, 1851, brother of Helen Ramsay in Aberdeen and son of John Ramsay of Barra. (SRO.SH.1851)

READ, William, son of William Read, merchant in Aberdeen, settled in New South Wales pre 1854. (SRO.SH.1854)

REID, JAMES, born 3.1.1777 son of William Reid, town clerk of Banff, and Margaret Innes, merchant in Gothenburg, Sweden, died there 17.3.1813. (NS7.1.147)

REID, John, from Aberdeen, member of the Scots Charitable Society of Boston 1747. (NEHGS)

REID, Robert, ex Aberdeen(?), overseer in Carriacou, Grenadines, 1773-. (PSAS.114.489)

RICE, William, soldier from Aberdeen, married Anna Geertruyt Tomassen from Groningen in Mastricht, Netherlands, 16.7.1662. (Mastricht Marriage Register)

RITCHIE, John, from Aberdeen, member of the Scots Charitable Society of Boston 1729. (NEHGS)

ROBERTSON, Alexander, born 13.5.1772 son of William Robertson and Jean Ross in Aberdeen, educated at King's College, Aberdeen, 1786-1787, to New York 1792, painter in New York, married Janet McLaren 6.8.1806, died 27.5.1841 New York.   (KCA.2.365)(ANY.I.307)

ROBERTSON, Archibald, son of William Robertson in Aberdeen, educated at King's College, Aberdeen, 1783, painter and author in New York. (KCA.2.361)

ROBERTSON, Charles, Aberdeen, pro 10.1697 Barbados RB6.1.22

ROBERTSON, Charles Williams, coffee planter in Ceylon, son of William Robertson, merchant tailor in Aberdeen, who died 18.8.1847. (SRO.SH.1867)

ROBERTSON, James, from Stonehaven, printer, member of the Scots
Charitable Society of Boston 1767. (NEHGS)
ROBERTSON, Thomas, born in Aberdeen 1768, customs officer and city
surveyor, died in Savanna, Georgia, 27.12.1810. (Savanna Daily
Recorder)
ROSS, George, in the Hague, burgess of Aberdeen 19.10.1658. (ABR)
ROSS, George, magistrate in Demerara, son of Charles Ross, merchant in
Aberdeen, 1843. (SRO.SH.1843)
ROSS, James, in Balnamore, Ireland, son of George Ross, carrier in Turriff,
1839. (SRO.SH.1839)
ROSS, Robert, from Aberdeen, merchant in Pensacola, West Florida, 1764-
1772, merchant and planter in Mississippi 1772-1778, American
Loyalist, settled in Shelburne, Nova Scotia, 1780s.
(PRO.AO13.26.414/423)
ROSS, William, from "Tain near Aberdeen", member of the Scots Charitable
Society of Boston 1755. (NEHGS)
ROY, George, born Banffshire 1751, "an early settler ofHalifax", died at
Merigomish, Halifax, North America, 1831. (GM.101.477)
RUSSEL, Errol, born 1773 son of Thomas Russel of Rathen and Anna Innes,
Lieutenant. Royal Marines, died in West Indies 7.1795. (Banff g/s)
RUSSEL, Roddam, born 1781 son of Thomas Russel of Rathen and Anna
Innes, midshipman, died St Domingo 31.10.1797. (Banff g/s)
RUSSEL, Thomas, son of Alexander Russel of Montcoffer, died in Aden
1791. (A.J.Obits.)
RUSSEL, Thomas, born 1772 son of Thomas Russel of Rathen and Anna
Innes, died Martinique 7.1794. (Banff g/s)
SCOTT, John, merchant in Stonehaven, settled in America 1817.
(SRO.CS233.s.1.45)
SCROGGIE, William, merchant in Coleraine, Ireland, grandson of John
Scroggie, dyer in Aberdeen, who died 7.10.1836. (SRO.SH.1865)
SEATON, John, son of William Seaton of Ranistoun and Jean Leith,
emigrated 1653, died in Lublin, Poland, birth brief 1672. (APB)
SEYMOUR, James, from Aberdeenshire, minister in Augusta, Georgia,
c.1775. (see below)
SEYMOUR, John, from Aberdeenshire, planter in St Stephen's parish, South
Carolina, pro 11.6.1775 S.C.
SHAND, David, born13.4.1733 son of James Shand in Forgue, member of the
Scots Charitable Society of Boston 1766. (NEHGS)
SHAND, John, merchant in the West Indies, died 1825. (Fettercairn g/s)

SHAW, David, son of Rev. Lachlan Shaw and Helen Stuart in Elgin, to New York on the Lovely Jane, 1759, merchant in New York, married Polly Dey 24.11.1761, father of Lachlan, William, Janet, and maria, died 1.10.1767 New York, buried in Hackensack graveyard. (ANY.I.84)

SHAW, Lachlan, born 27.1.1729 son of Rev. Lachlan Shaw and Anne Grant, settled in Jamaica, died in London. (F.6.390)

SHEED, George, born 28.9.1790 son of George Sheed and Isabel Murray in St Nicholas parish, Aberdeen, educated at Marischal College, Aberdeen, 1807, minister of Ancaster and Flamborough, Ontario, 1827-1832, died 1832. (F.7.650)

SHEPHERD, John, in Colesberg, Cape of Good Hope, son of Ann Wood, widow of John Shepherd, in Aberdeen who died 3.6.1869. (SRO.SH.1869)

SHERRIFS, David, in St George's Park, son of David Sherrifs in Aberdeen, died in Kingston, Jamaica, 1805. (A.J.Obits.)

SHINNIE, Alexander, born 1782 in Kincardineshire, millwright, settled in Charleston, South Carolina, 1821, naturalised in South Carolina 31.7.1831, died 31.10.1834. (Telescope, 9.11.1834)(US.NA.M1183)

SIBBALD, David, Lieutenant Colonel of the Swedish Army, son of John Sibbald of Keir and Janet Strachan, killed in Germany 9.1641, birth brief 1642. (APB)

"SIJERAER"(?), William, from Turriff, married Margen Aerts in Gouda, Netherlands, 12.5.1603. (Gouda Marriage Register)

SIM, James George, born 4.3.1804 son of James Sim and Elisabeth McKilligan in Banff, MD, HEICS, died 10.9.1830 Singapore. (Banff g/s)

SIM, John, late of Antigua, died 29.11.1807, aged 63. (Banff g/s)

SIMSON, David, of the Bengal Civil Service, son of Rev. Henry Simson, Chapel of Garioch, who died 30.1.1850. (SRO.SH.1866)

SIMPSON, George, born 1849 son of James Simpson and Margaret Milne in Banff, ship-carpenter, died in Adelaide, Australia, 12.1878. (Banff g/s)

SIMPSON, James, in Tobago, burgess of Banff 1773. (BBR)

SIMPSON, John, born 1829 son of James Simpson and Margaret Milne in Banff, shipmaster, died in Demerara 8.1867. (Banff g/s)

SIMPSON, William, born 1831 son of James Simpson and Margaret Milne in Banff, seaman, died in Calcutta 4.7.1853. (Banff g/s)

SIVERTSEN, Peter, from Aberdeen, married Aeltje Aerntsen in Utrecht, Netherlands, 2.4.1637. (Utrecht Marriage Register)

SKENE, George, son of Andrew Skene in Aberdeen, minister in Prince Frederick's parish, South Carolina, pro 14.11.1766 S.C.

SLATER, Andrew, soldier from Aberdeen, married Trijntgen Aryens in Schiedam, Netherlands, 6.3.1637. (Schiedam Marriage Register)

SMITH, Andrew, born in Banff 1.7.1762, farmer in St George's parish, Dorchester County, S.C., naturalised in South Carolina 7.2.1814. (US.NA.M1183)

SMITH, Edward, Fochabers, settled at Slave Lake, North America, pre 1812. (SRO.RS-Elgin, 827, 1812)

SMITH, George, son of Patrick Smith of Ardoyne and Margaret Glass, emigrated to Danzig 6.1687, settled in Colum of Prussia, birth brief 1697. (APB)

SMITH, George, Fochabers, settled at Pictou, Nova Scotia, pre 1812. (SRO.RS-Elgin, 827, 1812)

SMITH, George, born 22.12.1808 son of James Scott, farmer, and Jean Hutcheon in Old Deer, educated at King's College, Aberdeen, 1823 -1824, farmer in Turriff then a land speculator in Chicago. (KCA.2.450)

SMITH, James, from Banffshire, naturalised in South Carolina 21.1.1799. (US.NA.M1183)

SMITH, James, born 24.8.1816 son of Alexander Smith, shoemaker in Old Machar, and Isabella Main, settled Buffalo, New York, pre 1827. (Banchory Ternan g/s)

SMITH, Jean, born in Fordyce, housekeeper in Gothenburg, Sweden, 1759-, married Peter Engstrom, died in Sweden 1821. (NS7.1.147)

SMITH, John, merchant, formerly in Poland, burgess of Aberdeen 6.10.1658. (ABR)

SMITH, John, born in Forres, merchant in New York 1791-1818, married Agnes Wetzell 1793. (ANY.I.315)

SMYTH, Leslie, born in Aberdeen, naturalised Newberry County, South Carolina, 22.4.1843. (S.C.Archives)

SNAWIE, Elspeth, prisoner in Aberdeen Tolbooth, banished from Scotland 20.9.1800. (SRO.JC11.44)

SPEEDY, Peter, soldier from Forres, married Maertge Frericx in Schiedam, Netherlands, 14.6.1636. (Schiedam Marriage Register)

SPIDIMAN, Patrick, soldier from Forres, married Janneken Hutson in Schiedam, Netherlands, 13.6.1637. (Schiedam Marriage Register)

SQUYRE, John, born 1685, educated at Edinburgh University 1703, missionary in Carolina 1713-1718, died in Forres 27.1.1758. (F.6.422)

STEVENSON, David, from Aberdeen, resident in Wijnstraat, Rotterdam, married Aefge Jans from Bergen, in Rotterdam 21.2.1621. (Rotterdam Marriage Register)

STEWART, Gilbert, merchant in Amsterdam, burgess of Aberdeen 20.4.1697. (ABR)

STEWART, James, son of Alexander Stewart of North Colpnay and Isobel Leslie, emigrated from Aberdeen to Danzig, merchant in Poland, birth brief 1705. (APB)

STEWART, James, in Elnoch, Glen Muick, Aberdeenshire, prisoner in Aberdeen Tolbooth, sentenced to be transported beyond the seas 7.4.1796. (SRO.JC11.42)

STEWART, Peter, from Banffshire, member of the Scots Charitable Society of Boston 1759. (NEHGS)

STEWART, Robert, merchant in Bordeaux, burgess of Aberdeen 14.7.1673. (ABR)

STUART, Charles, son of John Stuart, educated at King's College, Aberdeen, 1811-1815, merchant in Quebec. (KCA.2.410)

STUART, James, minister in Georgetown and All Saints, South Carolina, Chaplain to the King's Rangers, died 1809. (Fasti Aberdonensis.215)

STUART, Patrick, Lieutenant Colonel of the 3rd West India Regiment, son of Alexander Stuart of Edinglassie, died in Barbados 21.1.1800. (A.J.Obits.)

SUTHERLAND, John, born 1569 in Aberdeen, son of Jack Sutherland, soldier, married Elisabeth Anderson, a Scot, in Breda, Netherlands, 1595. (Breda Marriage Register)

TARRAS, James, Elgin, to Tangiers 1678. (RPC.X.546)

TARRAS, John, born 16.3.1732, son of .... Tarras, merchant in Banff, and Margaret Gilchrist, merchant, settled Gothenburg, Sweden, 1758, married (1) ? (2) Anna Margarita Augustin, died in Gothenburg 5.5.1790. (NS7.1.147)

TAYLOR, James, born 17.6.1798, son of William Taylor, farmer in Coullie, Fordoun, and Helen Walker, merchant in Savanna, Georgia. (Fordoun g/s)

TAWSE, John, son of James Tawse, farmer in Towie, Aberdeenshire, educated at King's College, Aberdeen, 1817-1821, minister in Toronto. (KCA.2.431)

THAIN, Thomas, born 1779 son of John Thain (1739-1816), settled in Montreal, died 1832. (Forgue g/s)

'THILGER', Andrew, soldier from Aberdeen, married Margaret Kirkwood from Edinburgh, in Schiedam 29.12.1641. (Schiedam Marriage Register)

THOMAS, James, shoemaker from Aberdeen, admitted as a citizen of Leyden, Netherlands, 27.10.1623. (Leyden Citizenship book, S.A.II.155); married Magdalene Lievens of Leyden 13.4.1624, (Leyden Marriage Register, Vol. J, fo.203)

THOMAS, James, soldier from Aberdeen, married Elizabeth Milne from Aberdeen, in Rotterdam 14.1.1635. (Rotterdam Marriage Register)

THOMSON, Alexander, ba. 6.8.1795 son of George Thomson of Fairley and
Agnes Dingwall, soldier 1814-1825, Lieutenant of the Bengal Army,
died in Burma 11.5.1825. (BA.4.264)
THOMSON, Francis, born 27.4.1770 son of Rev. James Thomson and Helen
Anderson in Aberlour, planter in St Vincent. (F.6.335)
THOMSON, George, born 19.9.1799 son of George Thomson of Fairley and
Agnes Dingwall, soldier 1815-1841, Lieutenant Colonel of the
Bengal Army, married Anna Dingwall in Aberdeen 1830, died in
Dublin 10.2.1886. (BA.4.265)
THOMSON, James, born 17.10.1773 son of Rev. James Thomson and Helen
Anderson in Aberlour, surgeon in New South Wales. (F.6.335)
THOMSON, James, agriculturalist in County Tyrone, Ireland, brother of
Alexander Thomson, silk mercer in Aberdeen. (SRO.SH.1864)
THOMSON, John, ba. 17.2.1801 son of George Thomson of Culter and Agnes
Dingwall, soldier 1819-1840, died Ghazipur 12.8.1840. (BA.4.267)
THOMSON, William, in Jamaica, son of Baillie William Thomson of
Aberdeen, died in Philadelphia 3.7.1801. (A.J.Obits.)
THOMSON, William Gordon, in Elkadua, Kandy, Ceylon, son of William
Thomson, surgeon in Stonehaven, who died 21.4.1858. (SRO.SH.1867)
TULLOH, Robert, born 1763 probably son of Robert Tulloh of Bogton, Forres,
soldier 1783-1797, died Calcutta 6.5.1802. (BA.4.321)
TURNER, John, merchant in Przenorscenci, Poland, burgess of Aberdeen
18.8.1670. (ABR)
TURNER, John, son of John Turner of Turnerhall and Elizabeth Urquhart,
died in Grenada 2.6.1792. (TOF554)(A.J.Obits.)
TURNER, William Donaldson, born 26.2.1784 son of Robert Turner of Menie,
Belhelvie, and Euphemia Simpson, soldier 1800-1813, Captain
Lieutenant of the 15th Native Infantry, Bengal Army, died Mirzapur
24.6.1813. (BA.4.329)
URE, David, in Dunedin, New Zealand, brother of Duncan Ure, teacher in
Kincardine, who died 11.1831. (SRO.SH.1866)
URQUHART, John, born 1750, son of Captain John Urquhart of Craigston and
Jean Urquhart of Meldrum, planter in Carriacou, Grenadines, 1772-
1785. (PSAS.114.489/95)
URQUHART, Mary Isabella, or Pollard, in Kintuck, Ireland, daughter of
William Urquhart of Craigston, 1847. (SRO.SH.1847)
URQUHART, William, of Meldrum, planter in Carriacou, Grenadines, 1775-.
(PSAS.114.482)
URQUHART, William, born 1758, son of James Urquhart in Aberdeenshire,
surveyor in Carriacou 1771-, died 1790. (PSAS.114.519)

WALKER, Alexander, born 25.12.1845, son of Rev. Henry Walker and
Eleanora F. Julian in Urquhart parish, Morayshire, settled in
Australia. (F.6.411)
WALKER, James, from Aberdeen, member of the Scots Charitable Society
of Boston 1744. (NEHGS)
WALKER, James Fife, born 3.2.1814, son of Rev. Alexander Walker and
Elizabeth Grant in Urquhart parish, Morayshire, planter in Berbice,
died 6.8.1842. (F.6.411)
WALKER, John, born 4.12.1847, son of Rev. John Walker and Anne Duff in St
Andrew's parish, Morayshire, settled in Tasmania, died 10.9.1893.
(F.6.398)
WALKER, Robert Duff, born 15.3.1846, son of Rev. John Walker and Ann Duff
in St Andrew's parish, Morayshire, settled in Australia, died
29.12.1888. (F.6.398)
WALLACE, Alexander, merchant in Calcutta, grandson of Alexander
Wallace, farmer in Mormond, 1847. (SRO.SH.1847)
WALLACE, John, born 1760s son of John Wallace and Margaret Mair in
Fyvie, died in South Carolina. (TOF.134)
WALLIS, James, born 1823 son of William Wallis in Gartly, minister of
Woodside, Aberdeen, 1849-1854, minister in Demerara 1854-,
minister in New Zealand 1865-. (F.6.42)
WATSON, Jack, from Aberdeen, resident in Moelenstraat, Rotterdam,
married Cattelijne van der Luff from Antwerp in Rotterdam
5.1.1596. (Rotterdam Marriage Register)
WATSON, John, hotel keeper in Brisbane, Australia, son of Robert Watson
in Aberdeen who died 21 2.1849. (SRO.SH.1869)
WATT, Alexander, Banff, in Copenhagen 1832. (SRO.SH.1832)
WATT, John, from the Mearns, member of the Scots Charitable Society of
Boston 1740. (NEHGS)
WATT, John, from Aberdeen, member of the Scots Charitable Society of
Boston 1753. (NEHGS)
WATT, Captain John, in Banff, then in Batavia, 1832. (SRO.SH.1832)
WEIR, Alexander, in Ireland, brother of John Weir, farmer in Keith, 1858.
(SRO.SH.1858)
WEST, James, from Aberdeen, member of the Scots Charitable Society of
Boston 1765. (NEHGS)
WEST, John Morris, in Tuscany 1855, grandson of Major James Mercer of
Auchnacant, Aberdeenshire. (SRO.SH.1855)
WHITE, William, from Fraserburgh, shopkeeper in Charleston, South
Carolina, pro 19.7.1793 Charleston.
WILLIAMSON, John, in Rotterdam, burgess of Aberdeen 23.8.1614. (ABR)

WILLIAMSON, Robert, born 26.7.1806, son of Robert Williamson, farmer, and Elizabeth Williamson in Mains of Portlethan, Kincardineshire, died in Tobago 1827. (Banchory Devenick g/s)

WILSON, George, in Melbourne, Australia, son of David Wilson, builder in Aberdeen, who died 1838. (SRO.SH.1868)

WILSON, James, son of George Wilson and Margaret Phillip in Banff, died Port au Prince 20.6.1794. (Banff g/s)

WILSON, James Milne, son of John Wilson, shipowner in Banff, settled in Van Dieman's Land pre 1852. (SRO.SH.1852)

WOOD, Thomas, born 2.12.1759 son of James Wood and Margaret Barclay, died in America 1818. (Fetteresso g/s)

WRIGHT, James, from Grantown on Spey (?), settled St Thomas parish, South Carolina, pro 12.6.1790 Charleston.

WYAT, Rev. Robert, former minister in Skene, died in Dieppe, France, 1791. (A.J.Obits.)

EMIGRANTS AND ADVENTURERS
from
Aberdeen and North East Scotland

INTRODUCTION

For many centuries emigration has been a regular feature of the demography of north eastern Scotland. The intensity and direction of this has changed significantly from being relatively small scale and directed towards continental Europe in the early modern period to being substantial and channeled towards North America and Australasia from the mid-nineteenth century onwards. During the seventeenth century much of the movement of people from north eastern Scotland was determined by economic opportunity, especially as soldiers of fortune or as merchants in Sweden, Poland and the Netherlands but by the Victorian era emigration was motivated by opportunities in the colonies and in the United States as farmers, planters, merchants, administrators, physicians, teachers, clergymen and soldiers. While the broad picture is well known genealogists require highly specific data which is not generally available. This book, the second in a series, attempts to provide some of the answers.

David Dobson
St Andrews, 1994

The Emigration of Indentured Servants to America

For many prospective emigrants the cost of their passage across the Atlantic Ocean was prohibitative. This problem was soon overcome through modifying the long established system of indentureship under which a young person would contract to serve an employer for a period of apprenticeship in a trade or profession. People would now contract as indentured servants and in exchange for shipment to the American colonies would agree to work for a certain number of years there during which time the employer would not pay them but instead provide accommodation, food and clothing. Such contracts were often made with shipmasters or merchants in this country who would sell their rights under the contracts to farmers, merchants, or tradesmen in the colonies. The system worked but was subject to abuse - many such servants absconded soon after arriving in America while others were badly treated by their masters. Newspapers throughout the British Isles carried advertisements for indentured servants and Aberdeen was no exception as can be seen from the following extract.

"The good new snow The Antigua Pacquet of Aberdeen. Lewis Gellie commander, will sail precisely the sixteenth instant for Cork and Antigua. Any good tradesman or others who choose to indent for Antigua will meet with suitable encouragement on applying to Captain Gellie or the owners. Good accommodation for passengers"

Source: The Aberdeen Journal No.192
September 1751

REFERENCES

ARCHIVES

ABA   Aberdeen Burgh Archives, Aberdeen
           ABR   Aberdeen Burgess Roll
           APB   Aberdeen Proprinquity Book
SRO   Scottish Record Office, Edinburgh
           NRAS   National Register Archives, Scotland
           RD   Register of Deeds
           RS   Register of Sasines
           SH   Services of Heirs
USNA   United States National Archives, Washington

PUBLICATIONS

AJ   Aberdeen Journal
ANY   Biographical Register of the St Andrews Society
           of New York   [McBean, N.Y., 1911]
AP   Historical Account of the St Andrews Society of
           Philadelphia [Philadelphia, 1907]
BA   Officers of the Bengal Army. [Hodson,London, 1927]
CCMC   Colonial Clergy of the Middle Colonies
           [Weis, Baltimore, 1966]
CRA   Cess Roll of Aberdeen [Tayler, Aberdeen, 1932
F   Fasti Ecclesiae Scoticanae [Scott, Edinburgh,1920]
HBRS   Hudson Bay Record Society publications [London]
Imm.NE   Immigrants to New England [Bolton, Salem, 1931]
KCA   Officers and Graduates of King's College, Aberdeen
           [Anderson, Aberdeen, 1893]
MSC   Miscellany of the Spalding Society [Aberdeen, 1940]
RGS   Register of the Great Seal of Scotland, series
SIP   The Scots in Poland [Steuart, Edinburgh, 1913]
SP   The Scots Peerage [Paul, Edinburgh, 1904-]
TML   The MacLeods [Edinburgh, 1969]

ABBREVIATIONS

cnf   confirmation of testament
g/s   gravestone inscription

EMIGRANTS AND ADVENTURERS FROM

ABERDEEN AND NORTH EAST SCOTLAND

☐Part Two☐

ABERNETHY, GEORGE, merchant in Aberdeen and in Jamaica 1751. (SRO.RD4.177.311)

ADAM, JAMES STEWART, born 1846, son of John Adam and Jane Morrice, died in Africa 12.5.1868. (Banchory Ternan g/s)

AIRTH, SIMON, son of Gilbert Airth and Agnes Cordiner in Ardgrayne, Ellon, resident in "Wairkie", Poland, 1598. (MSC.II.45)

AITKEN, WILLIAM, born in Torpichen 28.2.1834, son of Robert Aitken, farmer, and Anne Anderson, educated at Edinburgh University, minister in Canada 1864-, died 13.12.1913. (F.7.624)

ALLAN, ALEXANDER, son of John Allan and Isobel Philp in Lauriston, died in Warso, Prussia, 2.1601. (MSC.II.59)

ALLAN, JOHN, Aberdeen, admitted as a citizen of Cracow 1573. (SIP39)

ALLARDYCE, ALEXANDER, late of Jamaica, 1783. [SRO.R.S.Kincardine, 24]

ALLARDYCE, DAVID, son of John Allardyce and Janet Allardyce in Blackford, Auchterless, settled in Danzig pre 1597. (MSC.II.42)

ALEXANDER(?), JOHN, son of James Alexander (?) and Marjory Douglas in Mounie, Daviot, burgess of Malmo, Denmark, 1593. (MSC.II.22)

ANDERSON, DUNCAN, born in Monymusk 1826, educated at King's College, Aberdeen, 1848, minister in Ontario 1854-. (F.7.625)

ANDERSON, GEORGE GILBERT, in Calcutta, son of George Anderson, writer in Peterhead, and Helen Blaikie who died 21.9.1879. (SRO.SH.1881)

ANDERSON, JAMES, M.D., settled in Melbourne, Australia, prior to 1856, son of James Anderson and Elspet Gow in Scroggiemill, Elgin. (SRO.SH.1856)

ANGUS, ANDREW, son of James Angus and Bessie Riddell in Inverurie, burgess of Stockholm, died 3.1589. (MSC.II.10)

ANGUS, ANDREW, son of Thomas Angus and Janet Myieden in Balgove, Tarves, settled in Cracow, Poland, 1590. (MSC.II.34)

ANGUS, JAMES, son of James Angus and Bessie Riddell in Inverurie, settled in Poland pre 1590. (MSC.II.10)

Emigrants and Adventurers from Aberdeen

ANNAND, ROBERT, son of Mr William Annand of Tollhill and Janet King, died in Carnova, Poland 9.1600. (MSC.II.55)

ANNAND, Mr THOMAS, son of Mr William Annand of Tollhill and Janet King, a student in Paris, France, 1601. (MSC.II.55)

ARDUTHIE, HENRY, son of Thomas Arduthie and Janet Merchant in Fetteresso, resident of Hamburg, died 1602. (MSC.II.62)

AULD, JAMES, traveller in Poland 1597. (MSC.II.41)

BAGRAY, ARCHIBALD, son of John Bagray, burgess of Banff, and Margaret Thomson, settled in Poland 1585. (MSC.II.33)

BAGRAY, WILLIAM, son of Andrew Bagray and Christian Mill in Troine, settled in Pomerania 1586. (MSC.II.31)

BANNERMAN, WILLIAM, son of William Bannerman and Katherine Ronaldson in Bogforlay, Aberdeenshire, burgess of Harisbrig, Germany, 1597. (MSC.II.40)

BARBER, WILLIAM MACLEOD, born in Fochabers 31.5.1827, son of Thomas Barber and Madeline MacLeod, emigrated to Newhaven, Connecticut, educated at Yale, minister, died in Malden, Massachusetts, 1889. (TML.2.39)

BARCLAY, PATRICK, Auchterless, educated at King's College, Aberdeen, 1846, minister in New Zealand. (KCA298)

BARCLAY, ROBERT, son of Walter Barclay of Mondurno and Margaret Leslie, in Hungary 1592. (MSC.II.17)

BARCLAY, THOMAS, son of Walter Barclay of Mondurno and Margaret Leslie, traveller in Poland 1592. (MSC.II.17)

BARNET, WILLIAM, from Poland, burgess of Aberdeen 9.12.1657. (ABR)

BARR, ANDREW, son of Andrew Barr and Agnes Hay in Old Aberdeen, settled in Poland by 1597. (MSC.II.43)

BARTHOLEMEW, JOHN, from Aberdeen, married Catrijn Pieters from Antwerp in Gouda, Netherlands, 15.5.1590. (Gouda Marriage Register)

BAYNE, RONALD, in Buenos Ayres, son of Reverend Charles J. Bayne and Jane Duguid (she died 17.2.1850) in Fodderty. (SRO.SH.1853)

BEATON, PATRICK, born 8.6.1825 in Lethenty, Fyvie, son of William Beaton and Margaret Cowieson, educated at King's College, Aberdeen, 1843, minister in Mauritius, New Zealand and Paris, died 11.10.1904. (KCA296)(F.7.535)

BEATON, WILLIAM, Longside, educated at King's College, Aberdeen, 1837, minister in Grenada 1851-1856, died in Aberdeen 1857. (KCA291)(F.7.667)

BIRNY, ALEXANDER, son of Alexander Birny, burgess of Aberdeen, and Catherine Bishop, settled in Denmark by 1595. (MSC.II.32)

BIRNIE, JAMES, planter in Tobago, later in Techmuiry, cnf 1799 Aberdeen

Emigrants and Adventurers from Aberdeen

BIRNIE, JAMES, born in Aberdeen 1799, to America 1816, married
Charlotte Beadeau, employee of the North West Company 1818-1821,
and the Hudson Bay Company 1821-1846, settled in Cathlamet,
Washington Territory, died 21.12.1864. [HBRS.3.429]
(American Armory and Blue Book)

BISSET, ALEXANDER, born in Ardlaw, Pitsligo, 1814, son of James Bisset,
farmer, educated at Marischal College, Aberdeen, 1832, minister in
Amsterdam, died 4.2.1864. (F.7.539)

BLACK, ROBERT, born 1839, died in Natal 2.12.1875. (Banchory Ternan g/s)

BLACKHALL, GILBERT, son of John Blackhall and Margaret Forbes in
Stonewood, died in Konigsberg 1601. (MSC.II.60)

BOWIE, JOHN HENRY, born in Aberdeen 1807, son of William Bowie, settled
in New York 1825, leather merchant, died Brooklyn 3.7.1859.
(ANY.2.264)

BRAND, GEORGE, born in Arbuthnott 4.12.1815, British Consul at St Paul de
Luanda and later in Lagos, Africa, died at sea 16.6.1860.
(Arbuthnott g/s)

BRANDER, ALEXANDER TERII NOHARIA TEPAN, of Papeete, Tahiti, heir of
Isabel Skene, widow of William Forsyth, tailor in Elgin, and to his
father John Brander of Papeete, Tahiti, who died 15.6.1877.
(SRO.SH.1880)

BRANDER, JAMES, merchant in Lisbon, son of John Brander, merchant in
Elgin, 1766. (SRO.RS29.VII.409)

BRANDER, JOHN, born in Cairney, Aberdeenshire, 1812, settled in
Alexandria, Virginia, died in Baltimore, Maryland, 24.1.1850.
(AJ.20.3.1850)

BRANDER, WILLIAM, carpenter on the Toyal or Elizabeth of Rotterdam,
master John Stevenson, cnf 1757 Edinburgh

BREMNER, ALEXANDER, born 1793, son of James Bremner, farmer, and
Isabel Ord, died in Demerara 14.2.1820. (Speymouth Dipple g/s)

BREMNER, GEORGE, Marnoch, educated at King's College, Aberdeen, 1840,
teacher at the Cape of Good Hope. (KCA293)

BROTCHIE, JAMES RAINY, born in Kintore 27.3.1843, son of John Brotchie,
educated at Aberdeen University 1863, minister in Ceylon 1869
-1876, died 10.2.1878. (F.7.566)

BROTCHIE, JOHN ALEXANDER, born in Kintore 22.10.1849, son of John
Brotchie, educated at Aberdeen University, minister, settled in New
South Wales 1883, died there 2.9.1908. (F.7.588)

BROWN, ANDREW, son of William Brown and Marion Anderson in the Mill of
Rubray, Forglen, Banffshire, traveller in Germany, 1599. (MSC.II.48)

BROWN, JAMES, born 1797, son of William Brown, bookseller in Aberdeen,
educated at Marischal College, Aberdeen, 1815, Indian chaplain 1821
-, died Malacca 23.9.1830. (F.7.570)

Emigrants and Adventurers from Aberdeen

BROWN, JOHN, son of James Brown and Margaret Shearer in Affleck, Kinnoir, settled in Kreustbrig, Hungary, pre 1597. (MSC.II.37)

BROWN, JOHN, former servant to Viscount Arbuthnott, merchant in Rotterdam, cnf 1731 Edinburgh

BRUCE, ALEXANDER, born in Aberdeen 1789, grocer, emigrated from Grangemouth to New York, naturalised in New York 18.4.1821.

BRUCE, JAMES, born 1849, son of Ransom Bruce and Catherine Murdoch, died in Calcutta 9.6.1879. (Fordoun g/s)

BUCHAN, ALEXANDER, son of Thomas and Elizabeth Buchan in Aberdeen, died in Siedmigrodski, Sebinow, Bialogrod, Poland 1602. (SIP40)

BUCHAN, WILLIAM, son of Thomas and Elizabeth Buchan in Aberdeen, citizen and merchant of Zamosc, Poland, 1602. (SIP40)

BURNET, ANDREW, son of Andrew Burnet of Campfield and Constance Pitcairn, burgess of Cracow, Poland, pre 1592. (MSC.II.16)

BURNET, JOHN, Aberdeen, admitted as a citizen of Cracow, Poland 1607. (SIP41)

BURNET, ROBERT, son of Andrew Burnet of Camphill and Christian Pitcairn, traveller in Poland, 1597. (MSC.II.42)

BURNET, THOMAS, trader from Aberdeen, admitted as a citizen of Cracow, Poland, 1617. (SIP41)

BURNET, WILLIAM, son of William Burnet of Gask and Janet Forbes, settled in Kulm, Poland, pre 1589. (MSC.II.6)

BURNET, WILLIAM, eldest son of Bishop Gilbert Burnet and Maria Scott, educated at Trinity College, Cambridge, Governor of New York and New Jersey 1720, Governor of Massachusetts and New Hampshire 1728, married (1) Maria Stanlope, (2) Maria Va Horn in New York, father of Gilbert, Mary, William and Thomas, died in Boston, Massachusetts, 17.9.1729.
["Family of Burnett of Leys" p140; Aberdeen, 1901]

CAMERON, Dr DONALD, physician in St Thomas, Jamaica, husband of Anne Cameron cnf 1792 Aberdeen

CAMERON, JAMES, Inveravon, educated at King's College, Aberdeen, 1855, minister in Amsterdam. (KCA307)

CARMICHAEL, JANE, possibly from Nairn, settled in New South Wales pre 1850. (SRO.SH.1850)

CARNEGIE, JOHN, Aberdeen, educated at King's College, Aberdeen, 1857, physician in China. (KCA308)

CASSIE, JOHN, educated at King's College, Aberdeen, 1805, minister of the Dutch Reformed Church at Caledon, South Africa, 1828-1850. (F.7.561)

CHALMER, ALEXANDER, son of Gilbert Chalmer and Marjory Gray in Kilbleyn, Batholny, Aberdeenshire, traveller in Poland, 1598. (MSC.II.44)

4

Emigrants and Adventurers from Aberdeen

CHALMERS, JAMES, in Cracow, Poland, son of Gilbert Chalmers of
Countesswells, admitted as a burgess of Aberdeen 22.8.1660. [ABR]

CHALMERS, JAMES, Aberdeen, educated at King's College, Aberdeen, 1806,
minister in the West Indies. (KCA269)

CHALMER, JOHN, son of Peter Chalmer, burgess of Aberdeen, and Bessie
Murray, in Poland 1589. (MSC.II.8); citizen of Cracow 1596. (SIP43)

CHALMER, JOHN, born 1673, son of William Chalmer in Kinedward, educated
at Marischal College, Aberdeen, minister in the Netherlands 1698-
1722, died 18.9.1729. (F.7.542)

CHALMER, ROBERT, Aberdeen, citizen of Cracow, Poland, 1621. (SIP43)

CHAPMAN, ANDREW, son of John Chapman and Elspet Forbes in Old Meldrum,
in Rossinburgh, Prussia, 1590. (MSC.II.10)

CHAPMAN, JAMES, son of William Chapman and Marjory Molleson at the
Kirk of Bathelny, traveller in Poland 1603. (MSC.II.63)

CHAPMAN, STEVEN, son of William Chapman and Marjory Molleson at the
Kirk of Bathelny, traveller in Poland 1603. (MSC.II.63)

CHEYNE, Dr ALEXANDER M., in Australia, son of Abigael Mackenzie or Cheyne
in Whitehall, Aberdeen, 1854. (SRO.SH.1854)

CHEYNE, GEORGE, Aberdeenshire, Lieutenant HEICS, died in India 1809.
(SRO.CS46.1834.21)

CHRISTIE, JAMES, Kildrummy, educated at King's College, Aberdeen, 1846,
missionary in Canada. (KCA298)

CLARK, JOHN, Aberdeen, citizen of Cracow, Poland, 1621. (SIP43)

COBBAN, ANDREW, son of William Cobban and Janet Angus in Meikle Larguy,
burgess of Aberdeen, married Katherine Anderson, father of Isabel
Cobban, died in Poland pre 1592. (MSC.II.17)

COBBAN, NICOLL, born in Kincardine, son of William Cobban and Janet
Angus, merchant, died in Danzig 12.1591. (MSC.II.15)

COCHAR, Mrs JESSIE, born in Stonehaven 7.2.1820, married James Cochar
shipbuilder, died in Sulkea, Bengal, 28.2.1845. [Sulkea g/s]

COLLIE, JAMES MOSSES, merchant in Seychelles, son of John Collie,
merchant in Aberdeen, 1855. (SRO.SH.1855)

COLLIE, JOHN, born 1786, son of James Collie and Janet Florence, died in
Dinapore, Bengal, 15.8.1816. (Maryculter g/s)

COLLIE, JOSEPH, Elgin, educated at King's College, Aberdeen, 1844,
insurance employee in Melbourne. (KCA296)

COLLIE, MARGARET, parish of Kincardine(?), married David Cunningham,
settled in Copenhagen, Denmark, pre 1591. (MSC.II.12)

COLT, ALEXANDER, son of David Colt and Marjory Irving in Fingask, Daviot,
Aberdeenshire, settled in Elsinore 1587. (MSC.II.31)

COOK, JOHN, son of Thomas Cook and Beatrice Dickie in Cocklaw,
Peterhead, servant in Ull, Latvia, died 9.1589. (MSC.II.23)

COPLAND, CHARLES, Aberdeen, cooper in Ostend, 1790. (SRO.S/H)

5

Emigrants and Adventurers from Aberdeen

COULL, GEORGE, born in Rathven 1831, son of John Coull, educated at King's College, Aberdeen, 1850, minister in Smyrna 1857-1870, lecturer in Nova Scotia and Quebec 1873-, died 1.1882. (KCA302)(F.7.614)

COW, WILLIAM, merchant in Zamosc, Poland, 1716. (SRO.RS.Banff.6.94)

CRAIG, JOHN, trader from Aberdeen, admitted as a citizen of Cracow, Poland, 1587. (SIP.43)

CRICHTON, JAMES, son of Robert Crichton of Condeland and Janet Con, to France 10.1602. (MSC.II.61)

CRUICKSHANK, ALEXANDER, draper in Melbourne, brother of James Cruickshank, grocer in Aberdeen, who died 23.9.1880. (SRO.SH.1881)

CRUICKSHANK, BRODIE, Aberdeen, educated at King's College, Aberdeen, 1831, settled at Cape Coast Castle. (KCA286)

CRUKSHANK, GEORGE, merchant of Aberdeen, admitted as a citizen of Cracow, Poland, 1646. (SIP44)

CRUKSHANK, JAMES, son of John Crukshank and Agnes Garwick in Kincousie, traveller in Holstein (?) 1593. (MSC.II.21)

CRUKSHANK, WILLIAM, son of John Crukshank and Agnes Garwick in Kincousie, traveller in Holstein (?) 1593. (MSC.II.21)

CRUKSHANK, WILLIAM, son of Andrew Crukshank in Meikle Durno and Beigge Lesly, settled in Wersoy, Prussia, by 1589. (MSC.II.7)

CRUKSHANK, WILLIAM, son of Malcolm Crukshank and Helen Leith in Aslink of Straloch, merchant burgess of Suntis, Poland, 1601. (MSC.II.54)

CUMMING, ANDREW, son of Alexander Cumming of Erneside and Gertie Blackater, traveller in foreign countries, 1594. (MSC.II.29)

CUMMING, BEROALD, son of Andrew Cumming in Tuchill, Deer parish, merchant traveller in Prussia, died 12.1588. (MSC.II.5)

CUSHNIE, JOHN, son of James Cushnie and Christia Bardane at Kirk of Cluny, settled in Konigsberg pre 1593. (MSC.II.26)

DAVIDSON, ANDREW, born 1799, son of Andrew Davidson, advocate in Aberdeen, and Barbara Forbes, died in Java 1831. (St Nicholas g/s)

DAVIDSON, GORDON FORBES, born 1807, son of Andrew Davidson, advocate in Aberdeen, and Barbara Forbes, died in New South Wales 17.10.1865. (St Nicholas g/s)

DAVIDSON, JOHN, son of Alexander Davidson, burgess merchant of Aberdeen, and Margaret Black, burgess of Cracow, Poland, 1597. (MSC.II.40)

DAVIDSON, JOHN, merchant in Rotterdam, 1764. (SRO.S/H)

DAVIDSON, JOHN, born 1792, son of Andrew Davidson, advocate in Aberdeen, and Barbara Forbes, died in Java 1841. (St Nicholas g/s)

DAVIDSON, JOHN, born 1869, son of William Davidson, farmer in Pittenkerrie, died in British Guiana 10.10.1893. (Banchory Ternan g/s)

Emigrants and Adventurers from Aberdeen

DAVIDSON, JONATHAN, born 1797, son of Andrew Davidson, advocate in Aberdeen, and Barbara Forbes, died in Mauritius 1854. (St Nicholas g/s)

DAVIDSON, RICHARD RICH MILFORD, born 1809, son of Andrew Davidson, advocate in Aberdeen, and Barbara Forbes, died in Singapore 1831, (St Nicholas g/s)

DAVIDSON, THOMAS, Old Deer, educated at King's College, Aberdeen, 1860, schoolmaster in U.S.A. (KCA.311)

DAVIDSON, WILLIAM, merchant in Rotterdam, later in Aberdeen, 1764. (SRO.S/H)

DEVINE, JAMES, Aberdeen, educated at King's College, Aberdeen, 1840, minister in Canada. (KCA293)

DICK-LAUDER, JOHN, born in Regulas, Edinkille, Morayshire, 21.4.1813, Lieutenant of the 47th Bengal Native Infantry, died in Bournemouth 23.3.1867. (BA.3.20)

DICKSON, ALEXANDER, trader from Aberdeen, admitted as a citizen of Cracow, Poland, 1599. (SIP44)

DICKSON, THOMAS, son of Thomas Dickson, burgess of Aberdeen, and Janet Leslie, merchant in Cracow, Poland, 1600. (MSC.II.50)(SIP44)

DONALD, WILLIAM, born 6.6.1807 in Edingight, Banffshire, son of John Donald and Janet McHattie, educated at Marischal College, Aberdeen, 1828, schoolmaster in Huntly, minister in New Brunswick 1849-, died 20.2.1871. (F.7.609)(KCA287)

DONALDSON, WALTER, born in Aberdeen, settled in Sedan, France, husband of Elizabeth Goffin, father of Alexander Donaldson MD, 1642. (RGS.IX.1250)

DOUN, DAVID, son of Thomas Doun and Marian Selby in Corshill, died in Konigsberg 7.1600. (MSC.II.56)

DOVERTIE, WILLIAM, from Tarves (?). "wes slaine ... in bolongze on ye frontier" 8.158-. (MSC.II.15)

DOWNIE, JAMES, son of Andrew Downie and Isobel Smalye in Manecht, resident in Warsaw, Poland, 1603. (MSC.II.62)

DUFF, JAMES, merchant in Cadiz, son of William Duff of Cromby, 1783. (SRO.S/H)

DUFF, JAMES, born 1741,'late of Madeira', died 1.4.1812. (Banff g/s)

DUFF, ROBERT, Banff, educated at King's College, Aberdeen, 1828, minister in Berbice. (KCA284)

DUN, ALEXANDER, son of Peter Dun and Margaret Simson in Slioch, Drumblade, settled in Prussia 1589. (MSC.II.43)

DUNCAN, ROBERT, born 24.4.1752 in Aberdeenshire, died in Calcutta 1.8.1808. [South Park g/s. Calcutta]

7

Emigrants and Adventurers from Aberdeen

DUNN, ALEXANDER, born 29.12.1859 in Leochel Cushnie, son of Peter Dunn, educated at Aberdeen University 1882, minister in Scotland, Ceylon and Belgium, died 23.3.1917. (F.7.534)

DUN, JOHN, son of James Dun and Margaret Mathewson in Parkhill, traveller in Danzig and Prussia 1589. (MSC.II.7)

DUN, JOHN, son of Thomas Dun, dyer burgess of Aberdeen, and Margaret Davidson, in Anderberg, Germany, 1602. (MSC.II.60)

DUNCAN, JAMES, son of Duncan Duncan and Anne Simpson in Newburgh, traveller in Neumark, Brandenburg, died there 5.1590. (MSC.II.14)

DUNCAN, THOMAS, born 2.8.1828 in Foveran, son of George Duncan and Elspet Webster, married Margaret Smart in Aberdeen 1.5.1858, to America 23.5.1860, died 19.1.1887 in Philadelphia. (AP.162)

DUTHIE, ALEXANDER, planter in Jamaica, later in Aberdeen, cnf 1769 Aberdeen

DYSART, ALEXANDER, son of William Dysart, burgess of Aberdeen, and Janet Whyte, traveller in Prussia, 1596. (MSC.II.33)

ELMSLIE, GEORGE, son of George Elmslie, burgess of Aberdeen, and Marjorie Cairns, traveller in Poland, 1598. (MSC.II.45); possibly the George Elmslie who was admitted as a citizen of Cracow, Poland, (SIP45)

ELMSLIE, WILLIAM, Aberdeen, educated at King's College, Aberdeen, 1857, physician in India. (KCA308)

ESTELL, ALEXANDER, son of George Estell and Katherine Steven at Bridge of Don, burgess of Wermer, Prussia, 1601. (MSC.II.56)

FALCONER, PATRICK, born 1775, son of William Falconer, farmer in Kinnermony, (1720-1793), and Anna Rose, (1743-1821), merchant in New York, died 1837. (Inveraven g/s)(ANY.2.15)

FALCONER, ROBERT, born 1782, son of William Falconer (1720-1793) and Anna Rose (1743-1821), merchant in New York, died 1851. (Inveraven g/s)

FALCONER, WILLIAM, born 1763, son of William Falconer, farmer in Kinnermony, (1720-1793), and Anna Rose, (1743-1821), merchant in New York, died 1818. (Inveraven g/s)

FALCONER, WILLIAM , born 1807, son of Captain D. Falconer and Catherine ..., died in Grenada 30.5.1844. (Rothes g/s)

FARQUHARSON, CHARLES, born 1779, son of James Farquharson in Ballintruan, Kirkmichael, and Anne Stewart, died in Baltimore, Maryland, 2.6.1860. (Inveraven Downan g/s)

FARQUHARSON, ROBERT, born 1777, son of James Farquharson in Ballintruan, Kirkmichael, and Ann Smart, died in Nashville, Tennessee, 28.6.1856. (Inveraven Downan g/s)

FERGUSON, ALEXANDER, in Genoa, great great grand-nephew of William Watt in Gilcomston, Aberdeen, who died 11.8.1822. (SRO.SH.1881)

Emigrants and Adventurers from Aberdeen

FERRIER, ALEXANDER, born Aberdeen 22.11.1850, son of Charles Ferrier and Isabel Greig, educated at Aberdeen University 1877, Indian chaplain 1878-1900. (F.7.572)

FINNIE, WILLIAM, Aberdeenshire, Lieutenant of the 61st Company, Royal Marines, died at Boston, Massachusetts, pro. 1775 PCC

FLEMING, JAMES WILLIAM, born in Ballindalloch, Inveraven, 28.8.1855, son of John Fleming and Ann Gradner, educated at Aberdeen University, minister in Argentina 1879-, died 14.6.1925. (F.7.681)

FORBES, Sir ARTHUR, of Craigievar, died in Boulogne sur Mer 27.2.1823. (SM.86.520)

FORBES, DUNCAN, merchant in Amoy, son of Alexander Forbes, wine merchant in Aberdeen, and Janet ... , 1853. (SRO.SH.1853)

FORBES, FRANCIS, Aberdeen, educated at King's College, Aberdeen, 1821, minister in British Guina. (KCA278)

FORBES, JAMES, born 1814 in Leochel Cushnie, educated at King's College, Aberdeen, 1836, minister, settled in Australia 1837, died there 12.8.1851. (F.7.588)

FORBES, JAMES LAWSON, born in Kincardine O'Neil 24.12.1853, son of James Forbes and Catherine Lawson, educated at Aberdeen University 1877, minister, settled in New South Wales 1882, married Eliza Murray, died post 1920. (F.7.588)

FORBES, JOHN, son of Arthur Forbes and Elizabeth Davidson in Tullibirlecht, Skene, traveller in Poland, 1594. (MSC.II.29); possibly the John Forbes admitted as a citizen of Cracow, Poland, 1588. (SIP46)

FORBES, JOHN, born in Banffshire, educated at Marischal College, Aberdeen, 1733, minister in New Jersey 1733-1736, died pre 9.11.1736. (CCMC)

FORBES, MARGARET, born 1823, died at Madura, East Indies, 10.12.1843. (Banchory Devenick g/s)

FORBES, ROBERT, son of James Forbes of Janetshall, Keith, and Margaret Blackadder, residnet in Cracow, Poland, 1598. (MSC.II.45)

FORBES, THOMAS, born in Banffshire, son of James Forbes and Sarah Gordon, partner in Panton, Leslie and Company, merchants in Florida, died 1808. ("Indian Traders of the south eastern Spanish Borderlands" p121, Coker Watson, Florida 1986)

FORBES, WILLIAM, son of Alexander Forbes of Whitehouse, burgess of Aberdeen, and Margaret Arthur, in Poland 1590. (MSC.II.8)

FORBES, WILLIAM, son of Sir William Forbes ofCraigievar, died in Calcutta 4.10.1820. [South Park g/s, Calcutta]

FORFAR, WILLIAM, Kincardineshire, settled in Greifswald, Pomerania, pre 1656. (SRO.SH.1656)

9

Emigrants and Adventurers from Aberdeen

FORSYTH, JOHN, born 19.9.1784, son of John Forsyth in Newhills,
    Aberdeenshire, settled in Newburgh, New York, married Jane Currie
    11.1.1810. ["American Army & Blue Book"]
FORSYTH, JOHN SMITH, born 1.1.1840 son of Rev. James Forsyth and
    Elizabeth Brown in St Nicholas parish, Aberdeen, died in Melbourne
    26.11.1885. (F.6.40)
FOTHERINGHAM, JOHN, son of James Fotheringham and Janet Martin,
    settled in Groningen, Friesland, pre 1596. (MSC.II.36)
FOWLIE, JOHN, born 1855 in New Deer, educated at St Andrews University,
    minister in New South Wales 1882-1885, later settled in Nova
    Scotia. (F.7.588)
FRASER, GILBERT, son of Mr Thomas Fraser of Clinterie and Marjory
    Watson, died in Konigsberg, Prussia, 1600. (MSC.II.56)
FRATER, ARTHUR WELLESLEY, born in Aberdeen 20.10.1852, son of James
    Frater and Mary Lowe, educated at Aberdeen University 1875,
    minister in Middelburg, Flushing and Belgium 1884-. (F.7.549)
FROSTER, THOMAS, son of John Froster and Christian Gray in Kellie,
    Methlick, traveller in Poland 1600. (MSC.II.50)
FYEN, GILBERT, son of Robert Fyen, burgess of Aberdeen, and Janet
    Lumsden, died in "Sanctanaberie", Saxony, 9.1599. (MSC.II.50)
GARDEN, ALEXANDER, born in Aberdeen 4.10.1794, educated at King's
    College, Aberdeen, M.D. 1813, surgeon HEICS, died in Calcutta
    24.4.1845. (KCA274)[St Andrew's Kirk, Calcutta, g/s]
GARDEN, JOHN, son of William Garden and Isabel King in Cairnbrogie,
    Tarves, traveller in Poland, 1597. (MSC.II.43)
GARDINER, JAMES, son of James Gardiner (1720-1790) and Elspet Wilson
    (1720-1795), settled in Jamaica pre 1813. (Banff g/s)
GARDINER, JOHN MILNE, born 1833, son of A. W. Gardiner in Greenskares,
    died in Bombay 29.7.1852. (Banff g/s)
GARDYNE, JOHN, son of Andrew Gardyne and Helen Walker in Carnbrokie,
    Tarves, traveller in Pomerania, 1593. (MSC.II.24)
GAULD, JOHN, Coldstone, educated at King's College, Aberdeen, 1844,
    minister in Canada. (KCA296)
GEDDES, JAMES, son of John Geddes and Margaret Slora in Suichanne,
    Petane parish, servant to John Brown jr in Danzig, 1595. (MSC.II.31)
GELLIE, FRANCIS, King Edward, educated at King's College, Aberdeen, 1856,
    HEICS. (KCA307)
GERARD, JAMES, Aberdeen, educated at King's College, Aberdeen, 1811,
    surgeon HEICS. (KCA272)
GERARD, JOHN, Aberdeen, educated at King's College, Aberdeen, 1803,
    HEICS. (KCA268)
GIB, JOHN, son of Robert Gib and Christian Lyell in Leys, Ardo, traveller in
    Poland, 1594. (MSC.II.28)

Emigrants and Adventurers from Aberdeen

GIBBON, HUGH, born in Aberdeen 19.10.1812, died in Gorockpore, Bengal, 19.11.1844. [Gorockpore g/s]

GILLESPIE, ALEXANDER, son of David Gillespie of Auchlech and Isobel Watt, died in Kniesen, Poland, 4.1589. (MSC.II.8)

GILLESPIE, DAVID, son of David Gillespie of Auchlech and Isobel Watt, to Denmark by 1589. (MSC.II.7)

GILLIES, THOMAS, surgeon HEICS, 1785. [SRO.R.S.Kincardine, 63]

GORDON, ALEXANDER, son of Patrick Gordon of Harlaw and Rachel Leslie, a merchant in Poland 1707. [CRA97]

GORDON, ALEXANDER, merchant in Amsterdam, son of Robert Gordon of Cairnfield, 1718. (SRO.S/H)

GORDON, ALEXANDER, born 1786, surgeon at Satara, died 2.5.1819. (St Nicholas g/s)

GORDON, CHARLES, born in Aberdeenshire 1666, educated in Aberdeen, minister in Veere 1686-1691, died in Ashkirk 19.4.1710. (F.2.164)

GORDON, FABIAN, Colonel in Polish Service 1788. (SRO.S/H)

GORDON, FRANCIS DRUMMOND, born 1833, son of Rev. John Gordon, Lieutenant of the 36th Madras Infantry, died at Kittool, Madras Residence, 5.1864. (Speymouth Dipple g/s)

GORDON, GEORGE, born 1789, surgeon in Bombay, died in Aberdeen 4.5.1832. (St Nicholas g/s)

GORDON, JAMES, son of Patrick Gordon of Harlaw and Rachel Leslie, a merchant in Poland 1707. [CRA97]

GORDON, JOHN, born 1790, Lieutenant of the Bombay Artillery, died in the Persian Gulf 8.1809. (St Nicholas g/s)

GORDON, LOCKHART, born 1732 youngest son of John, Earl of Aboyne, married Catherine Wallop 1770, died in Calcutta 24.3.1788. [South Park Street Burial Ground, Calcutta, g/s]

GORDON, WILLIAM, born 1780, settled in Tobago, died in Elgin 1831. (Rothes Dundurcas g/s)

GORDON, WILLIAM, born 1814, son of Rev. John Gordon, surgeon, died at Newcastle Barracks, Jamaica, 7.12.1836. (Speymouth Dipple g/s)

GRANT, ALEXANDER, Lumphanan, educated at King's College, Aberdeen, 1852, missionary in China. (KCA304)

GRANT, ALEXANDER WILLIAM, born 1822, son of Alexander Grant of Dellacaple, Ensign of the 11th Madras Light Infantry, died at Nudapapoor, East Indies, 10.2.1840. (Speymouth Essil g/s)

GRANT, DAVID, Morayshire, educated at King's College, Aberdeen, 1816, missionary in India. (KCA275)

GRANT, JAMES AUGUSTUS, born 1813, son of Alexander Grant of Dellacaple, died at Kishnagur, Bengal, 8.8.1838. (Speymouth Dipple g/s)

11

Emigrants and Adventurers from Aberdeen

GRANT, JAMES, born 1831, son of Robert Grant and Isabella Reid, died in Singapore 27.12.1846. (Banchory Devenick g/s)

GRAY, Reverend DAVID THOMPSON, chaplain in Nagpure, India, son of David Gray, Professor of Natural Philosophy in Aberdeen who died 10.2.1856. (SRO.SH.1880)

GRAY, ROBERT, son of Andrew Gray, burgess of Aberdeen, and Annabel Lawson, died in Jutland 1593. (MSC.II.30)

GREEN, ALEXANDER, born 1807, son of William Green and Helen Stewart, died in Jamaica 22.4.1834. (Aberlour g/s)

GREEN, JOSEPH, born 1802, son of William Green and Helen Stewart, died in Jamaica 14.7.1847. (Aberlour g/s)

GUTHRIE, GEORGE, Elgin, merchant, admitted as a citizen of Cracow, Poland, 1624. (SIP47)

HADDEN, DAVID, born 13.10.1773 in Aberdeen, son of Alexander Hadden and Elspet Young, arrived in New York 18.11.1806 on the packet boat New Guide, merchant in New York, died 3.6.1856. (ANY.2.17)

HALL, ALEXANDER, son of Thomas Hall in Mylloy and Marjory Mamrie, merchant in Poland 1581-1588, died in Leuschawis, Poland. (MSC.II.8)

HALL, MARGARET, daughter of Alexander Hall and Elspet Fraser in Monymusk, died in Elsinore, Denmark, 8.1677. (APB)

HARPER, WILLIAM I., educated at King's College, Aberdeen, 1860, minister in Demerara. (KCA.311)

HAY, JOHN, Tarves, educated at King's College, Aberdeen, 1834, settled in Sydney. (KCA289)

HAY, PETER SCOTT, born 12.3.1844 in Dufftown, Banffshire, son of John Hay and Catherine Green, educated at King's College, Aberdeen, minister in New Zealand 1877-, married Margaret Ross, father of Catherine, died 31.5.1925. (F.7.603)

HENDERSON, JAMES, son of William Henderson and Geils Cordiner in Mydill, resident in Konigsberg 1595. (MSC.II.32)

HENDERSON, JAMES, born Montquhitter 9.3.1852, son of James Henderson, educated at Aberdeen University 1874, Indian chaplain 1878-1905, died 5.10.1925. (F.7.573)

HENDERSON, WILLIAM, Aberdeen, educated at King's College, Aberdeen, 1822, minister in Newcastle, New Brunswick. (KCA279)

HORNE, GEORGE, son of Alexander Horne and Margaret Innes in Boyne, Fendraught, resident in Bublitz, Pomerania, 1594. (MSC.II.28)

HORNE, GEORGE, son of John Horne and Helen Douglas in Ladymyre, Logie, died in Cracow, Poland, 12.1596. (MSC.ii.38)

HORNER, PATRICK, son of Gilbert Horner of Carnedany and Margaret Bowie, settled in Cracow, Poland, pre 1596. (MSC.II.36)

Emigrants and Adventurers from Aberdeen

HUCHEON, ARTHUR, son of William Hucheon and Helen Philp in Leither, Turriff, traveller in Prussia, 1599. (MSC.II.48)

HUCKLEY, HENRY ROSE, in Veray, Switzerland, grand-nephew of Reverend Richard Rose in Drainie who died 23.6.1856. (SRO.SH.1856)

HUNTER, THOMAS, St Nicholas, educated at King's College, Aberdeen, 1852, missionary in Bombay. (KCA304)

HUSTWICK, CHARLES, born 28.4.1822, ships carpenter, died at Brown's Creek, New South Wales, 3.2.1890. (Speymouth Essil g/s)

HUSTWICK, WILLIAM, born 15.5.1813, shipmaster, son of William Hustwick, shipmaster in Garmouth, died 27.1.1896 at Dry Creek, Bonnie Doon, Victoria, Australia. (Speymouth Essil g/s)

HUTCHEON, ALEXANDER, son of Reverend John Hutcheon in Fetteresso, died in Kingston, St Vincent, 29.10.1812. (SM.75.158)

HUTCHISON, JOHN ROSS, born in Stonehaven 29.6.1792, to India 1810, Judge in the Bengal Civil Service, died in Calcutta 16.9.1838. [South Park g/s, Calcutta]

INKSON, THOMAS, Morayshire, educated at King's College, Aberdeen, 1813, physician in the West Indies. (KCA274)

INNES, DONALD, born 1834, son of John Innes in Newton of Glenlivet and Jane Grant, died in Granite, Virginia, 15.2.1899.
(Inveraven Downan g/s)

INNES, ROBERT, in Tarnovien, Poland, burgess of Aberdeen 19.1.1629. (ABR)

INNES, JOHN, son of ...... Innes and Mary Dawson, died in St Johns, New Brunswick, 8.187-. (Knockando g/s)

INVERARITY, JOHN, born 11.11.1783, son of John Inverarity and Henrietta Panton in Aberdeen, emigrated to Florida 1802, partner in the firm of Panton, Leslie and Company, and of John Forbes and Company, merchants, died 1854. [IT]

IRONSIDE, ALEXANDER, born in Auchterless 24.11.1845, son of Robert Ironside, educated at Aberdeen University 1867, minister in Amsterdam 1882-1894, died in Aberdeen 3.11.1915. (F.7.540)

IRONSIDE, GEORGE EDMUND, born in Aberdeen ca. 1766, educated at King's College, Aberdeen, 1781, married Helen ... in Aberdeen, to New York 1808, teacher, died in Washington 7.5.1827. (ANY.2.10)

IRVINE, Dr CHARLES, in St Thomas, Jamaica, later in Aberdeen, cnf 1794 Aberdeen

IRVINE, JOHN, in Gothenburg, later in Aberdeen, 1792, [SRO.R.S.Kincardine, 224]; cnf 1795 Aberdeen

IRVING, ROBERT, Captain of the Scots Regiment of the King of France's Guards, later in Rayne, Aberdeenshire, 1656. (RGS.X.525)

JAMIESON, Reverend WILLIAM, educated at King's College, Aberdeen, 1826, chaplain in Amsterdam, son of Andrew Jamieson, merchant in Turriff, 1850. (SRO.SH.1850)(KCA282)

13

Emiqrants and Aduenturers from Aberdeen

JOHNSON, PETER, from Aberdeen, married Tenneken Jans from Antwerp in Rotterdam 7.2.1588. (Rotterdam Marriage Register)
JOHNSTON, Reverend FRANCIS, in Vere, Jamaica, 1794. [SRO.R.S.Kincardine, 295]
JOHNSTON, JAMES, son of David Johnston and Marjory Barclay in Crimond, traveller in Poland 1597. (MSC.II.38)
JOHNSTON, JOHN, son of Andrew Johnston and Margaret Stern in Carnfochie, Tarves, died in Stralsund, Germany, pre 1592. (MSC.II.21)
JOHNSTON, WILLIAM, HEICS, son of James Johnston, merchant in Aberdeen then in USA, and Euphemia Cheyne, 1856. (SRO.SH.1856)
KAY, THOMAS, son of John Kay and Katherine Selby in Gardyne, Aberdeenshire, died in Melvin, Prussia, 1599. (MSC.II.51)
KAY, WILLIAM, son of Thomas Kay and Margaret Jamieson in "Lorresell", settled in Nynbrig, Poland, 1587. (MSC.II.34)
KELMAN, JOHN, born 1797, son of Peter Kelman and Isabella Milne, died in Van Dieman's Land 31.12.1841. (Banchory Devenick g/s)
KIDD, JAMES, New Deer, educated at King's College, Aberdeen, 1851, minister in New Brunswick. (KCA303)
KING, AGNES, daughter of Andrew King and Isobel Watson, residing with Thomas Steven, burgess of Danzig, 1601. (MSC.II.55)
KING, JAMES, son of William King and Marjory Gray in Ardconnand, traveller in Poland, 1593. (MSC.II.25)
KING, RONALD, son of William King and Marion Gray in Ardconan, Batholny, Aberdeenshire, burgess of Cracow, Poland, 1598. (MSC.II.44)
KING, THOMAS, son of Andrew King and Janet Forbes in Tollihill, traveller in Poland, 1594. (MSC.II.28)
KING, THOMAS, son of David King and Janet Forbes in Hillbrae, traveller in Poland, died in Saintsoii, Italy, 10.1600. (MSC.II.55)
KNIGHT, JOHN, born 1772, son of James Knight and Catherine Morgan, died in the East Indies 22.2.1790. (Fetteresso g/s)
KNOLLIS, ALEXANDER, son of James Knollis and Agnes Smith in Maryculter, "quha departit in ye eist partis" (Baltic states) pre 1592. (MSC.II.18)
LAIRD, JOHN, son of John Laird and Margaret Ogilvy in Fornety, Foveran, settled in Nynbrig, Poland, pre 1596. (MSC.II.34)
LAMONT, PATRICK B., born in Aberdeen 1787, painter in New York 1818-, died 7.5.1828. (ANY.2.69)
LAWSON, WILLIAM, burgess of Copenhagen 1593. (MSC.II.26)
LAWTIE, GEORGE URQUHART, born in Banff(?) 1751, Ensign of the Bengal Infantry, died in Calcutta 25.11.1807. (BA.3.30)
LAWTIE, JAMES, born in Banff(?) 1755, Lieutenant Colonel of the 27th Bengal Native Infantry, died in Cheltenham 28.6.1836. (BA.3.30)

Emigrants and Adventurers from Aberdeen

LAWTIE, PETER, born in Banff 25.2.1792, son of George Urquhart Lawtie and Sarah ....., Lieutenant of Engineers in Bengal, died Ratangarh, Rajputana, 4.5.1815. (BA.3.30)

LEDINGHAM, WILLIAM, son of William Ledingham and Margaret Bartlett, merchant in Buenos Ayres, died there 1871. (Dyce g/s)

LEGERTWOOD, ALEXANDER, born 1755, son of James Legertwood of Skelmuir and Agnes Dyce, Brevet Major of the Bengal Artillery, died in Cawnpore 19.9.1802. (BA.3.39)

LEITH, JAMES, son of James Leith and Jelis Leith at the Kirk of Crathie, settled in Prussia 1586. (MSC.II.29)

LEITH, WILLIAM, born in Aberdeenshire 1759, son of Margaret Leith, Lieutenant of the 1st Bengal European regiment, died in Calcutta 1781. (BA.3.41)

LESK, JOHN, educated at King's College, Aberdeen, 1667-1671, minister in Middelburg and Walcheren 1692-1697, died 1697. (F.7.548)

LESK, MAGNUS, son of John Lesk in Cremondmocat and Margaret Ferguson, died in Poland 1585. (MSC.II.11)

LESLIE, GEORGE, of Haddo, born 1734, in Jamaica, later in Aberdeen, died 26.3.1793, 1794. (SRO.S/H); cnf 1796 Aberdeen

LESLIE, JOHN, son of John Leslie and Janet Leslie in Balmadie, burgess of Berent, Danzig, 1593. (MSC.II.22)

LESLIE, NORMAND, son of John Leslie, portioner of Buchanstane, and Constance Leslie, traveller in Pomerania and Prussia 1591. (MSC.II.14)

LESLIE, PATRICK, son of Patrick Leslie of Drumtauss, resident in Danzig 1599. (MSC.II.46)

LESLIE, Sir WALTER, Colonel in Hungary, son of John Leslie of Balquhan and Jean Erskine, 1637. (RGS.IX.648)

LIDDEL, DUNCAN, born 1561, son of John Liddel burgess of Aberdeen, educated at King's College, Aberdeen, to Danzig 1579, physician and scholar in Helmstadt, Germany, died Aberdeen 17.12.1613. (St Nicholas g/s)

LITTLE, JOHN, merchant traveller in Poland 1596. (MSC.II.35)

LONGMORE, WILLIAM, Australia, son of William Longmore, banker in Keith, and Helen Lemmon, 1858. (SRO.SH.1858)

LOW, HENRY, son of John Low and Margaret Mealing in Coulinns, Drumoak, settled in Prussia 1584. (MSC.II.38)

LOW, JAMES, born in Aberdeen 8.3.1759, son of John Low, tutor in Rotterdam and Utrecht, educated at Utrecht University, minister in the Netherlands 1783-, died 20.11.1817. (F.7.539)

LUMSDEN, DAVID, merchant in Aberdeen, afterwards in Kingston, Jamaica, dead by 1763. (SRO.S/H)

Emigrants and Adventurers from Aberdeen

LUMSDEN, DAVID, Aboyne, educated at King's College, Aberdeen, 18..,
   accountant in South Africa. (KCA.311)
MCBEAN, JOHN, Nairn, educated at King's College, Aberdeen, 1832, minister
   in Columbo. (KCA287)
MACKIE, JOHN FLETCHER, born in Aberdeen 4.1806, agent for Jersey City
   Rolling Mills by 1831, died in Saugatuck, Connecticut, 4.1851.
   (ANY.2i.27)
MCCRINDELL, THOMAS, born in Aberdeen ca. 1794, son of George McCrindell
   and Margaret Cruickshank, via London to New York on the Venus
   27.4.1827, merchant in New York 1822-1837, died in London (?)
   (ANY.2.85)
MCDONALD, ALEXANDER, Aberdeen, Captain of the Florida Rangers,
   pro. 4.1805 PCC
MACDONALD, CHARLES, Aberdeen, educated at King's College, Aberdeen,
   1850, Professor in Halifax, Nova Scotia. (KCA302)
MACFARLANE, JAMES RUTHVEN, born Crathie 8.3.1819, son of Alexander
   MacFarlane, educated at King's College, Aberdeen, 1833, chaplain
   HEICS Madras, 1849, died 6.3.1866. (KCA288)(F.7.576)
MACFARLANE, WILLIAM,born 9.9.1839 in Boharm, Fochabers, son of Mungo
   MacFarlane and Margaret Christie, educated at King's College,
   Aberdeen, 1858, schoolmaster/minister in Amsterdam, died
   8.3.1905. (KCA309)(F.7.540)
MCGILLEVRAY, ALEXANDER, merchant in Charleston, South Carolina,
   husband of Lucy McIntosh, 1748. (SRO.RS38.X.88)
MCHENRY, JAMES, born in Forres, Morayshire, 1788, settled in America pre
   1806, partner in Andrew Low and Company of Savanna, Georgia, died
   in Lexington, Oglethorpe County, Georgia, 22.9.1826. (Georgia
   Republican 10.10.1826)
MCINTOSH, CHARLES, merchant in Gibralter, 1776. (SRO.RS38.XIII.413)
MCINTOSH, LACHLAN, merchant in Gibralter later in London, 1776.
   (SRO.RS38.XII.410)
MACHRAY, ROBERT, Aberdeen, educated at King's College, Aberdeen, 1851,
   Primate of Canada. (KCA303)
MACINTOSH, DUNCAN, born 1779, son of Andrew MacIntosh merchant in
   Forres, surgeon, died in Spain 10.5.1813. (SM.75.478)
MACIRVINE, GEORGE, Glass, educated at King's College, Aberdeen, 1849,
   minister in Mauritius. (KCA301)
MACKENZIE, SIMON, Old Machar, educated at King's College, Aberdeen,
   1848, minister in Brisbane. (KCA300)
MACKENZIE, WILLIAM, born 1847, son of William Mackenzie in Carron and
   Jane Thompson, died in Surinam 10.12.1893. (Aberlour g/s)

Emigrants and Adventurers from Aberdeen

MACKEY, ALEXANDER BERRY, born 1794 in Aberdeenshire, educated at
King's College, Aberdeen, 1814, minister in Amsterdam 1823, died
5.1.1835. (F.7.539)(KCA274)

MACKIE, PATRICK, son of John Mackie and Margaret Paterson in parish of
Drumblade, traveller in Pornluk, Poland, 1589. (MSC.II.7)

MCLEOD, JOHN, Aberdeen, educated at King's College, Aberdeen, 1810,
HEICS. (KCA272)

MCPHERSON, HUGH, Old Machar, educated at King's College, Aberdeen, 1837,
surgeon HEICS. (KCA291)

MCPHERSON, JOHN, Old Machar, educated at King's College, Aberdeen, 1833,
HEICS physician in Calcutta. (KCA287)

MCWILLIAM, JAMES, Old Machar, educated at King's College, Aberdeen,
1835, merchant in America. (KCA289)

MALCOLM, JOHN, son of James Malcolm and Elspet Ranzie in Bowhill,
Banchory, traveller in Prussia pre 1596. (MSC.II.36)

MANN, ALEXANDER, Aberdeen, educated at King's College, Aberdeen, 1819,
minister in Pakenham, Canada. (KCA277)

MANN, JAMES, born in Elgin 15.12.1795, son of John Mann and Janet Laing,
husbandman, to Philadelphia, settled in New England 1812,
naturalised in Rockingham County, New Hampshire, 11.3.1833.

MANTACH, Rev. JAMES, born 1792, son of John Mantach, farmer in
Dundurcas, and Jane Hossack, died on Boaz Island, Bermuda,
18.12.1854. (Rothes Dundurcas g/s)

MANTACH, ROBERT, Rothes, educated at King's College, Aberdeen, 1840,
minister in Bermuda. (KCA294)

MARSHALL, ALEXANDER, son of John Marshall and Helen Irving in Arbedie,
traveller in Pomerania, 1599. (MSC.II.49)

MARSHALL, ROBERT, son of John Marshall and Helen Irving in Arbedie,
traveller in Pomerania, 1599. (MSC.II.49)

MARTIN, JOHN, born in Aberdeen 1748, journeyman printer, died in New
York City 12.12.1778. (New York Gazette and Mercury 14.12.1778)

MELDRUM, JAMES, son of John Meldrum and Margaret Chalmer in Petty,
Fyvie, died in Konigsberg 7.1601. (MSC.II.60)

MELDRUM, JOHN, son of William Meldrum and Marjory Richard in Minnes,
Foveran, merchant, died in Wartha, Poland, 1591. (MSC.II.20)

MELDRUM, Captain WILLIAM, son of George Meldrum of Jackstoun and Jane
Ogilvie, died in Diesacht, Holland, pre 6.1592. (MSC.II.17)

MERCER, HUGH, born ca. 1725 in Aberdeen, son of Rev. William Mercer in
Pitsligo, educated at Marischal College, Aberdeen, 1744, physician,
Jacobite, arrived in Philadelphia 1746, settled in Franklin County,
Pennsylvania, General of the US Army, died 12.1.1777 after Battles
of Trenton and Princeton. (AP.278)

Emigrants and Adventurers from Aberdeen

MERCHANT, JAMES, son of James Merchant (1783-1869) and Elizabeth
Guthrie (1773-1862), settled in North America. (Arbuthnott g/s)

MERSON, CHARLES, born in Elgin 1820, educated at King's College,
Aberdeen, 1840, minister in Columbo, Ceylon, died 1869. (F.7.567)

MIDDLETON, PETER, born in Old Aberdeen, son of George Middleton and
Janet Gordon, emigrated to Poland 21.6.1693, married Susannah
Moer, father of Patrick etc, died in Cracow 1771. (SP.VI.178)

MIDDLETON, WILLIAM, born 26.1.1832 in Mid Strath, Birse, son of John
Middleton and Mary Harper, educated at Marischal College, Aberdeen,
1851, Indian chaplain 1861-1871, died at Hyderabad 22.11.1871.
(F.7.578)

MILL, JOHN, son of Andrew Mill and Janet Ligertwood in Meikle Creich,
Deer, traveller in Poland 1601. (MSC.II.58)

MILL, WILLIAM, son of Andrew Mill and Margaret Mill in Newton of Troine,
Abercharder, Banffshire, settled in Neustatyn, Pomerania, 1595.
(MSC.II.31)

MILL, WILLIAM, son of Andrew Mill and Janet Ligertwood in Meikle Creich,
Deer, traveller in Poland 1601. (MSC.II.58)

MILNE, DAVID, born in Aberdeen 26.12.1787, son of James Milne and Agnes
Copeland, educated at Aberdeen Grammar School and King's College,
Aberdeen, settled in Cincinnati, Ohio, 1827, merchant in Philadelphia
1829-, died 30.7.1873 in Philadelphia. (AP.281)

MILNE, JAMES, born in Ellon 1799, son of Thomas Milne a merchant,
educated at Marischal College, Aberdeen, 1818, minister in New
South Wales 1854-1885, married Jane Baird, died 1885. (F.7.595)

MILNE, JAMES, born 10.10.1810 in Aberdeen, son of David Milne and Helen
Forbes, merchant in Cincinnati and Philadelphia, died in Philadelphia
9.12.1865. (AP.282)

MILNE, JAMES, born Newhills, Aberdeenshire, 14.12.1865, son of William
and Ann Milne, educated at Aberdeen University, minister in
Australia and New Zealand 1890-. (F.7.595)

MILNE, JOHN, born in Aberdeen, settled in Savanna, Georgia, 1783, died
there 28.10.1811. (Savanna Republican 29.10.1811)

MITCHELL, HENRY LUMSDEN, born 9.9.1838, son of Henry Mitchell in
Montquhitter, educated at Marischal College, Aberdeen, 1853,
minister in Ceylon 1862-1870, died 3.5.1900. (F.7.568)

MITCHELL, THOMAS, son of Andrew Mitchell, burgess of Aberdeen, and
Margaret Cargill, died in Danzig (?) 4.1592. (MSC.II.16)

MITCHELL, WILLIAM, born 1728, son of Reverend James Mitchell in St
Machar's, educated at King's College, Aberdeen, 1745, schoolmaster
in Rotterdam, minister in Leyden, died 9.1807. (F.7.547)

MOIR, JOHN, son of Alexander Moir and Janet Clerk in Fintry,
Aberdeenshire, settled in France 1586. (MSC.II.23)

18

Emigrants and Aduenturers from Aberdeen

MOIR, WILLIAM, born in Aberdeen 1826, emigrated to USA 1835, watchmaker, died in New York 21.3.1896. (ANY.2.285)

MORGAN, JAMES, born in Arbuthnott 1783, son of James Morgan, farmer, educated at Marischal College, Aberdeen, 1802, minister in Dordrecht 1818-1840, died in Stonehaven 15.8.1869. (F.7.544)(Arbuthnott g/s)

MORGAN, Dr WILLIAM, Rector of Kingston, Jamaica, then Professor of Philosophy at Marischal College, Aberdeen, cnf 1789 Aberdeen

MORRISON, GEORGE, born in Glassaugh, Fordyce, 1768, son of George Morrison, educated at King's College, Aberdeen, 1791, minister in the Netherlands 1818-, died 23.7.1853. (F.7.545)

MORISON, JOHN, born in Aberdeenshire, emigrated from Londonderry to New England 1720, married Janet Steele, died 1736. (Imm.NE,140)

MORRISON, JOSEPH, King Edward, educated at King's College, Aberdeen, 1848, settled at Cape of Good Hope. (KCA300)

MORTIMER, ISABELLA, born 1842, widow of William Stalker, died in New Home, Pietermaritzburg, Natal, 24.7.1913. [Peterculter g/s]

MOWATT, GEORGE, settled in New York city, probate 17.3.1796 New York

MURISON, GEORGE, born 1675, educated at King's College, Aberdeen, 1701, schoolmaster in Albany, New York, 1703, minister in New York and Connecticut 1705-1708, died in Rye, New York, 12.10.1708. (CCMC)

MURRAY, ANDREW, born 26.5.1794, son of Andrew Murray and Isabel Milne in Mill of Clatt, Aberdeenshire, educated at Marischal College, Aberdeen, 1816, minister in South Africa 1822-1866, died 1866. (F.7.563)

MURRAY, JAMES, merchant in Veere, 1784. [SRO.R.S.Kincardine, 50]

MURRAY, JOHN, son of Alexander Murray, burgess of Turriff, and Margaret Lindsay, burgess of Kalmar, Sweden, 1597. (MSC.II.41)

MURRAY, JOHN, in Demerara, later in Portsoy, cnf 1795 Aberdeen

MURRAY, JOHN, flax dresser, emigrated from Aberdeen to America pre 1824, naturalised in New York 12.9.1840.

MUTRAY, GILBERT, son of Henry Mutray of Lochhills and Elisabeth Crukshank, traveller in Poland 1595. (MSC.II.32)

NAPIER, JOHN, born 3.11.1788 in Bervie, arrived in America 1815, merchant in New York 1817-1859, died in Brooklyn 23.6.1879. (ANY.2.73)

NICOLL, ALEXANDER, son of William Nicoll and Agnes Males in Grandholm, St Machar, traveller in Poland from 1589. (MSC.II.36)

NICOLL, WILLIAM, son of John Nicoll and Isobel Walker in Netherdell, Aberchirder, Banffshire, traveller in Masine, Poland, 1597. (MSC.II.41)

NORIE, ALEXANDER, son of William Norie, burgess of Aberdeen, and Margaret Allan, traveller in Poland, 1596. (MSC.II.34)

19

Emigrants and Adventurers from Aberdeen

OGG, ALEXANDER, land surveyor at Castle Fraser, emigrated to Australia 1850. (SRO.NRAS.2508.4.4.44)

OGG, CHARLES SIMMERS, born 10.4.1832 in Banchory Ternan, son of Rev. Charles Ogg, educated at King's College, Aberdeen, 1851, minister in New Brunswick 1861-, minister in New Zealand 1872-1903, died 21.8.1905. (F.7.605)(KCA303)

OGILVY, DAVID, born 1793, son of Reverend Dr Skene Ogilvy, on the Madras Medical Establishment, died 31.10.1814. [South Park g/s, Calcutta]

OGILVY, JAMES, born in Aberdeen 1760, teacher in Virginia and Kentucky, died in Aberdeen 18.9.1820. (ANY.2.47)

OGILVY, JOHN, son of George Ogilvy of Meldrum and Bessie Meldrum, traveller in Latvia 1598. (MSC.II.44)

OGILVY, JOHN, son of Alexander Ogilvy and Margaret Anderson in Countesswells, in Copenhagen, Denmark, 1602. (MSC.II.60)

ORAM, PATRICK, Aberdeen, trader, admitted as a citizen of Cracow, Poland, 1599. (SIP.53)

ORAM, THOMAS, Aberdeen, trader, admitted as a citizen of Cracow, Poland, 1607. (SIP54)

ORD, PETER, son of Bartholemew Ord and Agnes Chalmers in Skene, witness in Cracow, Poland, 1625. (SIP53)

PATTULLO, ROBERT ALEXANDER, born in Huntly 17.1.1740, emigrated to Nova Scotia 1780, married Mrs Elizabeth Robertson-Bartlett in Liverpool, Nova Scotia, 20.9.1794, died in Chester, Nova Scotia, 31.12.1833. (Patillo Families/Fort Worth, Texas, 1972)

PAUL, JAMES, Aberdeenshire (?), minister in Warwick, Bermuda, 1720-1750, died 1750. (F.7.661)

PAUL, JOHN L., Elgin, educated at King's College, Aberdeen, 1845, HEICS physician. (KCA297)

PORTER, WILLIAM, Forgue, educated at King's College, Aberdeen, 1835, merchant in St Vincent. (KCA290)

RAIT, ALEXANDER, son of Joseph Rait and Jelis Strachan in Haugh of Towie, settled in Prussia pre 1590. (MSC.II.10)

RANESON, ALEXANDER, son of Thomas Raneson and Effie Thom in Wester Kenny, Skene, resident of Danzig 1593. (MSC.II23)

RANNY, JOHN, son of William Ranny and Margaret Jamieson in Millhill, Tullinessill, traveller in Poland 1601. (MSC.II.59)

RAYNE, JOHN, son of William Rayne and Margaret Jamieson in Millhill, Tullinesle, traveller in Poland, 1595. (MSC.II.32)

REID, JOSEPH, Rothiemay, educated at King's College, Aberdeen, 1839, teacher at the Cape of Good Hope. (KCA293)

REID, WILLIAM, Kildrummy, educated at King's College, Aberdeen, 1833, minister in Toronto. (KCA288)

Emigrants and Adventurers from Aberdeen

RIACH, JOHN, born 1826, son of John Riach, farmer in Hillfolds, and Margaret Anderson, died in Toronto 5.2.1855. (Rothes g/s)

ROBB, ALEXANDER, Old Machar, educated at King's College, Aberdeen, 1848, minister in Jamaica. (KCA300)

ROBB, JOHN, sr, burgess of Ull, Latvia, 1593. (MSC.II.23)

ROBERTSON, ALEXANDER, son of William Robertson and Christian Tough at Mill of Tulleben, Culter, traveller in Poland 1592. (MSC.II.19)

ROBERTSON, ALEXANDER, fifth son of Thomas Robertson merchant in Peterhead, a cooper and wine merchant in Calcutta, died 31.12.1807. [South Park g/s, Calcutta]

ROBERTSON, ANDREW, son of William Robertson, burgess of Aberdeen, and Bessie Chalmer, died in Copenhagen 1593(?) (MSC.II.26)

ROBERTSON, EDWARD, son of John Robertson and Margaret Crag at the Mill of Corsinday, settled in Riesenberg, Prussia, by 1585. (MSC.II.16)

ROBERTSON, ISAAC, mill carpenter on Richmond Estate, St George's, Grenada, cnf 1791 Aberdeen

ROBERTSON, JAMES, merchant in Jamaica, son of James Robertson of Bishopmiln, 1768. (SRO.RSVIII.87)

ROBERTSON, JAMES, Marnoch, educated at King's College, Aberdeen, 1843, physician in Melbourne. (KCA296)

ROBERTSON, LEWIS, born 1816, son of Lewis Robertson, (1775-1828), and Jane Inkson, (1792-1864), died in Australia 25.1.1847. (Knockando g/s)

ROBERTSON, THOMAS, son of Master James Robertson and Agnes Cye in Fordyce, traveller in Poland, 1598. (MSC.II.44)

ROBERTSON, WILLIAM, son of Alexander Robertson in Coull, Mar, settled in Seilfeild, Poland, pre 1591. (MSC.II.13)

ROBERTSON, WILLIAM, born in Morayshire, educated at King's College, Aberdeen, 1828, minister of the Dutch Reformed Church in South Africa, died 1879. (F.7.564)

ROGER, JOHN MORRICE, Aberdeen, educated at King's College, Aberdeen, 1827, minister in Peterborough, Canada. (KCA283)

ROLLAND, THOMAS, son of Alexander Rolland and Margaret Elder, traveller in Poland 1596. (MSC.II.37)

ROSS, ALEXANDER, of Ankerville, merchant in Poland, husband of Sophia French, 1721. (SRO.RS38.VIII.34)

ROSS, JAMES, Peterhead, educated at King's College, Aberdeen, 1857, minister in New South Wales. (KCA.309)

ROSS, WILLIAM ("Willem Rijs") from Aberdeen, soldier under Colonel Erskine, married Anna Gertrude Tomassen from Groningen in Maastricht 16.7.1662. (Maastricht Marriage Register)

Emigrants and Adventurers from Aberdeen

ROSS, WILLIAM, born 1820 in Huntly, son of William Ross a watchmaker, educated at Marischal College, Aberdeen, 1840, minister in Australia 1846-1880, died in Scotland 8.1899. (F.7.597)

RUST, WILLIAM, son of Andrew Rust and Janet Symmer in Larkhill, Fintray, Aberdeenshire, died in Konigsberg 11.1598. (MSC.II.46)

RUXTON, ROBERT, born 1747 son of Robert Ruxton in Cairnhill, Esslemont, married Margaret Brown, Cononsyth,Carmyllie, 5.11.1780, emigrated to America 1788, father of William, died 1828. [BLG2898]

SADLER, WILLIAM, son of Alexander Sadler and Marjory Barker, traveller in "ye eist partis" (Baltic States) 1597. (MSC.II.41)

SANGSTER, JOHN, in Achridie (?), married Janet Gardyne, settled in Skeyne, Poland, pre 1592, father of Gilbert. (MSC.II.19)

SCOTT, JAMES, born at Pitarrow, Fordoun, 18.2.1778, son of Archibald Scott, to India 1797, Lieutenant Colonel of the Bengal Army, died 11.8.1820. (BA.4.35)

SCOTT, JOHN, merchant in Stonehaven, bankrupt - fled to America ca.1817. (SRO.CS233.Seqn.S1/45)

SCOTT, THOMAS, born 27.1.1853 in Old Machar, son of Alexander Scott, educated at Aberdeen University 1872, Indian chaplain 1881-1907. (F.7.580)

SELLAR, JAMES SYDNEY, in Elgin late in Pretoria, brother of Alexander Gordon Sellar, ironmonger in Elgin, who died 15.4.1879. (SRO.SH.1881)

SETON, WILLIAM, son of William Seton and Elizabeth Cecil in Tambeistane, Kinkell, Aberdeenshire, resident of Danzig, later in Konigsberg, 1600. (MSC.II.51/52)

SHAND, GEORGE, in Demerar, later in Aberdeen, husband of Mary Walker cnf 1793 Aberdeen

SHAND, JOHN, Kinardineshire, planter in Jamaica ca. 1800. (SRO.CS46/1852)

SHAND, ROBERT, son of Alexander Shand and Trednia(?) Mar in Aberdeen, settled in Rotterdam, Holland, pre 1596. (MSC.II.35)

SHAND, ROBERT, born in Aberdeenshire, educated at King's College, Aberdeen, 1819-1823, minister of the Dutch Reformed Church in South Africa 1834 -, died 21.11.1876. (F.7.564)

SHAND, WILLIAM, Mortlach, educated at King's College, Aberdeen, 1843, teacher at the Cape of Good Hope. (KCA296)

SHAND, WILLIAM, estate manager in Jamaica 1791-1823, later in Arnhall, Kincardineshire. (SRO.CS46.1852)

SHAW, JAMES, born 1822 in Abernethy, storekeeper, naturalised in Charleston, South Carolina, 5.4.1853. (US.NA.M1183, roll 1)

Emigrants and Adventurers from Aberdeen

SHEARER, GILBERT, burgess of Aberdeen, son of Andrew Shearer, baillie of Aberdeen, and Margaret Brabner, bound to the "eist pairtis" (Baltic States) 8.1601. (MSC.II.58)

SHEARER, JOHN, son of Thomas Shearer, burgess of Aberdeen, and Agnes Mathewson, burgess of Elsinore, Denmark, 1593, dead by 7.1597. (MSC.II.26/39)

SHEARER, PATRICK, son of William Shearer and Janet Brown in Auchinleck, Kinnoir, resident in Elbing, Prussia, 1599. (MSC.II.48)

SHEWAN, ALEXANDER, St Fergus, educated at King's College, Aberdeen, 1855, Professor in Montreal. (KCA307)

SHIRREFFS, LAUDERDALE, born 1837, died in Demerara 1854. (Banchory Ternan g/s)

SIM, JAMES, born in Banff 11.11.1759, settled in St Vincent, died 27.5.1825. (Banff g/s)

SIM, JAMES GEORGE, MD, HEICS, born in Banff 4.3.1804, died in Singapore 10.9.1830. (Banff g/s)

SIM, JOHN, born 1744, 'late of Antigua', died 29.11.1807. (Banff g/s)

SIME, ALEXANDER, born 1845, son of Alexander Sime, farmer in Ringorm, and Margaret Donaldson, died in Warrnambool, Australia, 24.6.1886. (Knockando g/s)

SIME, LEWIS, born 1848, son of Alexander Sime, farmer in Ringorm, and Margaret Donaldson, died in St Thomas, Canada, 15.3.1871. (Knockando g/s)

SIMPSON, WILLIAM, born 17.3.1863 in Alves, Elgin, son of Charles Simpson, educated at Aberdeen University 1883-, St Andrews University 1891, minister in Melbourne, minister in New Zealand 1900-1904, returned to Scotland. (F.7.605)

SIMS, ANDREW, sometime in Jamaica, died in Peterhead 9.2.1803. (Peterhead g/s)

SIMSON, THOMAS, son of James Simson, burgess of Aberdeen, and Christian Cults, died in Wilhelmsburg, Neumark, pre 8.1592. (MSC.II.19)

SKENE, ANDREW, factor in Veere, 1655. (RGS.X.363)

SKLAITT, ANDREW, son of Robert Sklaitt and Katherine Steven in Udny, Ellon, died in "Brynnusser", Premissill, Poland, 1599(?) (MSC.II.46)

SMITH, GEORGE, born Aberdeen 1811, an assistant in the Bhowanipore Factory, Bengal, died 22.5.1842. [Bhowanipore g/s]

SMYTH, GILBERT, son of William Smyth and Janet Davidson in Ardconan, Bathelny, Aberdeenshire, resident of Prussia 1603. (MSC.II.63)

SMYTH, JAMES, son of John Smyth, mariner burgess of Aberdeen, and Katherine Oswall, resident "in ye mouth of swunne", Norway, died 9.1593. (MSC.II.27)

SMITH, JOHN, in Antigua, later in Aberdeen, cnf 1795 Aberdeen

Emigrants and Aduenturers from Aberdeen

SMITH, THOMAS, born 10.1745 in Aberdeenshire, arrived in Pennsylvania 1768, settled in Bedford, Pennsylvania, Justice of the Supreme Court of Pennsylvania, died 31.3.1809. (AP.319)

SMITH, WILLIAM, born 7.9.1727 in Aberdeenshire, educated at the University of Aberdeen 1747, to America 1751, Provost of the College of Philadelphia 1754-1779, founder of Washington College, Maryland 1782, co-founder of the American Philosophical Society, died 14.5.1803 near Falls of Schullkill, Pennsylvania. (AP325)

SMITH, WILLIAM, born in Aberdeen, educated at King's College, Aberdeen, 1798-1802, teacher in New York 1806-1816, died in Port Jackson, Australia, 1826. (ANY.2.41)

SPRING, JOHN, son of Thomas Spring and Janet Burnet in Banchory, resident of Hendland (?), Poland, 1593. (MSC.II.27)

STALKER, JOHN, Aberlour, educated at King's College, Aberdeen, 1858, missionary in Pietermaritzburg. (KCA.309)

STEPHEN, ALEXANDER, son of John Stephen, baker in Rothes, (died 1854), and Anne Booth, (died 1841), settled in America pre 1877. (Rothes g/s)

STEVEN, ALEXANDER, son of William Steven and Elspet Moir in Drumnahoy, Cluny, traveller in Prussia, 1599. (MSC.II.49)

STEWART, CHARLES, Forres, educated at King's College, Aberdeen, 1846, merchant in America. (KCA298)

STEWART, FREDERICK, Rathen, educated at King's College, Aberdeen, 1859, H.M.I.S. Hong Kong. (KCA.310)

STEWART, JAMES, Captain in the 3rd Battalion the Royal Scots, son of Andrew Stewart of Auchlunkart, Banff, died at St Sebastian 2.9.1813. (SM.75.799)

STEWART, JOHN, son of Archibald Stewart, citizen of Old Aberdeen, and Isobel Chalmer, traveller in Germany, 1595. (MSC.II.30)

STEWART, MURDOCH, Contin, educated at King's College, Aberdeen, 1834, minister in Nova Scotia. (KCA289)

STEWART, WILLIAM, of Answanly, formerly a merchant in Gothenburg, later in Elgin, 1765. (SRO.RS29.VII.389)

STILL, ALEXANDER, born in Peterhead 17.1.1865, son of Peter Still and Joan Murray, educated at Edinburgh University 1888, Indian chaplain 1891-, died 30.5.1892. (F.7.581)

STRACHAN, Captain JOHN, son of Thomas Strachan and Helen Scott in Forgan, died in Flanders pre 9.1600. (MSC.II.54)

STRACHAN, WILLIAM, merchant in Rotterdam, later in Banff, cnf 1777 Aberdeen

STUART, ADAM, born 1836, son of John Stuart and Anne Rae, died off Cape Horn 13.2.1869. [Strachan g/s]

Emigrants and Adventurers from Aberdeen

STUART, ALEXANDER, Inveravon, educated at King's College, Aberdeen, 1843, minister in Halifax, Nova Scotia. (KCA296)

STUART, WILLIAM, born 1870, died in Johannesburg 20.4.1894. [Strachan g/s]

SUTHERLAND, JOHN, Duffus, educated at King's College, Aberdeen, 1841, planter in South Africa. (KCA295)

SYMMER, JOHN, son of John Symmer and Janet Wood in Halton of Fintray, burgess of Warkie, Poland, 1595. (MSC.II.32)

TAYLOR, JAMES, born 1855, son of William Taylor and Mary Ross, died in Sydney, Australia, 14.1.1888. (Banchory Ternan g/s)

THOM, ALEXANDER, son of William Thom, burgess of Kintore, and Mab Anderson, traveller in Poland, 1593. (MSC.II.27)

THOM, JOHN, born 1825, son of William Thom and Mary Burnett, died in Coraki, New South Wale, 2.9.1869. (Banchory Ternan g/s)

THOMSON, GEORGE, Aberdeen, educated at King's College, Aberdeen, 1822, minister in Macnab, Canada. (KCA279)

THOMSON, GEORGE, born 1866, son of James Thomson, died in Cromwell, Natal, 27.2.1906. (Banchory Ternan g/s)

THOMSON, JAMES, born 1819, son of Alexander Thomson, feuar in Fochabers, and Elspet Geddes, died in Adelaide, South Australia, 10.4.1878. (Speymouth Dipple g/s)

THOMSON, JOHN, son of Andrew Thomson and Elizabeth Blackhall in Carnequhyn, resident in Slap, Poland, 1600. (MSC.II.52)

THOMSON, ROBERT, born 1862, son of James Thomson, died at Umzinto, Natal, 27.5.1896. (Banchory Ternan g/s)

THOMSON, WILLIAM, born 1786, son of John Thomson, feuar in Dufftown, and Jane Grant, died in Jamaica 1811. (Aberlour g/s)

THOMSON, WILLIAM, born in Leslie, Aberdeenshire, 19.4.1862, son of John Thomson and Mary Elmslie, educated at Aberdeen University 1885, minister in Amsterdam 1895-. (F.7.540)

THOMSON, WILLIAM, born 19.12.1861 Inverallen, son of John G. Thomson and Jane T. Parker, educated at Aberdeen and Edinburgh Universities, minister in South Australia 1889-1892, died in Scotland 21.5.1914. (F.7.600)

TOD, WILLIAM, merchant in Rouen, later in Fraserburgh, 1652. (RGS.X.46)

TOPP, ALEXANDER, Morayshire, educated at King's College, Aberdeen, 1831, minister in Toronto. (KCA286)

TORRY, WILLIAM, Aberdeen, admitted as a citizen of Cracow, Poland, 1626. (SIP56)

TURNER, WILLIAM, son of John Turner and Margaret Collie, in Glesfennie, Drumoak, Kincardineshire, traveller in Prussia, 1591. (MSC.II.29)

25

Emigrants and Adventurers from Aberdeen

UDNY, JOHN, son of Robert Udny and Elspet King in Selby, traveller in Poland, 1594. (MSC.II.28); admitted as a citizen of Cracow, Poland, 1598. (SIP56)

WALKER, ALEXANDER, son of James Walker, burgess of Aberdeen, and Constance Fenton, burgess of Torun, Prussia, pre 1591. (MSC.II.15)

WALKER, ALEXANDER, son of John Walker and Elizabeth Harvie in Disblair, traveller in "ye eist partis" 1592. (MSC.II.20)

WALKER, GEORGE, merchant in Nassau, 1796. [SRO.R.S.Kincardine, 349]

WALKER, THOMAS, son of John Walker and Elizabeth Harvie in Disblair, resident of "Sanctanberie", Germany, 1592. (MSC.II.20)

WALKER, WILLIAM, son of John Walker and Elizabeth Harvie in Disblair, resident of "Sanctanberie", Germany, 1592. (MSC.II.20)

WALKER, WILLIAM G., son of Andrew Walker (1819-1901), farmer in Torphins, and Susan Gerrard (1819-1897), settled in OOkala, Hawaii. (Banchory Devenick g/s)

WALLACE, ALEXANDER, a merchant in Calcutta by 1847, grandson of Alexander Wallace, feuar of Mormond. [SRO.S/H]

WATSON, JAMES, Aberdour, educated at King's College, Aberdeen, 1843, minister in Kingston, Jamaica. (KCA296)

WATSON, THOMAS, son of John Watson and Isabel King in Boghead, Fyvie, to the "eist pairtis" (Baltic States) 1602. (MSC.II.61)

WEIR, GEORGE, Aberlour, educated at King's College, Aberdeen, 1848, Professor in Kingston, Canada. (KCA300)

WILLIAMSON, ALEXANDER, in Jamaica, later in Haugh of Edinglassie, cnf 1791 Aberdeen

WILLIAMSON, GEORGE, died in Carafraxa, Canada West, 1858. (Banchory Ternan g/s)

WILLIAMSON, JOHN, born 1805, son of John Williamson and Jane Russell, died in Jamaica 16.11.1850. (Speymouth Dipple g/s)

WILLOX, HENRY, son of John Willox and Isobel Donaldson in Ellon, resident of Danzig, 1594. (MSC.II.28)

WILSON, ALEXANDER, born 2.1.1742, son of James Wilson, minister in Gamrie, educated at St Andrews University 1770, minister in the Netherlands 1776-1789, died 3.5.1789. (F.7.542)

WILSON, GEORGE, Insch, educated at King's College, Aberdeen, 1841, teacher in America. (KCA295)

WILSON, JAMES, in Calcutta, 1780. (SRO.RS29.VIII.494)

WISEMAN, JOHN, son of James Wiseman, baker burgess of Aberdeen, and Isobel Burns, servant to William Rolland, resident of Danzig, 1593. (MSC.II.25)

WISHART, ROBERT, son of Alexander Wishart and Isobel Morris in Grandholm, settled in Konigsberg pre 1593. (MSC.II.26)

Emigrants and Adventurers from Aberdeen

WISLEY, Reverend GEORGE, in Malta, brother of William Wisley, physician in Nevie, Glenlivet, who died 16.11.1847. (SRO.SH.1881)

WOOD, JOHN, son of James Wood and Margaret Barclay, died in Calcutta 1791. (Cowie g/s)

WRIGHT, ALEXANDER MACLEAN, born 7.7.1852 in Elgin, son of George Wright, educated at Aberdeen University 1876, minister in New Zealand 1879-, died 16.12.1900. (F.7.605)

WRIGHT, JOHN, son of John Wright and Marjory Paterson in Newton of Balquhan, died in Prussia 2.1595. (MSC.II.30)

YOUNG, JOHN, in Montserrat, son of Dr William Young of Falside, 1784. [SRO.R.S.Kincardine, 57]

EMIGRANTS AND ADVENTURERS
from
Fife

INTRODUCTION

Emigration from Fife has occurred for centuries. Initially the flow was to the lands with which Fife had trading connections such as the Netherlands, France, Scandinavia and the Baltic states but from the late seventeenth century onwards the direction of emigration was westwards to the New World, and more recently to Australasia. During the seventeenth century Scots emigrants and religious or political refugees settled on the continent, some permanently others temporarily, often as merchants, factors, or soldiers of fortune. The first Fifer in America was a Thomas Henderson who settled at Jamestown, Virginia, around 1607, Emigration to North America was small scale prior to the late eighteenth century. From the mid nineteenth century onwards Australia and New Zealand began to rival Canada and the United States as major destinations for Scots emigrants.

Although the destinations and reasons for emigration are well known there is little available in print to identify individual emigrants or their specific places of settlement. This booklet, the first in a series, supplies some of such missing details.

David Dobson
St Andrews, 1994

REFERENCES

ARCHIVES
NEHGS	New England Historic Genealogical Society,	Boston
SRA	Strathclyde Regional Archives,	Glasgow
SRO	Scottish Record Office,	Edinburgh
B	Burgh Records	
CC	Commissariat Court	
CS	Court of Session	
GD	Gifts and Deposits	
NRAS	National Register of Archives, Scotland	
RD	Register of Deeds	
RS	Register of Sasines	
SC	Sheriff Court	
SH	Services of Heirs	
PRO	Public Record Office,	London
CO	Colonial Office	
E	Exchequer Records	
PCC	Prerogative Court of Canterbury	
USNA	United States National Archives, Washington	

PUBLICATIONS
ANY	Biographical Register of the St Andrews Society of New York
BLG	Burke's Landed Gentry
BPP	British Parliamentary Papers, London,
CAG	Compendium of American Genealogy
CF	Colonial Families of the United States
F	Fasti Scoticanae Ecclesiae
MAGU	Matriculation Albums of Glasgow University
SG	The Scottish Genealogist

ABBREVIATIONS
cnf	confirmation of testament
pro	probate
gs	gravestone

THE SCOTS OVERSEAS

EMIGRANTS AND ADVENTURERS
FROM FIFE
|Part One|

ADAM, GEORGE, born 1846 son of Alexander Adam, died Singapore 3.6.1876. (Dunfermline g/s)

ADAMSON, JAMES, born 1825 son of Alexander Adamson and Jane Hastie, died Grouse Island, America, 12.6.1847. (St Monance g/s)

ADAMSON, JOHN, born 1829 son of Alexander Adamson and Jane Hastie, died Calcutta 11.2.1863. (St Monance g/s)

ADAMSON, LAURENCE, born 1766 son of John Adamson and Sophia Key, died Bengal 4.1789. (St Andrews g/s)

ADAMSON, ROBERT KEY, youngest son of Dr Adamson in Cupar, died Kingston, Jamaica, 1827. (Blackwood's Magazine 23.664)

AITKEN, ANDREW, born 1835 son of Thomas Aitken and Mary Meldrum, died Havanna 10.9.1858. (Abercrombie g/s)

AITKEN, GEORGE, born 1801 son of George Aitken of Thornton and Janet Ponton, captain of the 13th Light Infantry, died Calcutta 1831. (Cupar g/s)

AITKEN, HENRY, Kinghorn, member of the Scots Charitable Society of Boston, Massachusetts,1740. (NEHGS)

AITKEN, ROBERT, born 1793, captain of the 6th Bengal Cavalry, died 21.12.1852. (Cupar g/s)

ALLAN, ISABELLA, wife of Peter Cleghorn, died Madras 1.6.1824. (Dunino g/s)

ALLAN, JAMES AARCHIBALD FINNIE, born 4.1.1832 son of George Allan and Mary Pagan, died Cien Fuegos, Cuba, 3.5.1865. (Ferry Port on Craig g/s)

ALLEN, GEORGE, Fife, member of the Scots Charitable Society of Boston, 1736. (NEHGS)

ALLERDYCE, ARCHIBALD, born 1818, died Sydney, New South Wales, 24.7.1890. (Forgan g/s)

ANDERSON, ALEXANDER JOHN, of Montrave, Captain HEICS, died Lucknow 9.3.1858. (St Monance g/s)

ANDERSON, ANNIE, born Newburgh 21.3.1786, died Cape of Good Hope 1813. (Abdie g/s)

ANDERSON, ANN, born 1792 daughter of Laurence Anderson and Jane Watson, died New York 24.11.1825. (St Andrews g/s)

Emigrants and Adventurers from Fife

ANDERSON, BALLANTYNE MITCHELL, born 1826, died Tirhoot, India, 25.1.1859. (Burntisland g/s)

ANDERSON, DAVID, Lochgelly, sentenced to transportation for 7 years, at Perth 15.9.1809. [SM.71.954]

ANDERSON, EBENEZER, farmer in Detroit, Michigan, ex Cupar, cnf 1892. (SRO.SC70.1.307)

ANDERSON, GEORGE, born 1830 son of Thomas Anderson and Charlotte Nicol, engineer died Amolree, India, 1865. (Newburgh g/s)

ANDERSON, JAMES, born 1797 son of Laurence Anderson and Jane Watson, died Newark, USA, 12.4.1830. (St Andrews g/s)

ANDERSON, JOHN, Dunfermline, settled Danbury, Connecticut, pro 6.3.1740 Connecticut

ANDERSON, JOHN, born 1790 son of James Anderson, died Halifax, North America, 17.7.1810. (Kilrenny g/s)

ANDERSON, JOHN, born 2.10.1796 Newburgh, minister died Nice 16.3.1834. (Newburgh g/s)

ANDERSON, JOHN, born 1819 son of Thomas Anderson and Charlotte Nicol, died Wai Wai, Auckland, New Zealand, 1883. (Newburgh g/s)

ANDERSON, JOHN DAVID jr., born 1819, died Bermuda 31.7.1857. (Burntisland g/s)

ANDERSON, ROBERT, born 1820 son of Thomas Anderson and Charlotte Nicol, died Darraweit, Cuim, Australia, 1885. (Newburgh g/s)

ANDERSON, ROBERT, Major in East India Company Service, 1788. [SRO.RS.Fife, 2031]

ANDERSON, WALTER FERGUSON, born 28.1.1822, Lieutenant Colonel in HM Bombay Army, died 1.8.1869. (Kirkcaldy g/s)

ANDERSON, WILLIAM, Dunfermline, settled Deerfield. Massachusetts, 1758, married Abigail Hitchcock, died 1810. (Imm.N.E.1700-1775,p3)

ANGUS, GEORGE, born 1830 son of John Angus and Mary Sime, died America 4.4.1869. (Cupar g/s)

ANGUS, JOHN, son of William Angus and Betty Gardner in North Grange, died on passage to Australia 1853. (Abdie g/s)

ANNAN, DAVID, born 1754 Cupar son of John Annan, married Mary Smith, settled Peterbrough, New Hampshire, died 1802 Ireland. (Imm.N.E.,p5)

ANNAN, THOMAS, born 1841 son of Thomas Annan and Ann Sharp, engineer died Calcutta 28.6.1866. (Moonzie g/s)

ANSTRUTHER, HENRY, born 4.6.1836, Lieutenant Royal Ulster Fusiliers, died Battle of Alma 20.9.1854. (St Monance g/s)

ARCHIBALD, ANDREW MURRAY, born 1829 son of John Archibald and Grace Murray, died Otago, New Zealand, 28.5.1859. (Burntisland g/s)

ARNOT, HARRY, son of Peter Arnot of Balcormo, settled Shillez, Danzig, pre 1605. (SRO.RS{Fife}.5.86)

Emigrants and Adventurers from Fife

ARNOT, JAMES, son of Peter Arnot of Balcormo, goldsmith in Schillez, Danzig, pre 1605. (SRO.RS{Fife}5.86)

ARNOT, WILLIAM, son of Peter Arnot of Balcormo, goldsmith in Shillez, Danzig, 1605. (SRO.RS.{Fife}5.87)

ARNOT, WILLIAM, son of Thomas Arnot in Fife, pro 17.11.1790 Charleston, South Carolina

ARNOTT, JOHN, born 6.11.1845 son of Robert Arnott, died melbourne 28.1.1877. (Auchtermuchty g/s)

ATKIN, GEORGE, Kirkcaldy, member of the Scots Charitable Society of Boston, 1730. (NEHGS)

ATKIN, HENRY, Kinghorn, member of the Scots Charitable Society of Boston, 1740. (NEHGS)

BAIN, JOHN, typefounder in St Andrews 1742, later in Camlachie, Glasgow, emigrated to America, type founder in Philadelphia. [SSA.86]

BALEASE, ROBERT, wright in Kirkcaldy, to America after 1823. (SG.33.2.184)

BALFOUR, ANN, born 1838 daughter of David Balfour and Elizabeth Morris, died Hokitika, New Zealand, 1.10.1885. (Anstruther Wester g/s)

BALFOUR, JAMES, born 1836 son of William Balfour and Mary Duncan, died America 30.7.1875 (Kilrenny g/s)

BALLANTINE, DAVID, born 1753 son of David Ballantine and Elisabeth Mitchell, died Kingston, Jamaica, 4.6.1777. (Burntisland g/s)

BARCLAY, CHARLES, born 1790 son of Reverend Peter Barclay and Margaret Duddingston in Kettle, died Guadaloupe 1819. (F.5.160)

BARCLAY, ELIZABETH CLELLAND, born 12.2.1792 Kettle daughter of Reverend Peter Barclay and Margaret Duddingston, wife of Thomas Martin, merchant in Antigua, died 4.12.1841. (F.5.160)

BARCLAY, JOHN, ex Carricou, Grenada, died Cupar 1801. (SRO.SC20.33.14)

BARCLAY, JOHN, born 9.7.1795 at Kettle son of Reverend Peter Barclay and Margaret Duddingston, minister educated Edinburgh University, settled Kingston, Ontario, died 29.9.1826. (F.5.160)

BARKER, JOHN, died Middelburg, Holland, 7.9.1888. (Kirkcaldy g/s)

BARRON, JAMES, born 1828 son of John Barron, shipmaster, died Cook Strait, New Zealand, 14.2.1869. (Ferry Port on Craig g/s)

BAXTER, GEORGE, born 21.1.1854 son of Thomas Baxter and Janet Wilson, died Silvertown, New South Wales, 16.5.1885. (Newburgh g/s)

BEALL, NINIAN, born 1625 Largo, soldier transported to Barbados 1650, settled Maryland, died Fife's Largo, Maryland, 1717, pro 28.2.1717 Maryland.

BELL, ALEXANDER, born 1649 St Andrews son of Alexander Bell and Margaret Ramsay, died Maryland 1744. (SG.28.4.189)

Emigrants and Adventurers from Fife

BELL, ANDREW, born 27.3.1753 St Andrews son of Alexander Bell and
Margaret Robertson, clergyman and teacher educated St Andrews
University, emigrated to Virginia 1774, later HEICS chaplain in
Madras, died 27.1.1832. (Westminster Abbey g/s)
BELL, AUGUSTUS CLIFFORD, son of Reverend David Bell and Sarah Scott,
clergyman, died Bangalore 21.4.1874. (Kennoway g/s)
BELL, CATHERINE, born 1817, wife of William Roy, died New Orleans
27.5.1858. (Cupar g/s)
BELL, CHARLES, late Governor of Annamabee, Africa, 1788.
[SRO.RS.Fife, 1989]
BELL, DAVID, 21st Fusiliers, died Bellary, East Indies, 16.7.1864.
(Kennoway g/s)
BELL, WILLIAM, born 1815 son of Thomas Bell and Mary Tod, died on voyage
to Bermuda 20.10.1842. (Kirkcaldy g/s)
BELL, Lieutenant ROBERT, son of Colonel George Bell, died Madras
25.9.1835. (St Andrews g/s)
BENNET, JAMES, born 1831, died Castle Point, Wellington, New Zealand,
17.2.1880. (Kilconquhar g/s)
BENNET, LAWRENCE, in Poland, son of William Bennett of Balgonie, 1617.
(SRO.RS{Fife}.1.30)
BENNET, WILLIAM, merchant in Keidon, Lithuania, son of Rev. James Bennet
in Auchtermuchty, 1672. (SRO.RD4.32.255)
BERWICK, DAVID, born 1829 son of David and Jean Berwick, died Oakland,
California, 12.2.1896. (St Andrews g/s)
BERWICK, JAMES, born 1835 son of James Berwick and Agnes Young, banker
in Hong Kong, died St Andrews 29.4.1881. (St Andrews g/s)
BETHUNE, Sir HENRY LINDSAY, born 12.4.1787, major general, died Persia
19.2.1851. (Kilconquhar g/s)
BEVERIDGE, HENRY, born 1798 son of Michael Beveridge in Kirkcaldy, died
1819 Demerara. (Blackwood's Magazine 7.231)
BEVERIDGE, JOHN, born 1847 son of Alexander Beveridge and Isabella
Pringle, died Antwerp 6.1.1875. (Dunnikier g/s)
BEVERIDGE, WILLIAM, born 1842 son of Alexander Beveridge and Isabella
Pringle, died St Thomas, West Indies, 24.8.1865. (Dunnikier g/s)
BIRRELL, GEORGE, Captain in East India Company Service, 1789.
[SRO.RS.Fife, 2124]
BISSET, ROBERT, born 1830, died Fiji 25.8.1884. (Dunfermline g/s)
BLACK, DAVID, born 1846 son of John Black and Elizabeth Deas, died Klip
Drift, South Africa, 14.1.1872. (Markinch g/s)
BLACK, JAMES TAYLOR, born 1850 son of Robert Black and Isabella Dow,
died Valparaiso 16.10.1894. (Ferry Port on Craig g/s)
BLACK, JOHN, born 11.3.1817, ex Hudson Bay Company, died 3.2.1879.
(St Andrews g/s)

Emigrants and Adventurers from Fife

BLACK, WILLIAM, born 1794, settled Charleston, South Carolina,
naturalised 1828 Charleston. (US.Nat.Arch.M1183.1)
BLACK, WILLIAM, born 1837 son of William Black and Christian Pyott, died
Livingstonia 7.5.1877. (Dunbog g/s)
BLAKE, RICHARD, born 1827 at Burn Mill, Leven, settled Dunedin, New
Zealand, died 24.3.1877 Leven. (St Monance g/s)
BONELLA, ANN, daughter of John Bonella and Margaret Fernie, died Kansas
19.9.1859. (Leuchars g/s)
BONTHRON, JOHN, born 1789, emigrated to Philadelphia 1817, naturalised
1828 Washington, D.C.
BOWER, ALEXANDER, son of Alexander and Helen Bower, mariner died
Batavia   8.12.1830. (St Andrews g/s)
BOWER, JOHN, born 1821 son of Alexander and Helen Bower, shipmaster
died Panama 22.4.1853. (St Andrews g/s)
BOWMAN, DAVID, Kirkcaldy, planter in Accomack County, Virginia, died
1785, pro 1786 Accomack.
BRAID, NORMAN, born 1791 son of John Braid and Catherine Porterfield,
surgeon died Borneo 22.7.1811. (St Andrews g/s)
BRIGGS, Major JAMES, died Bergen-op-Zoom 3.4.1855. (Largo g/s)
BRIGGS, JOHN, late of Calcutta, 1790. [SRO.RS.Fife, 2614]
BRIGGS, WILLIAM, Quartermaster 20th Bengal Native Infantry, died
Moorshedabad 1827. (Largo g/s)
BRODIE, ALEXANDER, late of Madras, 1789. [SRO.RS.Fife, 2121]
BROUGHTON, CICELIA ANNE, wife of Surgeon Major D. Wright, died
Kathmandu, Nepal, 17.2.1873. (St Andrews g/s)
BROWN, AGNES, born 1841 daughter of John Brown and Isabella Duncan,
wife of Reverend Andrew Baillie, died Lucea, Jamaica, 25.11.1872.
(St Andrews g/s)
BROWN, ALEXANDER, born 1815, engineer of the Netherlands India
Company,   died Surabaya, Java, 9.7.1863. (Balmerino g/s)
BROWN, ANN, daughter of William Brown and Janet Ogilvy, wife of
Laurence Constable Browne, died St Petersburg 16.6.1814.
(St Andrews g/s)
BROWN, DAVID, born 1785 son of David Brown and Helen Oswald, died
Jamaica 2.1.1830. (Kingsbarns g/s)
BROWN, GEORGE, St Andrews, member of the Scots Charitable Society of
Boston, 1744. (NEHGS)
BROWN, GEORGE, born 1832 son of Charles Brown and Mary Kinnear, died
Brooklyn 24.2.1874. (Ferry Port on Craig g/s)
BROWN, JAMES, born 1838 son of Thomas Brown and Margaret Balfour in
Cellardyke, died Antwerp 9.12.1889. (Anstruther Easter g/s)
BROWN, JOHN, born 1843 son of James Brown and Janet Gardner, died
Namino, British Columbia 12.4.1886. (St Monance g/s)

Emigrants and Adventurers from Fife

BROWN, SIMON, born 1801 son of James Brown and Margaret Arnot, shipmaster, died Port au Prince 19.4.1829. (Ferry Port on Craig g/s)

BROWN, THOMAS, merchant in Rotterdam, wife Beiges Johnston, 1608. (SRO.RS, Fife, XI.208)

BROWN, THOMAS, born 1835 son of John Brown and Mary Hodge, died Australia 25.3.1862 (Kilrenny g/s)

BROWN, THOMAS, born 1834 son of John and Jane Brown, died Melbourne 22.10.1879. (Kilconquhar g/s)

BROWN, WILLIAM, born 1829 son of James Brown and Janet Gardner, died New York 21.6.1866. (St Monance g/s)

BRUCE, Lord EDWARD, died Bergen op Zoom, Holland, 1613. (Culross g/s)

BRUCE, ROBERT, born 1832 son of William Bruce and Jean Anderson, died Korrit, Victoria, 16.10.1890. (Collessie g/s)

BRYCE, ALEXANDER, born 1848 son of William Bryce, died Charters Towers, Queensland, 28.1.1884. (Aberdour g/s)

BRYCE, WILLIAM, born 14.2.1830 son of William Bryce, Lieutenant Madras Fusiliers, died Calcutta 14.10.1852. (Aberdour g/s)

BUIK, ROBERT, born 1809 son of Robert Buik and Jean Dick, died St Louis, South America, 28.10.1832. (Cupar g/s)

BUIST, GEORGE, born 1778, minister educated at Edinburgh University, settled Charleston, South Carolina, 1793, died 1852. (F.

BUIST, HENRY, born 1804 son of Henry Buist and Rachel Robertson, died Canada 19.12.1876. (Strathmiglo g/s)

BURNS, PATRICK, born 2.1807, Auditor General of the Leeward Islands, died 2.7.1875. (St Andrews g/s)

BURT, JAMES, ex Kirkcaldy, soldier, married Helena Moor from St Andrews in Bergen-op-Zoom, Netherlands 1585. (Bergen op Zoom Marriage Register)

BUTE, JAMES, son of John Bute and Elizabeth Whyte, settled Houston, Texas, pre 1894. (Torryburn g/s)

BUTTERS, JOHN H., born 2.4.1798 Fife, to New York 28.8.1829, naturalised 26.9.1840 New York

CAMERON, ALLEN, born in Auchtermuchty, wife Mary Stewart, settled Bladen County, North Carolina, died 1800. (GBF)

CAMPBELL, DAVID, HEICS Madras, died St Andrews 27.1.1828. (St Andrews g/s)

CAMPBELL, JAMES DAVID LYON, died Melbourne 31.5.1844 (St Andrews g/s)

CAMPBELL, MARGARET, born 1846 daughter of Alexander Campbell and Agnes Reddoch, died America 23.3.1875. (Tulliallan g/s)

CANT, DAVID, born 1807 son of Reverend George Cant, died South Australia 13.5.1876. (Kingsbarns g/s)

CARSTAIRS, THOMAS, born Largo 1759, architect, settled Pennsylvania 1784. (Scots Overseas{Edinburgh, 1966}119)

Emigrants and Adventurers from Fife

CASSEL, JOHN, born 1779 in Cupar, minister and teacher educated
St Andrew's University, settled Nova Scotia 1811, died Bocca Bec,
St Patrick's, New Brunswick, 18.7.1850. [StAUL]

CATHCART, TAYLOR, son of James Cathcart of Pitcairly, educated Glasgow
University 1793, settled Jamaica. (MAGU171)

CATTON, JOHN EDWARD, born 1853, settled Punjab, died Braemar
17.8.1886. (Aberdour g/s)

CHALMERS, JAMES, Elie, member of the Scots Charitable Society of Boston,
1771. (NEHGS)

CHALMERS, THOMAS H., born Fife 1793, grocer, naturalised 7.5.1821 New
York.

CHALMERS, WILLIAM, born 1778 son of John Chalmers and Elizabeth Hall,
died on the Queen , Rio de Janeiro 1800. (Anstruther Easter g/s)

CHARLES, ALEXANDER H., born 1857 son of A.H.Charles and Jeanne Steel,
died Isle de Naos, Panama Bay 6.9.1885. (Burntisland g/s)

CHRISTIE, ANDREW, born 1788 son of Andrew Christie and Margaret
Dempster, died India 26.11.1821. (Cupar g/s)

CHRISTIE, JOHN, born 1833 son of George Christie and Christine Strobie,
died Rio de Janeiro 7.2.1853. (Ferry Port on Craig g/s)

CHRISTIE, ROBERT, of Durie, born 24.7.1818, Captain 5th Bengal Light
Cavalry HEICS, died 29.8.1896. (St Monance g/s)

CHRISTIE, WILLIAM, born 16.12.1817 son of John Christie and Janet
Jamieson, died Port of Spain, Trinidad, 4.4.1838. (Tulliallan g/s)

CLEGHORN, ALLAN MACKENZIE, son of Peter Cleghorn, 4th Madras Native
Infantry, died Hong Kong 4.11.1844. (Dunino g/s)

CLEGHORN, ISABELLA, born 1823 daughter of Peter Cleghorn, died Rome
1888. (Dunino g/s)

CLEGHORN, PETER, of Stravithie, barrister in Madras, died 9.6.1863.
(Dunino g/s)

CLEPHANE, JAMES, born 20.10.1790 son of Thomas Clephane, emigrated
from Kirkcaldy to Virginia 1817, settled Washington, D.C.,
naturalised 10.12.1833 Washington, D.C. (BLG2621)

COCHRANE, JAMES CHURCH, Bengal Civil Service, died Azamgarh 4.2.1874.
(Cupar g/s)

COCHRANE, JOHN, physician, educated St Andrews University, emigrated
pre 1744 to Kingston, Jamaica. (SRO.NRAS.726.5)

COCKBURN, WILLIAM, son of William Cockburn and Euphemia Hunter,
lieutenant of 24th Native Infantry, died India 1820. (Cupar g/s)

COLDSTREAM, ALEXANDER, born 1766 son of Alexander Coldstream and
Janet Goodfellow, died on passage from Dominica 6.8.1809.
(St Andrews g/s)

CONNACHER, WILLIAM, born 1844 son of William Connacher and Helen
Scott, died Gelong, Victoria, 12.9.1871. (Forgan g/s)

Emigrants and Adventurers from Fife

COOK, JOHN, born 8.8.1800, master mariner, died 14.11.1831, buried Holland. (Pittenweem g/s)

COOK, JOSEPH, born 1831 son of Joseph Cook and Isabella Girdwood, died Dunedin, Otago, New Zealand, 20.1.1886. (St Andrews g/s)

COOK, WALTER, born 1815 son of John Cook, Lieutenant HEICS, died Cape of Good Hope 7.11.1838. (St Andrews g/s)

COOK, WILLIAM, wife Margaret Symson, ex St Andrews, in Little Scotland, Danzig, cnf 1550 St Andrews

COOPER, JAMES LUNDIN, Madras Fusiliers, died Lucknow, 25.10.1857. (Kirkcaldy g/s)

CORNFOOT, ANDREW JAMES, born 1807 Largo, died Surinam 1830. (Blackwood's Magazine 28.574)

CORSTORPHINE, CHARLES, died Georgetown, Demerara, 12.8.1867. (St Andrews g/s)

CORSTORPHINE, GEORGE, born 1806 son of Thomas Corstorphine and Ann Johnston, died Barbados 20.9.1834. (St Andrews g/s)

COUL, JOHN, born 1821 son of John Coul and Ann Bissett, died Windsor, California, 3.12.1878. (Leuchars g/s)

COUSTON, MARGARET, daughter of William Couston and Catherine Brock, died Bombay 10.2.1896. (Torryburn g/s)

CRAWFORD, ANDREW, born 1827 son of Andrew Crawford and Jean Davidson, died Hong Kong 22.8.1861 (Kilrenny g/s)

CRAWFORD, JOHN, born 1828 son of Andrew Crawford and Jean Davidson, died Melbourne 4.4.1864 (Kilrenny g/s)

CRAWFORD, WILLIAM, born 1794 son of William Crawford, Lieutenant in the 16th Bengal Native Infantry, died Calcutta 6.4.1818. (St Andrews g/s)

CROLL, ANDREW, born 1821 son of Charles Croll and Janet Mitchell, died Quebec 18.6.1848. (St Andrews g/s)

CUMMING, JAMES, born 1829 son of George and Janet Cumming, shipmaster, died Barbados 27.5.1855. (Ferry Port on Craig g/s)

CUMMING, JOHN BALFOUR, born 1817, staff sergeant Bengal Artillery, died 12.1.1892. (Culross g/s)

CUNNINGHAM, JAMES, born 1722, soldier in Scots Brigade in Holland, died Brompton 1793. (Inverkeithing g/s)

CUTHBERT, JAMES, of Berthier, HM Legislative Councillor in Canada, son of David Cuthbert (1715-1781). (Culross g/s)

DAIRSIE, MARGARET, daughter of John Dairsie and Agnes Robertson, married William Sturgeon, died Westerly, Rhode Island, 5.1849. (Anstruther Easter g/s)

DALL, ALEXANDER, born 1815 son of James Dall and Agnes Black, customs officer, died Falmouth, Jamaica, 8.9.1840.(Leuchars g/s)(Cupar g/s)

Emigrants and Adventurers from Fife

DALL, WILLIAM, born 1797, died Racine, Wisconsin, 24.5.1877.
(Newburgh g/s)
DALRYMPLE, JOHN HAMILTON, born 1777, Customs Collector at Montego
Bay, Jamaica, died 7.8.1804. (St Andrews g/s)
DALRYMPLE, ROBERT, Burntisland, member of the Scots Charitable Society
of Boston, 1739. (NEHGS)
DAVIDSON, ALEXANDER, born 1788 son of John Davidson, mariner, died
Bengal 23.10.1809 (Kilrenny g/s)
DAVIDSON, Captain GEORGE, born 1774 son of John Davidson, died Isle de
France (Mauritius) 22.2.1810 (Kilrenny g/s)
DAVIDSON, JAMES, born 1823 son of John Davidson and Margaret Ramage in
Dunfermline, emigrated to Canada 1844. (SG.39.1.40)
DAVIDSON, JOHN, born 1834 son of John Davidson and Janet Sutherland,
died Adelaide, South Australia, 22.7.1881. (Burntisland g/s)
DAVIDSON, MARGARET, born 1805, wife of James Anderson, died Calcutta
1843. (Kennoway g/s)
DAVIDSON, ROBERT, ex Cupar, soldier, married Adriaen Michiels in Brda,
Netherlands, 1594. (Breda Marriage Register)
DEMPSTER, JAMES, born in Cupar, Fife, 1760, died in Georgia 18.10.1802.
(Georgia g/s)
DICKSON, THOMAS, shipmaster, died Dieppe 16.6.1866. (Crail g/s)
DOIG, JOHN, born 1809 son of James Doig and Anne Henderson, died
Hobarttown, Tasmania, 12.12.1859. (Burntisland g/s)
DOIG, Captain ROBERT FLEMING, adjutant 2nd Regiment of Infantry, died
Bolarum, Hyderabad Deccan, 12.8.1871. (Torryburn g/s)
DOIG, WILLIAM, born 1829 son of John Doig and Elizabeth Watson, died
Williamstown, Australia, 17.10.1882. (Kilrenny g/s)
DONALD, EBENEZER, born 1820 son of James Donald and Helen
Fotheringham, died at sea 22.4.1848. buried Old Castle, Dardanelles.
(Tulliallan g/s)
DONALD, THOMAS, born 1823 son of James Donald and Helen Fotheringham,
died 27.2.1882, buried Syria, Greece(sic). (Tulliallan g/s)
DONALDSON, THOMAS, Cupar, emigrated via Belfast to New York on the
Perseverance, Crawford, 1811. (NWI.2.335)
DOUGLAS, CHARLES HILL, born 1832, died Melbourne 30.3.1898.
(Dunfermline g/s)
DOUGLAS, JOHN, born 1784 Dunfermline, brewer, distiller and storekeeper,
settled Whitestown, Oneida County, New York, naturalised 2.5.1821
& 11.10.1830 New York.
DOUGLAS, ROBERT, in Jamaica and in Burntisland, cnf 20.8.1816
St Andrews. [SRO.CC20.30.204]
DRUMMOND, KATHERINE, daughter of James Drummond in Kelty, died
Kingston, Jamaica, 1806. (Scots Magazine 69.77)

Emigrants and Adventurers from Fife

DRUMMOND, THOMAS, born 1742 son of James Drummond of Lundin and
Rachel Bruce, settled New York 1768, Loyalist, died Bermuda 1780.
(Scots Peerage 5)
DRYSDALE, ALEXANDER, born 21.5.1870 son of James Drysdale and Euphane
Young, died Camillo, Spain, 21.2.1897, (Tulliallan g/s)
DUNCAN, JAMES, born 1772, son of William Duncan and Agnes Sime, died
Savannah, America, 1798 (Kilmany g/s)
DUNCAN, JAMES, born 1826, paymaster of the 13th Regiment of Foot, died
South Africa 5.11.1878. (St Andrews g/s)
DUNDAS, DAVID, ex St Andrews, admitted as a citizen of Cracow, Poland,
1576. ((Lib.Jur.Civ.Cracow 1555-1601, f.551)
DURHAM, Admiral Sir PHILIP CHARLES HENDERSON CALDERWOOD, of Largo,
born Largo 29.7.1763, died Naples 2.4.1845. (Largo g/s)
DUTCH, DAVID, born 1849 son of William Dutch and Helen Hay, died Sydney
3.12.1873. (Ferry Port on Craig g/s)
DUTCH, JOHN, born 1837 son of William Dutch and Helen Hay, died Cape
Horn 18.5.1853. (Ferry Port on Craig g/s)
EASON, JOHN, shipbuilder, son of Thomas Eason and Margaret Henderson,
settled Hobartstown, Van Diemen's Land pre 1854. (Anstruther
Easter g/s)
ECKFORD, JOHN, son of John Eckford and Janet Buntine, Captain of HEICS
ship Lady Dundas, died 1809. (Dunfermline g/s)
EDIE, ALEXANDER, born 1801, son of David Edie and Mary Stark, Lieutenant
HEICS, died India 1825 (Kilmany g/s)
EMMERSON, JAMES, born 1809 son of Thomas Emmerson and Elspeth
Fleming, died Melbourne 17.9.1864. (Crail g/s)
EMMERSON, THOMAS, born 1802 son of Thomas Emmerson and Elspeth
Fleming, died Calcutta 3.8.1831. (Crail g/s)
ERSKINE, ROBERT, born 7.9.1735 Dunfermline son of Reverend Ralph
Erskine and Margaret Simson, Geographer and Surveyor General of the
US Army, died America 2.10.1780. (F.5.30)
FAIR, JOHN, son of John Fair and Helen ...., paymaster, 63rd Foot, died
Barbados 4.7.1808 (Kilconquhar g/s)
FAIR, THOMAS, son of John Fair and Helen ..., Captain HEICS, died Goa
24.12.1822 (Kilconquhar g/s)
FAIRLEY, THOMAS, born 1800, died Marseilles 4.5.1855. (Culross g/s)
FALCONER, ALEXANDER, ex St Andrews, died Franklin County, North
Carolina, 17.3.1818. (Raleigh Register 3.1818)
FERNIE, GEORGE, son of William Fernie of Tillywhandland, Lieutenant of
10th Bengal Native Cavalry, died Jallalabad, Afghanistan, 29.7.1842.
(St Andrews g/s)
FERRIER, JAMES, son of George Ferrier and Elizabeth Bayne, settled
Montreal pre 1841. (Auchtermuchty g/s)

Emigrants and Adventurers from Fife

FINDLAY, THOMAS, of Balkirsty, son of James Findlay, settled Barbados pre 1741, father of Thomas, Isabella, Margaret and Helen, died 6.1760. (SRO.RD3.224.9)

FINLAY, WILLIAM, Fife, member of the Scots Charitable Society of Boston, 1739. (NEHGS)

FLEMING, ANDREW, wright in Kirkcaldy, to America after 1824. (SG.33.2.184)

FORBES, ALEXANDER, Wemyss, Jacobite transported to Jamaica 1747. (PRO.CO137.58)

FORBES, ALEXANDER, born 1830 son of John Forbes and Jean Dick, died Berbice, British Guina, 23.10.1876. (Anstruther Easter g/s)

FORBES, ROBERT, born 1855 son of William Forbes and Margaret Hopkins, died Leadville, Colorado, 10.12.1891. (St Andrews g/s)

FORDYCE or BALFOUR, EUPHEMIA KATHERINE, died Pau Basse, Pyrenees, 9.1.1852 (Markinch g/s)

FORREST, JAMES NAIRNE, born 1842 son of Thomas Forrest and Janet Alexander, surgeon, died Nagasaki 29.7.1873. (Elie g/s)

FORTUNE, JOHN, son of John Fortune and Margaret Gray, died Kingston, Jamaica, 1.10.1853. (St Andrews g/s)

FOSTER, ANDREW, born 25.6.1772 son of John Foster and Barbara Fairnie in Kinghorn, merchant in New York by 1798, married (1) Ann Giraud, (2) Ann Ten Eyck, father of Jacob, died New York 25.12.1849. (ANY.1.334)

FOULIS, PETER, born 1836 son of Robert Foulis, engineer RN, died Bermuda 31.10.1875. (Aberdour g/s)

FOWLER, ALEXANDER, born 1830 son of Robert Fowler and Elizabeth Rodger, died 5.9.1856 on the Northern Bride, River Hooghly. (Kilrenny g/s)

FOWLER, GEORGE SWAN, born 9.3.1835 son of James Fowler and Rhea Anderson, died Mitcham, South Australia, 1.10.1896. (Kilrenny g/s)

FRASER, DAVID, Parbroath, member of the Scots Charitable Society of Boston, 1743. (NEHGS)

FRASER, FINLAY, born 1826, gardener in Fife, arrived in Hobart, Tasmania, on the John Bell 4.12.1855. (SRA.TD292)

GALLOWAY, JAMES, born 1829 son of James Galloway in Springfield, died Melbourne 7.7.1860. (Collessie g/s)

GEDDES, JOHN, born 1829 son of Alexander Geddes and Jean Ramsay, died Westmoreland, Jamaica, 27.8.1857. (Cupar g/s)

GEDDIE, JOHN, Kinkell, Fife, soldier in Holland 1640. (SRO.SH1640)

GIBB, HENRY WILLIAM, born 1813 son of Henry Gibb, died Port Adelaide, New South Wales 8.1.1842. (Dunfermline g/s)

GIBB, WALTER, born 1838 son of Thomas Gibb, died India 15.10.1870. (Kennoway g/s)

Emigrants and Adventurers from Fife

GLASS, CUDBERT THORNHILL, born 1793, eldest son of Lt. Col. Glass in
St Andrews, died 14.12.1830. [South Park g/s, Calcutta]
GOODFELLOW, JOHN, born 1800 son of Thomas Goodfellow and Catherine
Farquharson, died New Granada 1860. (Ceres g/s)
GOODWILLY, DAVID, Cupar, transported 4.1752. (SRO.B59.26.11.5.13)
GORDON, JOHN SUTHERLAND, born 1821, planter in Demerara, died
19.8.1880. (Burntisland g/s)
GORRIE, WILLIAM, born 1842 son of David Gorrie and Barbara Bett, died Rio
de Janeiro 26.9.1872. (Ferry Port on Craig g/s)
GOVAN, GEORGE MONCRIEFF, brigade surgeon, died Almora, India, 1.4.1898.
(Cupar g/s)
GOVAN, JOHN GEORGE, died Darjeeling 5.3.1850. (Cupar g/s)
GRANT, ALEXANDER, MD, born 7.11.1827, died Bombay 18.11.1853.
(Kennoway g/s)
GRAY, CHARLES, born 1818 son of Major George Gray, RM, and Ann Roger,
died Narreb Narreb, Victoria, 27.1.1905. (Anstruther Wester g/s)
GRAY, JOHN, Creich, soldier in Georgia, pro 1770 PCC.
GRAY, MARY ANN, born Anstruther, daughter of Major George Gray and Ann
Roger, died Melbourne 21.2.1903. (Anstruther Wester g/s)
GRAY, THOMAS CARSTAIRS, born 17.1.1817 Anstruther, Lieutenant 29th
Bengal Native Infantry, died Meerut 11.10.1829. (Kingsbarns g/s)
GREENHILL, DAVID, son of David Greenhill and Agnes Hill in Russellmill,
died Hamilton, Canada West, 23.11.1873. (Cupar g/s)
GREENHILL, JOHN, born 1811 son of David Greenhill and Agnes Hill in
Russellmill, died Binbrook, Canada West, 15.2.1868. (Cupar g/s)
GREIG, DAVID, born 1801, Kilrenny, died Greenland 10.8.1832.
(Boarhills   g/s)
GRIM, GEORGE, ex Crail, soldier, married J.Wauchop in Schiedam,
Netherlands, 1636. (Schiedam Marriage Register)
GRUBB, JAMES, born 1815, shipmaster, died Philadelphia 21.5.1849. (Ferry
Port on Craig g/s)
GRUBB, Mrs JANET, born 1788 Fife, naturalised New York 20.5.1828.
GURLEY, Captain William, of Peterhop, born 1783, St Vincent, died
30.10.1824. (Inverkeithing g/s)
HALKETT, JOHN, of Pitfirran, born 1769, Governor of the Bahamas, died
1852. (Dunfermline g/s)
HASTIE, JOHN, born 1827 son of James Hastie and Agnes Cairns, died New
Zealand 12.2.1868. (Kettle g/s)
HAY, DAVID, born 1808 son of John Hay and Ann Tod, married Jane Berwick,
died Parua, New Zealand, 14.1.1889. (Leuchars g/s)
HAY, GRAHAM, born 1835, Lieutenant Colonel 62nd (Wiltshire) Regt., died
Morar, India, 10.5.1878. (St Andrews g/s)

Emigrants and Adventurers from Fife

HAY, HENRY, born 1838 son of David Hay and Helen Morris, died New
   Zealand 20.8.1893. (Leuchars g/s)
HAY, JAMES, born 1809 son of Alexander Hay and Jeannie Scott, died New
   Orleans 10.12.1835. (Kilconquhar g/s)
HEAD, JAMES, captain of the HEICS Canning died Calcutta River 1824.
   (Balcarres g/s)
HENDERSON, JAMES, born 1708 son of William Henderson, settled Augusta
   County, Virginia, pre 1760, died 1784. (RAV46)
HENDERSON, JAMES, born 1839 son of John Henderson and Elizabeth
   Orchard, died India 1.6.1878. (Cupar g/s)
HENDERSON, JOHN, in Dunfermline, late of Georgia, 1787.
   [SRO.RS.Fife, 1635]
HENDERSON, JOHN, born 1768 son of John Henderson and Elizabeth Hay,
   Captain in the 42nd Regiment, died Paullace, France, 7.7.1814.
   (Logie g/s)
HENDERSON, THOMAS, settled Jamestown, Virginia, 1607, father of
   Richard. (CAG.1.928)(CF.4.179)
HENDERSON, THOMAS, born 1802 son of George Henderson and Janet Tod,
   died Leghorn 11.10.1854. (Pittenweem g/s)
HENDERSON, THOMAS, born 1831 son of David Henderson and Margaret
   Miller, died Windermere, Victoria, 19.7.1866. (Balmerino g/s)
HERRON, JAMES, died Melbourne 24.2.1853. (Cairneyhill g/s)
HILL, JOHN, Colonel in the Madras Army, died Winberg, Cape of Good Hope,
   14.5.1866. (St Andrews g/s)
HIRD, WILLIAM, son of William Hird, physician in Rennes, Brittany, 1626.
   (SRO.SH1626)
HONEYMAN, DAVID, born 1827 son of Charles Honeyman and Angela Philp,
   died America 8.1849. (Monimail g/s)
HOOD, MARTIN, ex Burntisland, soldier, married Annette Antonis in Brielle,
   Netherlands, 1681. (Brielle Marriage Register)
HOPE, HARRY, born in Falkland 28.12.1800, died in Howrah 2.11.1840.
   [Howrah g/s, Bengal]
HOPE, WILLIAM, born in Falkland 1803, died in Howrah 18.6.1841.
   [Howrah g/s, Bengal]
HORSBURGH, JAMES, born Elie 23.9.1762, HEICS Hydrographer in Bombay,
   died 14.5.1836. (Elie g/s)
HORSBURGH, THOMAS PATE, born 1819 son of Andrew Horsburgh of Firth
   and   Christian Pollock, died Chatham Island, New Zealand, 11.1855.
   (Pittenweem g/s)
HOWDEN, JOHN, born 1783 son of Archibald Howden and Joan Manderson,
   merchant, died Savannah, Georgia, 26.10.1806. (St Monance g/s)
   (Savanna Death Register)

Emigrants and Adventurers from Fife

HUNT, JOHN, ex Dunfermline, settled Charleston, South Carolina, 1803, naturalised 1808. (South Carolina Court of Common Pleas Z3/150)

HUNTER, FRANCIS JEFFREY, born 1802 son of James Hunter and Jane Wilson, Lieutenant HEICS Bengal, died Calcutta 10.3.1833. (St Andrews g/s)

HUNTER, JAMES, born 1849, died Mobile, Alabama, 31.1.1886. (St Andrews g/s)

HUNTER, THOMAS, son of Thomas Hunter of Elie and Christina Morrison, settled New Zealand pre 1847. (Newburn g/s)

HUTCHISON, ANDREW, born 1786 son of Andrew Hutchison and Mary Malcolm, surgeon HMS Sapphire, died Chagre, Spanish Main, 17.9.1819. (Burntisland g/s)

HUTTON, JAMES, born 1747, factor, naturalised 1796 Charleston, South Carolina. (US.National Archives M1183/1)

HUTTON, JOHN, born 1852 son of James Hutton and Margaret Rogers, died at sea on voyage from New York to Leith 11.1868. (Crombie g/s)

HUTTON, MARY, born 1816 daughter of David Hutton, died California 25.1.1854. (Cupar g/s)

INGLIS, JAMES, son of John Inglis and Annie Robertson, died Australia 9.11.1884. (Burntisland g/s)

INGLIS, ROBERT, of Kirkmay, born 1813, died Allahabad 1841. (Crail g/s)

INNES, DAVID, born 1812, died 30.11.1835 on the Home on the banks of Newfoundland. (Anstruther Easter g/s)

IRELAND, GEORGE, born 1804 son of John Ireland and Mary Jackson, died St Petersburg 7.10.1819. (Ferry Port on Craig g/s)

IRELAND, ISABELLA, born 1818, Fife, arrived in Hobart, Tasmania, on the Ocean Chief 25.3.1855. (SRA.TD292)

IRELAND, JAMES, born 1827 son of William Ireland and Euphemia Roger, died East Oakland, California, 16.3.1884. (Ferry Port on Craig g/s)

IRELAND, PETER, born 1817, ploughman in Fife, arrived in Hobart, Tasmania, on the Ocean Chief 25.3.1855. (SRA.TD292)

IRELAND, WALTER FOGGO, son of Walter Foggo Ireland, Captain of the Bengal Police, died Narsinghpur 6.7.1865. (St Andrews g/s)

IZATT, ANDREW, born 1820, labourer in Fife, arrived in Hobart, Tasmania, on the John Bell 4.12.1855. (SRA.TD292)

JACK, DAVID WILLIAM, born 25.2.1785 son of William Jack in Cupar, settled St Andrews, New Brunswick. (American Armory and Blue Book: London 1903)

JACKSON, DAVID, born 1800 Kirkcaldy, settled Richmond, Virginia, 1822, naturalised Virginia 1825. (US.D/C.RB5./492)

JACKSON, GEORGE, born 1803 son of James Jackson and Margaret Bread, died Baltimore 15.7.1830. (Burntisland g/s)

JAMIESON, WILLIAM, born 1837 son of James Jamieson and Catherine

Emigrants and Adventurers from Fife

Hutcheson, died Kobe, Japan, 27.5.1882. (Kirkcaldy g/s)

JOHNSON, ALEXANDER, ex St Andrews, soldier, married Aechtge Willems in Rotterdam 1588. (Rotterdam Marriage Register)

KELLY, ALEXANDER, son of Alexander Kelly and Ann Tod, died Ballerat, Australia, 5.4.1882. (Aberdour g/s)

KENNEDY, DAVID, born 1773 son of Thomas Kennedy and Ann Gibb in Falkland, merchant in Philadelphia, died Germantown, Pennsylvania, 1798. (Falkland g/s)

KENNEDY, JESSIE ROBINA, died Narbong, India, 5.10.1880. (Kilconquhar g/s)

KETTLE, THOMAS YOUNG, born 27.11.1778 Leuchars son of Reverend Thomas Kettle and Sarah Young, settled Savannah, Georgia. (F.5.222)

KEY, WILLIAM INGLIS, born 1816 son of John Key, merchant in New Orleans 1856, died New Orleans 5.4.1868. (Crail g/s)

KIDD, JANET, born 1800 daughter of Thomas Kidd and Margaret Anderson, died Horsham, Victoria, 17.11.1855. (Newburn g/s)

KIDD, JOHN, born 1808 son of Thomas Kidd and Margaret Anderson, died Melbourne 18.3.1853. (Newburn g/s)

KIDD, ROBERT, born 1832 son of Robert Kidd and Elizabeth Smith, died Ephuca, Victoria, 23.9.1882. (Forgan g/s)

KING, JAMES, born 1797 son of James King and Helen Skinner, vinegrower in New South Wales, died London 29.11.1857. (Kilconquhar g/s)

KING, MARY, wife of William Carstairs, died Cape of Good Hope 7.3.1834. (Cupar g/s)

KING, MITCHELL, born Crail 1783, emigrated to America 1805, teacher and judge in Charleston, South Carolina, naturalised 1810 Charleston, died 1862. (US.National Archives M1183/1)

KINNINMONT, JOHN, born 1769, wife Catherine Carstairs, died France 1815. (Kilconquhar g/s)

KIRK, CATHERINE, born 1821 daughter of David Kirk and Janet Walls, died America 1856. (Burntisland g/s)

KIRK, GEORGE, born 1836 son of Alexander Kirk and Elizabeth Clark, died Hawkes Bay, New Zealand, 2.9.1894. (St Andrews g/s)

KIRK, GEORGE, born 1868 son of John Kirk and Margaret McLaren, died America 24.11.1893. (Rosyth g/s)

KIRK, JAMES, son of James Kirk and Elspeth Russell, merchant settled St Johns, New Brunswick, pre 1832. (Pittenweem g/s)

KIRK, JAMES, born 1825 son of Alexander Kirk and Elizabeth Clark, died Braidwood, New South Wales, 27.1.1859. (Pittenweem g/s)

KIRK, ROBERT, born 1841 son of Alexander Kirk and Elizabeth Clark, died at sea off Cape Colony 9.3.1880. (Pittenweem g/s)

KIRKE, ROBERT, born 1816 son of Robert Kirke and Helen Balfour, Greenmount, Burntisland, and Waterloo Nickery, Surinam, died 3.1.1894. (Cairneyhill g/s)

Emigrants and Adventurers from Fife

KYD, GEORGE, son of Captain Kyd in Elie, physician, died St Vincent 1775 (Scots Magazine 37.286)

LAING, PETER, draper in Newburgh, settled Cape of Good Hope, died 1813. (Abdie g/s)

LAIRD, MATTHEW, born 1825 son of Matthew Laird and Margaret Tavendale, died on voyage from Manilla to Sydney 3.9.1846. (Burntisland g/s)

LAMONT, NEIL, MD, member of the Scots Charitable Society of Boston, 1758. (NEHGS)

LATOU, ROBERT, son of Peter Latou and Janet Henderson, settled New York pre 1851. (Leuchars g/s)

LAW, WILLIAM, born 1829 son of Reverend John Law and Jane Murray, died Trinidad 21.8.1855. (Dunfermline g/s)

LAW, WILLIAM, born 1830 son of John and Mary Law, died Rio de Janeiro 1852. (Crail g/s)

LEE, JAMES, born St Andrews, settled New York pre 1795, married Mary Crookshank, father of James, died New York 9.10.1795. (ANY.2.83)

LEES, HENRY, born 1839 son of James Lees, died Chicago 1867. (Kilconquhar g/s)

LEITCH, Reverend WILLIAM, born 1815, 18 years Principal of Queen's College, Kingston, Ontario, wife Euphemia Paterson, died Monimail 9.5.1864. (Monimail g/s)

LEITH, ROBERT, former baillie of Pittenweem, settled Philadelphia pre 1751. (SRO.CS16.1.85)

LESLIE, ALEXANDER, born 1765 son of Andrew Leslie and Jean Orrock, died America 1818. (Burntisland g/s)

LESLIE, ALEXANDER, born 1767, farmer, settled Richmond, Virginia, naturalised 1799 Virginia. (US.D/C.1799.34)

LESLIE, JOHN, ex Kirkcaldy, soldier, married Belijtgie van Maaseyck in Schiedam, Netherlands, 1632. (Schiedam Marriage Register)

LESLIE, JOHN, born 1772 son of Andrew Leslie and Jean Orrock, died America 1818. (Burntisland g/s)

LESLY, DAVID, son of David Lesly and Jane Kinnear, shipmaster settled New York pre 1826. (Monimail g/s)

LESSELS, ANDREW, born 1829 son of George Lessels and Martha Henderson, died Panama 27.8.1868. (Newburgh g/s)

LESSELS, GEORGE, born 1825 son of George Lessels and Martha Henderson, died America 1847. (Newburgh g/s)

LESSELS, JAMES, born 1839 son of George Lessels and Martha Henderson died India 3.11.1845. (Newburgh g/s)

LESSLY, ANDREW, member of the Scots Charitable Society of Boston, 1752. (NEHGS)

Emigrants and Adventurers from Fife

LIDDELL, DAVID, born 1806 son of James Liddell and Agnes Leighton, Captain 10th Bombay Native Infantry, died at sea 21.4.1829. (Aberdour g/s)

LIDDELL, HENRY, born 1801 son of James Liddell and Agnes Leighton, Major 11th Native Infantry, died Bombay 27.12.1841. (Aberdour g/s)

LIDDELL, HENRY, born 1807, Bombay Civil Service, died Culross 29.9.1873. (Auchtertool g/s)

LIDDELL, JAMES, born 1798 son of James Liddell and Agnes Leighton, Major 1st Bombay Cavalry, died Kotra 3.6.1841. (Aberdour g/s)

LIDDELL, JOHN, born 1805 son of James Liddell and Agnes Leighton, Lieutenant Bombay Artillery, died Cape of Good Hope 14.10.1824. (Aberdour g/s)

LIDDELL, JOHN, born 1847 son of David Liddell and Elizabeth Davidson, died Sydney, New South Wales, 15.1.1873. (Auchtertool g/s)

LIDDELL, JOHN, born 1811, Major General Bombay Army, died 12.4.1879. (Auchtertool g/s)

LINDSAY, ADAM, of Nativity, born 1754, Lieutenant Colonel 7th Bengal Native Infantry HEICS, died 12.3.1812. (Dunfermline g/s)

LINDSAY, GEORGE, born 1737 son of George Lindsay of Wormiston and Margaret Bethune, writer, died Havanna, Cuba, 1762. (Scots Peerage.5.415)

LINDSAY, JAMES, born 1794 son of John Lindsay and Margaret Jackson, joiner, died New Orleans 28.8.1822. (Falkland g/s)

LINDSAY, JAMES HEAD, born 2.11.1828 son of Robert Lindsay and Frances Henderson, died Barrackpore, Bengal, 14.8.1856. (St Andrews g/s)

LINDSAY, JOHN, born 2.7.1694 Crail son of John Lindsay and Margaret Haliburton, merchant, settled New York after 1729, died Albany, New York, 12.10.1751. (Scots Peerage.5.415)(SRO.GD203)

LINDSAY, JOHN, born 1801 son of John Lindsay and Margaret Jackson, joiner, died New York 22.5.1855. (Falkland g/s)

LINDSAY, JOHN, born 1803 son of William Lindsay of Balmunzie and Mary Adamson, Lieutenant of 34th Madras Native Infantry, died Rangoon 12.10.1824. (St Andrews g/s)

LINDSAY, ROBERT, born 19.5.1827 son of Robert Lindsay and Frances Henderson, died Trichinopoly, Madras, 18.1.1849. (St Andrews g/s)

LINDSAY, ROBERT, son of Lieutenant General James Lindsay, died Genoa 18.12.1856. (Balcarres g/s)

LITSTER, HUGH, born 1678 son of Reverend Thomas Litster and Margaret Lindsay in Aberdour, sailor on the Rising Sun, died Charleston, South Carolina, 1699, cnf 1708 Edinburgh. (F.5.3)

LOCHTY, JAMES, born 1823 son of John Lochty and Isobel Moyes, died Sydney 23.10.1856. (Aberdour g/s)

Emigrants and Adventurers from Fife

LORIMER, JAMES, born 1852 son of Professor James Lorimer and Hannah
   Stoddart, died Grahamstown, South Africa, 1898. (Newburn g/s)
LOUDEN, Captain ROBERT, shipmaster in Limekilns, died Christiansand,
   Norway, 24.11.1884. (Rosyth g/s)
LOW, IRVINE, major in the Bangal Cavalry, died Simla 26.6.1881.
   (Kemback g/s)
LUKE, DAVID, born St Monance 13.5.1858 son of John Luke and Elizabeth
   Simson, died Melbourne, Australia, 17.9.1909. (Abercrombie g/s)
LUKE, ROBERT S., born 26.10.1859 son of John Luke and Elizabeth Simson,
   died Coolgardie, Western Australia, 13.10.19894. (Abercrombie g/s)
LUMSDAINE, JOHN, Major in East India Company Service, 1786.
   [SRO.RS.Fife, 1385]
LUMSDEN, JAMES, wright in Kirkcaldy, to America after 1827.
   (SG.33.2.184)
McCREDIE, WILLIAM, born 1806, staff assistant surgeon, died Bermuda
   13.10.1840. (Kirkcaldy g/s)
McDONALD, DONALD ALEXANDER, born 1820 son of Angus McDonald and
   Robina MacFarlane, died Furreedport, East Indies 20.9.1845.
   (Dysart g/s)
McDONALD, GORDON, Plantation Moy, Corome, Surinam, died Burntisland
   28.6.1859. (Burntisland g/s)
MACFARLANE, JOHN, born in Fife 1814, died 29.5.1834.
   [Scotch Burial Ground g/s, Calcutta]
MAKGILL, Sir JOHN, born 6.2.1836 son of George Makgill of Kemback, died
   Brackmont, Waiuku, New Zealand, 14.11.1906. (Kemback g/s)
McKENZIE, COLIN, born 1811 son of Colin McKenzie and Marjory Lumsden,
   carpenter on the Firth of Alloa, died China Sea 1836. (Dysart g/s)
McKENZIE, ROBERT, born 1803, "21 years in America", died Leslie
   24.4.1854. (Leslie g/s)
McKIBBIN, ROBERT, born 1840 son of William and Janet McKibbin, died
   Calcutta 7.5.1867. (St Andrews g/s)
McKINLAY, JAMES, mason in Kirkcaldy, to America 1827. (SG.33.2.183)
MACKIE, MARGARET, born 1793, naturalised Charleston, South Carolina,
   1837. (US.National Archives M1183/1)
McLAREN, WALTER, born 1848 son of Walter McLaren and Agnes Meiklejohn,
   died Indian Ocean 3.1876. (Tulliallan g/s)
McLEOD, DAVID, Fife, member of the Scots Charitable Society of Boston,
   1738. (NEHGS)
McNEISH, JOHN, born in Largo 1785, merchant, wife Janet, and five
   children, emigrated from Falkiek to USA, naturalised in New York
   5.2.1828.
McRUVIE, WILLIAM, son of Duncan McRuvie and Agnes Scott, died Ballston
   Spa, USA, 2.4.1888. (Kilconquhar g/s)

Emigrants and Adventurers from Fife

MAIN, GEORGE, ex St Andrews, soldier, married Margaret Brand from
Aberdeen in Geertruidenberg, Netherlands, 1638. (Geertruidenberg
Marriage Register)

MALCOLM, JAMES, Kirkcaldy, member of the Scots Charitable Society of
Boston, 1766. (NEHGS)

MALCOLM, JAMES, born 1809 son of Alexander Malcolm and Janet Allison,
died Adelaide, Australia, 28.10.1865. (Kirkcaldy g/s)

MAN, ANDREW, Dunfermline, emigrated via Glasgow to Pictou, Nova Scotia,
on the Hector 1773, settled in Noel, Nova Scotia.
[The Scots in Canada, p106]

MARTIN, JOHN, rioter in Cupar, transported to America 1773.
(SRO.B59.26.11.1.6.18)

MASON, WILLIAM, born 1764, merchant in Jamaica, died 1.12.1841.
(St Andrews g/s)

MATHER, ARCHIBALD, son of James Mather and Christine Melville, died
Hamburg 10.3.1850. (Ferry Port on Craig g/s)

MATHER, THOMAS, born 1822 son of James Mather and Christine Melville,
shipmaster, died River Gallegos, South America, 23.10.1850.
(Ferry Port on Craig g/s)

MATHESON, ALEXANDER, Anstruther, member of the Scots Charitable
Society of Boston, 1736. (NEHGS)

MATTHEWSON, AGNES, born 1817, widow of William G. Dobie, died Kansas
City, USA, 27.12.1898. (Dunfermline g/s)

MATTHEWSON, JOHN, son of George Matthewson and Elizabeth Melville,
settled New York pre 1854. (Dunnikier g/s)

MAXWELL, JOHN, born 1812 son of Alexander Maxwell and Elizabeth Dutch,
died Davis Strait 8.5.1837. (Ferry Port on Craig g/s)

MAYES, ALEXANDER, born 1740 son of Philip Mayes and Margaret Key,
settled in Newark, Carriacou, died Elie 21.4.1791. (St Monance g/s)

MEIKLEJOHN, ROBERT, born 1818 son of George Meiklejohn and Mary
Anderson, died Aghuay Coast, Guinea, 11.4.1842. (Tulliallan g/s)

MELDRUM, DAVID, born Dundee 22.2.1826 son of William Meldrum and Jane
Millar, died Rio de Janeiro 15.5.1850. (Ferry Port on Craig g/s)

MELDRUM, JEAN STENHOUSE SCOTLAND, born 1811 daughter of George
Meldrum and Janet Stenhouse, died Kulladehee, East Indies, 4.1833.
(Dunfermline g/s)

MELDRUM, JOHN BALFOUR, born 1810 son of James Meldrum, died Paterson,
New Jersey, 3.1883. (Leuchars g/s)

MELVILL, ALAN, Leven, son of Rev. Thomas Melvill in Scoonie, merchant,
settled in Boston 1748, member of the Scots Charitable Society of
Boston, 1749, father of Thomas born 1751. (NEHGS)(ANY.II.79)

MELVILL, JOHN, Leven, member of the Scots Charitable Society of Boston,
1757. (NEHGS)

Emigrants and Adventurers from Fife

MELVILLE, JOHN, born 1794, wife Willemina Durie, shipmaster, died
St Vincent 18.6.1834. (Pittenweem g/s)
MELVIN, JAMES, Pittenweem, member of the Scots Charitable Society of
Boston, 1730. (NEHGS)
MERCER, JAMES, son of Robert Mercer, died Middelberg, South Africa,
8.3.1895. (Torryburn g/s)
MERCER, WILLIAM, shipmaster, died Port au Prince, San Domingo, 1.1839.
(Tulliallan g/s)
METHVEN, ALEXANDER, son of Thomas Methven and Mary Symers, surgeon,
died South Carolina 1807. (St Andrews g/s)
METHVEN, ALEXANDER MELDRUM, born 1806 son of Thomas Methven and
Helen Larbert, Lieutenant in 56th Bengal Native Infantry, died Mhow
24.8.1833. (St Andrews g/s)
METHVEN, Captain CATHCART, son of Thomas Methven and Mary Symers,
died Calcutta 1832. (St Andrews g/s)
MILES, THOMAS, born 1832 son of Thomas Miles and Margaret Thomson,
died North Fork, America River, California, 24.5.1852.
(St Andrews g/s)
MILL, CHARLES, son of Thomas Mill of Blair and Janet Young, Lieutenant
Colonel 55th Regiment of Foot, died Coorg, India, 20.2.1780.
(Crombie g/s)
MILLER, ALEXANDER, chief mate of barque Henry Tanner of London died
Cape Ras Haffoon, north east Africa, 18.8.1858. (Tulliallan g/s)
MILLER, GEORGE, son of George Miller and Janet Morrison, died Savannah
28.9.1839. (Tulliallan g/s)
MILLER, JOHN, son of Alexander Miller, died Cape Ras Haffoon, north east
Africa 18.8.1858. (Tulliallan g/s)
MILLER, STOCKS, son of Walter Miller and Sarah Stocks, died Moorcroft,
Wyoming, 8.1890. (Logie g/s)
MILLER, HARRIET, born 1839, wife of John Davidson, died Adelaide, South
Australia, 21.12.1883. (Burntisland g/s)
MILLER, WILLIAM, son of George Miller and Janet Morrison, died Melbourne
5.4.1871. (Tulliallan g/s)
MILLIE, WILLIAM JAMES, born 1842, died Chittagong, India, 10.4.1874.
(Dunnikier g/s)
MILLIGAN, GEORGE, son of Reverend George Milligan and Agnes Colville,
captain of the Bengal Horse Artillery, died Buyukdere 24.6.1865.
(Elie g/s)
MITCHELL, ALEXANDER, born 1799 son of George Mitchell and Elizabeth
Chiene, Lieutenant of Madras Native Infantry, died at sea 31.3.1827.
(St Andrews g/s)
MITCHELL, ARCHIBALD, born 1856 son of John Mitchell and Janet Nicolson,
marine engineer, died Singapore 28..1904. (Ceres g/s)

Emigrants and Adventurers from Fife

MITCHELL, ROBERT, born 24,8,1817, late of Auckland, New Zealand, died 3.1898. (St Andrews g/s)

MITCHELL, THOMAS, ex Cupar, soldier, married Iffijen Kry in Haarlem 1597. (Haarlem Marriage Register)

MITCHELL, THOMAS, born 1800 son of George Mitchell and Elizabeth Chiene, commander of the Sultan of Calcutta, died off Saugor Island 22.5.1833. (St Andrews g/s)

MITCHELL, THOMAS, son of Robert Mitchell and Margaret Carmichael, died Montreal 10.8.1848. (St Andrews g/s)

MOIR, JAMES, minister, ex Auchtertool(?), died 31.12.1766 Edgecombe County, North Carolina. (Scots Magazine 28.615)(SRO.CS16.1.134)

MONCREIFF, ELIZABETH, spouse of Thomas Brown in France, formerly in Crail, 1672. (SRO.RD4.31.320)

MONRO, JOHN, born 1830 son of Arthur Monro and Helen Reid, died Hamburg 5.12.1859. (Rosyth g/s)

MOODIE, THOMAS, Cocklaw, Beith, Fife, wife Ann McKenzie, settled Georgia 1750, Secretary to the Governor. (Houstouns of Ga. p134)

MORE, JOHN BERWICK, born 1860 son of Robert More and Jessie Berwick, died Adelaide, South Australia, 1884. (St Andrews g/s)

MORRIS, DAVID, born 1793 son of William Morris and Elizabeth Simpson, died Dominica 18.5.1818. (Kemback g/s)

MORRISON, JOHN, born 1781, merchant, naturalised 1807 Charleston, South Carolina. (US.National Archives M1183/1)

MORRISON, SIMON, born 1796, cabinetmaker, naturalised Charleston, South Carolina, 1830. (US.National Archives M1183/1)

MORRISON, THOMAS, West Wemyss, settled Leyden, Holland, pre1636. (SRO.SH1636)

MORTON, J. A. THOMSON, son of Robert Morton and Elizabeth Anderson, died Bermuda 7.5.1861. (Strathmiglo g/s)

MORTON, THOMAS CAMPBELL, born 1772, merchant in New York 1793-, died in New York 30.4.1833. [ANY.I.341]

MOULTRIE, JOHN, born 1702 son of John Moultrie and Catherine Craik in Culross, educated Edinburgh University, settled Charleston, South Carolina, 1729, died 1771. (South Carolina Historical and Genealogical Magazine 5.242)

MUIRHEAD, THOMAS, Linktown of Abbotshall, merchant in Rotterdam 1688. (SRO.RD4.62.816)

MUNRO, CATHERINE, born 1778 daughter of Robert and Margaret Munro , settled Charleston, South Carolina, pre 1807 naturalised 1828. (US.National Archives M1183/1)(Crail g/s)

MUNRO, JAMES, mariner, naturalised 1796 Charleston, South Carolina, (US.National Archives M1183/1)

Emigrants and Adventurers from Fife

MURRAY, ALEXANDER, born 1797 son of Andrew Murray and Janet Mackie, died Jamaica 1821. (Auchterderran g/s)(F5.77)

MURRAY, ANDREW, born 1806 son of Andrew Murray and Janet Mackie, died Bombay 1833. (Auchterderran g/s)

MURRAY, CHARLES, born 1812 son of Andrew Murray and Janet Mackie, died Louisiana 1853. (Auchterderran g/s)

MURRAY, GEORGE, born 1844 son of James Murray, captain, died Shanghai 9.3.1882. (Cupar g/s)

MYLES, ELIZA CRAIG, born 1848 daughter of Robert Myles and Helen Cellars, died Emerson, Mills County, Iowa, 15.5.1874. (Cupar g/s)

NICHOLSON, WILLIAM, born 1749, died Macao 1801. (Burntisland g/s)

OGILVIE, CHRISTINA MURRAY, born 1833, wife of John White, died Teviot Junction, New Zealand, 25.9.1869. (Ferry Port on Craig g/s

OSWALD, HENRY, son of Thomas Oswald in Kirkcaldy, pro 1726 Essex County, Virginia.

OSWALD, JAMES, born 1830, died on the Marco Botsares in the Black Sea 30.6.1859, buried at Constantinople, (Boarhills g/s)

OSWALD, ROBERT C. B., born 1784 son of J. T. Oswald of Dunnikier, Lieutenant Colonel of Greek Light Infantry, died 1848.(Kirkcaldy g/s)

PARK, ALEXANDER, Captain in East India Company Service, 1786. [SRO.RS.Fife, 1464]

PATERSON, ROBERT, born 1779 son of Robert Paterson and Rosetta Maitland, died Great Courland Estate, Tobago, 23.7.1803. (St Andrews g/s)

PATERSON, WILLIAM, in Bergen, Norway,1627, ex Kirkcaldy(?) (SRO.SH1627)

PATON, ALEXANDER, born 26.11.1786, surgeon in Bombay, died 26.4.1852. (Torryburn g/s)

PATON, DAVID, born 1862 son of Thomas Paton, died Texas 21.2.1886. (Balgonie g/s)

PATON, THOMAS, born 1865, farmer in Fife, with wife and 2 children, settled in Saltcoats, Assiniboia, North West Territories, 15.5.1888. [BPP.Emi.9/185]

PATTERSON, JAMES, born 1835, shipmaster, died Rangoon 19.12.1874. (Rosyth g/s)

PATTERSON, JOHN, born 1838 in Fife, farmer and butcher, with his wife, 1 son and 2 daughters, settled in Saltcoats, Assiniboia, North West Territories, 22.5.1888. [BPP.Emi.9/185]

PATTON, ALEXANDER, born 13.12.1779 Auchtermuchty, cooper, settled New York 22.6.1801. (SG.32.3)

PEARSON, DAVID, died in St Petersburg. (no date) (Anstruther Easter g/s)

PEARSON, ELSPETH, rioter in Cupar, transported to America 1773. (SRO.B59.26.1.6.18)

Emigrants and Adventurers from Fife

PEATIE, THOMAS, born 1827 son of Thomas Peatie and Mary Cairns, died
Saldhana, Africa, 7.4.1845. (St Andrews g/s)
PEDDIE, JOHN SMART, born 1.2.1816 son of James Peddie, surgeon RN
sailed on HMS Terror on Franklin's Arctic Expedition 1845.
(Inverkeithing g/s)
PEIRSON, JOHN, born 1789 son of John and Margaret Peirson, lieutenant in
the 3rd Native Infantry regiment, died Cannanore, East Indies,
18.2.1812. (Kettle g/s)
PHILLIPS, JOHN, born 1834, corporal 74th Regiment, died Hong Kong
7.8.1878. (Aberdour g/s)
PHILP, BELLA, born 1846 daughter of David Philp and Anne Lowe, wife of
John Martin, died 26.11.1869 Brisbane. (Aberdour g/s)
PHILP, CHRISTINA, born 1844, daughter of David Philp and Anne Lowe, wife
of Alexander Kelly, died Brisbane, Queensland, 23.3.1888.
(Aberdour g/s)
PHILP, ROBERT HAIG, born 1827 son of Andrew Philp and Magdalene Haig,
died Queensland 13.11.1863. (St Andrews g/s)
PITCAIRN, JOHN, born 1722 in Dysart son of Reverend David Pitcairn and
Catherine Hamilton, Major RM, died Bunker's Hill, New England,
19.4.1775. (F.5.87)
PITCAIRN, ROBERT, tavernkeeper in Newburgh, settled Spanish Town,
Jamaica, pre 1780. (SRO.GD1.675.113)
PITTENDREICH, DAVID, born 1798 son of Robert Pittendreich and Catherine
Gay, died off the coast of Africa 1833. (Cupar g/s)
PLAYFAIR, CHARLES, born 7.6.1795 son of Rev James Playfair and Grizel
Duncan in Bendochy, died in America. (F.5.254)
PLAYFAIR, GEORGE, born 1782, Inspector General of the Bengal Hospitals,
wife Jessie Ross, died 26.11.1846. (St Andrews g/s)
PLAYFAIR, GEORGE WILLIAM, born 1827 son of William Davidson Playfair,
Colonel Madras, died Edinburgh 26.11.1876. (St Andrews g/s)
PLAYFAIR, JAMES OCTAVIUS, born 1839 son of George Playfair, died
Buenos Ayres 19.8.1864. (St Andrews g/s)
PLAYFAIR, JAMES, born 1818 son of William Davidson Playfair, died
Calcutta 6.4.1845. (St Andrews g/s)
PLAYFAIR, ROBERT HALDANE, born 1836 son of William Davidson Playfair,
died Buenos Ayres 3.6.1865. (St Andrews g/s)
PLAYFAIR, WILLIAM DAVIDSON, born 1784, Lieutenant Colonel HEICS
Bengal, died 31.1.1852. (St Andrews g/s)
PLAYFAIR, WILLIAM DALGLEISH, born 1822 son of Sir Hugh Lyon Playfair,
Lieutenant Indian Army, died Sobraon 16.2.1846. (St Andrews g/s)
PLAYFAIR, WILLIAM, born 1831 son of William Davidson Playfair, Major
General Bengal, died Surrey 1.11.1891. (St Andrews g/s)

Emigrants and Adventurers from Fife

POTTER, WILLIAM, born 1871 son of John Potterand Christian Webster, died on the Benlaric of Leith in the Mediterranean 20.9.1893. (Rosyth g/s)

PRINGLE, ROBERT McROBERT, born 1853 son of James and Marion Pringle, died New Plymouth, New Zealand, 3.11.1881. (Aberdour g/s)

RAE, ANN BELL, born 1844, died Dow City, Iowa, 20.6.1888. (Kettle g/s)

RAE, ISOBELLA, born 1855 daughter of Thomas Rae and Janet Bell, died Dow City, Iowa, 3.1888. (Kettle g/s)

RAMSAY, JOHN, son of David Ramsay and Helen Wemyss in Fife, shopkeeper in Charleston, South Carolina, pro 20.7.1734 South Carolina.

RANKINE, DAVID, born 1866 son of Andrew Rankine and Joanna Currie, medical missionary, died I-Chang, China, 4.7.1899. (Auchterderran g/s)

REDDIE, Captain JOHN, HEICS, died 31.10.1826. (Dysart g/s)

REEVE. THOMAS CAMPBELL TWISS, born 1813 son of Thomas Reeve and Helen Campbell, died India 25.1.1840. (Cupar g/s)

REID, ANDREW, born 1798 son of William Reid, HEICS, died Chittagong, Bengal, 16.3.1822. (Creich g/s)

REID, JOHN, son of John Reid in Culross, thief, transported to America 1763. (SRO.B59.26.11.6.41)

REID, WILLIAM, born 1821 son of William Reid, HEICS, died 22.4.1825. (Creich g/s)

RENWICK, EDWARD, son of Henry and Jane Renwick, Major, died Santander, Spain, 12.1.1836. (St Andrews g/s)

RICHARD, JAMES WALTER, born 1844, banker in Hoblee, died Bombay 12.7.1881. (St Andrews g/s)

RICHARD, MELVILLE, son of William Richard and Catherine Bell, captain of the Jane of Glasgow, died Black River, Jamaica, 26.7.1817. (St Andrews g/s)

RITCHIE, JOHN, born 1795, captain of the Caledonia of Dundee, died Elsinore 18.6.1842. (St Andrews g/s)

ROBERTSON, GEORGE ADAM LYON, born Lindores 19.12.1832 son of James Robertson and Janet Edmiston, died South Yarrah, Melbourne, 24.3.1882. (Abdie g/s)

ROBERTSON, JAMES, Newbigging, Lieutenant General, pro 22.3.1788 New York; pro 5.4.1788 New Jersey. (New Jersey Archives.Lib.38/520)

ROBERTSON, JAMES, born 1796, merchant in Charleston, South Carolina, naturalised Charleston 1823. (US.National Archives M1183/1)

ROBERTSON, JAMES, born Lindores 5.2.1835 son of James Robertson and Janet Edmiston, died South Yarrah, Melbourne, 20.6.1893. (Abdie g/s)

ROBERTSON, WILLIAM, son of William Robertson and Rachel Anderson, died Ballarat, Australia, 25.4.1888. (Cupar g/s)

Emigrants and Adventurers from Fife

RODGER, W. H., son of James Rodger and Bessie Halliday, settled Buenos Ayres pre 1879. (Dunnikier g/s)

ROLLAND, HENRY, son of James Rolland in Culross, carpenter, settled Charleston, South Carolina, pre 1774. (SRO.CS16.1.137)

ROLLO, FRANCIS, born 1843 son of Alexander Rollo and Elizabeth Duncan, drowned St Petersburgh 28.6.1863. (Balmerino g/s)

ROY, ALEXANDER, born 10.10.1843 son of Alexander Roy and Elizabeth Keeler, cabinetmaker, died Lithgow, New South Wales, 4.10.1893. (Dunfermline g/s)

ROY, JAMES, born in Fife, died 25.7.1818 Augusta, Georgia. (Colonial Museum & Savanna Advertiser 4.8.1818)

RUSSELL, JAMES, mariner in Philadelphia, 1791. [SRO.RS.Fife, 2943]

RUSSELL, JAMES, born 26.9.1859 son of George Russell, died Barunah Plains, Victoria, 31.1.1911. (Kilconquhar g/s)

RUSSELL Lieutenant Colonel, HEICS 7th Native Infantry, born 21.11.1781, died 10.7.1839. (Pittenweem g/s)

RUSSELL, DAVID, son of David Russell and Mary Black, died Jamaica 24.4.1867. (St Andrews g/s)

RUSSELL, HENRY, son of Henry Russell and Agnes Beaton, died Baltimore 2.1846. (Kettle g/s)

RUSSELL, JAMES, born 23.4.1708 son of James Russell and Anne Wightman in Kingseat, Slipperfield, settled Nottingham, Prince George County, Maryland, 1730. (Maryland Historical Magazine 72/165)

RUSSELL, JAMES, born 1829, coffee planter in South Coorg, India, died Aberdour 15.8.1879. (Aberdour g/s)

RUSSELL, JAMES, born 1868 son of James and Barbara Russell, died San Francisco 22.11.1897. (Cupar g/s)

RUTHERFORD, THOMAS, born 1766 son of Thomas Rutherford and Janet Meldrum in Kirkcaldy, educated Glasgow University, settled Virginia 1784, died 1790. (BAF)

RYMER, JAMES, born St Andrews, settled South Carolina 1753, minister, died Walterborough, South Carolina, 1755. (SC Gazette 10.7.1755)

SALMOND, JOHN BROWN, born 9.10.1843, died Point de Galle, Ceylon, 29.9.1867. (Dunnikier g/s)

SANG, DAVID, born 1800, wife Helen Brodie, died New York 15.10.1842. (St Andrews g/s)

SANG, JOHN, born 1833 son of David Sang and Helen Brodie, died Brisbane, Australia, 15.1.1872. (St Andrews g/s)

SCOTLAND, ROBERT, born 1847 son of William Scotland and Helen Sorley, died Melbourne 25.5.1894. (Burntisland g/s)

SCOTT, DAVID, born 1838 son of David Scott and Janet Todd, died Melbourne 29.8.1885. (Cupar g/s)

Emigrants and Adventurers from Fife

SCOTT, ELIZABETH DOW, born 1824 daughter of William Scott and
Elizabeth Bell, died Melbourne 1916. (Ferry Port on Craig g/s)
SCOTT, HENRY, Cupar, via Belfast to New York on the Perseverance, 1811.
(NWI.2.343)
SCOTT, JOHN, son of John Scott, schoolmaster, (1750-1813) and Jane
French (1750-1816), died in America. (Monimail g/s)
SCOTT, ROBERT, born 1831 son of William Scott and Elizabeth Bell, died
Cape Town 1890. (Ferry Port on Craig g/s)
SCOTT, THOMAS, Major in East India Company Service, 1782.
[SRO.RS.Fife, 1782]
SETON, JOHN, son of Sir David Seton of Parbroath and Mary Gray, emigrated
via London to Virginia 7 August 1635. (PRO.E157.20)(AOF196)
SETON, JOHN, in Collessie, late of Jamaica, 1782. [SRO.RS.Fife, 268]
SHAW, ROBERT, son of Alexander Shaw and Isabella Wishart, died Port
Elizabeth 16.12.1887. (Dunfermline g/s)
SHEPHERD, ALEXANDER, born 1843 son of James Shepherd and Cecilia
Wilson, died Havannah 11.7.1858. (Balmerino g/s)
SHEPHERD, DAVID, son of William Shepherd (1792-1832), settled New
Orleans, Louisiana, pre 1847. (Dunfermline g/s)
SHEPHERD, ROBERT, born 1810, died Calcutta 10.9.1839. (Burntisland g/s)
SHIELDS, ALEXANDER, minister in St Andrews, emigrated to Darien 1699,
died Port Royal, Jamaica, 1700. (F7.655)
SHIELDS, HENRY, merchant in Charleston, USA 1819, son of Henry Shields,
farmer in Coaltown of Balmull, naturalised Charleston, South
Carolina, 1813. (US.National Archives M1183/1)
SIMMONS, ALEXANDER, ex Anstruther, soldier, married Marieken Jansen In
Rotterdam, 1588. (Rotterdam Marriage Register)
SIMPSON, DAVID, wife Marie Lentron, ex Dysart, in Stockholm, Sweden,
1688. (SRO.RD2.69.311)
SIMSON, JOHN, born 1800, third son of George Simson in Fife, died in
Calcutta 19.9.1820. [South Park g/s, Calcutta]
SIMPSON, JOHN, son of James Simpson and Christian Whyte, died New
Orleans 16.10.1843. (Kirkcaldy g/s)
SIMSON, JAMES, born 1821 son of Robert Simson and Elizabeth Carstairs,
died Brim Brim, Victoria, 15.8.1858. (Anstruther Wester g/s)
SKINNER, ISABELLA SMITH, daughter of William Skinner and Isabella
Davidson, died Florida 1.12.1886. (Kirkcaldy g/s)
SKINNER, JAMES, son of George Skinner and Jean Laing, died Madras
26.9.1846. (St Andrews g/s)
SMART, LAURENCE, ex Dunfermline, admitted as a citizen of Cracow,
Poland, 1593. (Lib.Jur.Civ.Cracow 1556-1612, f.354)
SMITH, DAVID, born 1796 son of Robert Smith and Janet Henderson,
merchant in New Orleans, died Perth 27.12.1882. (Logie g/s)

Emigrants and Adventurers from Fife

SMITH, JAMES, born 1838 son of Peter Smith and Christina Swinton, died
Auckland, New Zealand, 1.11.1872. (Largo g/s)
SMITH, JOHN, born 1793 son of David Smith and Euphame Ramsay, died
Jamaica 1820. (Dunnikier g/s)
SMITH, JOHN, born 1832 son of John and Helen Smith, died Bangalore
13.11.1894. (Saline g/s)
SMITH, JOHN, born 1840 son of William D. Smith and Janet Morrison, died
Nickerie, Surinam, 16.5.1872. (Burntisland g/s)
SMITH, JOHN ELDER, son of John Smith and Ann Hutton Elder, died New York
28.4.1887. (St Monance g/s)
SMITH, MARGARET, born 1839 daughter of John and Helen Smith, died
Bangalore 8.7.1889. (Saline g/s)
SMITH, ROBERT, born 1798 son of David Smith and Euphame Murray, died
Calcutta 28.9.1844. (Dunnikier g/s)
SMITH, ROBERT, born 1837 son of Peter Smith and Chistina Swinton, died
Auckland, New Zealand, 30.8.1882. (Largo g/s)
SMITH, ROBERT LESLIE, born 1863 son of John J. Smith and Isabella Walker,
died Providence, Rhode Island, 21.2.1895. (St Andrews g/s)
SMITH, THOMAS WALKER, born 1852 son of John J. Smith and Isabella
Walker, died Moulmein, Burma, 5.2.1879. (St Andrews g/s)
SPEARS, CATHERINE, born 1809 daughter of Robert Spears of Kininmont
and Margaret Millie, died Paris 21.5.1827. (Cupar g/s)
SPEARS, THOMAS, born 1807 son of Robert Spears of Kininmont and
Margaret Millie, died Calcutta 22.12.1845. (Cupar g/s)
SPEARS, THOMAS, born 25.5.1807. Kirkcaldy, died 22.12.1845.
[Scotch Burial Ground g/s, Calcutta]
SPEARS, THOMAS, born 1814 son of Thomas Spears and Margaret Roy, died
Rangoon 14.2.1868. (Kirkcaldy g/s)
SPRATT, DANIEL, settled Urbanna, Middlesex County, Virginia, pro 1807
Williamsburg, Virginia.
SPRATT, ROBERT BEVERLEY, settled Urbanna, Middlesex County, Virginia,
pro 1805 Williamsburg, Virginia.
STEVENS, JOHN, ex Crail, soldier, married Immitge Lucas 1601 in Delft,
Netherlands. (Delft Marriage Register)
STEWART, JAMES, ex St Andrews, soldier, married Janneke Anthonis in
Bergen op Zoom 1586. (Bergen op Zoom Marriage Register)
STEWART, JAMES AFFLECK, son of Robert and Ann Stewart, captain in the
11th Hussars, died Brantford, Canada West, 15.5.1867. (Forgan g/s)
STEWART, ROBERT, born in Fife 1752, died in Calcutta 11.3.1811.
[North Park g/s, Calcutta]
STEWART, ROBERT, born 1817 son of Alexander Stewart and Christine
Scott, died Isle de France (Mauritius?) 19.1.1845. (Burntisland g/s)

Emigrants and Adventurers from Fife

STEWART, SAMUEL, born 1813 son of Alexander Stewart and Christine Scott, died on voyage to Bombay 12.4.1866. (Burntisland g/s)

STIRLING, ANDREW, born 1818 son of John Stirling of Eldershaw and Elizabeth Willing, died Western Australia 5.11.1844. (St Andrews g/s)

STIRLING, CHARLES, born 3.6.1862, Lieutenant R.N., died Malta 28.8.1894. (St Andrews g/s)

STIRLING, JOHN, born 1836 son of John Stirling of Eldershaw and Elizabeth Willing, died Inkerman 5.11.1854. (St Andrews g/s)

SWAN, JAMES, born 1837 son of James Swan and Jean McRitchie, died Melbourne 17.4.1855. (Cupar g/s)

TAYLOR, JOHN, born 1767, mariner, naturalised 1799 Charleston, South Carolina. (US.National Archives M1183/1)

TAYLOR, JOHN, born 1788 son of John Taylor, Colonel HEICS Bengal, died St Andrews 26.7.1841. (St Andrews g/s)

TAYLOR, ROBERT, wife Elisabeth Henderson, and family emigrated from Auchtermuchty to Canada ca. 1832. (SG.39.2/81)

TAYLOR, Captain THOMAS, born 1799, died in Bahia 19.3.1850. (Anstruther Easter g/s)

THOMPSON, ALEXANDER, born 1810, Kirkcaldy, died 15.3.1840. [Scotch Burial Ground g/s, Calcutta]

THOMSON, ANDREW, of Kinloch, writer, died Saratoga, USA, 1831. (WS)

THOMSON, ANDREW, born 1789 son of John Thomson of Prior Letham, writer, died Florida 1841. (WS)

THOMSON, GEORGE EBENEZER, born 1839 son of George Thomson and Josephine Watt, died Melbourne 1860. (St Andrews g/s)

THOMSON, JOHN THOMAS, born 1836 son of George Thomson and Josephine Watt, died Shanghai 1864. (St Andrews g/s)

THOMSON, JAMES, born 1828 son of Andrew Thomson and Ann White, died River St Lawrence 26.9.1856. (Methilhill g/s)

THOMSON, JAMES, born 1823 son of David Thomson and Ann Spens, died Fitzroy Town Hall, Melbourne, 10.9.1881. (Cupar g/s)

THOMSON, JOHN COUPAR, born 1843 son of John Thomson and Euphemia Coupar, died Australia 1892. (St Andrews g/s)

THOMSON, PETER, son of John Thomson in Burntisland, died Kingston, Jamaica, 1803. (Gentleman's Magazine.72.374)

THOMSON, WILLIAM ADAM ANSTRUTHER, born 4.12.1822, lieutenant colonel, wife Isabella Steel, died Calcutta 3.8.1865. (Kilconquhar g/s)

THOMSON, WILLIAM HENRY, born 1840 son of George Thomson and Josephine Watt, died Victoria, Australia, 1871. (St Andrews g/s)

TODD, GEORGE, born 1808 son of David Todd and Christine Fair, died Bengal 22.7.1876. (Cupar g/s)

Emigrants and Adventurers from Fife

TOSH, JAMES, Kirkcaldy, member of the Scots Charitable Society of
Boston, 1771. (NEHGS)
TOSH, THOMAS, born 1794 son of Thomas Tosh and Sophia Henderson, died
Calcutta 24.11.1859. (Carnbee g/s)
TRAILL, THOMAS, born 1720, settled Dominica, died 7.1763.
(St Andrews g/s)
TURCAN, JAMES, born 1822 son of William Turcan and Catherine Watt,
died Danzig 23.3.1875. (Tulliallan g/s)
TURCAN, WILLIAM, born 1826 son of George Turcan and Agnes Mercer, died
Rio de Janeiro 2.3.1852. (Tulliallan g/s)
TURNBULL, DAVID, son of David Turnbull (1720-1788) and Janet Whyte
(1731-1784), died Jamaica. (Dunfermline g/s)
WALKER, ALEXANDER, son of Livingston Walker and Mary Ballingall,
shipbuilder in Grenada pre 1810. (Dunino g/s)
WALKER, ALEXANDER, son of Samuel Walker (1797-1870) and Elspeth
Oswald (1799-1874), died Australia aged 47. (St Andrews g/s)
WALKER, ANDREW, born 1819 son of Andrew Walker and Isobel Landale,
died Buninyong, Victoria, 8.1887. (Cupar g/s)
WALKER, ISOBEL, born 1771 daughter of Reverend William Walker and
Margaret Manderston in Collessie, died Jamaica 1853. (F5.135)
WALKER, JAMES, son of John Walker, died Lisbon 4.12.1841.
(St Andrews g/s)
WALKER, MARGARET, daughter of John Walker, died New York 8.1849.
(St Andrews g/s)
WALKER, MARGARET, widow of John Walker, died New York 8.1875.
(St Andrews g/s)
WALKER, PARTHINIA, widow of John Carmichael, died New York 1855.
(St Andrews g/s)
WALKER, WILLIAM, born 1768 son of Reverend William Walker and Margaret
Manderston in Collessie, attorney, died Jamaica 1799. (F5.135)
WALKER, WILLIAM, born 1810 son of Andrew Walker and Isobel Landale,
died Williamsburgh, New York, 9.1853. (Cupar g/s)
WALLACE, DAVID, born 21.8.1791 Pittenweem, wife Helen ..., resident
Calcutta, died Pittenweem 17.12.1839. (Pittenweem g/s)
WALLACE, DAVID, son of David Wallace of Balmeadowside and Margaret
Meldrum, died Copmanhurst, Clarence River, New South Wales,
19.11.1845. (Creich g/s)
WALLACE, ROBERT, son of Laurence Wallace and Cecilia Taylor, died New
Zealand 3.2.1845. (St Andrews g/s)
WALLACE, THOMAS, born 1794 son of William and Esther Wallace, died
Amazon 12.10.1863. (St Andrews g/s)
WANN, DAVID, born 1850 son of William Wann and Elizabeth Muir, died
London, Ontario, 22.5.1873. (Monimail g/s)

Emigrants and Adventurers from Fife

WANN, JOHN, born 1838 son of Alexander Wann and Janet Johnston, died Calcutta 7.11.1859. (Balmerino g/s)

WATSON, ALEXANDER, born 1795, planter, naturalised 1825 Charleston, South Carolina. (US.National Archives M1183/1)

WATSON, DAVID, born 1820, shipmaster in Anstruther, wife Anne Sharp, died on way to St George Sound, Western Australia, 27.11.1870 (Kilrenny g/s)

WATSON, JAMES, born 1782, mariner, naturalised 1807 Charleston, South Carolina. (US.National Archives M1183/1)

WATSON, KATHERINE, Cupar, transported to America 1777. (SM.38.511)

WATSON, ROBERT, son of Andrew Watson and Ann Hutton, died St Vincent 1803. (St Andrews g/s)

WATSON, ROBERT, born 1849 son of David Watson and Anne Sharp in Anstruther, died Adelaide 7.4.1869 (Kilrenny g/s)

WATSON, THOMAS, son of Alexander Watson and Agnes Key, died India 13.8.1802. (St Andrews g/s)

WATT, ARCHIBALD, son of Cumberland Watt and Julia Landale, died Port Adelaide, South Australia, 9.1.1887. (Auchtertool g/s)

WATT, JAMES, born 1838 son of George Watt and Helen Meikle, died Kansas 29.3.1884. (Dunfermline g/s)

WEBSTER, ROBERT FARQUHAR, born Balgarvie 24.9.1826, died Algiers 25.2.1889. (Cupar g/s)

WELSH, JOHN, born 1827 son of Walter Welsh, died Mobile 8.4.1860. (Auchtertool g/s)

WEMYSS, ROBERT, born 1796 commander of Bombay Castle in India, died Edinburgh 19.2.1860. (St Andrews g/s)

WEST, JAMES, born 11.6.1791 son of John West In Kirkcaldy, emigrated to America 1815, settled Wood County, West Virginia, died 1851 Fox Township, Ohio. (OVG125)

WHYTE, JAMES, born 1777 in Kirkcaldy, emigrated via Liverpool to America, a merchant, to settle in Mississippi, naturalised 6.1.1819 in New York.

WIGHTMAN, CHARLES, son of Charles Wightman in Anstruther, merchant in Tobago 1778. (SRO.CS16.1.174)

WILKIE, ANDREW, died Melbourne 7.1863. (Cults g/s)

WILKIE, JOHN, MD, Inspector General of Hospitals, died Nynee-Tal, Bengal, 23.5.1870. (Cults g/s)

WILKIE, JOHN, captain 49th Regiment, Bengal Native Infantry, died Dinapur, 10.8.1824. (Cults g/s)

WILSON, ANDREW, born 1820 son of James Wilson and Elizabeth Whyte, died Demerara 19.4.1856. (Newburgh g/s)

WILSON, DAVID, born 1794 son of David Wilson and Margaret Duncan, died Calcutta 1815. (Carnbee g/s)

Emigrants and Adventurers from Fife

WILSON, JAMES, born 1768 son of Walter Wilson, Major HEICS, died
Bangalore. (St Andrews g/s)
WILSON, JAMES, born 1828 son of James Wilson and Elizabeth Whyte, died
Australia 1848. (Newburgh g/s)
WILSON, JAMES ATKINSON, born 1830 son of John Wilson and Janet
McLachlan, doctor of medicine, died West Coast of Africa 4.4.1851.
(Dunfermline g/s)
WILSON, JOHN, baker, settled New York 1778, died at sea on the brig Peace
between Jamaica and New York 19.8.1809. (ANY.1.225)
WILSON, Captain JOHN, born 1854, died Baltic Sea 1889. (Rosyth g/s)
WILSON, ROBERT, born Cupar 2.4.1736, surgeon-apothecary in Burntisland,
emigrated via London to South Carolina 1753, married Ann Chisholm
1759 in Charleston, died 26.8.1815. (BLG2978)
WILSON, ROBERT, born 1801 son of Alexander Wilson and Helen Kellock,
died Bombay 20.1.1859. (Burntisland g/s)
WILSON, THOMAS, son of Walter Wilson, Lieutenant HEICS, died India
10.5.1759. (St Andrews g/s)
WILSON, Lieutenant General THOMAS, born 1779 son of Dr Charles Wilson
and Elizabeth Stark, HEICS, died Wales 4.1856. (St Andrews g/s)
WILSON, THOMAS, born 1802 son of Alexander Wilson and Helen Kellock,
died Melbourne 1859. (Burntisland g/s)
WILSON, WILLIAM, born 1811 son of Alexander Wilson and Helen Kellock,
died Bombay 7.2.1852. (Burntisland g/s)
WRIGHT, ANDREW, born 1835, died New York 1.2.1873. (Tulliallan g/s)
WRIGHT, GEORGE TOD, born 1823 son of Rev. George Wright and Mary
Blundell, HEICS Straits Settlements, died 5.1.1883.
(St Andrews g/s)
WRIGHT, HELEN GRAY, died at sea 22.9.1867, buried Foo Chow Foo
3.11.1862. (Tulliallan g/s)
WRIGHT, ROBERT, carpenter in America, ex Limekilns, cnf 1829 Edinburgh
(SRO.SC70.1.352).
WYLIE, DAVID, born 21.9.1810 son of Robert Wylie and Jane Primrose, died
Moscow 1.6.1836. (Tulliallan g/s)
WYLLIE, HALDANE, born 1843 son of Haldane and Mary Wyllie, died on
voyage to New York 1869. (Tulliallan g/s)
WYLLIE, WILLIAM, born 1812 son of Walter Wyllie and Elizabeth Scott, died
Rio de Janeiro 19.11.1852. (Tulliallan g/s)
YOUNG, ALEXANDER, naturalised Camden, South Carolina, 1806.
(SC.Citizenship Book.54)(S.C.Arch.Misc.Records, Vol.8)
YOUNG, GEORGE, born 1804 son of Nathaniel Young, shipmaster, died
St Petersburg 3.10.1844. (Ferry Port on Craig g/s)
YOUNG, Captain GEORGE, master of the brig Gowrie of Dundee died
Acapulco 30.10.1852, wife Mary Oswald. (Kingsbarns g/s)

Emigrants and Adventurers from Fife

YOUNG, JOHN, born 1851 son of David Young and Barbara Forgan, banker,
    died Melbourne 1.11.1879. (St Andrews g/s)
YOUNG, PETER, son of John Young and Helen Walls, died Honduras
    18.12.1808. (Burntisland g/s)
YOUNGER, ANDREW, born 1820 son of John Younger and Margaret Horne, died
    Buenos Ayres 26.12.1844. (St Monance g/s)

EMIGRANTS AND ADVENTURERS
from
Moray and Banff

REFERENCES

Archives

	BA	Barbados Archives, Bridgetown
	RB	Register Book
	ML	Montrose Library
	MBR	Montrose Burgess Roll
	NEHGS	New England Historic Genealogical Society, Boston SCS-MSS, B/S.36r6
	PRO	Public Record Office, London
	PCC	Prerogative Court of Canterbury
	SAB	Stats Arkivet, Bergen
	SRO	Scottish Record Office, Edinburgh
	CC	Commissary Court
	NRAS	National Register of Archives, Scotland
	RD	Register of Deeds
	RH	Register House
	RS	Register of Sasines
	SH	Services of Heirs
	USNA	United States National Archives, Washington, DC

Publications

	AJ	Aberdeen Journal
	ANY	Biographical Register of the St Andrews Society of New York, R McBean [NY, 1922]
	BA	List of Officers of the Bengal Army 1758-, VCP Hodson [London, 1945]
	BBR	Banff Burgess Roll F McDonnell [St Andrews, 1994]
	BLG	Burke's Landed Gentry

CCMC Colonial Clergy of the Middle
Colonies, FL Weis
[Baltimore, 1983]
ESG Early Settlers of Georgia
EMCoulter [Baltimore,1983]
F Fasti Ecclesiae Scoticanae
H Scott [Edinburgh, 1920s]
IT Indian Traders of the South
Eastern Spanish Borderlands
W Coker [Florida, 1986]
KCA Officers and Graduates of the
University and King's College,
Aberdeen, P J Anderson
[Aberdeen, 1893]
MSC Records of Marischal College,
Aberdeen, 1593-1860.
PJ Anderson[Aberdeen, 1898]
SG The Scottish Genealogist
SIP Scots in Poland, 1576-1793
A Steuart [Edinburgh1915]
SM Scots Magazine
TML The MacLeods
[Edinburgh 1969]

Abbreviations cnf confirmation
g/s gravestone inscription
pro probate

Emigrants and Adventurers from

MORAY and BANFF

ABERCROMBY, ARTHUR, appointed to a Dutch East India ship bound for China 1758. [SRO.NRAS.0002]

ABERCROMBY, GEORGE, brother of Sir George Abercromby of Birkenbog, a doctor in Mexico ca.1770, father of John an officer in the Spanish Army and Mary Louise. [SRO.NRAS.0002]

ABERNETHIE, JOHN, son of Captain John Abernethie in Bengal, admitted as a burgess of Banff 1777. [BBR]

ADAMSON, WILLIAM, merchant from Banff, died in Brighton, Melbourne, 30.4.1875. [AJ6652]

ALLAN, ALEXANDER, born 1798 in Morayshire, housecarpenter in Charleston, naturalised in South Carolina 16.8.1847. [USNA.M1183/1]

ALLAN, ALEXANDER, born 1825, son of John Allen and Helen Allen, died in Jamestown, South Australia, 14.2.1879. [Inveraven g/s]

ALLAN, ANNIE, daughter of Alexander Allan in Banff, married John Stuart, Vegeria Estate, Rakwane, in Columbo, Ceylon, 15.5.1875. [AJ6651]

ANDERSON, ALEXANDER, born 25.2.1782, son of Reverend Joseph Anderson and Jean Craig in Birnie, died on the Hercules in the West Indies 9.1803. [F.6.380]

ANDERSON, ANDREW, Major General in East India Company Service, 1832. [SRO.RS.Elgin & Forres, 63]

ANDERSON, ARCHIBALD, born 10.6.1785, son of Reverend Joseph Anderson and Jean Craig in Birnie, surgeon in the Honourable East India Company Service, died 1817. [F.6.380]

ANDERSON, GEORGE, surgeon HEICS 1787, grandson of George Anderson a merchant in Forres. [SRO.R.S.Caithness, 85]
ANDERSON, JAMES, born 1834, son of Alexander Anderson, farmer in Carsemoor, died 18.10.1857 in Calcutta. [Bellie g/s]
ANDERSON, JAMES, born 1789 in Cullen, Banffshire, member of the firm Anderson, Wallace and Company, died 24.4.1843, husband of Margaret, born in Cullen 1805, died 16.3.1843. [Scotch Burial Ground g/s. Calcutta]
ANDERSON, JAMES, M.D., son of James Anderson and Elspet Gow in Scroggiemill, Elgin, settled in Melbourne, Australia, by 1856. [SRO.SH1856]
ANDERSON, JOHN, from Boharm, Banffshire, a surgeon in St Michael's parish, Barbados, pro. 2.12.1714 Barbados [RB6.41.9]
ANDERSON, Dr JOHN, in St Kitts, 23.7.1792. [SRO.RS.Banff.292]
ANDERSON, ..., emigrated from Morayshire to Prince Edward Island, Canada, on the John and Elizabeth 1775, shipwrecked in Flat River, Prince Edward Island. [HMS][TIM.18.30]
ASHER, JOHN GORDON, born 1833, son of Reverend William Asher and Katherine F Gordon, surgeon major of the Bombay Army, died 2.3.1880. [Inveraven g/s]
ASHER, ROBINA AGNES, born 1837, daughter of Reverend William Asher [1791-1874] and Katherine Forbes Gordon [1799-1880], wife of Captain G J Skinner of the Bengal Army, died in Dinapure, Bengal, 7.8.1876. [Inveraven g/s]
BAGRAY, ARCHIBALD, son of John Bagray burgess of Banff and Margaret Thomson, settled in Poland by 1585. [MSC.II.33]
BALMER, ROBERT, born 1830, son of Thomas Balmer and Agnes Stuart, Lieutenant of the Honourable East India Company, died 26.1.1853 in India. [Bellie g/s]
BARBER, THOMAS, born 1830, son of Thomas Barber and Madelina McLeod, died in Andersonville, Georgia, 9.9.1864. [Bellie g/s]
BARBER, WILLIAM MCLEOD, born 31.5.1827 in Fochabers, son of Thomas Barber and Madeline McLeod, emigrated to Newhaven, Connecticut, educated at Yale University, minister, died 1889 in Malden, Massachusetts. [TML.2.39]
BENNET, JAMES GORDON, born 1795 in Enzie, Banffshire, founder of The New York Herald, died 2.6.1872 in New York. [ANY.II.138]
BETHUNE, Dr GEORGE, in Tobago, admitted as a burgess of Banff 1800. [BBR]

BLACK, PETER, born 1823, son of Peter Black, farmer in
Pennycairn, and Anne Skeen, died on Fonte Bella Estate,
Port Maria, Jamaica, 23.11.1845. [Inveraven g/s]
BLANE, ROBERT, Lieutenant Colonel on Honourable East India
Company Service, 4.6.1792. [SRO.RS.Elgin & Forres.328]
BOWIE, ROBERT, a merchant in Bordeaux, 23.4.1785. [SRO.RS.Elgin
& Forres.123]
BRANDER, ALEXANDER TERII NOHARIA TEPAN, of Papeete, Tahiti,
heir to Isobel Skene, widow of William Forsyth, tailor in
Elgin, and to his father John Brander of Papeete, Tahiti,
who died 15.6.1877. [SRO.SH1880]
BRANDER, ALEXANDER, a carpenter in Australia by 1856.
[SRO.S/H]
BRANDER, JAMES, merchant in Lisbon, son of James Brander,
merchant in Elgin, ca1760. [SRO.RS29{Elgin}VII.409]
BREMNER, ALEXANDER, born 1793, son of James Bremner, farmer,
and Isabel Ord, died 14.2.1820 in Demerara.
[Speymouth Dipple g/s]
BREMNER, JOHN, born 1792, son of Joseph Bremner, feuar in
Fochabers, and Mary Allan, mariner then a merchant in
Nassau, New Providence, Bahamas, died 30.8.1818 Nassau.
[Bellie g/s]
BREMNER, JOSEPH, born 1799, son of Joseph Bremner, feuar in
Fochabers, and Christina Ross, merchant in Samarang, Java,
died 13.5.1831 in Java. [Bellie g/s]
BRODIE, ALEXANDER, born 1738, son of Alexander Brodie of
Windyhills and Ann Dawson, merchant in Windyhills,
St Mary's parish, Antigua, married Ann Kidder [1730-1801]
in 1766, died 1800 in Antigua. ["Caribeanna".1.98]
BRODIE, ALEXANDER, in Madras, admitted as a burgess of Banff
1785. [BBR]
BRODIE, LOUISA, Morayshire, wife of H. Cotton a surveyor in Van
Diemen's Land 1843-1850. [SRO.NRAS.0021]
BRODIE, WILLIAM, British Consul in Malaga, admitted as a
burgess of Banff 1799. [BBR]
BROWN, ANDREW, son of William Brown and Marion Anderson in
the Mill of Rubray, Forglen, Banffshire, a traveller in
Germany 1599. [MSC.II.48]
BROWN, GORDON, M.D., born 2.7.1784, son of Reverend Alexander
Brown and Isabella Ord in Spynie, educated at Marischal
College, Aberdeen, 1799-1802, a physician in Demerara,
died there 16.7.1813.[F.6.407][Records of Marischal College
and the University of Aberdeen, 1593-1860,Aberdeen,1898]

BROWN, JAMES, bon 1809, son of John Brown, feuar in Fochabers, and Helen Gray, died 1834 in New York. [Bellie g/s]
BROWN, LOUISA, born 22.6.1795 in Spynie, daughter of Reverend Alexander Brown and Isabel Ord, wife of William Willox, died in Sierra Leone 21.3.1826. [F.6.407]
BRYANT, WILLIAM, in Kingston, Jamaica, admitted as a burgess of Banff 1774. [BBR]
BURD, JOHN, born in Portsoy 24.9.1795 son of Charles Burd and Mary Johnston, settled in Copenhagen 1818, a shipmaster trading to the East Indies, married (1) Mette Marie Grefson 7.10.1826, (2) Karie Caroline Winning, appointed as Danish Consul in Hong Kong 1845, died 7.2.1855. [Danish East India Company Papers, National Archives, Copenhagen]
BURGESS, JAMES, son of William Burgess in Rothes [died 11.1831], settled in Demerara and Essequibo. [SRO.SH.1867]
BURNET, JAMES, in Batavia, admitted as a burgess of Banff 1771. [BBR]
CALDER, ARCHIBALD, Commissary of Stores in Antigua, admitted as a burgess of Banff 1768. [BBR]
CAMPBELL, JAMES, in Dowan Vale, Jamaica, admitted as a burgess of Banff 1783. [BBR]
CARSTAIRS, ALEXANDER, Rotterdam, admitted as a burgess of Elgin 1686. [Elgin BUrgess Roll]
CHALMERS, JAMES, son of James Chalmers of Balnellan, Boharm, a planter in St Thomas in the Vale, Surrey County, Jamaica, ca1766. [Consistorial Processes and Decreets 1658-1800 {SRS/Grant/Edinburgh/1909}]
CLAYTON, Captain JOSEPH, born 1781, died 18.5.1818 at Miramachi. [Banff g/s]
COLLIE, JOSEPH, Elgin, graduated MA at King's College, Aberdeen, 1844, an officer of the Victoria Insurance Company in Melbourne. [KCA296]
COLVIN, ENEAS MACKINTOSH, third son of Alexander Colvin in Earlsmill, Forres, died of sunstroke on way from Mussoori to Calcutta 27.5.1874. [AJ6600]
COMBIE, JAMES, died in Montreal 18... [Banff g/s]
COULL, THOMAS DUNARD, born 20.12.1815, youngest son of James Coull of Ashgrove, Elgin, died 20.5.1837. [Scotch Burial Ground g/s, Calcutta]
CRAUFORD, PATRICK, in Rotterdam, admitted as a burgess of Banff 1776. [BBR]

CROMBIE, WILLIAM, Morayshire, member of the Scots Charitable Society of Boston, Massachusetts, 1745. [NEHGS:MSS.B/S.36v6]

CRUICKSHANKS, ALEXANDER, Banffshire, member of the Scots Charitable Society of Boston, Massachusetts, 1769. [NEHGS]

CRUICKSHANKS, Captain CHARLES, in Haverford, Pennsylvania, later in Elgin, cnf 13.8.1785 Moray.

CRUICKSHANKS, WILLIAM, born 1775 in Morayshire, shoemaker, naturalised 15.8.1805 in South Carolina. [USNA.M1183]

CUMING, LACHLAN, in Demerara, 24.1.1799. [SRO.RS.Elgin & Forres.494]

CUMING, THOMAS, in Demerara, 3.6.1799. [SRO.RS.Elgin & Forres.508]; in Elgin, late of Demerara, cnf 19.5.1813. [SRO.CC16.5.2.26]

DAVIDSON, PETER, born 1789, Findhorn, Morayshire, late of Bhaugulpore, died in Calcutta 29.7.1821. [South Park g/s, Calcutta]

DAVIDSON, ROBERT, born 1786, son of Robert Davidson and Isabella Davidson in Findhorn, Morayshire, late of Calcutta, died 20.8.1841. [New Burial Ground g/s, Circular Road, Calcutta]

DICK-LAUDER, JOHN, born in Regulas, Edinkille, Morayshire, 21.4.1813, Lieutenant in the 47th Bengal Native Infantry, died 23.3.1867 in Bournemouth. [BA.3.20]

DINGWALL, JOHN, born 1745 in Duthil, son of Alexander Dingwall in Knockelgranish, emigrated to America before 1776, Loyalist, settled at Riviere aux Raisins, Glengarry, Canada, 1783, father of Ann and Sophia. {possibly emigrated on the John and Elizabeth 1775}[HMS][DF

DONALDSON, WILLIAM, Carolina, admitted as a burgess of Elgin 1776. [Elgin Burgess Roll]

DUFF, JAMES, born 1741, merchant in Madeira, admitted as a burgess of Banff 1779. [BBR]; died 1.4.1812. [Banff g/s]

DUFF, JAMES, merchant in Cadiz, son of William Duff of Cromby. [SRO.SH.1783]

DUFF, PATRICK, Captain of Artillery on East India Company Service in Bengal admitted as a burgess of Banff 1774. [BBR]; Colonel, HEICS, 9.10.1790. [SRO.RS.Banff.232]

DUFF, ROBERT, Banff, educated at King's College, Aberdeen, 1828, minister in Berbice. [KCA284]

DUFF, WILLIAM, Banffshire, member of the Scots Charitable Society of Boston, Massachusetts, 1760. [NEHGS]

DUFF, WILLIAM, in St George's, Grenada, admitted as a burgess of Banff 1797. [BBR]

DUNBAR, LOUISA, born 24.8.1812 Duffershouse, Morayshire, daughter of Sir A. Dunbar of Northfield, wife of Reverend R. B. Boswell, died in Calcutta. [South Park g/s, Calcutta]

DUNBAR, CHARLES CUMMING, ba.9.8.1808 in Duffus, son of Sir Archibald Dunbar of Northfield and Helen Penuel, Ensign of the Bengal Army, died in Barrackpore 2.7.1828. [BA.2.95]

DUNBAR, STEPHEN, son of Walter Dunbar in Forres, died in Jamaica 9.1780. [SM.42.617]

DUNBAR, WILLIAM, born 13.11.1740, son of Robert Dunbar in Dyke, Forres, member of the Scots Charitable Society of Boston, Massachusetts, 1766. [NEHGS:MSS.B/S.36v6]

DUNBAR, WILLIAM, born in Moy and Culbin parish, son of Reverend Robert Dunbar of Ballinspink, [1707-1782], and Jean Miller, [died 1788], sometime in Grenada, died in London. [F.6.413]

DUNBAR, WILLIAM, born 1749 in Morayshire, son of Sir Archibald Dunbar of Thunderton, Elgin, {1693-1769} and Anne Bain. Emigrated to Philadelphia 1771. Trader there and later at Fort Pitt. Planter in Florida, later in Louisiana, settled in Natchez, Adams County, Mississippi, 1773. Died 1810. [Dunbar Papers, University of North Carolina]

DUNCAN, JAMES, Elgin, settled in Charleston, South Carolina, naturalised 23.4.1839 in South Carolina. [USNA.M1183]

DUNCANSON, ROBERT, merchant in Fredericksburg, Virginia, died there 1764, brother of Thomas Duncanson, a surgeon in Forres, Morayshire. [Spotsylvania Deed Book G, 7.7.1764, Virginia]

ERSKINE, MARIA, born in the East Indies 9.11.1791, died in Banff 25.5.1807. [Banff g/s]

FALCONER, PATRICK, born 1775, son of William Falconer, farmer in Kinnermany, [1720-1793] and Anna Rose [1743-1821], merchant in New York, died 1837. [Inveraven g/s]

FALCONER, ROBERT, born 1782, son of William Falconer, farmer in Kinnermany, [1720-1793], and Anna Rose [1743-1821], merchant in New York, died 1851. [Inveraven g/s]

FALCONER, ROBERT, born 22.12.1780 in Pitchash, Inveraven, educated at Aberdeen University, emigrated to America ca1800, settled in Sugar Grove, Pennsylvania, father of Robert and James. [BLG2679]

FALCONER, WILLIAM, born 1763, son of William Falconer, farmer in Kinnermony, [1720-1793], and Anna Rose, [1743-1821], merchant in New York, died 1818. [Inveraven g/s]

FALCONER, WILLIAM FYER, born 1807, son of Captain D. Falconer
and Catherine ..., died 30.5.1844 in Grenada. [Rothes g/s]
FARQUHARSON, CHARLES, born 1779, son of James Farquharson
and Ann Stuart in Ballinstruan Kirkmichael, died 2.6.1860
in Baltimore, Maryland. [Inveraven Downan g/s]
FARQUHARSON, JOHN, son of James Farquharson of Coldrach, died
14.10.1808 in Jamaica. [SM.71.237]
FARQUHARSON, ROBERT, born 1777, son of James Farquharson and
Ann Stuart in Ballinstruan, Kirkmichael, died 28.6.1856 in
Nashville, Tennessee. [Inveraven Downan g/s]
FINDLATOR, ALEXANDER STEPHEN, son of James Findlater in
Jamaica, admitted as a burgess of Banff 1777. [BBR]
FINDLATOR, MARY WILLIAMSON, daughter of James Findlator in
Balvenie, Banffshire, married James Burnet in Montreal
13.11.1872. [AJ6515]
FORBES, CHARLES, Captain of the 60th Regiment of Foot, died
at Ticonderoga, New York, 1758. [Banff g/s]
FORBES, JOHN, Banffshire, educated at Marischal College,
Aberdeen, 1733, Episcopal minister in New Jersey 1733-
1736, died before 9.11.1736. [CCMC]
FRASER, ALEXANDER or ANGUS, brother of William Fraser of
Belnain, in Mexico 1760s. [SRO.NRAS.0002]
FRASER, ALEXANDER, born 26.9.181, son of Alexander Fraser,
merchant in Forres, and Jane Warden, officer in the Bengal
Army 1827-1843, died in Benares 20.7.1843. [BA.2.215]
FRASER, HUGH, born 1769 in Morayshire, Professor of Divinity at
Georgetown, naturalised 21.2.1817 in South Carolina.
[USNA.M1183]
FRASER, JOHN, born 1816, Forres, died 3.4.1845. [Scotch Burial
Ground g/s, Calcutta]
FRASER, ROBERT WARDEN, son of Alexander Fraser merchant in
Forres {died 27.10.1816} and Jean Warden, Captain of the
45th Bengal Native Infantry 1851. [SRO.S/H]; born 3.1.1806
in Forres; officer of the Bengal Army 1821-1853; died in
Edinburgh 30.6.1876. [BA.2.220]
FRASER, WILLIAM TULLOH, son of Alexander Fraser merchant in
Forres {died 27.10.1816} and Jean Warden, a merchant in
Calcutta 1851. [SRO.S/H]
FRASER, WILLIAM, Boharm, graduated MA at King's College,
Aberdeen, 1859, a minister in Newcastle, New South Wales.
[KCA310]
FYFE, DAVID, in Jamaica, admitted as a burgess of Banff 1775.
[BBR]

GAIRDYN, GEORGE, attorney in St Mary's, Jamaica, admitted as a burgess of Banff 1784. [BBR]

GARDINER, JAMES, born 1760, late in Jamaica, died in Banff 22.5.1820, husband of Margaret Aven (1762-1831). [Banff g/s]; cnf 30.10.1830. [SRO.CC1.6.W993]

GARDYNE, SAMUEL, in Charlestown, South Carolina, admitted as a burgess of Banff 1785. [BBR]

GEDDES, ALEXANDER, born 1800, son of John Geddes [1753-1817] and Helen Tod [1771-1837], died 1.4.1864 in Jamaica. [Bellie g/s]

GEDDES, GEORGE, born 1808, son of John Geddes [1753-1817] and Helen Tod [1771-1837], died 24.5.1864 in Jamaica. [Bellie g/s]

GEDDES, JAMES, son of Alexander Geddes and Margaret Innes in Morayshire, settled in Georgia ca1737. [SG.33/3.233]

GEDDES, JOHN, in Virginia, son of William Geddes, minister in Urquhart, ca1710. [SRO.RS29{Elgin}V.210]

GEDDES, JOHN, born 1788, son of John Geddes and Margaret Anderson, assistant surgeon of the 54th Regiment, died 11.1808 in Jamaica. [Bellie g/s]

GEDDES, JOHN, born 1821, son of John Geddes and Margaret Anderson, Secretary to the Governor of the Cape Coast, died 31.7.1839.[Bellie g/s]

GILLIARD, JOHN, in Charlestown, South Carolina, admitted as a burgess of Banff 1785. [BBR]

GORDON, ADAM, born 11.10.1812, son of Reverend William Gordon and Catherine Brodie, died 23.3.1832 on Richmond Estate, St Vincent. [F.6.391]

GORDON, ALEXANDER, born 30.1.1750, son of Reverend George Gordon and Agnes Brodie in Alves, died in India. [F.6.376]

GORDON, ALEXANDER, merchant in St Martins, France, 1740. [SRO.RS29{Elgin}VI.468]

GORDON, ALEXANDER, and Company, merchants in Bordeaux, ca1740. [SRO.RS29{Elgin}VI.413]

GORDON, ALEXANDER, son of Reverend Harry Gordon [1730-1764] in Ardesier, a planter in Tobago, died aged 26. [F.6.434]

GORDON, ALEXANDER, born 29.5.1805, son of Reverend William Gordon and Catherine Brodie in Elgin, died in America. [F.6.391]

GORDON, CATHERINE, born 1804, daughter of William Gordon and Margaret Stuart, died 18.12.1883 in Paris. [Bellie Tynet g/s]

GORDON, CHARLES, born 28.1.1777, son of Reverend Lewis Gordon and Elizabeth Logan in Elgin, died on the Harriet on the homeward voyage from India. [F.6.391]

GORDON, FRANCIS DRUMMOND, born 1833, son of Reverend John Gordon, Lieutenant of the 36th Madras Infantry, died at Kittool Madras Residency, 5.1864. [Speymouth Dipple g/s]

GORDON, GEORGE, Banff, citizen of Bergen, Norway, 1700.[SAB]

GORDON, GEORGE, son of Dr William Gordon, physician in St Croix, admitted as a burgess of Banff 1767. [BBR]

GORDON, JAMES COSMO, born 13.8.1756 son of John Gordon of Birkenbush, officer of the Bengal Army 1781-1792, died in Calcutta 31.12.1792. [BA.2.288]

GORDON, JAMES LEWIS JOSEPH, born 13.8.1844, son of Reverend George Gordon and Anna Stephen in Birnie, army captain, died 7.5.1886 in Nani Tal, India. [F.6.380]

GORDON, JOHN, born 5.6.1775, son of Reverend Lewis Gordon and Elizabeth Logan in Elgin, died 7.2.1802 in Calcutta. [F.6.391]

GORDON, JOHN, born 19.5.1795, son of Reverend William Gordon and Catherine Brodie in Elgin, surgeon in Honourable East India Company Service, died 2.3.1821 in the Persian Gulf. [F.6.391]

GORDON, LEWIS, born 19.10.1780, son of Reverend Lewis Gordon and Elizabeth Logan in Elgin, Lieutenant in the Honourable East India Company Service, died 5.12.1801 in India. [F.6.391]

GORDON, STEPHEN, born 6.3.1850, son of Reverend George Gordon and Anna Stephen in Birnie, a merchant in Smyrna. [F.6.380]

GORDON, WILLIAM, born 1780, settled in Tobago, died 1831 in Elgin. [Rothes Dundurcas g/s]

GORDON, WILLIAM, factor in Veere, admitted as a burgess of Elgin 1686. [Elgin Burgess Roll]

GORDON, WILLIAM, M.D., born 26.10.1804, son of Reverend William Gordon and Margaret Anderson, Honourable East India Company Service. [F.6.410]

GORDON, WILLIAM, born 1814, son of Reverend John Gordon, surgeon, died at Newcastle Barracks, Jamaica, 7.12.1836. [Speymouth Dipple g/s]

GRANT, ALEXANDER, ba. 7.8.1793 in Morayshire, son of Robert Grant of Wester Elchies, officer of the Bengal Army 1809-1829, died in Edinburgh 13.8.1835. [BA.2.311]

GRANT, ALEXANDER, born 1820, son of Robert Grant [1785-1852] and Eliza Grant [1797-1881], mariner, died 2.1874 in Melbourne. [Inverallan g/s]

GRANT, ANNA, born 1.8.1762, daughter of Reverend John Grant and Anna Grant in Elgin, wife of James Brice, Collector of Revenue in Washington, Pennsylvania, later in Pittsburg. [F.6.394]

GRANT, DAVID, late merchant in Grantown, died 1846 in Jamaica. [Inverallan g/s]

GRANT, DAVID, Morayshire, educated at King's College, Aberdeen, 1816, a missionary in India. [KCA275]

GRANT, DONALD, Grantown, settled in America 1814, father of Donald Cameron Grant. [BLG2719]

GRANT, EUPHEMIA, daughter of Lieutenant Edward Grant, Royal Navy, [died 6.11.1857], Rockhouse, Lossiemouth, wife of Reverend Louis A. Sery of the French National Reformed Church. [SRO.SH.1861]

GRANT, GEORGE, late in Jamaica, 22.1.1796. [SRO.RS.Elgin & Forres.410]

GRANT, GEORGE, born 16.4.1825, son of Reverend James Grant and Christina Macintosh in Nairn, a merchant in Rangoon. [F.6.444]

GRANT, JAMES, soldier from Elgin, married Ann Lindsay, from Dundee, in Schiedam, Netherlands, 19.12.1637. [Schiedam Marriage Register]

GRANT, Colonel JAMES, Governor of East Florida ca1770. [SRO.RS29{Elgin}VIII.202]

GRANT, JAMES, born 1783, son of John Grant, farmer in Croft, and Jean Fraser, wright in North Carolina, died 1828. [Cromdale g/s]

GRANT, JAMES, born 1817, son of Alexander Grant, postmaster of Ballindalloch, and Ann Grant, died 1834 in Africa. [Inveraven g/s]

GRANT, Colonel JAMES AUGUSTUS, born 11.4.1827, son of Reverend James Grant and Christina Macintosh in Nairn, an African explorer, died 11.2.1891 in Nairn. [F.6.444]

GRANT, JAMES THOMAS, in the East Indies, son of Sir James Grant of Grant, 30.9.1803. [SRO.RS.Elgin & Forres.620]

GRANT, JAMES, born 1785, Lynstock, Grantown, died 20.9.1829. [Scotch Burial Ground g/s. Calcutta]

GRANT, JOHN, in Jamaica, admitted as a burgess of Banff 1775. [BBR]; in Jamaica then in Banff, cnf.19.11.1807. [SRO.CC1.6.W329]

GRANT, JOHN, Captain formerly in East India Company Service, admitted as a burgess of Banff 1778. [BBR]

GRANT, JOHN, son of Peter Grant, [1760-1838], merchant in Grantown, and Isabella Ross, [1785-1855], died 1858 in Canada. [Inverallan g/s]

GRANT, JOHN, born 1829, son of Alexander Grant, postmaster of Ballindalloch, and Ann Grant, died 1856 in Africa. [Inveraven g/s]

GRANT, LUDOVICK, born 2.8.1786 in Duthil, son of Ludovick Grant, officer in the Bengal Army, died 30.8.1818 in Calcutta. [BA.2.318]

GRANT, MAGGIE, born 1831, daughter of William Grant [1798-1879] and Elspet Grant [1807-1886], died 1865 in Australia. [Inverallen g/s]

GRANT, ROBERT, of Kincorth, born 3.3.1752, son of David Grant and Margaret Grant, original member of the North West Company of Canada, died in Kincorth 10.8.1801. [Cromdale g/s]

GRANT, ROBERT, born 1837, son of William Grant [1798-1879] and Elspet Grant [1807-1886], died 1889 in Australia. [Inverallan g/s]

GRANT, W.R., son of William Grant [1800-1890] and mary Grant [1807-1891], settled in Buenos Ayres pre 1889, died 1902 in Edinburgh. [Advie g/s]

GRAY, JAMES, born 1827, son of James Gray and Margaret Taylor, died 1.11.1876 in Philadelphia. [Bellie g/s]

GREEN, ALEXANDER, born 1807, son of William Green and Helen Stewart, died 22.4.1834 in Jamaica. [Aberlour g/s]

GREEN, GEORGE, born 1835, son of James Green, carpenter in Fochabers, and Susan Bremner, died in Bernardstown, Massachusetts, 1.7.1860. [Bellie g/s]

GREEN, JOSEPH, born 1802, son of William Green and Helen Stewart, died 14.7.1847 in Jamaica. [Aberlour g/s]

GUTHRIE, GEORGE, merchant from Elgin, admitted as a citizen of Cracow 1624. [SIP47]

HAY, JAMES, born 1819, son of James Hay and Isabella Steinson, Lieutenant of the 3rd Regiment of the Madras Light Infantry, died 22.1.1842 in Hyderabad. [Bellie g/s]

HAY, PATRICK, Major on Honourable East India Company Service, 15.5.1794. [SRO.RS.Elgin & Forres.368]

HAY, PETER SCOTT, born 12.3.1844 in Dufftown, son of John Hay and Catherine Green, educated at King's College, Aberdeen, a minister in New Zealand 1877-, died 31.5.1925. [F.7.603]

HAY, WILLIAM G., born 1818, son of James Hay and Isabella Steinson, Lieutenant of the 35th regiment of Madras Native Infantry, died 4.1841 in Secunderabad. [Bellie g/s]

HENDERSON, ALEXANDER, merchant in St Kitts, admitted as a burgess of Banff 1770. [BBR]

HENDERSON, ROBERT, in Jamaica, later in Elgin, cnf 28.5.1824. [SRO.CC16.4.10.497]

HOSACK, ALEXANDER, born 1728 in Elgin, son of Alexander Hosack and Margaret Cook, soldier in the French and Indian Wars, settled in New York as a merchant in 1763, married Jane Arden, father of David, William, Alexander, James, and Jane, died in Hackensack, New York, 9.1.1826. [ANY.I.206]

HOUSTOUN, ALEXANDER CRUICKSHANK, born 25.3.1829 in Kirkton of Inverallen, Lieutenant of the 62nd Regiment of Bengal Native Infantry, died 29.5.1855 at Fort Abouzie, Punjab. [Cromdale g/s]

HOYES, ALEXANDER, son of Reverend John Hoyes [1744-1834] and Janet Reid in Kinloss, a merchant in the West Indies. [F.6.425]

HOYES, JOHN, son of Reverend John Hoyes [1744-1834] and Janet Reid in Kinloss, a merchant in the West Indies. [F.6.425]

HUDSON, JOHN, born in Elgin, married Mayken Adrians, born in Arnemuiden, in Arnemuiden, the Netherlands, 13.4.1630. [Arnemuiden Marriage Register]

HUSTWICK, CHARLES, born 28.4.1822, ships carpenter, died 3.2.1890 at Brown's Creek, New South Wales. [Speymouth Essil g/s]

HUSTWICK, WILLIAM, born 15.5.1813, son of William Hustwick, ships carpenter in Garmouth, died 27.1.1896 in Dry Creek, Bonnie Doon, Victoria. [Speymouth Essil g/s]

INGRAM, GEORGE, Banff, settled as a smith in Trinidad before 1842. [SRO.S/H]

INKSON, THOMAS, Morayshire, graduated King's College, Aberdeen, 1813, a physician in the West Indies. [KCA274]

INNES, ALEXANDER, chief carpenter at HM Dockyard, Port Royal, Jamaica, 31.8.1784. [SRO.RS.Elgin & Forres.99]

INNES, DONALD, born 1834, son of John Innes, Newton of Glenlivet, and Jane Grant, died 15.2.1899 in Granite, Virginia. [Inveraven Downan g/s]

INNES, JOHN, son of ..... Innes and Mary Dawson, died 8.187- in St Johns, New Brunswick. [Knockando g/s]

INNES, ROBERT, born 14.9.1745, son of Robert Innes, town clerk of Banff, and Margaret Gilchrist, a merchant in Gothenburg by 1765, a burgess of Montrose 1791, a burgess of Newcastle 1795. [MBR][Northern Scotland, Vol.7.1.146]

INNES, THOMAS, Banff, member of the Scots Charitable Society of Boston, Massachusetts, 1748. [NEHGS]

IRVINE, JOHN, late in Gothenburg, now in Aberdeen, 20.6.1792. [SRO.RS.Banff.287]

JAMIESON, THOMAS, Moray, a citizen of Bergen, Norway, 1632. [SAB]

KEITH, JAMES, formerly in Charleston, South Carolina, died in Blairshinnock, Banffshire, 14 August 1788. [Aberdeen Journal 2119]; probate 8.1810 PCC

KEITH, WILLIAM, son of William Keith, surgeon in South Carolina, admitted as a burgess of Banff 1764. [BBR]

LAURENCE, ..., in Jamaica, admitted as a burgess of Banff 1770. [BBR]

LESLIE, JAMES, possibly from Elgin, died in Jamaica ca1783. [Elgin Town Council minutes, 15.11.1783]

LESLIE, JAMES, born 31.5.1797 in Elgin, son of Reverend William Leslie and Margaret Sinclair, died 4.7.1819 in Bermuda. [F.3.397]

LESLIE, JOHN, ba. 13.10.1749 in Rothes, son of Alexander Leslie of Balnageith and Anna Duff, a merchant in St Augustine, East Florida, 1786. [IT.21][Florida Historical Review.18.1]

LESLIE, ROBERT, bap. 3.2.1758 in Rothes, son of Alexander Leslie of Balnageith and Anna Duff, settled in Florida, partner in Panton, Leslie and Company, 1792. ["Indian Traders of the South Eastern Spanish Borderlands", p19: Coker Watson; Florida, 1986]

LESLIE, WILLIAM, born 2.7.1794, son of Reverend William Leslie and Margaret Sinclair in Lhanbryd, Honourable East India Company Service surgeon, died 10.6.1831 in India. [F.6.397]

LESLIE, WILLIAM, born 26.12.1798 in Duffus, Morayshire, member of the firm of Gibson and Company tailors, died 11.6.1841. [Scotch Burial Ground g/s, Calcutta]

LOGIE, Major WILLIAM, son of Alexander Logie [1756-1836] and Agnes Cluny [1757-1823], settled in America. [Speymouth Essil g/s]

LOGIE, WILLIAM, born 10.8.1781, son of James Logie and Elizabeth Gordon in Boat of Bog, Speymouth, Bengal Army officer, died 13.1.1828 in Saugor, Bengal. [BA.3.74]

LONGMORE, WILLIAM, settled in Australia before 1858, son of William Longmore, banker in Keith, and Helen Lemmon. [SRO.SH.1858]

MACKIE, JAMES, in St Vincent, admitted as a burgess of Banff 1778. [BBR]

MACKIE, THOMAS, in Quebec, son of James Mackie a merchant in Findhorn, 1.8.1801. [SRO.RS.Elgin & Forres.567]

MACKIE, WILLIAM, in Jamaica, later in Forres, cnf. 11.9.1820. [SRO.CC16.5.3.189]

MAITLAND, CHARLES, Major on Honourable East India Company Service, 15.5.1794. [SRO.RS.Elgin & Forres.367]

MANN, JAMES, born in Elgin 15.12.1795, son of John Mann and Janet Laing, husbandman, emigrated to Manchester, Essex County, Massachusetts, via Philadelphia, settled in New Chester, New Hampshire, 1812, moved to Danby, New Hampshire, 10.1820, later in Hampstead, New Hampshire, 11.1828, naturalised 11.3.1833 Rockingham,New Hampshire.

MANN, WILLIAM, born in Elgin 1777, son of John Mann and Janet Laing, a ships carpenter in the service of the Honourable East India Company, stranded off the coast of Africa, rescued and landed at Salem, Massachusetts, 1803, settled in Essex County, Massachusetts. [The Highlander]

MANTACH, Reverend ROBERT, born 1792, son of John Mantach, farmer in Dundurcas, and Jane Hossack, died 18.12.1854 on Boaz Island, Bermuda. [Rothes Dundurcas g/s]

MARSHALL, GEORGE, son of William Marshall and Jean Giles, Lieutenant of the 92nd Regiment, died 1812 in Spain. [Bellie g/s]

MARSHALL, JOHN, son of William Marshall and Jean Giles, army captain, died 1829 in Madras. [Bellie g/s]

MERSON, CHARLES, born 1820 in Elgin, graduated King's College, Aberdeen, 1840, minister in Columbo, Ceylon, died 1869. [F.7.567]

MILL, JOHN, son of Andrew Mill and Janet Ligertwood in Meikle Creich, Banffshire, a traveller in Poland 1601. [MSC.II.58]

MILL, WILLIAM, son of Andrew Mill and Jnaet Ligertwood in Meikle Creich, Banffshire, a traveller in Poland 1601. [MSC.II.58]

MILL, WILLIAM, son of Andrew Mill and Margaret Mill in Newton of Troine, Abercharder, Banffshire, settled in Neustadtyn, Pomerania, 1595. [MSC.II.31]

MILNE, ALEXANDER, in Banff formerly in New York, son of John Milne a carter in Banff, 1840. [SRO.S/H]

MILNE, JAMES, born 1848, son of John Milne and Margaret
Paterson, died 29.6.1897 in Texas. [Bellie Tynet g/s]
MILNE, MOSES, son of James Milne, merchant in Bergen, admitted
as a burgess of Banff 1769. [BBR]
MILNE, THOMAS, merchant in Batavia, son of James Milne of
Milnefield, Elgin, 1830. [SRO.RS.Elgin & Forres, 371]
MILNE, WILLIAM, son of James Milne, merchant in Bergen,
admitted as a burgess of Banff 1764. [BBR]
MITCHELL, DONALD, M.A., born 6.1.1792, son of Reverend Donald
Mitchell and Christian Gordon in Ardclach, a missionary in
India, died 20.11.1823. [F.6.432]
MITCHELL, JOHN, born 22.11.1793, son of Reverend Donald
Mitchell and Christian Gordon in Ardclach, a missionary in
Ceylon. [F.6.432]
MITCHELSON, DAVID, late of New York, 4.12.1800. [SRO.RS.Elgin &
Forres.549]
MOORE, JOHN, Forres, husband of Betty Taylor, settled in
Moresville, Delaware County, New York, 1772. [New York
Genealogical and Biographical Record, Volume 25]
MORTIMER, EDWARD, born 1768 son of Alexander Mortimer,
burgess of Forres, and Mary Smith, a merchant in Pictou,
Nova Scotia, died there 10.10.1819.
[Chronicles of Keith {Glasgow, 1880}]
MORTIMER, EDWARD, born 5.3.1847 son of Edward and Margaret
Mortimer in Banff, died in Ceylon 8.2.1871. [Banff g/s]
MUNRO, Reverend JAMES, born 1747 in Orbiston, Morayshire,
educated at King's College, Aberdeen, 1772, minister in
Nottingham, Maryland 1785-, in Antigonish, Nova Scotia
1807-1819, died 17.5.1819 in Antigonish. [F.6.396]
[History of the Presbyterian Church {Toronto, 1885}]
MUNRO, WILLIAM, late of Jamaica, died in Forres 10.1.1809.
[SM.71.158]; cnf 9.11.1809. [SRO.CC16.4.1.172]
MURRAY, ALEXANDER, born 10.6.1757 in Duffus, son of Reverend
Alexander Murray and Isabel Gordon, Bengal Army officer,
died 6.12.1796 in Calcutta. [BA.3.357]
MURRAY, JAMES, a soldier from Forres, married Anna Holms in
the English Church in Middelburg 14.12.1617. [Arnemuiden
Marriage Register]
MURRAY, JOHN, born 12.3.1781 in Morayshire, son of Andrew
Murray and Jean Grant, Bengal Army officer, died 25.4.1802
in Cawnpore. [BA.3.361]
MURRAY, JOHN, in Demerara later in Portsoy, cnf Aberdeen 1795.

MURRAY, WILLIAM, Banff, member of the Scots Charitable Society of Boston, Massachusetts, 1751. [NEHGS]

MURRAY, WILLIAM, in Latiune, Jamaica, admitted as a burgess of Banff 1799. [BBR]

MCANDREW, ALEXANDER, born 4.6.1808 in Elgin, son of James McAndrew, commission agent in Portugal, Canada and New York, settled on Staten Island, New York, died 10.4.1883 in England. [ANY.II.240]

MCANDREW, GEORGE SHIRLEY, son of James McAndrew a merchant in Elgin, educated at Marischal College ca1812, settled in Jamaica. [Records of Marischal College and the University of Aberdeen, 1593-1860, {Aberdeen, 1898}]

MCBEAN, ARCHIBALD, born 1709, farmer in Aberlour, wife Catherine Cameron born 1714, father of Alexander, emigrated from Inverness to Georgia on the Prince of Wales, master William Dunbar, 20.10.1735, dead by 1740. [ESG83]

MCBEATH, Mr, America, admitted as a burgess of Elgin 1787. [Elgin Burgess Roll]

MCDONALD, FRANCIS, born 1795, died 19.6.1833 at Morant Bay, Jamaica. [Inveraven g/s]

MCDONALD, JAMES, born 1794, late of Morant Bay, Jamaica, died 6.4.1836 in Charleston of Aberlour. [Inveraven g/s]

MACEWEN, ROBERT HALDANE, born 1.1848, son of Reverend John MacEwen and Mary MacIntosh in Moy and Culbin, an indigo planter in India, died 1893. [F.6.417]

MACFARLANE, WILLIAM, born 9.9.1839 in Boharm, Fochabers, son of Mungo MacFarlane and Margaret Christie, graduated MA at King's College, Aberdeen, 1858, a schoolmaster and minister in Amsterdam. [KCA309][F.7.540]

MCGREGOR, CHARLES, son of Grigor McGregor [1770-1854] and Ann .... [1787-1838], settled in Trinidad. [Cromdale g/s]

MCGREGOR, GEORGE, born 1837, son of Alexander McGregor [1792-1846] and Maragret Cameron [1800-1881], died 14.5.1870 in Calcutta. [Inveraven g/s]

MACGREGOR, GRIGOR, son of Colquhoun MacGregor [died 1847] and Margaret Leslie [died 1810], merchant in Mauritius. [Cromdale g/s]

MCHENRY, JAMES, born 1788 in Forres, merchant in Savanna, Georgia, died 22.9.1826 in Lexington, Oglethorpe County, Georgia. ["Georgia Republican" 10.10.1826]

MCINNES, JOHN, Lieutenant Colonel in East India Company Service, 1831. [SRO.RS.Elgin & Forres, 1/3]

16

MCINTOSH, CHARLES, physician in Jamaica, admitted as a burgess of Banff 1770. [BBR]

MACINTOSH, DUNCAN, born 1779, son of Andrew MacIntosh a merchant in Forres, a surgeon, died in Spain 10.5.1813. [SM.75.478]

MCINTOSH, JAMES, born 1754 in Strathdearn, son of William Roy McIntosh of Dell and Marjory McIntosh, emigrated to New York 1776, merchant in New York, died there 4.11.1811. [ANY.I.176]

MACINTOSH, JAMES, Nairn, graduated MA at King's College, Aberdeen, 1846, a missionary in Madras. [KCA298]

MACKAY, GEORGE, born 1833, son of Reverend George MacKay and Helen Johnstone in Altyre, a banker in Shanghai, died 1867. [F.6.428]

MACKAY, HUGH MACPHERSON, M.A., born 1821, son of Reverend George MacKay and Helen Johnstone in Altyre, a planter in Ceylon, died 1859 in Forres. [F.6.428]

MACKAY, JOHN, born 1819, son of Reverend George Mackay and Helen Johnstone in Altyre, officer of the 33rd Bengal Infantry, died 13.1.1842 in Afghanistan. [F.6.428]

MCKENZIE, ROBERT, son of Peter McKenzie [1808-1871] and Janet Grant [1811-1866], settled in New South Wales before 1886. [Inveraven g/s]

MACKENZIE, WILLIAM, born 1847, son of William MacKenzie and Jane Thompson in Carron, died 10.12.1893 in Surinam. [Aberlour g/s]

MCKINNON, ALEXANDER, merchant in Leghorn, admitted as a burgess of Banff 1786. [BBR]

MACLEAN, LACHLAN, merchant in Danzig, admitted as a burgess of Banff 1786. [BBR]

MCLEOD, ALEXANDER, born 1792, son of Captain William McLeod [1761-1833], Lieutenant Colonel of the 61st Regiment, died 18.8.1849 in India. [Bellie g/s]

MCPHERSON, JOHN, Strathspey, member of the Scots Charitable Society of Boston, Massachusetts, 1758. [NEHGS.MSS.B/S.36v6]

MACPHERSON, ROBERT, born 1711, farmer in Alvie, emigrated from Inverness to Georgia on the Prince of Wales, master William Dunbar, 20.10.1735. [ESG87]

NICOL, ALEXANDER, indentured servant for Georgia who may have absconded, 19.7.1738. [Elgin Kirk Session Register]

OGILVIE, CHARLES, Banffshire, in South Carolina 1770s. [SRO.NRAS.0426, box 8, bundles 31-34]

OGILVIE, JAMES, born 1747, son of William Ogilvie and Helen Baird, died 6.6.1774 in Jamaica. [Banff g/s]

OGILVIE, JAMES T. born in Banff 1819, a clerk in Charleston, South Carolina, naturalised there 27.7.1846. [USNA,MII83.1]

OGILVIE, JOHN, born 1753 son of William Ogilvie and Helen Baird, died 30.8.1770 in Antigua. [Banff g/s]

OGILVIE, MATTHEW, a merchant, second son of John Ogilvie saddler in Banff, died in Charleston, South Carolina, 11.8.1872. [AJ9504]

OGILVIE, WILLIAM, born 1742, son of William Ogilvie and Helen Baird, died 9.5.1783 in Bassora. [Banff g/s]

PATERSON, ROBERT, born 17.7.1782, son of Reverend Robert Paterson and Margaret Collie in Spynie, Honourable East India Company Service surgeon, died 12.1829 in Calcutta. [F.6.407]

PAUL, ALEXANDER, born 3.5.1848 in Banff, drowned while yachting in Lake Huron 7.1870. [Banff g/s]

PURSS, JOHN, born 12.12.1732 in Elgin, son of Alexander Purss, a tailor, and Isabel Blenshel, settled in Canada before 1762, a merchant and public official there, died in Quebec 8.4.1843. [Dictionary of Canadian Biography]

REID, JAMES, born 3.1.1777, son of William Reid, town clerk of Banff, and Margaret Innes, a merchant in Gothenburg, died there 17.3.1813. [Northern Scotland, Volume 7.1.147]

RIACH, JOHN, born 1826, son of John Riach, farmer in Hillfolds, and Margaret Anderson, died 5.2.1855 in Toronto. [Rothes g/s]

RICHARDSON, JOHN, Aberlour, graduated MA at King's College, Aberdeen, 1856, in the service of the East India Company. [KCA308]

ROBERTSON, ALEXANDER, in Jamaica, son of James Robertson of Bishopmills, 1768. [SRO.RS29{Elgin}VIII.87]

ROBERTSON, ELIZABETH, born 1830, daughter of William Robertson, farmer in Cuttlebrae, and Elizabeth Sutherland, died 16.1.1861 in New York. [Bellie g/s]

ROBERTSON, ISABELLA, born 1828, daughter of William Robertson, farmer in Cuttlebrae, and Elizabeth Sutherland, died 19.11.1869 in Grimsby, Canada. [Bellie g/s]

ROBERTSON, JAMES, merchant in Jamaica, son of James Robertson of Bishopmills, ca1740. [SRO.RS29{Elgin}VI.449]

ROBERTSON, JAMES, in Jamaica, 24.4.1784/7.3.1788. [SRO.RS.Elgin & Forres. 88/211]

ROBERTSON, JOHN, Banff, applied for citizenship of Bergen, Norway, 1636. [Bergen State Archives]
ROBERTSON, LEWIS, born 1816, son of Lewis Robertson [1775-1828] and Jane Inkson [1792-1864], died 25.1.1847 in Australia. [Knockando g/s]
ROBERTSON, LEWIS DUNBAR BRODIE, born 16.11.1823, son of Reverend William Robertson and Margaret Robertson in Kinloss, died 14.1.1848 in Ceylon. [F.6.426]
ROBINSON, ALEXANDER, third son of James Robinson, Bishop Mill, Morayshire, Naval Officer of Kingston, Jamaica, died in Port Royal Harbour, Jamaica, 19.9.1791. [SM.53.568]
ROSE, CHARLES, born in Alves, Morayshire, a clergyman in Virginia from 1736 to 1761, died there 1761. [SA31]
ROSE, JOHN, from Forres, settled in Essex, America, by 1747. [SRO.RH1/2/861]
ROSE, ROBERT, born 12.2.1704 in Alves, Morayshire, a minister in Virginia from 1725 to 1751, died there 1751. [SA31]
ROY, GEORGE, born 1751 in Banffshire, 'an early settler of Halifax', died in Merigomish, Halifax, Nova Scotia, 1831. ["Gentleman's Magazine".101.477]
RUDDACH, JOHN, at Montego Bay, Jamaica, admitted as a burgess of Banff 1800. [BBR]
RUSSEL, ERROL, born 1773, son of Thomas Russel of Rathe and Anna Innes, Lieutenant of the Royal Marines, died in the West Indies 7.1795. [Banff g/s]
RUSSEL, RODDAM, born 1781, son of Thomas Russel of Rathen and Anna Innes, a midshipman, died at St Domingo 31.10.1797. [Banff g/s]
RUSSEL, THOMAS, born 1772, son of Thomas Russel of Rathen and Anna Innes, died in Martinique 7.1794. [Banff g/s]
RUSSELL, Major R., in Antigua, 3.10.1783. [SRO.RS.Elgin & Forres.71]
SCOTT, JAMES, clerk in Prince William County, Virginia, son of Reverend John Scott of Lochs, in Dipple, ca1712. [SRO.RS29{Elgin}V.228]
SELLAR, DAVID PLENDERLEITH, born 27.4.1833, son of Patrick Sellar of Westfield, Morayshire, educated at Edinburgh Academy, a banker in New York, died 22.10.1921. [Edinburgh Academy Register 1824-1914, p.127 {Edinburgh 1914}]
SHAND, JOHN, Elgin, graduated MA at King's College, Aberdeen, 1854, Professor of Classics in Dunedin. [KCA306]

SHAND, WILLIAM, Mortlach, graduated MA at King's College, Aberdeen, 1843, a teacher at the Cape of Good Hope. [KCA396]

SHAW, DAVID, born 1728 in Elgin, son of Reverend Lachlan Shaw and Helen Stuart, emigrated to New York on the brig Lovely Jane, master John Walker, 1759, merchant in New York, married Polly Dey 24.11.1761, father of Lachlan, William, Janet and Maria, died 1.10.1767, buried in Hackensack churchyard, New York. [ANY.I.84][F.6.390]

SHAW, LACHLAN, born 27.1.1729, son of Reverend Lachlan Shaw and Helen Stuart in Elgin, emigrated to Jamaica, died in London. [F.6.390]

SHERIFF, ALEXANDER, master of Elgin Grammar School, settled in Jamaica 1765. [Elgin Town Council Minutes, 24.10.1765]

SHERAR, JOHN, born 1792, Banffshire, died in Westminster, Ontario, 11.2.1872. [AJ6480]

SIM, JAMES, born in Banff 11.11.1759, late of St Vincent, died 27.5.1825, husband of Elizabeth McKilligan (1761-1826). [Banff g/s]

SIM, JAMES GEORGE, born in Banff 4.3.1804, physician in East India Company service, died 10.9.1830 in Singapore. [Banff g/s]

SIM, JOHN, born 1744, late of Antigua, died 29.11.1807, husband of Mary Stephen (1755-1847). [Banff g/s]

SIME, ALEXANDER, born 1845, son of Alexander Sime, farmer in Ringorm, and Margaret Donaldson, died 24.6.1886 in Warrnamboul, Australia. [Knockando g/s]

SIME, LEWIS, born 1848, son of Alexander Sime, farmer in Ringorm, and Margaret Donaldson, died 15.3.1871 in St Thomas, Canada. [Knockando g/s]

SIMPSON, GEORGE, a clerk in Kingston, Jamaica, son of George Simpson, a merchant in Elgin, 1788. [SRO.RD4.244.318]

SIMPSON, GEORGE, born 1849, son of James Simpson and Margaret Milne in Banff, a ships carpenter, died in Adelaide, Australia, 12.1878. [Banff g/s]

SIMPSON, JAMES, in Tobago, admitted as a burgess of Banff 1773. [BBR]

SIMPSON, JOHN, born 1829, son of James Simpson and Margaret Milne in Banff, a shipmaster, died in Demerara 8.1867. [Banff g/s]

SIMPSON, JOHN, born 1799, son of Alexander Simpson and Jean Smith, died in Canton 10.11.1822. [Banff g/s]

SIMPSON, WILLIAM, tailor in Gerbity, Dundurcas, married Janet
Winchester 16.2.1759, with family emigrated from Rothes,
Morayshire, to Canada on the John and Elizabeth in 1775,
shipwrecked in Flat River, Prince Edward Island.
[TIM.18.30][HMS]
SIMPSON, WILLIAM, a carpenter in St Catherine's parish,
Middlesex County, Jamaica, son of George Simpson, a
merchant in Elgin, 1788. [SRO.RD4.244.318]
SIMPSON, WILLIAM, born 1831, son of James Simpson and
Margaret Milne in Banff, a seaman, died in Calcutta
4.7.1853. [Banff g/s]
SMITH, EDWARD, Fochabers, settled at Slave Lake, North
America, by 1812. [SRO.RS{Elgin}827]
SMITH, GEORGE, from Portsoy, a seaman on the Dolphin of
Philadelphia, Captain O'Bryen, was captured by Algerian
pirates and imprisoned in Algiers in July 1785. He was
still in captivity in July 1790. [AJ2230]
SMITH, GEORGE, Fochabers, settled in Pictou, Nova Scotia, before
1812. [SRO.RS{Elgin}827]
SMITH, JEAN, born in Fordyce, a housekeeper in Gothenburg 1759·
married Peter Engstrom, died in Sweden 1821.
[Northern Scotland, Volume 7.1.147]
SMITH, JOHN, born in Forres, merchant in New York 1791-1818,
married Mrs Agnes Wetzell 1793. [ANY.I.315]
SMITH, ROBERT GORDON, born 29.4.1864, son of Reverend Robert
Smith and Helen Gordon in Altyre, a farmer in Australia.
[F.6.429]
SPEEDY, PETER, soldier from Forres, married Maertge Frerix in
Schiedam, Netherlands, 14.6.1636. [Schiedam Marriage
Register]
SPENCE, JAMES, minister in Castlemartyrs, Ireland, son of
Alexander Spence, minister in Birnie, ca1710.
[SRO.RS20{Elgin}V194, etc]
SPENCE, MICHAEL, of Stankhouse, attorney in the Court of
Common Pleas in Dublin, 1708. [SRO.RS29{Elgin}IV.231]
SPIDIMAN, PATRICK, soldier from Forres, married Janniken
Hutson in Schiedam, Netherlands, 13.6.1637. [Schiedam
Marriage Register]
SQUYRE, JOHN, born 1685, educated at Edinburgh University
ca. 1685, a missionary in Carolina 1713-1718, died in
Forres 27.1.1758. [F.6.422]

STALKER, JOHN, Aberlour, graduated MA at King's College, Aberdeen, 1858, a missionary in Pietermaritzburg. [KCA309]

STEPHEN, ALEXANDER, son of John Stephen, baker in Rothes, [died 1854], and Ann Booth, [died 1841], settled in America before 1877. [Rothes g/s]

STEPHEN, JAMES ALEXANDER, born 29.11.1857, son of Reverend Thomas Stephen and Anne MacIver in Kinloss, emigrated to Australia. [F.6.426]

STEVEN, ALEXANDER, in Tobago, 19.1.1795. [SRO.RS.Banff.336]

STEWART, CHARLES, Forres, graduated MA at King's College, Aberdeen, 1846, a merchant in America., [KCA298]

STEWART, DAVID, born 1712, surgeon in Cromdale, emigrated from Inverness to Georgia on the Prince of Wales, master William Dunbar, 20.10.1735. [ESG97]

STEWART, GREGOR, son of Adam Stewart and Marjory Grant in the Mains of Dalvey, surgeon of the 18th Regiment, died 18.8.1846 in Hong Kong. [Advie g/s]

STEWART, JOHN, Colonel of the Regiment of Foot in the service of the United Provinces, brother of James, 8th Earl of Moray, ca1760. [SRO.RS29{Elgin}VII.416]

STEWART, JOHN D., Logie, Morayshire, Major General of the Bombay Army, died in Rome 1874. [AJ6589]

STEWART, PETER, Banffshire, member of the Scots Charitable Society of Boston, Massachusetts, 1759. [NEHGS]

STEWART, WILLIAM, of Aswanly, formerly a merchant in Gothenburg, then resident in Elgin, and his wife Barbara King, 1760. [SRO.RS29{Elgin}VII.389, etc]

STIMSON, THOMAS, late of Banff, Chief Officer of the Onward of Hong Kong, married Margaret, youngest daughter of John McKenzie builder in Fortrose, in Melbourne 11.1.1872. [AJ6481]

STRAITON, ALEXANDER, in Dort, admitted as a burgess of Banff 1776. [BBR]

STUART, ALEXANDER, Inveravon, graduated MA at King's College, Aberdeen, 1843, minister in Halifax, Nova Scotia. [KCA296]

STUART, Reverend JAMES, late of Carolina, admitted as a burgess of Banff 1783. [BBR]

TARRAS, JAMES, in Elgin, to Tangiers 1678. [RPC.X.546]

TARRAS, JOHN JACOB, son of Laurence Tarras, merchant in Gothenburg, admitted as a burgess of Banff 1802. [BBR]

TAYLOR, BETTY, Elgin, wife of John Moore, settled in Moresville, Delaware County, New York, 1772. [New York Genealogical and Biographical Record, Volume 25]

TAYLOR, JAMES, Fochabers, applied to settle in Canada 2.3.1815. [SRO.RH9]

THOMSON, ALEXANDER, born 1836, son of John Thomson, merchant in Fochabers, and Mary Stewart, died 12.11.1860 in Melbourne. [Bellie g/s]

THOMSON, ALEXANDER, farmer in Fochabers, wife Elizabeth Hay, and son John {born 1853}, emigrated to America 1854, settled in Marison, Wayne County, New York. [DAB.XVIII.485]

THOMSON, WILLIAM, born 1786, son of John Thomson, feuar in Dufftown, and Jane Grant, died 1811 in Jamaica. [Aberlour g/s]

TOD, ROBERT, son of William Tod [1745-1821] and Helen Ogilvie [1746-1801], surgeon of the 1st Light Dragoons, died 20.2.1824 in Kaira, Bombay. [Bellie g/s]

TROUP, JAMES, late of Jamaica, 15.3.1785. [SRO.RS.Elgin & Forres.120]

TULLOH, ROBERT, born 1763, son of Robert Tulloh of Bogton, Forres, soldier in the Bengal Army, died 6.5.1802 in Calcutta. [BA.4.321]

TURNBULL, Mrs, Fochabers, died in Demerara 1.2.1801. [Glasgow Courant, 1519]

TWEED, ALEXANDER, merchant in Carolina, admitted as a burgess of Banff 1776. [BBR]; son of William Tweed, (1683-1760), merchant in Banff and Jean Jaffrey,(1692-1769).[Banffg/s]

WALKER, ALEXANDER, born 20.1.1811, son of Reverend Alexander Walker and Elizabeth Grant in Urquhart, surgeon in Honourable East India Company Service, died 5.9.1850 in Boharm. [F.6.411]

WALKER, ALEXANDER, born 25.12.1845, son of Reverend Henry Walker and Eleanora Julian in Urquhart, Morayshire, settled in Australia. [F.6.411]

WALKER, JAMES FIFE, born 3.2.1814, son of Reverend Alexander Walker and Elizabeth Grant in Urquhart, Morayshire, a planter in Berbice, died 6.8.1842. [F.6.411]

WALKER, JOHN, born 4.12.1847, son of Reverend John Walker and Anne Duff in St Andrew's parish, Morayshire, settled in Tasmania, died 10.9.1893. [F.6.398]

WALKER, ROBERT DUFF, born 15.3.1846, son of Reverend John Walker and Anne Duff in St Andrew's parish, Morayshire, settled in Australia, died 29.12.1888. [F.6.398]

WALKER, WILLIAM, born 19.10.1809, son of Reverend Alexander
Walker and Elizabeth Grant in Urquhart, a planter in
Berbice, died there 25.4.1843. [F.6.411]
WALLACE, GEORGE, merchant in Banff, applied for citizenship of
Bergen, Norway, 1711. [Bergen State Archives]
WALLACE, JAMES, merchant in Banff, applied for citizenship of
Bergen, Norway, 1727. [Bergen State Archives]
WATSON, JOHN, merchant in St Petersburg, Russia, 1780.
[SRO.RS29{Elgin}VIII.450]
WEIR, GEORGE, Aberlour, graduated MA at King's College,
Aberdeen, 1848, Professor of Classics in Kingston, Quebec.
[KCA300]
WENHAM, FRANCIS, third son of William Wenham factor in
Troup, Banffshire, murdered in Moboli, Solomon Islands
10.5.1872. [AJ6511]
WILSON, ANDREW, born in Banff 1795, died in Calcutta
16.5.1845. [Scotch Burial Ground g/s, Calcutta]
WILSON, JAMES, in Calcutta, 1780. [SRO.RS29{Elgin}VIII.494bis]
WILSON, JAMES, son of George Wilson and Margaret Phillip in
Banff, died in Port au Prince 20.6.1794. [Banff g/s]
WILSON, PETER, born 1794, late of Aberchirder, Banffshire,
died at Duke Street, Dunedin, Otago, New Zealand,
26.3.1876. [AJ6699]
WRIGHT, ALEXANDER MCLEAN, born 7.7.1852 in Elgin, son of
George Wright, educated at Aberdeen University 1876,
minister in New Zealand 1879-, died 16.12.1900. [F.7.605]
WRIGHT, JAMES, possibly from Grantown on Spey, settled in
St Thomas parish, South Carolina, pro. 12.6.1790,
Charleston, S.C.

EMIGRANTS AND ADVENTURERS
from
Angus and Perth

INTRODUCTION

Emigration has been for many centuries an established feature of Scottish demography. The degree and destination of emigration has changed from being relatively small scale and directed towards continental Europe in the sixteenth and seventeenth centuries to being substantial and predominently to North America during the eighteenth century and worldwide but mainly to Australasia and North America thereafter. During the early modern period there was a continuous trickle of scholars, merchants, tradesmen, and soldiers of fortune through the ports of Dundee, Perth and Montrose to destinations in north west Europe. Emigration directly from the region to America dates from August 1684 when the Thomas and Benjamin sailed from Montrose to East New Jersey. This book the first of a series, attempts to identify individual emigrants from the counties of Angus and Perth to worldwide destinations and is based on research in Scotland and elsewhere into primary and secondary sources

David Dobson, St Andrews, 1996

REFERENCES

ARCHIVES

GSA	Georgia State Archives
MCA	Montgomery County Archives, New York
	DFpp Duncan Fraser Papers
MPL	Montrose Public Library
	ArBR Arbroath Burgess Roll
	MBR Montrose Burgess Roll
NCSA	North Carolina State Archives, Raleigh
NEHGS	New England Historic Genealogical Society, Boston
NJA	New Jersey Archives, Trenton, New Jersey
PRO	Public Record Office, London
	HCA High Court of the Admiralty of England
	PCC Prerogative Court of Canterbury
SAB	Stats Arkivet, Bergen, Norway
SRA	Strathclyde Regional Archives, Glasgow
SRO	Scottish Record Office, Edinburgh
	CC Commissariot Court
	GD Gifts and Deposits
	NRAS National Register of Archives, Scotland
	RD Register of Deeds
	RS Register of Sasines
	SC Sheriff Court
	SH Services of Heirs
TRA	Tayside Regional Archives, Dundee
	DBR Dundee Burgess Roll
USNA	United States National Archives, Washington, DC

PUBLICATIONS

AJ	Aberdeen Journal, series
ANY	Biographical Register of the St Andrews Society of New York
AUPC	Annals of the United Presbyterian Church
BA	List of Officers of the Bengal Army 1758-1834
BLG	Burke's Landed Gentry
CCMC	Colonial Clergy of the Middle Colonies
Col Fams	Colonial Families of the USA
CGS	The Campbells and other Glengarry, Stormont and Harrington Pioneers
EEC	Edinburgh Evening Courant, series
F	Fasti Ecclesiae Scoticanae
HBRS	Hudson Bay Record Society
ImmNE	Immigrants to New England
RGS	Register of the Great Seal of Scotland
RPCS	Register of the Privy Council of Scotland
SIP	The Scots in Poland

Emigrants and Adventurers from

Angus and Perth

ABERCROMBIE, ALEXANDER, son of Thomas Abercrombie of Gourdie and
Grissel Sibbet, settled in Falkenburg in the Duchy of Brandenburg, by
1606. (TRA: Dundee birthbrief 16.6.1606)

ADAM, JOHN, born 1792 in Forfar, educated at Edinburgh University, HEICS
surgeon in Bengal 1817-1830, died in Calcutta 29.7.1830
[South Park g/s, Calcutta]

ADAMSON, Reverend Dr JAMES, Monzie, settled at the Cape of Good Hope
before 1846. [SRO.S/H]

AINEEL, NATHANIEL, Newmiln, Perthshire, soldier, banished from Holland
and Zealand 1611. (Leiden Judicial Archives vol.6, fo 234)

AINSLIE, JOHN, a merchant in Rotterdam, a burgess of Arbroath 1791.
[ArBR]

ALISON, ROBERT, settled in New South Wales prior to 1859, son of Robert
Alison, customs officer in Dundee, who died 7.11.1855.
(SRO.SH.1859)

ANDERSON, ANDREW, in Beckwith, Canada, 1831. [SRO.S.C.Perth.29/158]

ANDERSON, JAMES, of the Bengal Civil Service 1875.
[SRO.S.C.Perth.74/194]

ANDERSON, JAMES A., an architect in Detroit 1878. [SRO.S.C.Perth.78/171]

ANDERSON, ROBERT, Montrose, a merchant in Sydney by 1843. [SRO.S/H]

ANDERSON, WILLIAM, Depute Manager of the Oriental Bank, Calcutta, 1849.
[SRO.S.C.Perth.49/91]

ANDREW, ROBERT, son of Robert Andrew and Eupham Makie in Myreton of
Brichty, a weaver in Copenhagen, 1608. [TRA: Dundee Birth Brief,
2.4.1608]

ARCHER, WILLIAM, born in Perthshire 1778, saddler, died in Savanna,
Georgia, 18.10.1805. (Savanna Death Register)

ARCHIBALD, ROBERT, born 1802 in Dundee, accountant in the HEIC New
Mint, died 14.5.1832. [South Park g/s, Calcutta]

ARTHUR, Captain JAMES, born 1798 son of .... Arthur and Elizabeth Herald,
died in New York 4.1838. [St Andrews g/s, Dundee]

BAILLIE, GEORGE, son of George Baillie and Janet Sinclair at the Mill of
Melgund, a trafficker in Poland, 1608. [TRA: Dundee Birth Brief,
15.4.1608]

BAIN, JAMES, born in Madderty 1802, son of Peter Bain an articifer,
educated at Glasgow University, to Canada 1854, minister in Ontario
1854-1874, died in Markham, Ontario, 9.12.1885. (F.7.625)

BAIRD, JANET, in Tarbolton, Canada, 1846. [SRO.S.C.Perth.46/51]

BAKER, JAMES, a merchant in Philadelphia, 1822. [SRO.S.C.Perth.17/77]

BARCLAY, JAMES, born in Montrose 1790, died in Bermuda 11.3.1831,
buried in St Peter's, St George parish, Bermuda. [Bermuda g/s]

BARCLAY, THOMAS THOMSON, skipper in Montrose, citizen of Bergen,
Norway, 1708. [SAB]

BARRY, CHARLES HENDERSON, in Jefferson, New York, 1845.
[SRO.Perth.S.C.45/60]

BARRIE, JAMES, born in Moneydie, Perthshire, 1785, died in Savanna,
Georgia, 10.10.1817. (Savanna g/s)

BEATON, DONALD, in Vaughan, York, Canada, 1860. [SRO.S.C.Perth.61/101]

BEGG, JAMES, born in Dundee 24.9.1814, son of .... Begg and Margaret
Ramsay, emigrated from Leith to Quebec 1.4.1827, settled in
Glengarry County, Ontario. (CGS28)

BELL, DAVID, born 1817 son of Alexander Bell, surgeon, and Anne Ruthven
Leven, a coffee planter, died in Kandy, Ceylon, 26.9.1849.
[Howff g/s, Dundee]

BETT, JOHN, born in Coupar Angus 1825, son of William Bett, settled on
Staten Island, New York, 1864, died in St Andrews, Scotland,
14.3.1910. (ANY.2.273)

BIRRELL, JAMES, in Emerald Hill, Melbourne, 1865. [SRO.S.C.Perth.66/14]

BISSET, THOMAS, in Guina, 1815. [SRO.S.C.Perth.10/177]

BLACK, GEORGE, in Melbourne, Victoria, 1858. [SRO.S.C.Perth.59/158]

BLACK, GEORGE, in Tarwin Station, Stockyard Creek, Gipps Land,
Victoria, 1881. [SRO.S.C.Perth.81/129]

BLAIR, GEORGE, born in Perth 1818, educated at St Andrews University
1835, school superintendent in Canada, missionary in the Alleghany
Mountains, USA, died 2.1897. (F.7.627)

BLAIR, JOHN, born in Perthshire 1718, to America 1735, settled in
northern New Jersey, died 20.5.1798. (BLG2563)

BLUES, JANE, in Tagenrog, Russia, niece of John Blues, shipmaster in
Montrose who died 9.6.1851. (SRO.SH.1880)

BLUES, MARGARET, in Tagenrog, Russia, niece of John Blues, shipmaster in
Montrose who died 9.6.1851. (SRO.SH.1880)

BLUES, REBECCA, in Tagenrog, Russia, niece of John Blues, shipmaster in
Montrose who died 9.6.1851. (SRO.SH.1880)

BLYTH, ROBERT, born 1840, an engineeer, died in Calcutta 3.5.1869.
[Dundee, Western g/s]

BOWES, ROBERT, a surgeon in Virginia, son of Robert Bowis, minister of
Rattray 1699-1741, and Margaret Campbell. [F.4.171]

BOWES, ROBERT, Brechin, member of the Scots Charitable Society of
Boston 1748. (NEHGS)

BRAKENRIDGE, DAVID, surgeon HEICS then in Perth, 1869.
[SRO.S.C.Perth, 69.100]

BRAND, WILLIAM, born in Dundee 10.1813 son of James Brand and Isabella
Nicoll, a linen merchant in New York 1841-1865, died near Dundee
11.12.1882. [ANY.2.205]

BRECHIN, ALEXANDER, son of David Brechin and Elizabeth Duncan in
Monifieth, settled in Lumberg, Pomerania, by 1633. (TRA: Dundee
birthbrief 13.8.1633)

BRODIE, ALICE LINDSAY, daughter of James Brodie in Perth, wife of David
Prophet a solicitor, died in St Kilda, Melbourne, 18.9.1875. [AJ6674]

BRODIE, JOHN, born in Perthshire 1767, slater, wife Elizabeth Archibald,
daughter Lindsay 1798, sons John 1800, James 1802, emigrated
from Liverpool to New York, naturalised in New York 15.11.1819.

BROUGH, JAMES, in South Clutha, Otago, New Zealand, 1856.
[SRO.S.C.Perth, 56.260]

BROWN, ANDREW, merchant burgess of Perth, to France 1633.
[StAUL.MS36220.679]

BROWN, EDWARD, merchant, 22 Gore Street, Melbourne, 1875.
[SRO.S.C.Perth, 74.162]

BROWN, GEORGE, Oararm, Otago, 1875. [SRO.S.C.Perth, 74.222]

BROWN, JOHN, born 1807, son of Reverend William Brown (1774-1829) and
Christine Whyte (1775-1862), died at Montego Bay, Jamaica,
24.1.1845. [Perth Greyfriars g/s]

BROWN, LAWRENCE, Dundee, merchant in St Petersburg, 1803. (SRO.S/H)

BROWN, PATRICK, born 1778, died in India 25.6.1811. [Howff g/s, Dundee]

BRUCE, STEPHEN, son of James Bruce and Gilles Will, settled in Prussia by
1612. (TRA: Dundee birthbrief 5.1612)

BUCHANAN, GEORGE, born in Perthshire, to Canada, minister in Beckwith,
Ontario, 1822-, died 1835. (F.7.628)

BUCHANAN, JAMES, late of St Thomas, a burgess of Montrose 1783.[MBR]

BUCHANAN, JAMES, ba. 6.11.1769 son of David Buchanan and Margaret
Grubb in Montrose, merchant in New York, died in New York 1786.
(ANY.I.219)

BUICK, KIRKWOOD H., in Melville, North Dakota, 1891.[SRO.S.C.Perth, 90/87]

BUIST, Dr GEORGE, in Bombay by 1846, son of the Reverend John Buist in
Tannadice. [SRO.S/H]

BURDEN, HENRY, born 22.4.1791 Dunblane, son of Peter Burden and
Elizabeth Abercrombie, settled in Troy, New York, 1819, died 1871.
(BLG2591)
BURGH, WILLIAM, son of William Burgh of Craigie and Janet Gellatly,
resident in Konigsberg 1612. [TRA: Dundee Birth Brief, 17.8.1612]
BURN, DAVID, Angus, member of the Scots Charitable Society of Boston
1748. (NEHGS)
BURNETT, ANDREW, Angus, member of the Scots Charitable Society of
Boston 1737. (NEHGS)
BUTCHART, JOHN, son of Thomas Butchart and Janet Watt in Grange of
Cossins, a merchant in Konigsburg, 1615. [TRA: Dundee Birth Brief,
20.5.1615]
BUTTAR, WILLIAM, near Dundee, member of the Scots Charitable Society of
Boston 1762. (NEHGS)
CAIRNS, JAMES MILN, born in Longforgan 1806, schoolmaster in New York,
died 24.7.1832. (ANY.2.27)
CAITHNESS, or VOLKMAN, ELIZABETH, in Norway, daughter of Charles
Caithness, shipmaster in Dundee, 1831. (SRO.SH.1831)
CAITHNESS, or ULICH, MARGARETin Norway, daughter of Charles Caithness,
shipmaster in Dundee, 1831. (SRO.SH.1831)
CAITHNESS, MARY, in Ask, Norway, daughter of Charles Caithness,
shipmaster in Dundee, 1831. (SRO.SH.1831)
CAMERON, JAMES WATSON, Dundee, a merchant in New York during 1840s,
settled on Staten Island, possibly died in Dundee. [ANY.2.201]
CAMERON, JOHN MCAFEE, born in Rannoch 1730, to America on the Pearl
1773, settled on the Kingsborough Patent, New York, soldier of the
Royal Regiment of New York 1776-1783, settled in Fairfield,
Lancaster, Glengarry County, Ontario. (DFpp)
CAMPBELL, ALEXANDER, Killin, emigrated to Canada on the Harmony 1817,
settled in Mariposa, Ontario. (CGS274)
CAMPBELL, ALEXANDER, born in Killin 14.11.1734, son of James Campbell
and Elizabeth Buchanan, officer of the Black Watch, to New York
1756, married (1) Catherine Vedder (died 1767) in New York
12.10.1765, settled in Schenectady, New York, married (2) Magdalene
Van Sice 23.5.1768, merchant in Schoharie, New York, Loyalist,
settled in Ontario 1785, died 1800, buried in New Johnstown,
Edwardsburgh, Ontario. (CGS432)
CAMPBELL, ARCHIBALD, born in Glen Lyon 16.11.1779, son of Donald
Campbell and Mary Campbell, emigrated to Saratoga, New York, 1798,
married Mary Grant 30.6.1806, settled in Albany, New York, died
there 14.7.1865. (CCS/USA)
CAMPBELL, COLIN, Perthshire, member of the Scots Charitable Society of
Boston 1747. (NEHGS)

CAMPBELL, DUNCAN, born near Loch Tay 1771, married Catherine McIntyre (1779-1873), emigrated to Canada 1816, settled in Glengarry County, Ontario, died 1844. (CGS204)

CAMPBELL, JOHN, born in Killin, emigrated to Canada on the Harmony 1817, settled in Galt, Ontario. (CGS274)

CAMPBELL, MALCOLM, born in Killin 1772, stonemason, married Ann Anderson (1774-1856), emigrated to Canada on the Harmony 1817, settled in Dominionville, Ontario, died 1864, buried in Maxville. (CGS274)

CAMPBELL, MARK, Dunkeld, died in Grenada 2.12.1791. (EEC.24.3.1792)

CAMPBELL, MARY, born in Glen Lyon 1753, daughter of Peter Campbell and Margaret Stewart, married Donald Campbell (1750-1782), emigrated to New York 1798, died in York, Genessee County, New York, 1823. (CCS/USA)

CAMPBELL, PETER, Killin, emigrated to Canada on the Harmony 1817, settled in Glovesville, New York. (CGS274)

CARGILL, CHARLES, engineer in Australia, son of Susan Wightman or Cargill in Arbroath who died 16.11.1879. (SRO.SH.1880)

CARMICHAEL, JAMES, son of Robert and Margaret Carmichael in Dundee, admitted as a citizen of Cracow, Poland, 5.12.1625. (SIP42)

CARMICHAEL, JOHN, a soldier from Dundee, married Anneken Jans in Heusden, Netherlands, 18.5.1636. (Heusden Marriage Register)

CARR, ROBERT, Montrose, member of the Scots Charitable Society of Boston 1731. (NEHGS)

CHRISTIE, ANDREW, born in Montrose 1620, citizen of Bergen 1654, died in Bergen, Norway, 1694. [SAB]

CHRISTIE, JOHN, born 1745, married Janet McGregor (1757-1852), emigrated from Killin to America, settled at Creek Road, Mumford, New York, 1797, died 3.7.1843. ("Genealogy of Miller and Tillotson", Scottsville, New York, 1951)

CHRISTIE, ROBERT, son of James Christie and Agnes Scugall in Adamstown, settled in Lauenburg, Pommerania, by 1607. (TRA: Dundee birthbrief 22.8.1607)

CLARK, JOHN, Perth, settled in Australia by 1859. [SRO.S/H]

COCHRAN, WILLIAM J., born in Dundee 1.5.1797, son of John Cochran and Helen Thornton, tailor, emigrated from Dundee to America 1.5.1820, naturalised in New York 27.3.1834.

COLLIE, WILLIAM, son of William Collie, burgess of Arbroath, and Marjory Futhie, settled in Denmark by 1612. (Arbroath Burgh Testimonial 28.6.1612)

COMRIE, ALEXANDER, born in Perthshire, married Christine McIntyre in Breadalbane, emigrated to New York before 1776, settled in Johnstown, New York. (SPW)

COOK, ANDREW, farm labourer in Dundee, arrived in Hobart, Tasmania, on the Marco Polo 1855. (SRA.TD292)
COUTTS, DAVID, Logiealmond, divinity student 1823, minister in Canada. (AUPC)
COUTTS, JAMES, a merchant in Philadelphia, burgess of Montrose 1709. [MBR]
CREE, ALEXANDER, HEICS, son of James Cree in Perth, cnf Edinburgh 1792.
CRICHTON, MATILDA JACKSON or, in Dunkirk, France, daughter of Helen Scott or Jackson in Dundee who died 7.11.1880. (SRO.SH.1881)
CRICHTON, WILLIAM, late of Jamaica then in Dundee, son of Patrick Crichton of Ruthven, 1786. [SRO.GD48.box 17, fo812/813]
CROW, JOHN, HEICS in Bengal, later in Dundee, cnf 12.6.1819. [SRO.CC3.3.5.293]
CUMMING, ROBERT, born in Montrose 1701, son of John Cumming, a writer, emigrated to New Jersey, married (1) Mary Van Hook, (2) Mary Noble 1746, died in Freehold, New Jersey, 15.4.1769. (New Jersey Archives)
DALL, WILLIAM, Forfar, member of the Scots Charitable Society of Boston 1760. (NEHGS)
DAVIDSON, DAVID, son of David Davidson a slater in Dundee who died 14.12.1853, a slater in Melbourne 1854. [SRO.S/H]
DAVIDSON, WILLIAM, of Muirhouse, born 1713, son of Reverend Thomas Davidson and Janet Rodger, a merchant in Rotterdam, died 20.9.1794. [F.5.316]
DEMPSTER, ELIZABETH, Brechin, married Alexander Stewart, a soldier from Glasgow, in Schiedam, Netherlands, 27.4.1635. (Schiedam Marriage Register)
DICK, JAMES CHARLES, born 23.8.1792, fourth son of Dr Dick of Tullymet, Perthshire, died 17.11.1831. [Bareilly g/s, Bengal]
DICKSON, DAVID, from Errol, woolcomber in Leiden, Netherlands, married Marytgen Kaene from Kortrijk, Flanders, in Leiden, 12.10.1596 (Leiden Marriage Register, C.166); admitted as a citizen of Leiden 17.10.1608. (Leiden Citizenship Book II.37/6)
DONALD, Mrs ANN, died in New orleans 1.5.1858. [Howff g/s, Dundee]
DONALDSON, JAMES, merchant in Riga then in Montrose, cnf Brechin 1783.
DONALDSON, JAMES, born 1801, son of William Donaldson and Elizabeth Hill, died in Sydney 17.3.1857. [Dundee, Old Mains g/s]
DONALDSON, JOHN, son of Archibald Donaldson and Christian Ferrier, settled in Prussia by 1610. (TRA: Dundee birthbrief 21.5.1610)
DONALDSON, ROBERT, son of John Donaldson, burgess of Dundee, and Bessie Ireland, settled in Germany by 1606. (TRA: Dundee birthbrief 26.6.1606)

EMIGRANTS FROM ANGUS AND PERTH

DOUGAL, JOHN, merchant in Calcutta, son of Thomas Dougal, banker in
    Montrose. (SRO.SH.1830)
DOUGAL, THOMAS, born in Montrose 23.8.1807, died in Calcutta 11.4.1832.
    [South Park g/s, Calcutta]
DOUGLAS, CATHERINE, relict of John Douglas a planter in Charleston, South
    Carolina, cnf 16.9.1816. [SRO.CC3.3.14.307]
DRUMMOND, ANDREW shoemaker in Muthill, Perthshire, member of the
    Scots Charitable Society of Boston 1767. (NEHGS)
DRUMMOND, DAVID, son of John Drummond a banker in Crieff, settled in
    Sydney before 1848. [SRO.S/H]
DRUMMOND, RACHEL, daughter of James Drummond of Comrie, in Oporto,
    Portugal, pro 27.5.1746 Edinburgh
DRUMMOND, WILLIAM, Dundee, soldier, married Adriaenke Adriaens in
    Dordrecht, Netherlands, 22.3.1587. (Dordrecht Marriage Register)
DUFF, ANTHONY D., born in Dundee 1781, son of Robert Duff, emigrated to
    New York 1806, wine merchant, died 20.2.1825. (ANY.I.392)
DUNCAN, ALEXANDER, born 26.5.1805, son of Alexander Duncan of Parkhill,
    Arbroath, emigrated via Liverpool to New York 1821 on the Amity,
    educated at Yale and Brown Universities, a lawyer in Canandaigua
    and in Rhode Island, settled in England 1863, died in London
    14.10.1889. [ANY.2.298]
DUNCAN, JAMES, born in Alyth 1827, merchant in Dundee and New York,
    died at Jordanston, Alyth, 29.1.1909. (ANY.2.251)
DUNCAN, JOHN, son of John Duncan, a mariner, and Bessie Vauss, a
    traveller in Prussia, 1607. [TRA: Dundee Birth Brief, 13.7.1607]
DUNCAN, JOHN, born in Perthshire 1790, merchant, wife Jane born in
    Dundee 1786, children Ann born in Fife 1816, Ellen born in Fife 1818,
    David born in Fife 1820, daughter Jane born in New York City 1822,
    naturalised in New York 20.2.1823.
DUNCAN, ROBERT, son of David Duncan and Katherine Lecky in Fowlis,
    settled in Pomerania by 1606. (TRA: Dundee birthbrief 16.6.1606)
DURWARD, WILLIAM, son of Charles Durward and Margaret Gray in
    Balneaves, settled in Mecklenburg by 1616. (TRA: Dundee birthbrief
    9.9.1616)
EDGAR, THOMAS, born in Angus 19.10.1681, son of David Edgar of Keithock,
    married Janet Knox, settled in Elizabeth, New Jersey. (BLG2671)
ELDER, ALEXANDER, born in Milnathort 27.6.1804, son of William Elder and
    Christiana Mailer, educated at Glasgow University 1830, physician,
    settled in New York, died in New Jersey 3.2.1875. (ANY.2.276)
ELDER, WILLIAM, married Christiana Mailer pre 1804, Milnathort, Kinross,
    emigrated to New York 1828, settled West Farms, Schenectady
    County, New York. (ANY.II.276)

7

FERGUSON, JOHN, born 1830, labourer in Perthshire, arrived in Hobart, Tasmania, on the John Bell 4.12.1855. (SRA.TD292)

FERNIE, PETER, born in Perthshire 1793, accountant, emigrated from Belfast to America, naturalised in New York 2.4.1821.

FERRIER, ALEXANDER, Angus, member of the Scots Charitable Society of Boston 1738. (NEHGS)

FIFE, ROBERT, Dundee, burgess of Bergen, Norway, 1631, dead by 1642. [SAB]

FINLAYSON, THOMAS, a soldier from Brechin, married Elizabeth Peters from Gorinchem, in Heusden, Netherlands, 24.8.1628. (Heusden Marriage Register)

FRASER, ANDREW, son of Alaster Fraser of Glenshee and Elspeth Spalding, settled in Mecklenburg by 1616. (TRA: Dundee birthbrief 13.7.1616)

FRASER, JAMES FYFE, born in Coupar Angus 1827 son of John Fraser and Cecilia Fyfe, a merchant in New York, died in Perth 20.8.1856,. [ANY.2.231]

FRASER, PATRICK, probably from Perth, settled in Long Island, Bahamas, pro. 3.1795 PCC

FRASER, THOMAS, a soldier from Dundee, married Lubberich Reyers in Harderwijk, Netherlands, 15.2.1607. (Harderwijk Marriage Register)

FYFFE, ALEXANDER, son of James Fyffe of Dron, Angus, merchant in Savanna, Georgia, pro. 29.12.1766 Georgia.

FYFFE, DAVID, in Dundee, late of Jamaica, 1781. [SRO.RS.Forfar, 39]

FYFFE, ELIZABETH, Dundee, settled in St George's parish, Georgia, 14.11.1777. (GSA: Miscellaneous Bonds KK2.489)

FYFFE, MAGDALENE, Dundee, settled in St George's parish, Georgia, 14.11.1777. (GSA: Miscellaneous Bonds KK2.489)

GARDINER, JOHN, Dundee, settled in Virginia, pro. 11.1816 PCC

GARDYNE, JOHN, died in Samostye, Poland, 1618. [TRA: Dundee Birth Brief, 7.8.1618]

GAVIN, DAVID, merchant in Middelburg, Holland, 1750. (SRO.RS35.17.289)

GEIKIE, JAMES HENRY, Arbroath, settled on Colonel's Island, Glynn County, Georgia, married Catherine Amelia Gamble, father of Catherine Caroline Eleonora, born 11 8.1807, baptised 24.3.1811. [Arbroath OPR]

GELLATLY, JOHN, son of Walter Gellatly and Janet Smart, a traveller in Mehlsack, Konigsberg, 1608. [TRA: Dundee Birth Brief, 20.4.1608]

GELLATLY, THOMAS, son of George Gellatly and Katherine Man, resident in Danzig 1615. [TRA: Dundee Birth Brief, 28.4.1615]

GENTLEMAN, DAVID, Montrose, member of the Scots Charitable Society of Boston 1716. (NEHGS)

GEORGESON, GEORGE, Dundee, burgess of Bergen, Norway, 1615. [SAB]

GEORGESON, JAMES, Dundee, burgess of Bergen, Norway, 1615. [SAB]

GIBB, DAVID, born 1833, son of Alexander Gibb and Margaret Addison, died in Australia 8.5.1857. [Dundee, Western g/s]

GOLD, DAVID, coachmaker in Demerara, later in Crieff, cnf 29.10.1829. [SRO.CC7.9.4.412]

GORDON, THOMAS, merchant in Madeira, 1782. [SRO.RS.Forfar, 127]

GRAHAM, JAMES, Perthshire, member of the Scots Charitable Society of Boston 1761. (NEHGS)

GRAHAM, JAMES, tailor, near Crieff, Perthshire, member of the Scots Charitable Society of Boston 1767. (NEHGS)

GRAHAM, PATRICK, Redford, Perthshire, apothecary in Josephstown, Georgia, land grant in Savanna 19.5.1736, wife Ann Cuthbert, pro 27.8.1755 Georgia

GRANT, PETER GUILLAN, born in Dundee 21.1.1862, son of Reverend Peter Grant and Helen Guillan, died in Victoria, British Columbia, 16.5.1897. [F5.329]

GRAY, ALEXANDER, surgeon in Poospesang, Sumatra, son of Reverend Robert Gray and Anne Swinton in Brechin, 1752. (SRO.S/H)

GRAY, JACK, Dundee, resident of Newhaven, Rotterdam, married Bessie Jones, from Dysart, in Rotterdam, Netherlands, 1.9.1619. (Rotterdam Marriage Register)

GRAY, SAMUEL, born 23.12.1794 in Dundee, died in Serampore, Bengal, 14.12.1820. [Danish Cemetery, Serampore]

GRAY, WILLIAM, Angus, member of the Scots Charitable Society of Boston 1740. (NEHGS)

GUILD, DAVID, born 1795, a merchant, died in Philadelphia 5.3.1830. [Howff g/s, Dundee]

GUTHRIE, GEORGE, son of Walter Guthrie from Montrose, enobled in Sweden before 1684. [SRO.GD188.box 2]

GUTHRIE, HENRY, Montrose, citizen of Bergen, Norway, 1650. [SAB]

GUTHRIE, JAMES, born 20.4.1669 in Dundee son of Reverend John Guthrie and Isabel Lamb, a merchant in Stockholm, died 1711. [F.5.320]

GUTHRIE, JOHN, of Westhall, born in Arbirlot, Angus, 5.4.1664, son of Reverend John Guthrie and Isabel Lamb, a merchant in Stockholm. [F.5.319]

HALIBURTON, THOMAS, in Prince of Wales Island, later in Dundee, cnf 9.8.1823. [SRO.CC3.3.16.40]

HAY, DANIEL, son of James Hay, merchant in Dundee, died in Philadelphia 4.7.1797. (BLG2735)

HAY, Dr JOHN, in Grenada, a burgess of Arbroath 1790. [ArBR]

HELT, ALEXANDER, Montrose, burgess of Bergen, Norway, 1641. [SAB]

HENRY, Dr JOHN, in St Croix, a burgess of Arbroath 1791. [ArBR]

HERCULESSON, ANDREW, Arbroath, burgess of Bergen, Norway, 1628. [SAB]

HERIOT, JOHN, son of Andrew Heriot and Helen Gray in Phesemilne, a traveller in Muhlhausen, Konigsberg, 1617. [TRA: Dundee Birth Brief, 27.3.1617]

HOOD, MARGARET, died in Quebec 3.11.1861. [Howff g/s]

HOWDEN, ARTHUR, in Elsinore, a burgess of Arbroath 1791. [ArBR]

INVERARITY, CHARLES MILLER, in New Zealand, son of Alexander Inverarity, manufacturing foreman in Dundee, who died 25.11.1869. (SRO.SH.1881)

INVERARITY, JAMES, born in Brechin 18.8.1777, son of John Inverarity and Henrietta Panton, to West Florida 5.1796, merchant, died 3.10.1847. ("Indian Traders of the south east Spanish Borderlands" pp18/19, Coker Watson, Florida 1986)

INVERARITY, JOHN, born 8.1749, tanner in Brechin, married Henrietta Panton in Brechin 26.7.1776, to America pre 6.1792, merchant in firm of Panton, Leslie and Company in Florida, died in London 1805, ("Indian Traders of the south eastern Spanish Borderlands" pp18/19, Coker Watson, Florida 1986)

IRVINE, CLEMENTINA JANET, youngest daughter of Reverend Alexander Irvine in Blair Atholl, married Charles Blake Winchester in Surat, Bombay, 28.12.1874. [AJ6630]

JAY, JOHN, merchant in Rotterdam, a burgess of Arbroath 1791. [ArBR]

JOHNSON, PETER, Dundee, burgess of Bergen, Norway, 1625. [SAB]

JOHNSON, THOMAS, Dundee, burgess of Bergen, Norway, 1632. [SAB]

JOHNSTONE, ANDREW, merchant of Dundee, admitted as a citizen of Cracow, Poland, 1602. (SIP49)

JOHNSTON, GEORGE, Kirriemuir, sought in New York 1782. (New York Gazette and Weekly Mercury 20.5.1782)

JOHNSTONE, JAMES, surgeon HEICS, son of Provost James Johnstone of Dundee, admitted as a burgess of Dundee 1799. (Dundee Burgess Register)

JUST, JOHN, born in Perthshire, settled in New York by 1868, died there 14.9.1893. (ANY.2.267)

KEILLER, ALEXANDER BENNET, born 1824 son of John Keiller and Ann Bennet, died in Tobago 27.4.1848. [Howff g/s]

KEILLER, JESSIE BENNET, born 1802, wife of Robert Hood a merchant in Missouri, died in Dundee 24.5.1843. [Howff g/s]

KELT, JAMES, Carse of Gowrie, member of the Scots Charitable Society of Boston 1817. (NEHGS)

KETTLE, MARY, born in Dundee 1824, emigrated to Prince Edward Island 1842, died there 1918. [SPI.99]

KIDD, Major ROBERT, in Calcutta, 1780. (SRO.RS35.28.165)

KIDD, WILLIAM, born in Dundee 1654, {probably son of John Kidd and Bessie Butchart} master mariner, settled in New York 1688. (PRO.HCA.Vol.81:Jackson & Jacobs V. Noell, 1695)

KINLOCH, FRANCIS PEREGRINE, born 1748, son of Sir James Kinloch, died 24.8.1806. [South Park g/s, Calcutta]

KINNAIRD, ALEXANDER, in Stockholm, son of Sir George Kinnaird of Rossie, 1677. [SRO.GD48.1109]

KYD, WILLIAM ANDERSON, born in Dundee 23.4.1841, son of David Kyd and Margaret Anderson, educated at St Andrews University 1867, minister in New Zealand 1893-, died in Glasgow 1916. (F.7.604)

LANGLANDS, WILLIAM, a merchant in Dundee, son of John Langlands (1751-1838) and Christian Thoms (1771-1850), died in Melbourne 21.1.18.. aged 79. [Dundee, Constitution Road g/s]

LAURENSON, GEORGE SIMSON, born in Kinnettles, Angus, 18.2.1803, son of John Laurenson and Margaret Simson, Brevet Colonel of the Bengal Artillery, died in Cape Town, South Africa, 26.6.1856. (BA.3.29)

LAW, JAMES, born 1810, Dundee, died 20.3.1845. [Scotch Burial Ground g/s, Calcutta]

LAWSON, CHARLES, born 1812, son of James Lawson and Elizabeth Smart, died in Craigie, New South Wales, 6.4.1875.
[Dundee, Constitution Road g/s]

LAWSON, DAVID, son of John Lawson merchant in Dundee, settled in Naumsburg, Prussia, by 1616. (TRA: Dundee birthbrief 22.8.1616)

LAWSON, WILLIAM, born 1808 in Dundee, a merchant in New York, died in Brooklyn 15.10.1852. [ANY.2.245]

LECKIE, DAVID, born in Forfar 1807, accountant in Charleston, South Carolina, naturalised in South Carolina 12.7.1843. (US.NA.M1183.1)

LEIGHTON, JOHN, Dundee, Moravian preacher and schoolteacher, died in Bethlehem, Pennsylvania. 8.1756. (CCMC)

LESLIE, JAMES, from Dundee, a witness in Cracow, Poland, 1625. (SIP42)

LESLIE, PETER, possibly ba. 12.3.1777 in Forfar, son of John Leslie and Agnes Ferrier, shopkeeper, died in Savanna, Georgia, 15.8.1805. (Georgia Courier 11.9.1805)(Savanna Death Register)

LEVIE, ROBERT, Montrose, member of the Scots Charitable Society of Boston 1732. (NEHGS)

LIDDELL, DAVID, Brechin, admitted as a citizen of Cracow, Poland, 1592. (SIP52)

LINDSAY, ALEXANDER, Forfar, settled in Portland, New Hampshire, married Lydia Cross 3.12.1719. [Imm.N.E.113]

LINDSAY, ANNE, Dundee, married James Grant, a soldier from Elgin, in Schiedam, Netherlands, 19.12.1637. (Schiedam Marriage Register)

LINDSAY, ELIZABETH, Brechin, married Henry Muir, a soldier from Brechin, in Schiedam, Netherlands, 17.7.1638. (Schiedam Marriage Register)

LOVELL, GEORGE, Dundee, soldier, married Janneker Claes in Bergen-op-Zoom, Netherlands, 26.10.1602. (Bergen-op-Zoom Marriage Register)

LOVELL, ROBERT, son of John Lovell of Brunsie and Margaret Murdoch, a burgess of Radaune, Poland, 1611. [TRA: Dundee Birth Brief, 10.2.1611]

LOW, JOHN, born 1820, son of Joseph Low and Magdalene Hovell, died in Calcutta 5.9.1841. [Dundee, Constitution Road g/s]

LUCKIE, ALEXANDER, born 1771 son of William Luckie and Isabel Chalmers, died on HMS Valiant, Port Royal, Jamaica, 2.7.1799. [Howff g/s, Dundee]

LYALL, JOHN, Dundee, woolcomber in Leiden, Netherlands, married Ponsette le Feu from France, in Leiden 6.11.1603. (Leiden Marriage Register, E.86)

LYALL, JOHN, born 1836, died in Santa Crux, West Indies, 18.3.1856. [Howff g/s, Dundee]

MAYNE, EDWARD, Logie Perthshire, merchant in Lisbon, died 3.1743. 1743. (SRO.S/H)

MELLISH, JOHN, born in Perthshire 1771, geographer, to America 1809, died in Philadelphia 30.12.1822. (Georgia Republican 13.1.1823)(SSA76)

MELLIS, WILLIAM, born in Perthshire, merchant in Savanna, Georgia, died in Darien, Georgia, 7.8.1811. (Colonial Museum and Savanna Advertiser 5.9.1811)

MILNE, EDWARD PATRICK, born in Cortachy 6.12.1875, son of Reverend George Gordon Milne and Jessie Gavin, died in New Zealand 24.7.1915. [F.5.281]

MITCHELL, ROBERT, born in Perth 1.7.1776, merchant in Savanna, Georgia, died 26.12.1830, buried in the Old Colonial Cemetery, Savanna. (Savanna G/s)

MOWAT, GEORGE, Logie Pert, Angus,(?), settled in New York city, pro 17.3.1796 New York

MOWAT, JOHN, born in Montrose 11.8.1740, son of Alexander Mowat and Anne Walker, cabinetmaker and ironmonger in New York 1777-1829, died in New York 15.3.1829. (ANY.I.265)

MURRAY, JOHN, Perthshire, settled in Swataca, Pennsylvania, father of John born 1738. (ANY.I.214)

MCARTHUR, JOHN, born 1745 Perth, married Mary Miller, settled in Livingston, Maine, died 1816. [Imm.N.E.118]

MCCOWAN, JOHN, Dundee, member of the Scots Charitable Society of Boston 1758. (NEHGS)

MCCOWAN, JOHN, Methven, Perthshire, member of the Scots Charitable Society of Boston 1766. (NEHGS)

MCCULLOM, WILLIAM, born in Perth 1778, mariner, died in Savanna,
Georgia, 6.12.1806. (Savanna Death Register)
MCDONALD, DONALD, born in Drumcastle, Rannoch, educated at St Andrews
University, minister in Canada 1824-, died at Orwell Head, Prince
Edward Island, 21.2.1867. (F.7.621)
MACDONALD, FINLAY, born in Logerait 1781, son of Donald MacDonald and
Christine Stewart, emigrated to Prince Edward Island ca1825.
["Skye Pioneers" p83]
MCGRANE, MICHAEL, in Bordeaux, a burgess of Arbroath 1791. [ArBR]
MCINNES, BENJAMIN, born in Perthshire 1812, a smith in Charleston, South
Carolina, naturalised in South Carolina 7.1.1847. (US.NA.M1183.1)
MCINTYRE, JAMES MCGREGOR, surgeon in Swan Hill, Victoria, nephew of
Hugh McGregor of Fonab who died 19.10.1880. (SRO.SH.1881)
MCINTYRE, PETER, born in Perth 1791, hotelkeeper, naturalised in South
Carolina 18.7.1839. (US.NA.M1183.1)
MCKENZIE, COLIN, of Strathcathro, formerly a merchant in Jamaica, son of
Kenneth McKenzie of Dalmore, 1763. (SRO.RS35.20.355)
MCLEAN, DUNCAN, born 1749, a merchant in Petersburg, Virginia, died
there 10.4.1814. [Howff g/s, Dundee]
MACPHERSON, ALLAN, son of Allan MacPherson and Elizabeth MacPheson in
Blairgowrie, to Berbice 1804, a planter, soldier and chaplain in the
West Indies and in India. [SRO.NRAS.0057.bundle 8/10]
MACPHERSON, WILLIAM, son of Allan MacPherson and Elizabeth MacPherson
in Blairgowrie, a planter in Brbice 1806-. [SRO.NRAS.bundle 8/10]
MALCOLM, JOHN, son of Jean Malcolm in Madderty, settled in Norfolk, North
America, pro. 12.1793 PCC
MALTMAN, JAMES, Dunblane, member of the Scots Charitable Society of
Boston, Massachusetts, 1766. [NEHGS]
MANCOR, ANDREW, brn 1825, died in Melbourne 1.1853. [Howff g/s, Dundee]
MARSHALL, JOHN, formerly in Jamaica, 1776. (SRO.RS35.26.181)
MARSHALL, WILLIAM, son of William Marshall, merchant in Dundee, and
Christian Pilmore, died in New Orleans 23.12.1803.
[Howff g/s, Dundee]
MASTERTON, ALEXANDER, born in Forfar 29.2.1796, stonecutter, emigrated
via Halifax, Nova Scotia, to New York City, naturalised in New York
2.5.1829.
MATHER, ROBERT ALEXANDER, clerk in Bahia, Brazil, grandson of Alexander
Mather, wright in Arbroath, who died 22.1.1881. (SRO.SH.1881)
MELISH, JOHN, born in Perthshire 1771, geographer, emigrated to America
1809, died in Philadelphia 30.121822. ["Scots and their descendents
in America", p76, New York 1917]["Georgia Republican" 13.1.1823]
MENZIES, JAMES, jr., rioter at Castle Menzies, sentenced to seven years
transportation, at Perth 7.5.1798. [AJ2627]

MILL, ROBERT, merchant in Montrose, citizen of Bergen, Norway, 1695.
[SAB]
MILLER, DAVID, surgeon in Bristol, formerly in Westmoreland, Jamaica,
1750. (SRO.RS35.17.546)
MILLER, DAVID, born 1808, son of William Miller and Isabella Gilchrist,
drowned in the St Lawrence River, Canada, 12.5.1827.
[Howff g/s, Dundee]
MILLER, JAMES, born in Dundee 1787, died 4.5.1829.
[Scotch Burial Ground g/s, Calcutta]
MILLER, JOHN, Clunie, Perthshire, member of the Scots Charitable Society
of Boston 1817. (NEHGS)
MILLER, ROBERT, born 1817, son of David Miller and Isabella Gilchrist, died
in New Orleans 6.12.1850. [Howff g/s, Dundee]
MILLER, WILLIAM, born 1802 son of David Miller and Isabella Gilchrist,
died in Jamaica 1817. [Howff g/s, Dundee]
MITCHELSON, DAVID, Kirriemuir, member of the Scots Charitable Society
of Boston 1767. (NEHGS); born in Kirriemuir 26.1.1732, "late of New
York", died at Fyfe Place, Leith Walk, Edinburgh, 24.10.1802.
[Canongate g/s]
MONCUR, THOMAS, [? ba.9.11.1707 son of David Moncur, Liff], Dundee,
member of the Scots Charitable Society of Boston 1739. (NEHGS)
MORRISON, DAVID, merchant and shipowner in Montrose, and his wife
Elizabeth Mitchell from Aberdeen, settled in New Orleans in 1790,
died there 1808. [ANY.2.202]
MORISON, WILLIAM, born in Auchlines, Perthshire, 1748, minister in
Londonderry, New Hampshire 1783-, wife Jean Fullarton, died
9.1829. (Imm.NE.140)
MOWAT, JOHN, born 11.8.1740, son of Alexander Mowat and Anne walker in
Montrose, married Jane Quereau 7.1765, cabinetmaker and
ironmonger in New York 1777-1829, died in New York 15.3.1829.
[ANY.I.265]
MUDIE, ROBERT, Montrose, member of the Scots Charitable Society of
Boston 1746. (NEHGS)
MUIR, HENRY, Brechin, soldier, married Elizabeth Lindsay, Brechin, in
Schiedam, Netherlands, 17.7.1638. (Schiedam Marriage Register)
MURRAY, EDWARD, born 9.6.1714, son of John, Marquis of Atholl, died in
Port Royal, Jamaica, 2.2.1737. Pro.16.6.1737 PCC
MURRAY, JOHN, Perthshire, settled in Swataca, Pennsylvania, father of
John born 1738. [ANY.I.214]
MURRAY, JOHN, thief, banished to the Plantations for life, at Perth
10.1775. [Aberdeen Journal.1449]

NICOL, ALEXANDER, labourer at the Mains of Melgund, Angus, indentured as a servant to Sir John Ogilvie for work in Antigua 22.11.1783. (TRA.Dundee R/D.1783.fo1463)

NICOL, DAVIDSON, Montrose, died in Sydney 21.5.1880. [S.11395]

NORRIE, ADAM, born in Montrose 13.2.1796, settled in New York by 1827, died there 6.6.1882. (ANY.2.24)

OCHTERLONY, DAVID, Montrose, mariner in Boston, Massachusetts, member of the Scots Charitable Society of Boston 1752, wife Catherine ..., pro 7.3.1766 Boston.

OUCHTERLONY, JOHN, merchant in Riga, son of John Ouchterlony of the Guynd, Angus, 1793. (SRO.S/H)

OUCHTERLONY, MARY E., Guynd, Angus, settled in Riga before 1844. [SRO.S/H]

OGILVIE, DAVID, Arbroath, member of the Scots Charitable Society of Boston 1742. (NEHGS)

OGILVY, WALTER, a soldier from Dundee, married Grietgen Jacobs, from France, in Schiedam, Netherlands, 21.3.1637. (Schiedam Marriage Register)

ORD, WILLIAM, born in Perth, citizen of Paris, banker in Channerrie Street, St Eustace, Paris, pro. 1684 PCC

PARKER, JOHN, son of Patrick Parker and Beatrix Kinmond in Bandean, a merchant in Poland, 1615. [TRA: Dundee Birth Brief, 20.5.1615]

PARKER, PATRICK, son of William Parker of Ballindean and Elizabeth Anderson, a traveller in Poland, 1616. [TRA.Dundee Birth Brief, 16.3.1616]

PATERSON, GEORGE, late of Bengal, 1778. (SRO.RS35.27.61)

PEARSON, JAMES, merchant in Riga, son of Robert Pearson of Balmadies, advocate, 1767. (SRO.RS35.22.440)

PEARSON, THOMAS, Montrose, member of the Scots Charitable Society of Boston 1745. (NEHGS)

PETERSON, PETER, Dundee, burgess of Bergen, Norway, 1635. [SAB]

PETRIE, JAMES STURROCK, born in Arbroath 2.3.1809 son of John H. Petrie, a merchant in New York, died there 1860. [ANY.2.226]

PETRIE, JAMES, son of Henry Petrie and Helen Douglas, died in Melbourne 1859. [St Andrews g/s, Dundee]

PETRIE, JOHN, son of Henry Petrie and Helen Douglas, died in Meadville, USA, 1833. [St Andrews g/s, Dundee]

PHILP, JOHN, Governor of St Martins (Dutch West Indies), brother of James Philp of Almerieclose, Arbroath, 1733. (SRO.RS35.15.37)

PHIN, A.C.,born in Dundee 1811, druggist in Charleston, South Carolina, naturalised in South Carolina13.1.1847. (US.NA.M1183.1)

PIRNIE, JOHN, born in Perthshire 22.7.1791, distiller in New York 1831, died there 20.2.1862. (ANY.2.27)

PORTEOUS, JOHN, Muthill, Perthshire, settled in Herkimer County, New York, pro 13.6.1799 New York

PORTEOUS, JOHN, born 1802, son of David Porteous in Crieff, died 24.7.1834. [Scotch Burial Ground g/s, Calcutta]

PROUDFOOT, JAMES, born in Perth 1732, emigrated to Boston, Massachusetts, 1754, Associate Presbyterian minister in Pennsylvania and New York 1757-1799, died in Salem, New York, 22.10.1802. (CCMC)

RAIT, FRANCIS, standardbearer to Captain James Ruthven of the Scots Regiment in the Netherlands, son of William Rait of Cononsyth, 1680. (SRO.RD2.51.702)

RAMSAY, JOHN, Lieutenant of the Scots Brigade in Dutch Service, son of John Ramsay of Kinnalty, 1782. [SRO.RS.Forfar, 181]

RANKINE, JAMES, planter and merchant in Jamaica 1788-1814, merchant in Dundee 1819-1820. (SRO.CS230.Sed.Bk.4/2)

RASMUSSEN, RASMUS, Dundee, burgess of Bergen, Norway, 1615. [SAB]

REID, ALEXANDER, Pitnacre, Perthshire, member of the Scots Charitable Society of Boston 1767. (NEHGS)

REID, CHARLES, born in Forfar, settled in Norfolk, Virginia, before 1827. [ANY.2.261]

REID, JOHN, Dundee, member of the Scots Charitable Society of Boston 1747. (NEHGS)

REID, THOMAS, in Dundee, formerly a merchant in Jamaica, son of Thomas Reid of Drumgeith, 1766. (SRO.RS35.21.439)

RENNY, JAMES, merchant in Hamburg, burgess in Montrose 1767. (MBR)

RENTS, HERCULES, Arbroath, admitted as a citizen of Cracow, Poland, 1579. (SIP54)

RICHARDSON, COLIN, Perthshire, member of the Scots Charitable Society of Boston 1818. (NEHGS)

RITCHIE, ELIZABETH, or Allport, in Hobart Town, Tasmania, 1862. [SRO.S.C.Perth.63/27]

ROBERT, ..., glover in Brechin, citizen of Bergen, Norway, 1641. [SAB]

ROBERTSON, ALEXANDER, Edranyte, Perthshire, settled near the Wicocomico River, Somerset County, Maryland, before 1769. [SRO.NRAS.0247]

ROBERTSON, HUGH, born in Perthshire 1791, emigrated from Greenock to New York, grocer, naturalised in New York 17.4.1821.

ROBERTSON, JAMES, born in Perthshire 1791, grocer in Charleston, South Carolina, naturalised in South Carolina 13.10.1834. (US.NA.M1183.1)

ROBERTSON, THOMAS, Dundee, member of the Scots Charitable Society of Boston 1753. (NEHGS)

RORISON, JAMES, son of .... Rorison of Ardoch and Elizabeth Douglas, married Margaret Shanters 23.12.1756, settled in Pennsylvania pre 1776. (Col.Fams.VI.451)

RUXTON, ROBERT, born 1747, son of Robert Ruxton in Cairnhill, Esslemont, married Margaret Brown in Cononsyth, Carmyllie, 5.11.1780, to America 1788, died 1828. (BLG2898)

SANDEMAN, JOHN, born 6.4.1809 in Redgorton, son of William John Sandeman, bleacher in Luncarty, and Elizabeth Steuart, to India 1828, Lieutenant of the Bengal Army, died at Landour 20.1.1841. (BA.4.12)

SANDEMAN, ROBERT TURNBULL, born 1.10.1804 in Perth, son of William Sandeman and Catherine Turnbull, to India 1825, Major General of the 33rd Native Infantry, Bengal Army, died London 25.7.1876. (BA.4.12)

SANDEMAN, ROBERT, born in Perth 1718, emigrated to New England 1764, minister in New Hampshire and Connecticut, died in Danbury, Connecticut 2.4.1771. (Imm.NE,173)

SANDERSON, ALEXANDER, Dundee, burgess of Bergen, Norway, 1615. [SAB]

SCOTT, ALEXANDER, born in Dundee 7.1821, emigrated from Liverpool to New York 1841, settled in Greenville, South Carolina. (Greenville County Records)

SCOTT, DUNCAN GORDON, born in Auchterhouse 5.12.1788, son of Reverend James Scott and Margaret Munro, to India 1805, Lieutenant General of the Bengal Army, died in Roxburghshire 5.4.1863. (BA.4.31)

SCOTT, JAMES, son of Thomas Scott and Helen Jago in Dichty, in Berent near Danzig, 1608. [TRA: Dundee Birth Brief, 11.4.1608]

SCOTT, JAMES, born in Kinclaven, Perthshire, 14.10.1792, son of Reverend John Scott and Ann Swan, Captain of the British Legion in Columbian Service, killed at the Battle of Carabobo in South America 24.6.1821. [F4.163]

SCOTT, JOHN JAMIESON, Montrose, citizen of Bergen, Norway, 1694.[SAB]

SCOTT, ROBERT, son of John Scott and Elizabeth Neish in Mill of Mains, a traveller in Berent near Danzig, 1606. [TRA: Dundee Birth Brief, 7.1606]

SCRYMGEOUR, WILLIAM, born in Perth 23.2.1807, emigrated to New York 1836, died in Brooklyn 10.6.1885. (ANY.2.286)

SHEPHERD, THOMAS, born in Perth 1792 son of John Shepherd and Ann Jamieson, a merchant in New York, died there 7.3.1854. [ANY.2.205]

SIME, ALEXANDER, born 1839, son of William Sime, died in Lambayeque, Peru, 20.5.1901. [Dundee, Western g/s]

SIME, CRAWFORD, son of William Syme (1797-1863), died in Rio de Janeiro aged 21. [Dundee, Western g/s]

EMIGRANTS FROM ANGUS AND PERTH

SIME, JAMES PULLER, born 1841, son of William Sime, died in Invique,
Chile, 22.10.1898. [Dundee, Western g/s]
SINCLAIR, ALEXANDER, born in Perthshire 1793, son of Donald Sinclair,
married Christina McLaren (1809-1879), settled in Maxville,
Glengarry County, Ontario, died 1841. (CGS64)
SINCLAIR, FINLAY, born in Perthshire 1792, son of Donald Sinclair, married
Mary McLaren (1797-1870), settled in Glengarry County, Ontario,
1816, died 1869. (CGS64)
SKIRLING, PETER, Dundee, member of the Scots Charitable Society of
Boston 1747. (NEHGS)
SMART, JOHN, Dundee, burgess of Bergen, Norway, 1639. [SAB]
SMITH, ALEXANDER, in Stralsund, 1782. [SRO.RS.Forfar, 156]
SMITH, JAMES, of Strouckhill, Arbroath, husband Margaret Gavin, then in
Middelburg, Holland, 1709. (SRO.RS35.12.9)
SMITH, JAMES, born in Fowlis Wester 1825, son of Thomas Smith, educated
at Glasgow University, minister in Argentina 1850- , died 9.10.1906.
(F.7.683)
SMITH, JAMES, born 1818, died in Melbourne 21.6.1895.
[Dundee, Western g/s]
SOUTAR, THOMAS, merchant burgess of Lowites, Poland, son of Thomas
Soutar of Alyth, 1637. (RGS.IX.659)
SOUTAR, WILLIAM, son of David Soutar and Elizabeth Lindsay, a traveller in
Germany and Danzig by 1609. (TRA: Dundee birthbrief 11.3.1609)
SOUTTER, ROBERT, Dundee, and his wife Margaret Taylor from Forfar
settled in Norfolk, Virginia, before 1810.[ANY.2.220]
SPALDING, JAMES, born in Ashantilly, Perthshire, 1735, emigrated to
Georgia 1760, settled in St Simon's Island, Georgia, married Margery
McIntosh 1772, father of Thomas born 1774, politician, died 1794.
(Georgia g/s)
SPENCE, GEORGE, in Albany Fort, North America, son of George Spence,
maltman in Dundee, 1741. (SRO.RS35.16.117)
SPINK, JAMES, born in Arbroath 1800, settled in Darien, Georgia, died in
Savanna, Georgia, 16.11.1823. (Daily Georgian 21.11.1822)
STEPHEN, JAMES, merchant in Hamburg, burgess of Montrose 1753. (MBR)
STEWART, ANGUS, born in Perthshire 1792, innkeeper in Charleston, South
Carolina, naturalised in South Carolina 4.10.1832. (US.NA.M1183.1)
STEWART, CHARLES, born 3.8.1783 in Airlie, son of John Stewart and
Isabel Ellis, married Isabella ..., father of John 1810-, farmer,
settled in New York state, naturalised 2.10.1819 New York.
STEWART, CHARLES, born in Perth, resident of New York, died in Georgia
12.8.1800, (Georgia g/s)(Colonial Museum and Savanna Advertiser
15.8.1800)

STEWART, JAMES GILLESPIE, born in Blair Atholl 29.9.1813, son of
Reverend John Stewart and Ann Wight, died in the West Indies.
(F.4.145)

STEWART or MCCULLOCH, JOHN, rioter at Castle Menzies, sentenced to
seven years transportation, at Perth 7.5.1798. [AJ2627]

STEWART, JOHN, born 1798 in Blair Atholl, a Hudson Bay Company
employee 1816-1824, returned to Scotland on the Pow 1824
[HBRS.2.459]

STEWART, JOHN, born in Little Dunkeld 4.1800, educated at Edinburgh
University, minister in Nova Scotia 1835-1880, died 4.1880.
(F.7.618)

STEWART, JOHN, of Kinnaldy, shepherd to the 7th Duke of Atholl,
emigrated to New Zealand 1863. (SRO.NRAS.234.6478.3)

STEWART, PETER, born in Perth 1787, mason, emigrated via Guernsey to
USA, naturalised 25.1.1827 New York.

STEWART, RANDALL, born in Callander, Perthshire, 1756, married Margaret
Smith, to America 1806, settled in Buncombe County, North Carolina,
later in Bibb County, Georgia, died there 1844. (NCSA.2.103)

STEWART, WILLIAM, born in Foss 5.1831, educated at the Universities of
St Andrews and Edinburgh, minister in Nova Scotia 1863-1905, died
26.5.1920. (F.7.618)

STIRLING, GEORGE, Dundee, admitted as a citizen of Cracow, Poland, post
1591. (SIP55)

STIRLING, JOHN, Dundee, married Clara Maartsen in Harlem, Netherlands,
16.10.1601. (Harlem Marriage Register)

STOKES, JOHN, in Sandhurst, Victoria, grandson of John Smith and Janet
Robertson in Blairgowrie, 1881. (SRO.SH.1881)

STRACHAN, DAVID, goldsmith from Dundee, admitted as a citizen of
Cracow, Poland, post 1621. (SIP56)

STRACHAN, JAMES, Montrose, died in USA, father of George Blair Strachan,
pro 6.1844 PCC

STRATTON, WILLIAM, glover in Montrose, citizen of Bergen, Norway, 1657.
[SAB]

STRONG, DUNCAN, born in Perthshire 1776, grocer, emigrated from
Greenock to USA, naturalised in New York 18.4.1821.

STURROCK, DAVID, a soldier from Dundee, married Josijntie Pieters in
Hulst, Netherlands, 24.8.1657. (Hulst Marriage Register)

STURROCK, JAMES, merchant in Tobago, son of James Sturrock (1707-
1765) and Isabel Mudie (1712-1780). (Arbirlot g/s)

TAINSH, ROBERT DOUGLAS CLARKE, son of Robert Tainsh surgeon in Crieff,
settled in Demerara before 1841. [SRO.S/H]

TAYLOR, MICHAEL, Perth, emigrated via Belfast to New York on the brig
Shannon 18.1.1816. ["Passengers from Ireland"

TAYLOR, WILLIAM, born 1790, son of William Taylor a merchant, emigrated
to New York 1803, died in New York 23.3.1811. [Howff g/s, Dundee]
TENNESON, ELIZABETH, born in Dundee 1576, married John Thomas
Robertson, a soldier from Edinburgh, in Breda, Netherlands.
14.3.1598. (Breda Marriage Register)
THAYNE, ANDREW, son of Thomas Thayne and Katherine Barbour in Gourdie,
resident in Danzig 1612. [TRA: Dundee Birth Brief, 5.1612]
THOMSON, ALEXANDER, Dundee, burgess of Bergen, Norway, 1618. [SAB]
THOMSON, ALEXANDER, Montrose, member of the Scots Charitable Society
of Boston 1734. (NEHGS)
THOMSON, GORDON(?), Dundee, married Margaret Turner, a Scot, in
Steenbergen, 20.6.1620. (Steenbergen Marriage Register)
THOMSON, WILLIAM, son of Thomas Thomson and Christian Wichton, a
skinner in Danzig 1614. [TRA: Dundee Birth Brief, 27.6.1614]
THORNTON, THOMAS JOHNSON, Dundee, burgess of Bergen, Norway, 1614.
[SAB]
TRAILL, JOHN, Dundee, member of the Scots Charitable Society of Boston
1739. (NEHGS)
TRAPP, ELIZA, wife of Thomas Barker in Botany, Sydney, daughter of
Michael Trapp, fishmonger in Perth. (SRO.SH.1851)
TURNBULL, GEORGE, born in Perthshire, Ensign in General Marjorybank's
Scots Regiment - discharged 18.4.1756, officer in the 60th [Royal
American] Regiment 1756-1772 and in the New York Volunteers,
settled in New York 1788, died 13.10.1810 Bloomingdale, New York.
[ANY.I.48]
TURNBULL, GEORGE, born in Perthshire 1757, Officer in the Royal Navy,
settled in New York 1783, married (1) Marian Maxwell (2) Samatha
Van Horne, (3) Margaret Maxwell, Director of the Bank of New York
1800, died in New York 13.11.1825. [ANY.I.191]
WARDROPER, ANDREW, Dundee, merchant in Rotterdam 1685. (RPCS.X.131)
WATSON, JAMES, son of William Watson and Elizabeth Wallace, a merchant
traveller in Poland, 1636. [TRA: Dundee Birth Brief, 16.7.1636]
WATSON, WILLIAM, son of Mathew Watson, a merchant, and Janet Bomer, a
merchant traveller in Poland, 1636, [TRA: Dundee Birth Brief,
16.7.1636]
WATT, ALEXANDER, son of Isaac Watt a merchant burgess of Dundee, Major
HEICS, admitted as a burgess of Dundee 4.1.1851. [DBR]
WEBSTER, ARTHUR, a merchant in Montreal, son of Thomas Webster and
Margaret Webster [1740-1819]. [Dundee, Howff g/s]
WEBSTER, GEORGE, son of Charles Webster in Forfar, died in Madras
30.6.1824. [AJ4018]
WELSH, JAMES, in Kingston, Jamaica, a burgess of Arbroath 1789.[ArBR]

WHITE, JAMES FARQUHAR, born in Letham, Angus, 1820, a merchant in New
York pre 1864, died in Balruddery, near Dundee, 5.9.1884. [ANY.2.200]
WILKIE, ROBERT, Arbroath, member of the Scots Charitable Society of
Boston 1752. (NEHGS)
WILLIAM, ..., Montrose, citizen of Bergen, Norway, 1653. [SAB]
WILLIAMSON, ROBERT, Arbroath, burgess of Bergen, Norway, 1630. [SAB]
WILLIAMSON, WILLIAM, Dundee, burgess of Bergen, Norway, 1614. [SAB]
WILLISON, GEORGE, Dunnichen, a portrait painter in Madras, 1782.
    [SRO.RS.Forfar, 124]
WILSON, DAVID WILKIE, son of Edward Wilson an upholsterer in Dundee,
    died in Adelaide 29.4.1881. [Dundee, Western g/s]
WINTON, GILBERT, Dundee, burgess of Bergen, Norway, 1640. [SAB]
WOOD, ANDREW, Angus, chaplain HEICS, pro 1634 PCC (SRO.GD188.24.6.5)
WOOD, MARTIN BRYDEN, born 1837 in Broughty Ferry, son of Reverend John
    Wood and Annabella Bryden, died in Sydney 15.4.1918. [F.5.312]
WRIGHT, FRANCES, born in Dundee 1785, emigrated from Liverpool to
    America, naturalised in New York 16.11.1818.
WRIGHT, JAMES, son of John Wright and Margaret Turnbull in Bryddeston, a
    traveller in Poland 1615. [TRA: Dundee Birth Brief, 20.5.1615]
WYLLIE, DAVID, merchant in Hamburg, burgess of Montrose 1773. (MBR)
WYLLIE, JAMES, born 2.1.1795, son of William Wyllie and Annie Stupart,
    died in Russia 21.10.1850. [Howff g/s, Dundee]
YEAMAN, PATRICK, son of William Yeaman and Katherine Rodger in Rattray,
    a traveller in Poland 1609. [TRA: Dundee Birth Brief, 16.4.1609]
YOUNG, ALEXANDER, merchant in Montrose, citizen of Bergen, Norway,
    1704. [SAB]
YOUNG, GEORGE, born in Cortachy, Angus, 1789, merchant, emigrated from
    London to America, settled in Alabama, naturalised in New York
    10.11.1817.
YOUNG, JAMES, born in Dundee 1800, son of George Young, weaver, and Mary
    Young, educated at St Andrews University, minister in British Guiana
    1841-1844, died in Broughty Ferry 3.11.1882. (F.7.676)
YOUNG, JOHN, born 1814, porter in Dundee, died in Sydney 20.8.1861.
    [Dundee, St Peter's g/s]
YOUNG, WILLIAM, born 1828, son of William Young and Isabella Tutin, died
    in St Ann's, Barbados, 19.12.1848. [Howff g/s, Dundee]
YOUNG, WILLIAM, born 1829, son of William Young and Marjory Turnbull,
    died in New South Wales 1861. [St Aidan's g/s, Broughty Ferry]

EMIGRANTS AND ADVENTURERS
from
Southern Scotland

INTRODUCTION

This book deals with emigration from southern Scotland to all parts of the world outside the British Isles prior to 1900. The term "southern Scotland" refers to the current Regions of Borders and of Dumfries and Galloway, which together embrace the former counties of Berwickshire, Roxburghshire, Peeblesshire, Selkirkshire, Dumfriesshire, Kirkcudbrightshire and Wigtownshire.

Southern Scotland has experienced a relatively high level of out migration over the centuries. Within the British Isles movement of population has occurred from the region west to Ireland, south to the industrial north of England and north to the industrial heartland of Scotland. Emigration outwith the British Isles was relatively small scale until the late eighteenth century when groups left for North America and by the mid nineteenth century increasing numbers headed to Australasia. While the emphasis of emigration was to those areas people from southern Scotland could be found throughout the British Empire and beyond. This book, the first of a series, attempts to identify specific emigrants, their origins and places of settlement.

DAVID DOBSON
St Andrews, 1994

REFERENCES

ARCHIVES
DSA	Delaware State Archives
MSA	Maryland State Archives
NEHGS	New England Historic Genealogical Society
NJA	New Jersey State Archives
PRO	Public Record Office, London
	CO Colonial Office
	PCC Prerogative Court of Canterbury
SAB	Stats Arkivet, Bergen, Norway
SRA	Strathclyde Regional Archives, Glasgow
SRO	Scottish Record Office, Edinburgh
	CS Court of Session
	NRAS National Register Archives Scotland
	RD Register of Deeds
	RS Register of Sasines
	SH Services of Heirs
USNA	United States National Archives

PUBLICATIONS
AJ	Aberdeen Journal
ANY	Biographical Register of the St Andrew's Society of New York [McBean, N.Y., 1911]
BA	Officers of the Bengal Army [Hodson, London, 1927]
BLG	Burke's Landed Gentry [Townsend, London 1939]
Col. Fams	Colonial Families of USA. [Mackenzie, Md., 1966]
CCMC	Colonial Clergy of Middle Colonies[Weis,MD, 1977]
EEC	Edinburgh Evening Courant
F	Fast Ecclesiae Scoticanae [Scott, Edinburgh, 1920s]
ImmNE	Immigrants to New England 1700-1775 [Salem, 1931]
MAGU	Matriculation Albums of Glasgow University, 1727-1858 [Addison, Glasgow, 1913]
NCSA	North Carolina Scots Ancestry [Fort Worth, 1992]
SG	The Scottish Genealogist
SSP	Records of Scottish Settlers on the River Plate [Dodds, Buenos Ayres, 1897]

ABBREVIATIONS
cnf	confirmation of testament
g/s	gravestone inscription
pro	probate

EMIGRANTS AND ADVENTURERS FROM SOUTHERN SCOTLAND

[PART ONE]

ADAIR, JOHN, born in Portpatrick 3.7.1824, emigrated to Quebec 1848 on the Collingwood, settled in New York 1850, died in Newark, New Jersey, 10.11.1912. (ANY.2.287)

ADAMS, RICHARD, 32, architect, wife Anna, and 4 children, emigrated from Leith to Argentina on the Symmetry, master William Cochrane, 22.5.1825. (SSP18)

ADARE, ROBERT, Galloway, pro 29.12.1692 Barbados. (RB.6.3.63)

AFFLECK, JAMES, minister in Middelburg, Holland, then in London, later in Dumfries, cnf 1800 Dumfries

AIRD, JAMES, 28, carpenter, wife Mary, and 1 child, emigrated from Leith to Argentina on the Symmetry, master William Cochrane, 22.5.1825. (SSP18)

ALEXANDER, HELEN SCOTT or, in Melbourne, daughter of George Alexander in Jedburgh who died 8.5.1871. (SRO.SH.1880)

ALEXANDER, ROBERT, Dumfries, member of the Scots Charitable Society of Boston 1758. (NEHGS)

ALEXANDER, WILLIAM, Galloway, merchant in Cecil County, Maryland, pro 17.. Maryland (MSA.Willv24 f75)

ALLEN, THOMAS, Kirkbean, Galloway, member of the Scots Charitable Society of Boston 1819. (NEHGS)

ANDERSON, DAVID, 50, farmer, wife Mary, and 2 children emigrated from Leith to Argentina on the Symmetry, master William Cochrane, 22.5.1825. (SSP18)

ANDERSON, HUGH HATHORN, born in Stoneykirk 18.1.1826, son of Reverend James Anderson and Mary McGhie, wool merchant, died in Australia. (F.2.355)

ANDERSON, JAMES, born in Stoneykirk 5.11.1821, son of Reverend James Anderson and Mary McGhie, vine grower, died in Valparaiso, Chile. (F.2.355)

ANDERSON, JOHN, HEICS, Prince of Wales Island, East Indies, later settled at Farthingrush, Dumfriesshire, 1820s. (SRO.CS231.Misc.20.3)

ANDERSON, JOHN, librarian in Hokitika, New Zealand, son of Thomas Anderson, blacksmith in Hawick, who died 21.3.1873. (SRO.SH.1881)

ANDERSON, WILLIAM, born in Dumfries, planter in St Joseph's parish, Georgia, pro.7.2.1772 Georgia

ARMSTRONG, GEORGE, born 1788 in Roxburghshire, emigrated to America 1819, settled in Ovid, New York. [SG.32.3]

ARMSTRONG, THOMAS, Roxburghshire, emigrated to America 1819, settled in Ovid, New York. [SG.32.3]

ARMSTRONG, WILLIAM, Roxburghshire, emigrated to New York 1819, settled in Ovid, New York. [SG.32.3]

ARMSTRONG, WILLIAM, born in Kirleton, Gilnockie, Dumfriesshire, son of David Armstrong the Sheriff of Dumfries, British Army officer 1775- 1783, settled in New York 1790, married (1) Margaret Marshall 1793 (2) Elizabeth Roberts 1810, died in Elizabethtown, New Jersey, 27.1.1830. (ANY.1.284)

BALFOUR, JOHN, born in Bowden 25.9.1798, son of Reverend William Balfour and Mary Mein, died in Boston, USA, 15.8.1844. (F.2.172)

BALIEFF, JOSEPH, born 1819, drowned near New York 21.11.1836. (St Michael's Dumfries g/s)

BAIRD, JAMES OLIVER, born 26.3.1853, son of Reverend John Baird and Elizabeth Hughes, died in Hanover, Germany, 25.1.1872. (F.2.96)

BAXTER, HARRIET, born in Lilliesleaf 27.11.1816, daughter of Reverend David Baxter and Ann Campbell, married Joseph French, chemist in Australia, died 15.7.1890. (F.2.183)

BAXTER, HELEN FRANCES, born in Lilliesleaf, daughter of Reverend David Baxter and Ann Campbell, married E.N.Houstoun, surgeon in Australia, died 17.10.1902. (F.2.183)

BAXTER, JEMIMA NICOLINA, born in Lilliesleaf 20.7.1814, daughter of Reverend David Baxter and Ann Campbell, married William King, minister in Nelson, Ontario, died 1887. (F.2.183)

BECK, JOHN, son of William Beck in Balmangan, settled in New South Wales before 1857. [SRO.S/H]

BECK, WILLIAM JOHNSTON, born in Dumfries 14.5.1820, son of Thomas Beck of Tynron, died at West Farms, New York, 4.1877. (ANY.2.242)

BELSHES, JOHN, son of William Belshes, Fort St David's, India, 1760. (SRO.RS18.14.256)

BELL, JOHN, Annan, applied to settle in Canada 10.5.1827. [PRO.CO384.5.751]

BELL, PETER, soldier from Duns, married Jenneken Wouters from Hervert, in 'S-Hertogenbosch 16.5.1632. ('S-Hertogenbosch Marriage Register)

BELL, WILLIAM, Annandale, member of the Scots Charitable Society of Boston 1732. (NEHGS)

BERTHAM, ALEXANDER, born in Berwickshire 1795, died in Augusta, Georgia, 27.11.1827. (Georgia Courier 29.11.1827)

BEVERIDGE, ANDREW, born in Caerlaverock 11.11.1747, son of Reverend Andrew Beveridge and Jean Ferguson, died in Accra, Africa, 15.10.1767. (F.2.259)

BLACK, EDWARD, born 10.12.1793, son of James Black in Penningham, Wigtownshire, educated at Edinburgh University, minister in Montreal 1822-, died 6.5.1845. (F.7.627)

BLACKADDER, ADAM, born in Troqueer, son of Reverend John Blackadder and Janet Haining, merchant in Sweden and Edinburgh. (F.2.302)

BLACKADDER, ROBERT, born in Troqueer, son of Reverend John Blackadder (died 1686) and Janet Haining, merchant in New England. (F.2.302)

BLAIKIE, JAMES, Eccles, Berwickshire, member of the Scots Charitable Society of Boston 1775. (NEHGS)

BLAIR, JAMES BUCHANAN, born in Colmonell 19.8.1825, son of Reverend Thomas Blair and Anne McFadyen, farmer in New Zealand. (F.2.334)

BLAIR, PETER, Cockburnspath, settled in Salem, Massachusetts, pre 1752, married Sarah Baker in Marblehead 5.10.1752. (Imm.NE.220)

BLAKE, GEORGE ALEXANDER BRYCE, born 30.1.1855 in Stobo, son of Rev. James L. Blake and Janette Bryce, merchant in America. (F.2.24)

BLAKIE, JANE, born 1736, married William Spiden, merchant in Bowden, died in Kentucky 1819. [Bewlie, Selkirkshire, g/s]

BOSTON, ROBERT, born in Kelso 1779, slater in New York 1806-1813, naturalised in New York 17.4.1811, died 11.12.1813. (ANY.II.7)

BOYD, JAMES, born in Kirkcowan, Wigtownshire, married Jean McMaster, to America 1774, settled in Albany, New York, father of David and James. (ANY.2.39)

BOYD, JOHN, of Mairton Hall, Galloway, died in Bridgetown, Barbados, 27.6.1798. [AJ2647]

BRAND, JAMES, born in Dumfries 31.1.1822, son of John Brand and Jean McQueen, merchant in Ceylon and later in New York, died in New York 12.5.1897. (ANY.2.242)

BROACH, JAMES, 24, farmer, and his sister, emigrated from Leith to Argentina on the Symmetry, master William Cochrane, 22.5.1825. (SSP18)

BROADFOOT, WILLIAM, a merchant in Norfolk, Virginia, 1799, great grandson of John Broadfoot, a merchant in Wigton. [SRO.RS.Wigton, 544]

BRODIE, GEORGE, born in Meggatdale, Selkirkshire, 1814, emigrated to America 1846, settled in New York, died there 2.5.1866. (ANY.2.289)

BRODIE, JAMES, born in Selkirkshire 1804, distiller, emigrated from Greenock to America, naturalised in New York 14.5.1828.

BROMFIELD, ROBERT, born in Sprouston 14.3.1846, son of Reverend Robert Orange Bromfield and Mary Weatherstone, sheep farmer in Queensland, died 3.1.1888. (F.2.91)

BROMFIELD, THOMAS, born in Sprouston 20.10.1849, son of Reverend Robert Orange Bromfield and Mary Weatherstone, sheep farmer in Queensland. (F.2.91)

EMIGRANTS AND ADVENTURERS FROM SOUTHERN SCOTLAND

BROWN, ADAM, Wigton, member of the Scots Charitable Society of Boston 1736. (NEHGS)
BROWN, DAVID, born in Sanquhar, educated at Edinburgh University, minister in Valcartier, Quebec, 1833-1837. (F.7.628)
BROWN, JAMES, born in Annan 1786, a minister in Calcutta 1823-, died in Malacca 23.9.1830. [St Andrew's Kirk, Calcutta, g/s]
BROWN, JOHN, surgeon in Coldstream, Berwickshire, settled in Williamsburg, Virginia, by 1753, father of Robert. (SRO.RS18.13.314)
BROWN, JAMES MURRAY, born in Kirkmabreck 6.4.1767, son of Reverend Samuel Brown and Margaret Smith, died in Virginia. (F.2.368)
BROWN, JOHN, born in Dumfriesshire 1821, planter in Charleston, South Carolina, naturalised in South Carolina 5.7.1849. (US.NA.M1183.1)
BROWN, WILLIAM DAWSON, born 19.10.1802, son of Reverend David Brown and Janet Dawson, died in Montreal 1.9.1875. (F.2.108)
BUCHAN, JAMES, born in Harelaw Mains, parish of Linton, Roxburghshire, 3.9.1812, emigrated from Leith to Montreal 1833, settled in New York 1835, died there 29.4.1887. (ANY.2.235)
BUCHAN, THOMAS, Berwickshire, Lieutenant Colonel of Colonel McKay's Regiment in Holland 1687. (SRO.RS18.5.26)
BURNETT, JOHN SMITH, born in Dumfries, educated at Edinburgh University, minister in Canada 1866-, died 8.3.1908. (F.7.628)
BURNSIDE, JAMES, born in Dumfries 18.4.1788, son of Reverend William Burnside and Anne Hutton, died in India 1815. (F.2.267) (St Michael's Dumfries g/s)
CAMPBELL, ALEXANDER MUIR, son of Matthew Campbell in Wigtown, assistant surgeon, died in Nagpore, India, 5.6.1820. (EEC.1820)
CAMPBELL, EDWARD, born in Lilliesleaf 6.7.1765, son of Reverend William Campbell and Margaret Hume, died in the East Indies 1789. (F.2.183)
CAMPBELL, PATRICK, of the Oriental Bank in China, son of Abram Campbell, steamboat agent in Stranraer, 1856. (SRO.SH.1856)
CAMPBELL, WILLIAM, born in Kirkinner, Wigtownshire, 1727, son of Reverend William Campbell and Margaret Reid, physician in Antigua, died 1798. (F.2.365)
CARNOCHAN, JANE, born in Galloway, settled in McIntosh County, Georgia, married William McMasters 9.4.1826. (Daily Georgia 11.4.1826)
CARNOCHAN, JOHN, born in Dumfries 1778, emigrated from Scotland to Nassau, later settled in Georgia, married Harriet F. Putnam, father of John Murray Carnochan born 1812, died 1841. (BLG2602)
CARNOCHAN, WILLIAM, born 1774 Gatehouse of Fleet, Stewartry of Kirkcudbright, settled in Darien, Georgia, 1810, died there 28.11.1825. (Daily Georgian 3.12.1825)

CARNS, MUNGO, Ackford, member of the Scots Charitable Society of
   Boston, Massachusetts, 1756. [NEHGS]
CARR, ANDREW, born in Auchencairn, Kirkcudbrightshire, 1745, emigrated
   from London to New York 1784, shipbuilder, died in New York
   12.4.1812. (ANY.I.304)
CARRUTHERS JAMES, born in Dumfries, merchant in Savanna, Georgia, died
   in Augusta, Georgia, 9.9.1820. (Colonial Museum & Savanna
   Advertiser 19.9.1820)
CARRUTHERS, JOHN, settled in Antigua, died 1700, pro 5/740; 11/449, PCC
CARRUTHERS, JOSEPH, born Scotland 1783, settled in Savanna, Georgia,
   1804, died 19.10.1823. (Daily Georgia 28.10.1823)
CARRUTHER, MARY, born 1839, nurse in Dumfries, arrived in Hobart,
   Tasmania, on the White Star 1855. (SRA.TD292)
CARTER, WALTER, born in Earlston 19.5.1823, son of Thomas Carter and
   Agnes Ewing, emigrated to America 1831, settled in Saratoga
   County, New York, died Montclair, New Jersey, 19.5.1823.
   (ANY.2.254)
CHALMERS, JOHN STEELE, born in Ashkirk 1.1.1876, son of Reverend John
   Chalmers and Margaret Steele, settled in South Africa. (F.2.171)
CHRISTISON, ALEXANDER, born 17.4.1826 in Foulden, son of Reverend
   Alexander Christison and Helen Cameron, died in Australia. (F.2.49)
CHRISTISON, CAMERON, born 30.1.1839 in Foulden, son of Reverend
   Alexander Christison and Helen Cameron, killed by pirates in China.
   (F.2.49)
CHRISTISON, THOMAS MCKNIGHT, born 15.4.1835 in Foulden, son of
   Reverend Alexander Christison and Helen Cameron, sheep farmer in
   Australia, died there 1886. (F.2.49)
CHRISTISON, WILLIAM CAMERON, born 18.6.1827 in Foulden, son of
   Reverend Alexander Christison and Helen Cameron, died in
   Queensland 3.2.1874. (F.2.49)
CLARK, DAVID, born in Auchencairn, Kirkcudbright, lumber merchant in
   New York 1799-1833, married Mary Buchan 2.1803, died in New York
   30.12.1835. (ANY.I.358)
CLAPPERTON, SAMUEL SPENCE, born 1576 in Coldstream, son of Reverend
   John Clapperton and Joanna Spence, Colonel of Horse under Gustavus
   Adolphus, and Governor of Finland, died in Womer 1622. (F.2.40)
COCHRAN, CHARLES PATTERSON, born 6.1.1804 in Kirkcudbright, son of
   Robert and Elizabeth Cochran, educated at Edinburgh University,
   physician in Jamaica 1825-1834, merchant in New York, died in New
   York 28.12.1869. (ANY.II.250)
COCHRAN, FERGUS, born in Kirkcudbright 12.1804, son of Robert Cochran
   and Elizabeth Guthrie, merchant in New York 1830, died in St Croix
   8.12.1831. (ANY.II.135)

COCHRAN, JAMES BLAIR, born in Kirkcudbright 25.11.1799, son of Robert
Cochran and Elizabeth Guthrie, importer in New York 1831-, died
Sing Sing, New York, 25.4.1859. (ANY.2.266)

COCKBURN, JOHN, soldier from Jedburgh, married Anneken Hermans, in
Heusden, Netherlands, 22.4.1633. (Heusden Marriage Register)

COCKBURN, WILLIAM, born 7.1736 Duns, son of William Cockburn and
Barbara Home, settled in America. [Cockburn Family Records p256]

COLBRE, ANDREW, Berwick-on-Tweed, woolcomber in Leiden, banished
from Leiden, Netherlands, 17.6.1628 for smuggling. (Leiden Judicial
Archives, II.266)

COLTRANE, DAVID, Galloway, settled in Edgecombe County, North Carolina,
by 1738, married Mary Trotter, died pre 1745. (NCSA.2.93)

CONKIE, DAVID, Twynholm, Galloway, member of the Scots Charitable
Society of Boston 1767. (NEHGS)

COOK, GEORGE FREDERICK, born 1755, Berwick-on-Tweed, tragedian, died
in New York 26.9.1812. (Gentleman's Magazine.82.494)

COOK, GEORGE, born 17.3.1876 in Longformacus, son of Reverend George
Cook and Helen Lorrain, planter in Ceylon. (F.2.26)

COOK, JOHN, born 13.4.1805 in Sanquhar, son of John Cook, educated at the
Universities of Glasgow and Edinburgh, minister and academic in
Quebec and Ontario 1836-, died in Quebec 1.4.1892. (F.7.631)

COOK, WALTER LORRAIN, born 18.11.1880 in Longformacus, son of Reverend
George Cook and Helen Lorrain, Canadian Pacific Railway employee.
(F.2.26)

COSKRY, NATHANIEL, born in Kelton Hill, Kirkcudbright, hosier and
haberdasher in New York 1807, died at sea 8.1811. (ANY.2i.6)

COURTNEY, THOMAS, Foggo, member of the Scots Charitable Society of
Boston 1770. (NEHGS)

COWAN, JOHN, born Kirkcudbright 1790, died in Savanna, Georgia, 7.9.1820.
(Colonial Museum and Savanna Advertiser 14.9.1820)

CRAW, JAMES, at the Cape of Good Hope, son of Reverend Peter Craw in St
Boswell's, Roxburghshire, who died 21.3.1834. (SRO.SH.1849)

CRAWFORD, PATRICK, Berwickshire, merchant in Rotterdam 1775.
(SRO.RS18.16.443)

CRICHTON, MARION, from Sanquhar, married James Logan, soldier from
Ayr, in Dordrecht 5.8.1590. (Dordrecht Marriage Register)

CUNNINGHAM, GEORGE, born 14.11.1804 in Duns, son of Reverend George
Cunningham and Hyndmer Barclay, died in Canada. (F.2.11)

CURRIE, ALEXANDER, born in Galloway 1775, died Georgia 12.2.1813, buried
Old Colonial Cemetery, Savanna, Georgia. (Savanna g/s)

CURRIE, JOHN, born in Galloway 1762, settled in Savanna, Georgia, died
27.9.1799, buried in the Old Colonial Cemetery, Savanna. (Colonial
Museum and Savanna Advertiser 1.10.1799)(Savanna g/s)

EMIGRANTS AND ADVENTURERS FROM SOUTHERN SCOTLAND

DAVIDSON, ALEXANDER, born 21.1.1849 in Abbey St Bathans, son of
Reverend Thomas Davidson and Henrietta Proudfoot, banker in South
Africa. (F.2.3)
DAVIDSON, ISAAC, born in Sorbie 25.7.1804, son of Reverend Elliot W.
Davidson and Mary McTaggart, surgeon HEICS, died 25.6.1833.
(F.2.377)
DAVIDSON, WILLIAM, Peeblesshire, Captain of the 52nd Regiment of Foot,
died in Boston, Massachusetts, pro. 1776 PCC
DAVIDSON, WILLIAM jr., born in Dumfriesshire 1799, merchant in
Charleston, South Carolina, naturalised in South Carolina 6.5.1834.
(US.NA.M1183, roll 1)
DAVIDSON, WILLIAM PROUDFOOT, born 18.9.1853 in Abbey St Bathans, son
of Reverend Thomas Davidson and Henrietta Proudfoot, died in
Queensland 29.12.1914. (F.2.3)
DENNISTOUN, JAMES, son of James Dennistoun merchant in Dumfries,
educated at Glasgow University, minister in Jamaica 1842-1847, in
Constantinople 1847-1848, in Malta 1849-1851, in Jamaica 1851
- 1890+. (F.7.669)
DICK, JAMES, born in Dalry, Kirkcudbright, son of Reverend Alexander Dick
and Janet Martin, died in South Carolina 1771. (F.2.408)
DICK, ROBERT, Galloway, member of the Scots Charitable Society of
Boston 1737. (NEHGS)
DICKSON, WILLIAM, born in Whitslaid, Berwickshire, 1719, emigrated to
Jamaica 1748, settled in Philadelphia, Pennsylvania, 1763.
(BLG2659)
DINWIDDIE, ROBERT, born in Dumfries 23.7.1811, banker, settled in New
York 1835, died there 12.7.1888. (ANY.2.255)
DODD, JAMES, master of the Nancy and of the Holbeach of Boston,
Massachusetts, died in Boston, son of William and Margaret Dodd in
Berwick on Tweed, pro. 1774 PCC
DONALDSON, ROBERT, born in Barnkiss, Dumfries, 4.3.1764, son of John
Donaldson and Margaret Tait, married Sarah Henderson in North
Carolina 26.3.1795, merchant in New York, died in Brunswick County,
North Carolina, 8.7.1808. (ANY.I.391)
DOUGLAS, GEORGE, born at Castle Douglas, son of John Douglas and Mary
Heron, merchant in New York, died in Peerskill, New York, 9.10.1799.
(ANY.I.163)
DOUGLAS, SAMUEL, probably from Galloway, formerly in Savanna, Georgia,
late of Jamaica, pro. 4.1823 PCC
DOUHTON, ROBERT, soldier from Kelso, married Elizabeth Black, born in
Scotland, in Schiedam 25.4.1637. (Schiedam Marriage Register)

7

DOUGLAS, ROBERT, Berwick on Tweed, former soldier in the 68th Regiment, wife and two children, applied to settle in Canada 3.10.1827. [PRO.CO384.5.807]

DOW, ALEXANDER, Berwickshire, Colonel HEICS, 1777. (SRO.RS18.17.143)

DUNCAN, WILLIAM, born in Smailholm 31.12.1747, son of Reverend Alexander Duncan and Helen Home, Colonel HEICS, died in London 1.3.1830. (F.2.162)

DUNLOP, Colonel WILLIAM, born 16.3.1785 in Whitmuirhall, Selkirk, Quartermaster General of the Bengal Army, EIC, died 5.11.1841 in Allahabad. [St Andrew's Kirk, Calcutta, g/s]

DYSON, DUNBAR SMITH, born in Kirkcudbrightshire 1806, settled in New York by 1831, died in New Orleans 22.12.1848. (ANY.2i.27)

EDGAR, JOHN, Dumfries, member of the Scots Charitable Society of Boston 1694. (NEHGS)

ELDER, JAMES, born 1824, farm labourer in Peebles, arrived in Hobart, Tasmania, on the White Star 28.7.1855. (SRA.TD292)

EWART, AGNES, born in Kirkconnel 25.9.1755, daughter of Reverend John Ewart and Mary Corrie, married James Carson, merchant in South Carolina, 4.8.1784. (F.2.303)

EWART, JOHN, son of Isabella Lanford or Ewart in Berwick on Tweed, settled In Albany, North America, pro 5.1825 PCC

FAIRBAIRN, JOHN, son of Reverend John Fairbairn in Greenlaw, merchant in Rockhampton, Queensland, died 1.1.1901. (F.2.21)

FALL, JOHN, born in Roxburghshire 1777, carpenter, emigrated from London to America, naturalised in New York 16.6.1825.

FERGUSON, THOMAS, born in Inch, Wigtownshire, 12.9.1799, son of Reverend Peter Ferguson and Marion Murray, educated at Glasgow University 1817, surgeon, settled in St John, Antigua, died 21.5.1845. (F.2.337)(MAGU272)

FLEMING, Sir ALEXANDER, son of the Earl of Wigtown, Ensign of a Scots regiment in Holland, married Helena Neilson in Schiedam 24.54.1637. (Schiedam Marriage Register)

FORREST, JOHN, Berwickshire, in Poland 1700. (SRO.RS18.6.81)

FORSYTH, AMBROSE, born 1840, son of William Forsyth (1797-1846), died in Jamaica 28.2.1870. (St Michael's Dumfries g/s)

FORSYTH, NATHANIEL, born in Smailholm Bank, Dumfries-shire, 1769, a minister in India 1798-, died 11.2.1816. [Union Chapel, Dhurrumtollah, Calcutta. g/s]

FORSYTH, WILLIAM, born 1797, planter in the West Indies, died at Ladyfield, Dumfries, 29.11.1846. (St Michael's Dumfries g/s)

FOWLER, THOMAS, Dumfries, member of the Scots Charitable Society of Boston 1734. (NEHGS)

FRASER, CHARLES, son of William Fraser of Balmakewan, an Ensign of the 45th Native Infantry 1853. [SRO.S/H]

FRASER, JAMES, born in Kelso, indigo planter, died in Calcutta 16.4.1832. [South Park g/s, Calcutta]

FRASER, WALTER, Falshope, Selkirkshire, tailor in New York, married Jemima Carter 1784, died 5.1793. (ANY.I.203)

FRENCH, ROBERT, merchant in Kilpatrick, Annandale, member of the Scots Charitable Society of Boston 1685. (NEHGS)

FULTON, GEORGE, Coldingham, member of the Scots Charitable Society of Boston 1762. (NEHGS)

GALBRAITH, THOMAS, 28, farmer, wife Jane, and 1 child, emigrated from Leith to Argentina on the Symmetry, master William Cochrane. 22.5.1825. (SSP18)

GALLOWAY, GEORGE, born in Kirkcudbright 1802, son of George Galloway, educated at Edinburgh University, minister in Warwick, Bermuda, 1833-1834, died 12.3.1834. (F.7.660)

GARR, ANDREW, born 1745 in Auchincairn, Kirkcudbrighthshire, via London to New York 1784, shipbuilder, married (1) .... Sheffield, (2) Mary Ogden, (3) Margaret Garr, father of Andrew and Janet, died in New York 12.4.1812. (ANY.I.304)

GARRETT, JAMES, born Inch, Galloway, 1797, son of Robert Garrett, farmer, educated at Glasgow University, to Australia 1828, minister in Tasmania 1830-, died 1874. (F.7.601)

GIBSON of KELTON, JAMES, born in Colvend 23.7.1729, son of Reverend Luke Gibson and Marion Gilchrist, merchant in Virginia. (F.2.261)

GILLESPIE, GARNET, born in Kirkgunzeon 2.5.1875, son of Reverend James E. Gillespie and Agnes Murray, merchant's clerk in Melbourne. (F.2.281)

GILLESPIE, MURRAY, born in Kirkgunzeon 29.11.1870, son of Reverend James E. Gillespie and Agnes Murray, died in Grahamstown, South Africa, 18.9.1895. (F.2.281)

GILLESPIE, ROBERT, born 30.12.1778, son of Reverend John Gillespie and Dorothea McKean, Kells, Kirkcudbright, a merchant in New York, died 20.9.1830. [F.2.412]

GORDON, ALEXANDER, minister in Wigtownshire 1745-1760, married Agnes Christian 1747, father of Thomas, Patrick, William, Jean and Robert, emigrated to America 1760. [F.2.360]

GORDON of THREAVE GRANGE, DAVID, officer of the 67th Regiment later in the Russian Army, died in Russia 1771. [SRO.NRAS.0241.VI.22]

GORDON, ELIZABETH, Dumfries, emigrated from Belfast to New York on the Shannon 18.1.1816. ("Passengers from Ireland"

GORDON, JAMES, son of Alexander Graham and Anna Stroyan, Mains of Penningham, Wigtownshire, settled in Charleston, South Carolina, died 1817. ["Gordons of Craichlaw", p29, Dalbeattie, 1924]

GORDON, JOHN, Dumfries, emigrated from Belfast to New York on the Shannon 18.1.1816. ("Passengers from Ireland"

GORDON, JOHN, born in Twynholm 8.9.1839, son of Reverend John Gordon and Penelope Murdoch, merchant in New Zealand. (F.2.429)

GORDON, ROBERT, born in Dumfries 17.11.1829, son of William Gordon and Sarah Walker, educated at Glasgow University 1845, settled in New York 1849, financier, died in England 16.5.1918. (ANY.2.257)

GOWAN, PETER, born in Galloway 1797, watchmaker in Charleston, South Carolina, naturalised in South Carolina 5.7.1848. (US.NA.M1183, roll 1)

GOWDIE, FRANCIS, born in Earlston 7.8.1747, son of Reverend John Gowdie and Katherine Scott, Major General HEICS Madras, died 12.9.1813. (F.2.149)

GOWDIE, WALTER, born in Earlston 4.12.1740, son of Reverend John Gowdie and Katherine Scott, surgeon in Bengal, died in India. (F.2.149)

GRACIE, JAMES, son of James Gracie and Jean Cowan, Brevet Major of the 21st Infantry, died at the Battle of Baltimore 13.9.1813. (St Michael's Dumfries g/s)

GRAHAM, JAMES, born 1798 Dumfriesshire, married Isabella Glendenning, settled in Streetsville, Ontario, pre 1830. [SG.30.2.71]

GRAHAM, JOHN, born 1777, son of Thomas Graham, farmer, and Christian Halliday, Burnswark, Ecclesfechan, to New York 1792, merchant, married Ann McQueen 1804, died in New York 18.1.1843. (ANY.1.378)

GRAHAM, MANNERS HAMILTON, born in Rutherford 3.8.1866, son of Reverend M.H.N.Graham and Margaret Ritchie, fruit rancher in USA, died 6.8.1902. (F.2.186)

GRAHAM, SIMON, Dumfriesshire, emigrated from Greenock to New York on the Maria of New York 27.3.1795. [SRO.SC15.55.2]

GRANT, ALEXANDER, Berwickshire, merchant in Jamaica then in London, 1773. (SRO.RS18.16.228)

GRANT, ANDREW, Berwickshire, merchant in Jamaica then in London, 1774. (SRO.RS18.16.317)

GRANT, WILLIAM, Berwickshire, merchant in Rotterdam, 1754. (SRO.RS19.13.394)

GRIERSON, JAMES, born in Glencairn 3.6.1788, son of Reverend William Grierson and Margaret Walker, surgeon HEICS. (F.2.315)

GRIERSON, WILLIAM, 32, farmer, wife Catherine, and 3 children, emigrated from Leith to Argentina on the Symmetry, master William Cochrane, 22.5.1825. (SSP18)

GROSSET, or MUIRHEAD, JAMES, of Breadisholm, Berwickshire, merchant in Lisbon 1766. (SRO.RS18.15.224)

HAIG, BARBARA, Bemersyde, Berwickshire, in Italy 1858. [SRO.S/H]

HAIG, JAMES, miller in Van Dieman's Land, son of Helen Haig in Coldstream Bridge Toll, 1831. (SRO.S/H)

HAIG, MARY, Bemersyde, Berwickshire, in Italy 1858. [SRO.S/H]

HAIG, SOPHIA, Bemersyde, Berwickshire, in Italy 1858. [SRO.S/H]

HAIG, WILLIAM, born 28.3.1646, second son of David Haig of Bemersyde, married Mary, daughter of Gavin Lawrie, in London 1673, died 29.7.1688 in West New Jersey. ["Haigs of Bemerside", p441 {Edinburgh, 1881}]

HAIG, WILLIAM, born 20.6.1670, son of Anthony Haig of Bemersyde, merchant in Antigua. (Haigs of Bemersyde, p443 {Edinburgh:1881})

HALIBURTON, JOHN, born in Castleton 17.9.1754, son of Reverend Simon Haliburton of Howcleugh and Elizabeth Elliot, Captain HEICS, died in India. (F.2.170)

HALL, GEORGE, born in Roxburghshire 1780, merchant in Charleston, South Carolina, naturalised in Charleston 15.6.1812. (US.NA.M1183.1)

HANNAH, JOHN, born 1761, merchant in the West Indies, died 20.7.1841. (St Michael's Dumfries g/s)

HANNAY, WILLIAM, housecarpenter and merchant in Spanish Town, Jamaica, thereafter in Wigtown, cnf 1800 Wigtown

HARDCASS of HARDCASS, JOHN, member of the Scots Charitable Society of Boston 1718. (NEHGS)

HARDIE, ROBERT, born in Hawick 20.10.1805, son of John Hardie farmer, educated at Glasgow University, minister in British Guiana 1837, died 24.10.1837. (F.7.675)

HARKNESS, JAMES, eldest son of James Harkness, manufacturer in Sanquhar, matriculated at Glasgow University 1800, minister of St Andrew's Presbyterian Church, Quebec, 1820. [MAGU.196]

HAY, ALLAN, born in Kelso 8.1813, settled in New York 1834, died there 9.9.1900. (ANY.2.238)

HAY, JAMES, born in Kelso son of Allan Hay, soap manufacturer in New York, died there 24.8.1907. (ANY.2.299)

HAY, THOMAS, born in Kelso 1821, tallow chandler in New York, died there 17.7.1896. (ANY.2.299)

HENDERSON, GEORGE, merchant in Kingston, Jamaica, son of George Henderson in Newton Stewart, 1787. [SRO.RS.Wigton, 177]

HEPBURN, WILLIAM, born 1712, son of Provost Hepburn, physician in Jamaica, died in Dalscairth 30.5.1775. (St Michael's Dumfries g/s)

HERON, PATRICK, born in Kirkgunzeon 4.12.1798, son of Reverend James Heron and Mary Donaldson, died in St Kitts 10.11.1824. (F.2.280)

EMIGRANTS AND ADVENTURERS FROM SOUTHERN SCOTLAND

HETHERINGTON, IRVING, born in Whaite, Ruthwell, son of Richard Hederton
and Louisa Carruthers, educayed at Edinburgh University, to
Australia 24.3.1837, minister in New South Wales and Victoria
1837 -, died 5.7.1875. (F.7.590)
HILLS, JAMES, born in Berwickshire, settled in Savanna, Georgia, 1804,
died 17.7.1829. (Georgia Republican 20.8.1829)
HILL, ROBERT, son of James Hill and Agnes Muirhead, surgeon, died in
Jamaica 26.7.1737. (F.2.285)
HOLIDAY, WILLIAM, possibly from Dumfriesshire, settled in Goose Creek,
South Carolina, pro. 5.1810 PCC
HOME, ALEXANDER, Berwickshire, in St Kitts 1769. (SRO.RS18.15.371)
HOME, NINIAN, of Paxton, Berwickshire, in Grenada pre 1766.
(SRO.RS18.15.227)
HOPE, JOHN, Galashiels, member of the Scots Charitable Society of Boston
1819. (NEHGS)
HOUSTOUN, ALEXANDER, late a merchant in Grenada, husband of Helen
McKie, 1784. [SRO.RS.Wigton,66]
HOUSTOUN, WILLIAM, merchant burgess of Whithorn, burgess and
guildsbrother of Glasgow, merchant in Newcastle, Delaware, died
1707, pro. 11.12.1711 Newcastle, Delaware. (DSA.Misc.1.178)
HUNTER, ROBERT, born in Galloway 1759, naturalised in New York
19.11.1804
HUNTER, SAMUEL, born in Dumfries 1685, absconded from William Bradford
in New York City 1735. (New York Gazette 2.6.1735)
IRVINE, ANDREW, Dumfriesshire, theological student 1806-1809,
emigrated to America 1811. ["The Reformed Presbyterian Church in
Scotland" p162: Edinburgh, 1925]
JAFFRAY, JANE, born 29.5.1773, daughter of Reverend Andrew Jaffray and
Agnes Armstrong in Ruthwell, married ..... Renwick in New York 1794,
died 1850. [F.2.214]
JAIRDEN, WILLIAM, merchant in Dumfries, member of the Scots Charitable
Society of Boston 1684. (NEHGS)
JAMESON, JOHN CARMICHAEL, born in St Mungo 5.9.1812, son of Reverend
Andrew Jameson and Elizabeth Carmichael, surgeon in Melbourne.
(F.2.222)
JELLY, WILLIAM, born ca.1770, father of William born 8.9.1794 in
Kirkcudbright, also John, Charles, Samuel, Elizabeth, and Mary,
emigrated to America on the brig Elizabeth 8.8.1795, landed at Derby
Wharf, Salem, Massachusetts. (SG.1/1/22)
JOHNSTONE, GEORGE, born in Earlston 2.11.1780, son of Reverend Laurence
Johnstone and Esther Lauriston, staff surgeon of the Connaught
Rangers, died in Corfu 1833. (F.2.149)

JOHNSTON, HENRY HAMILTON, born 23.9.1858, son of Reverend Michael Johnston and Lilias McKelvie, manager of the Colorado Cattle Company in USA. (F.2.373)

JOHNSTON, JAMES, born 13.9.1685, second son of Lewis Johnston and Janet Rankin, married Janet Nisbet in Dumfries 1722, physician in the Royal Navy, settled in Georgia around 1750. ["History of the Johnstons - Supplement", Glasgow 1925]

JOHNSTON, JOHN, druggist formerly in Edinburgh by 1687 in East New Jersey, son of William Johnston in Lauderdale. [SRO.RD4.67.97]

JOHNSTON, JOHN, born 1781, son of John Johnston in Kirkcudbrightshire, emigrated to New York 1804, married Margaret Taylor. ["History of the Johnstons"]

JOHNSTON, ROBERT, born in Kirkcudbrightshire 1804, emigrated from Liverpool to America, accountant, naturalised in New York 29.10.1821.

JOHNSTONE, THOMAS, born 11.1.1829 Garrell, Dumfriesshire, son of William Johnstone and Elizabeth Renwick, educated at St Andrews University, to Australia 1856, minister in New South Wales 1856 -1903, died 3.2.1909. (F.7.590)

JOHNSTON, WILLIAM, born in Kirkcudbrightshire 1800, emigrated from Greenock to America, merchant, naturalised in New York 27.10.1821.

JOHNSTON, WILLIAM, married Margaret Thomson in Canonbie 24.4.1811, settled in Ontario before 1830. [SG.32.2/63]

JOHNSTON, WILLIAM, born 1803, died in St Bartholemew, West Indies, 21.11.1827. (St Michael's Dumfries g/s)

KEIR, ALEXANDER, Newton Stewart, Wigtownshire, via Londonderry to New York on the Barkley 14.8.1816. (NWI.2.358)

KENNEDY, JOHN, Kirkcudbright, died on passage from New York 5.1.1797. (Gentleman's Magazine.67.165)

KENNEDY, ROBERT, Tweeddale, member of the Scots Charitable Society of Boston 1762. (NEHGS)

KENNEDY, WALTER, son of Reverend Hugh Kennedy and Margaret Scott in Cavers, planter in Surinam, died in London 1777. (F.2.106)

KERR, JAMES, born 1754 Dumfries, emigrated to New York, Loyalist officer, settled in Parrsboro, Nova Scotia, died in Amherst, Nova Scotia, 6.6.1830. ["The Scots in Canada" p130]

KEVAN, ANDREW, born in Kirkcudbright 1757, shoemaker in New York, married Jean Dill 22.6.1806, father of Mary, died 25.4.1827. (ANY.I.363)

KEVAN, SAMUEL, born in Kirkcudbrightshire, master slater in New York by 1827, married Mary Tannahill in Schenectady 1831. (ANY.I.117)

KEVAN, WILLIAM, born in Kirkcudbright 1765, leather and shoe merchant in New York 1808, died there 7.12.1847. (ANY.2i.6)

KIMMINGS, ALEXANDER, Stranraer, settled in Upper Freehold, Monmouth County, New Jersey, pro 13.1.1784. (NJA.Lib.26/342)

KINCAID, PATRICK, a merchant in Cadiz, 1790. [SRO.RS.Wigton, 245]

KING, CHARLES, born in Dumfriesshire 1800, slater, wife Mary born in Galloway 1798, daughter Elizabeth born in Dumfries 1825, emigrated from Port Patrick via Belfast to America, naturalised in New York 20.10.1826.

KIRKPATRICK, SAMUEL, Dumfries, member of the Scots Charitable Society of Boston 1769. (NEHGS)

KIRKPATRICK, WILLIAM ESCOTT, in Brussels, nephew of Jane Kirkpatrick in Nithbank, Dumfries. (SRO.SH.1859)

LAIDLAW, JOHN, born in Roxburghshire 1794, teacher, wife Agnes born in Edinburgh 1794 a teacher, emigrated from Leith to America, settled in Brooklyn, naturalised in New York 24.7.1820.

LAIDLAW, WALTER, in Bombay, son of William Laidlaw, grocer in Hawick. (SRO.SH.1854)

LAIDLIE, ARCHIBALD, born in Kelso, educated at Edinburgh University 1730, Dutch Reformed minister in New York 1734-1776, died at Red Hook, New York, 1779. (CCMC)

LAING, GILBERT, Dumfriesshire, merchant in St Petersburg 1775.(SRO.S/H)

LAING, ROBERT, wife Ann Jesson, emigrated from Berwickshire to Canada 1810, settled in Peterborough County, Ontario. [SG.32.3]

LAING, WILLIAM, wife Helen Mabon, emigrated from Berwickshire to Canada 1810, settled in Peterborough County, Ontario. [SG.32.3]

LAMB, JAMES, Teviotdale, member of the Scots Charitable Society of Boston, 1750. (NEHGS)

LAMBERT, ANTHONY, born in Berwick on Tweed 5.8.1758, son of Charles Lambert and Jane Malcolm, Ensign of the Bengal Infantry, died in London 17.1.1800. (BA.3.5)

LAMBERT, ANTHONY, born in Berwick on Tweed 3.2.1785, son of Anthony Lambert and Cecily Proctor, Lieutenant of the 15th Bengal Native Infantry, killed at the Battle of Laswari 1.11.1803. (BA.3.5)

LAMONT, JOHN, born in Kirkpatrick Durham 27.12.1805, son of Reverend David Lamont and Anne Anderson, advocate and later a brewer in London, died in Wangaratta, Victoria, 7.1873. (F.2.285)

LAURIE, GILBERT, of Crossrig, educated at Edinburgh University 1673, to America 1686-, returned to Scotland, minister in Hutton and Fishwick 1696-1727, died 3.9.1727. (F.2.52)

LAURIE, THOMAS, born in Tynwald 27.4.1793, son of Reverend James Laurie and Rachel Carlyle, Lieutenant of the 15th Bengal Native Infantry, died in Sitapur, India, 30.11.1815. (BA.3.21)

LAW, DAVID, Innerleithen, member of the Scots Charitable Society of Boston 1734. (NEHGS)

EMIGRANTS AND ADVENTURERS FROM SOUTHERN SCOTLAND

LAWRIE, WALTER, born in Ewis Duris 18.4.1805, son of Reverend John
Lawrie and Anne Grieve, surgeon of the 4th Madras Light Cavalry,
died in Anantapur, India, 24.4.1844. (F.2.235)
LAWSON, ROBERT, son of Robert Lawson of Knockhorrock (1728-1800) and
Helen Hannah, died in St Kitts aged 24. (St Michael's Dumfries g/s)
LECKIE, JOHN MCRITCHIE, born in Parton 26.1.1851, son of Reverend
Thomas Leckie and Katherine McRitchie, sheepfarmer in Australia.
(F.2.422)
LEGGAT, WALTER, born in Hawick 1785, merchant in New York 1827, died
there 30.9.1850. (ANY.2.24)
LENNOX, PATRICK, born in Portpatrick 4.1750, emigrated to New England,
married Margaret McNear in Newcastle, Maine, 1785, father of
Robert, Thomas and Patrick, died 17.4.1831. (Imm.NE.111)
LENNOX, ROBERT, born in Kirkcudbright 31.12.1759, son of James Lennox
and Elizabeth Sproat, emigrated to America 1770, settled in New
York 1783, merchant, died in New York 13.12.1839. (ANY.I.173)
LILLIE, Rev. JOHN, born in Kelso 18.12.1812, educated at Edinburgh
University 1833, minister and schoolmaster in New York, died in
Kingston, New York, 23.2.1867. (ANY.2.239)
LILLIE, WILLIAM, born in Kelso 4.2.1802, emigrated to New York 1835,
leather merchant there, died in Edinburgh 16.1.1863. (ANY.2.239)
LITTLE, ARCHIBALD, merchant in Teneriffe, son of Matthew Little,
merchant in Langholm, 1794. (SRO.S/H)
LIVINGSTON, ROBERT, born in Ancrum, Roxburghshire, 13.12.1654, son of
Reverend John Livingston and Janet Fleming, to America 1673,
settled in Charlestown, Massachusetts, and later Albany, New York,
merchant and civil servant, died 1.10.1728. (Colonial Families,
Vol.6, p334)
LOCKHART, SAMUEL, late surgeon HEICS, eldest son of Ephriam Lockhart of
Barmaghan, died in Madras 23.4.1797. [AJ2615]
LUNDIE, GEORGE ARCHIBALD, born in Kelso 31.12.1819, son of Reverend
Robert Lundie and Mary Gray, missionary in Samoa, died 9.1841.
(F.2.73)
MCCARR, JOHN, born in Newton Stewart, Wigtownshire, 1757, merchant
tailor in New York, died there 1843. (ANY.I.306)
MCCLYMONT, JOHN, 25, farmer, wife Catherine, and 2 children, emigrated
from Leith to Argentina on the Symmetry, master William Cochrane,
22.5.1825. (SSP18)
MCCOMB, ARCHIBALD, late a smith in Glasserton, then in New York state,
1796. [SRO.RS.Wigton, 481]
MCCRAKEN, JAMES, born in Treqhair, Kirkcudbrightshire, 29.6.1785, son of
John McCraken and Mary Anderson, Lieutenant of the 14th Bengal
Native Infantry, died in Cawnpore 1.8.1816. (BA.3.113)

15

MCCRACKAN, JAMES, Galloway, settled in Cambridge, South Carolina, died 11.7.1818. (Abbeville District Will Book II pp46/50)

MCCREADY, JOHN, a runaway, a blacksmith/currier aged around 30, recently arrived from the Isle of Whithorn on the Golden Rule, Captain Cragg, - a reward offered by Patrick McMiking, 1774. (New York Mercury 5.9.1774)

MACCULLOCH, D., born in Dumfriesshire 1795, died 27.6.1822. [North Park g/s, Calcutta]

MCCULLOCH, EDWARD, born in Kirkcudbrightshire, son of David McCulloch and Janet Corsane, Lieutenant of the Bengal Infantry, died in Scotland 22.6.1796. (BA.3.114)

MCCULLOCH, HAWTHORN, born in Glasserton, Wigtownshire, 1772, son of Andrew McCulloch, emigrated from Greenock to America 1802, settled in New York 1803. (BLG2806)

MCCULLOCH, JAMES, Dumfries, member of the Scots Charitable Society of Boston 1747. (NEHGS)

MCCUNE, THOMAS, son of Samuel McCune in Wigtownshire, educated at Glasgow University, minister in British Guiana 1845, died 1845. (F.7.675)

MCEWEN, JAMES, Torthorwald, Nithsdale, member of the Scots Charitable Society of Boston 1767. (NEHGS)

MACGEOCH, GRACE, Glen Luce, Wigtownshire, emigrated from Belfast to New York on the Lorenzo 2.5.1816. (NWI.2.361)

MACGEOCH, SAMUEL, Glen Luce, Wigtownshire, emigrated from Belfast to New York on the Lorenzo 2.5.1816. (NWI.2.361)

MACGOWAN, BERNARD, Newton Stewart, Wigtownshire, emigrated from Newry to New York on the Leda 1815. (NWI.2.361)

MACKIE, JOHN, born in Makerstoun 15.2.1849, son of Reverend Andrew Mackie and Elizabeth Hewat, died in Bombay 2.3.1892. (F.2.79)

MACKINTOSH, ROBERT AIREY, third son of James Mackintosh of Lamancha, died aged 16, 18.. [Scotch Burial Ground g/s, Calcutta]

MACKINTOSH, SARAH, born 1786, wife of James Mackintosh of Lamancha, died 6.10.1846. [Scotch Burial Ground g/s, Calcutta]

MCKNAIGHT, THOMAS, in Grenada, 1791. [SRO.RS.Wigton, 287]

MCLACHLAN, ALEXANDER, in Dominica 1787, son of William McLachlan and Anne McGhie in Kirkcudbright. (Laing Charters 3268)

MCLAGAN, HECTOR, born in Melrose 26.6.1768, son of Reverend Frederick McLagan and Christian Turnbull, died in Jamaica 11.9.1808. (F.2.188)

MCMASTER, JAMES, Old Glenluce, Galloway, member of the Scots Charitable Society of Boston 1767. (NEHGS); merchant in Halifax, Nova Scotia, 1783. (Loyalists in Nova Scotia, p155)

MCMASTER, PATRICK, Glenluce, Galloway, member of the Scots Charitable
Society of Boston 1774. (NEHGS); settled in Portsmouth, New
Hampshire, 1767, merchant, Loyalist, settled Halifax, Nova Scotia,
1776, later in St Johns, New Brunswick, drowned in the Bay of
Fundy 1797. (Loyalists of Massachusetts, p209)
MCMASTER, WILLIAM, born in Galloway, settled in Boston, Massachusetts,
1765, merchant, Loyalist, settled in Shelborne, Nova Scotia.
[Loyalists of Massachusetts, p209]
MCMASTERS, WILLIAM, born in Galloway, settled in McIntosh County,
Georgia, married Jane Carnochan 9.4.1826.
(Daily Georgian 11.4.1826)
MCMEIKINE, ROBERT, a merchant in Kingston, Jamaica, 1801, son of Gilbert
McMeikine, a merchant in Glenluce, and Jean McHaffie.
[SRO.RS.Wigton, 623]
MCMILLAN, JOHN, born in Sanquhar, merchant in New Orleans, father of
Robert born in Charleston, South Carolina, 1813. (ANY.II.218)
MCMILLAN, JOHN, of Glen Lee, Kirkcudbrightshire, died before 1781 in
Spanish Town, Jamaica. [SRO.NRAS.0473.bundle 1]
MCMILLAN, JOHN, born in Dumfriesshire 1782, merchant in Charleston,
South Carolina, naturalised in South Carolina 5.10.1832.
(US.NA.M1183.1)
McNISH, JOHN, born in Galloway, merchant in Savanna, Georgia, died
in Georgia 19.12.1826. (Georgia Republican 20.12.1826)
MCWHIR, BRYCE JOHNSTONE, born in Urr 21.1.1816, son of Reverend John
McWhir and Jane Fraser, physician, died in Comercolly, Bengal,
12.6.1839. (F.2.307)
MAITLAND, DAVID, born in Kirkcudbrightshire 1802, emigrated from
Liverpool to America, merchant, naturalised in New York 15.3.1821.
MAXWELL, Major BRYCE, son of Provost Edward Maxwell and Charlotte
Blair, died in Martinique 1809. (St Michael's Dumfries g/s)
MAXWELL, JAMES THOMAS, born in Thornhill, Dumfriesshire, 10.4.1823, son
of Dr Robert Maxwell and Anne Young, emigrated to America 1835,
died in New York 2.3.1860. (ANY.2.246)
MENZIES, JEANNIE NEWBIGGING, born in Hoddam 23.9.1845, daughter of
Reverend Robert Menzies and Martha Coldstream, died in Hyeres,
France, 8.3.1892. (F.2.249)
MENZIES, LAWRIE, born in Hoddam 16.6.1848, son of Reverend Robert
Menzies and Martha Coldstream, engineer, died in Alexandrowsk,
South Russia, 11.12.1914. (F.2.249)
MILLER, JOHN, 38, farmer, wife Anne, and 1 child, emigrated from Leith to
Argentina on the Symmetry 22.5.1825. (SSP18)
MILLIGAN, WILLIAM, Kirkbean (?) Dumfriesshire, settled in Charleston,
South Carolina, died in Madeira 1819. (SRO.CS46.1834.150)

MILROY, DAVID, born in Crailing 16.12.1831, son of Reverend Andrew
Milroy and Margaret Bryce, phyician and surgeon, died in Bermuda
3.9.1864. (F.2.109)

MITCHELSON, WILLIAM, born 1798, son of Andrew Mitchelson and Helen
Grierson, Bengal Medical Staff, died 27.3.1866. (St Michael's
Dumfries g/s)

MORLAND, WILLIAM, Stranraer, member of the Scots Charitable Society of
Boston 1762. (NEHGS)

MORRINE, WILLIAM, born in Dumfries 1781, storekeeper, died in Savanna,
Georgia, 10.8.1805. (Georgia Courier 4.9.1805)(Savanna Death
Register)

MORRISON, JAMES, merchant in Jamaica, husband of Mary Allan, 1791.
[SRO.RS.Wigton, 283]

MORRISON, JOHN, merchant in Antigua then in Dumfries, pro 7.5.1770
Dumfries

MORTON, WALTER, born in Kelso, haberdasher in New York, died there
15.4.1891. (ANY.2.302)

MUIR, FREELAND, son of Andrew Muir, merchant in Kirkcudbright, and Anne
Blair, died in St Vincnet 6.1797. [AJ2609]

MUIR, JOHN MCCULLOCH, born in Kirkmabreck 2.5.1835, son of Reverend
John Muir and Gloriana Pearson, died in Denver, Colorado, 17.3.1899.
(F.2.369)

MUIR, WILLIAM, born 1754, emigrated from Kirkcudbright to America
1774, settled in New York, married Mary Ritchie, died 9.2.1809.
(BLG2837)

MUIRHEAD, EBENEZER, physician in Providence, Rhode Island, pre 1754,
eldest son of William Muirhead of Crochmore and Janet Richardson,
Dumfriesshire. (SRO.RS23.17.17)

MUNDELL, JOHN, Dumfries, member of the Scots Charitable Society of
Boston 1694. (NEHGS)

MURRAY, ANDREW, born in Melrose 11.5.1839, son of Reverend William
Murray and Agnes Cunningham, died in Burwood, New South Wales,
8.2.1895. (F.2.189)

MURRAY, DAVID, Philiphaugh, settled in Christchurch parish, Georgia, pro
17.2.1770 South Carolina.

MURRAY, JAMES, Roxburghshire, member of the Scots Charitable Society of
Boston 1765. (NEHGS)

MURRAY, Lieutenant Colonel WALTER, in Busch, Brabant, father of
Alexander Murray. (SRO.SH. {Roxburghshire}.1669)

NICHOLSON, THOMAS, born in Dumfriesshire 1799, physician, married Mary
Paterson in Thornhill, settled in St John, Antigua, 1822, died
8.7.1877. (Caribbeana.2.287)

NEILSON, CHARLES, Galloway, citizen of Bergen, Norway, 1719. [SAB]

NIVISON, ALEXANDER, born in Roberton, 17.7.1828, son of Reverend
Alexander Nivison and Christiana Thomson, died in Melbourne 1861.
(F.2.190)
NIVISON, DAVID THOMSON, born in Roberton 5.1.1834, son of Reverend
Alexander Nivison and Christiana Thomson, died in Calcutta
20.8.1867. (F.2.190)
OGILVIE, GEORGE, born in Galloway 1762, died in Georgia 7.12.1794.
(Georgia Gazette 15.12.1797)
OLIVER, JAMES, born in Berwick-on-Tweed 1774, planter, died in Savanna,
Georgia, 26.5.1808. (Savanna Republican 28.5.1808)
ORR, JOHN, son of Reverend Alexander Orr in Ecclefechan (1686-1767),
merchant in Virginia. (F.2.249)
PALMER, JOHN, born in Kelso (?), settled in New York 1799, merchant,
married Margaret Given, died 1.2.1858. (ANY.1.370)
PANTON, Reverend GEORGE, formerly in Shelborne, Nova Scotia, and New
York, late in Kelso, pro. 10.1810 PCC
PATON, EDWARD, born in Ancrum 5.12.1834, son of Reverend John Paton
and Mary Paton, merchant in Pernambuco, Brazil. (F.2.101)
PATON, JAMES, born in Ancrum 1.6.1839, son of Reverend John Paton and
Mary Paton, settled in Canada. (F.2.101)
PATON, JOHN, born in Ancrum 26.5.1831, son of Reverend John Paton and
Mary Paton, banker in New York, died 30.3.1908. (F.2.101)
POTTS, JOHN, Dumfries, died 15.2.1798 at Ballard's River, Clarendon,
Jamaica. [AJ2635]
PRINGLE, JAMES, Teviotdale, member of the Scots Charitable Society of
Boston 1753. (NEHGS)
PRINGLE, JOHN, Merse, member of the Scots Charitable Society of Boston
1739. (NEHGS)
RAE, JOHN, born in Wigtown, shipmaster in New York, died 3.10.1819.
(ANY.II.6)
REID, JOHN, Captain HEICS in Bengal, 1798. [SRO.RS.Wigton, 527]
RENWICK, WILLIAM, born in Roxburghshire, married Jane Jeffrey, settled in
New York 1794, merchant there. (ANY.II.25)
RIDDELL, JOHN, born 18.2.1836 in Longformacus, son of Reverend Henry
Riddell and Elizabeth Horne, settled in Geelong, Australia. (F.2.11)
RIDDELL, WILLIAM, born 5.8.1838 in Longformacus, son of Reverend Henry
Riddell and Elizabeth Horne, planter in Tirhoot, India. (F.2.11)
RIDOUT, JOSEPH, born in Berwick 1774, mariner, died in Savanna, Georgia,
2.1811. (Savanna Death Register)
ROBB, JAMES, Whithorn, Galloway, member of the Scots Charitable Society
of Boston 1756. (NEHGS)

EMIGRANTS AND ADVENTURERS FROM SOUTHERN SCOTLAND

ROBERTSON, ALEXANDER KEITH, born 9.2.1825, son of Reverend George Home Robertson and Elizabeth Kennedy, Berwickshire, killed at Harper's Ferry, USA, 1865. (F.2.55)

ROBERTSON, JAMES, Kirkcudbright, member of the Scots Charitable Society of Boston 1759. (NEHGS)

ROBERTSON, JOHN ALEXANDER, born 29.8.1868 in Whitsome, son of Reverend John Alexander Robertson and Helen Stenhouse, physician, died in Matjesfontein, Cape Colony, 22.9.1903. (F.2.65)

ROBERTSON, JOHN PARISH, born in Roxburghshire, settled in Argentina, 1813, later in Monte Grande, Buenos Ayres, 1825 (SSP3)

ROBERTSON, WILLIAM PARISH, born in Roxburghshire, settled in Argentina, 1813, later in Monte Grande, Buenos Ayres, 1825. (SSP3)

ROBINSON, DOUGLAS, born in Orchardton, Kirkcudbrightshire, 24.11.1824, son of George Rose Robinson, to Philadelphia 1842, later settled in Herkimmer County, New York, died at sea on the Kaiser Wilhelm III 25.11.1893. (ANY.2.235)

RODDICK, JAMES, born in Gretna 28.5.1852, son of Reverend James Roddick and Mary Dickson, minister in Adelaide, Australia. (F.2.248)

RODICK, Captain JOHN, master of the Thetis of Maryport, drowned at Bic Island, River St Lawrence, 18.10.1870. (St Michael's Dumfries g/s)

ROME, THOMAS, merchant in Antigua, 5.7.1714. (SRO.RS23{Kirkcudbright}105.448)

RORISON, JAMES, son of ....Rorison of Ardoch and Elizabeth Douglas, married Margaret Shanters in Castle Douglas 23.12.1756, settled in Pennsylvania pre 1776. (Colonial Families.VI.451)

ROSS, ALEXANDER, son of John Ross in Clairnbrock, Kirkham, Galloway, settled in New Jersey, pro 3.6.1780. (NJA.Lib.23/196)

ROSS, JAMES, Galloway, member of the Scottish Charitable Society of Boston 1732. (NEHGS)

ROYLE, MARY, born 1684, kidnapped in Dumfriesshire and shipped to America 8.1697, indentured servant in Chester, Pennsylvania, married (1) William Coles, (2) Jeremiah Brown, mother of William, Joshua. (Scottish Antiquary.X.146)

RUSSELL, ALEXANDER, Tweeddale, member of the Scots Charitable Society of Boston, Massachusetts, 1749. [NEHGS]

RUTHERFORD, WILLIAM, Teviotdale, member of the Scots Charitable Society of Boston, Massachusetts, 1748. [NEHGS]

SCOON, JOHN, born in Hawick 27.4.1771, settled in Geneva, New York, 1820, married Margaret Renwick, father of William born 1823, died 26.1.1861. (BLG2904)

SCOTT, HENRY, in Calcutta 1786. [SRO.RS.Wigton, 124]

SCOTT, JAMES, from Hawick, married Neeltge Jacobs in Schiedam 21.7.1652. (Schiedam Marriage Register)

SCOTT, JAMES, born in Ewis Duris12.2.1764, son of Reverend Richard Scott and Mary Turnbull, merchant in New York 1780-, died 24.12.1826, buried in Prospect Cemetery, Jamaica, Long Island, New York. (ANY.2.186)(F.2.234)

SCOTT, WALTER, born 1817, second son of Walter Scott of Wauchope, Roxburghshire, an assistant surgeon HEICS, died in Allahabad, Bengal, 17.8.1844. [Allahabad g/s]

SHANTERS, MARGARET, married James Rorison in Castle Douglas 23.12.1756, settled in Pennsylvania pre 1776. (Col.Fams.VI.451)

SINCLAIR, JOHN, late in Carsebuie, then a planter in Faquier County, Virginia, 1801, grandson of John Sinclair, a merchant in Newton Stewart, [SRO.RS.Wigton, 617]

SLIMMON, ROBERT, born in Sanquhar 1819, settled in New York 1840, merchant, died there 8.11.1870. (ANY.2.282)

SMITH, JAMES, born 1669 Glencairn, Nithsdale, maried Ann .... (1658-1741), died in Boston, Massachusetts, 2.4.1732. (Imm.N.E.183)

SMITH, JAMES, born in Kelso 5.4.1836, son of Reverend James Smith and Agnes Fyffe, died in Aleppo 17.11.1857. (F.2.73)

SMITH, JOHN FYFFE, born in Kelso 26.2.1838, son of Reverend James Smith and Agnes Fyffe, died in Tangiers 8.7.1858. (F.2.73)

SMITH, WILLIAM, born in Dumfries 1717, died in New York 1768. (Matthew's American Armory and Blue Book, London 1903)

SMYTH, KIRKPATRICK DICKSON, born in Barscar, Dumfriesshire, educated at Edinburgh University, minister in Bathurst, New South Wales, 1835 -1854, died in Scotland 1863. (F.7.598)

SOMERVILLE, ALEXANDER, born 1772 Roxburghshire son of Dr Archibald Somerville, bookseller in New York 1798, died in New Orleans 4.9.1804. (ANY.II.342)

SOMERVILLE, JAMES, born in St Boswells, son of Reverend Robert Somerville and Constantia Williamson, settled in Buenos Ayres. (F.2.193)

SPENCE, ALEXANDER, merchant in Duns, bankrupt - absconded to America ca.1796. (SRO.CS230.Seqn.s2/3)

SPRATT, JOHN, merchant in Wigton, Galloway, member of the Scots Charitable Society of Boston 1685. (NEHGS)

STEVEN, JAMES, born in Inch 1748, married Mary Dalrymple, emigrated from Stranraer to North Carolina on the Jackie 1774, Loyalist, sergeant of the Royal North Carolina Regiment ca1781, died in Robeson County, North Carolina, 1826. (NCSA.2.7)

STEVENSON, HAY, born in the Borders, merchant in New York 1783-, married Jessie Graham 29.7.1790, father of John Graham Stevenson, died 24.9.1799. (ANY.II.189)

STEWART, THOMAS, born in Dumfries 1777, architect in Augusta, Georgia, died in Camp Hope, Milledgeville, Georgia, 9.1826. (Georgia Republican 30.9.1826)

SWAN, JAMES, born in Dumfriesshire 1786, died in Savanna, Georgia, 26.8.1817. (Savanna Republican 26.8.1817)

TAIT, JOHN, born in Moffat 1809, son of William Tait and Catherine Beattie, educated at Glasgow University 1833, to New South Wales 1837, minister in Victoria and New South Wales 1837-1860, died 19.3.1860. (F.7.599)

TEMPLETON, HELEN, born in 1820, servant in Roxburghshire, arrived in Hobart, Tasmania, on the White Star 1855. (SRA.TD292)

THRESHIE, Major CAIRNS, son of Robert Threshie (1764-1836) died in Peshawur, India. (St Michael's Dumfries g/s)

THOMSON, ROBERT, born 1817, son of James Thomson, missionary in Tahiti, died 1.1.1854. (St Michael's Dumfries g/s)

TULLOH, THOMAS, Barrackpore, son of Robert Henry Tulloh of Ellieston, Roxburghshire, who died 22.12.1853. (SRO.SH.1855)

WALKER, JAMES, born in Legerwood 9.8.1838, son of Reverend John Hunter Walker, educated at Edinburgh University, minister of Channelkirk 1862-1885 then a farmer in British Columbia. (F.2.148)

WALKER, ROBERT, in St James parish, Jamaica, 1790. [SRO.RS.Wigton, 263]

WALKER, WILLIAM C., born in Dumfries 1823, merchant in New York by 1848, died at Hampstead, Long Island, 3.10.1873. (ANY.2.241)

WALLACE, ROBERT, born in Kirkpatrick-Durham, son of Reverend Robert Wallace and Elizabeth Smith, died in Mobile, Louisiana, 14.8.1867. (F.2.267)

WALLACE, DAVID LAMONT, born in Kirkpatrick-Durham 25.7.1826, son of Reverend Robert Wallace and Elizabeth Smith, merchant in New York, died in Louisville, Kentucky, 2.3.1895. (F.2.267)

WALLACE, GEORGE, born in Durisdeer 14.6.1831, son of Reverend George Wallace and Matilda Lennock, died in Otago, New Zealand, 24.9.1851. (F.2.314)

WALLACE, JAMES, born in Kirkpatrick-Durham 6.5.1828, son of Reverend Robert Wallace and Elizabeth Smith, merchant in USA, died 25.10.1887. (F.2.267)

WALLACE, WILFRED, born in Kirkpatrick-Durham 24.11.1824, son of Reverend Robert Wallace and Elizabeth Smith, merchant in New York, died 12.4.1893. (F.2.267)

WANLESS, ARCHIBALD, born in Roxburghshire 1798, saddler in Charleston, South Carolina, naturalised in South Carolina 11.10.1834. (US.NA.M1183.1)

WATSON, JAMES, Berwickshire, merchant in Jamaica 1769. (SRO.RS18.15.353)

WATSON, WILLIAM, son of James and Jane Watson in Duns, Berwickshire, planter in Baton Rouge, West Florida, pro 1781 South Carolina.

WELLS, JOHN, born in Dumfriesshire 1832, son of Robert Wells, educated at Glasgow University 1856, minister in New Brunswick 1861-. (F.7.612)

WHITE, JAMES, 24, farmer, wife Margaret, emigrated from Leith to Argentina on the Symmetry, master William Cochrane, 22.5.1825. (SSP18)

WHITE, WILLIAM, 22, farmer, wife Janet, and 1 child, emigrated from Leith to Argentina on the Symmetry, master William Cochrane, 22.5.1825. (SSP18)

WHITEWRIGHT, WILLIAM, born in Balmaghie, Kirkcudbrightshire, 8.7.1783, settled in New York by 1831, died there 8.5.1874. (ANY.2i.27)

WILLIAMSON, WILLIAM, born in Kirkmaiden-in-Rhinns 22.7.1849, son of Reverend William Williamson and Mary McDowall, settled in Detroit, USA. (F.2.342)

WOODHOUSE, ROBERT, Dalbeith, Galloway (?), merchant in Savanna, Georgia, died 1800, pro 10.7.1800 Chatham County, Georgia. (Will Book A)

WOTHERSPOON, JOHN, Writer to the Signet, in Australia, brother of Agnes Wotherspoon in Borgue, Kirkcudbrightshire. (SRO.SH.1857)

WOTHERSPOON, OSWALD, Sydney, brother of Agnes Wotherspoon in Borgue, Kirkcudbrightshire. (SRO.SH.1857)

WRIGHT, JAMES, Newton Stewart, Wigtownshire, emigrated from Sligo, Ireland, to New York on the Juno 16.8.1816. (NWI.2.368)

WRIGHT, ROBERT, born 4.9.1757, son of Reverend William Wright and Jean Allen, died in the West Indies. (F.2.294)

WYPER, JAMES, in Australia, son of Reverend William Wyper in Thornhill, and Janet Ann Hardie who died 19.5.1869. (SRO.SH.1881)

YAIR, ARCHIBALD MCDOUGALL, born in Eckford 30.12.1843, son of Reverend Joseph Yair and Helen McDougall, customs house officer in New York, died 6.7.1909. (F.2.111)

YAIR, JOSEPH, born in Eckford 20.1.1800, son of Reverend Joseph Yair and Helen McDougall, accountant in Canada. (F.2.111)

YOUNG, JAMES HUME, born in Eckford 11.10.1819, son of Reverend James Young and Marion Hume, missionary in Amoy, China, died in Musselburgh 2.1855. (F.2.111)

YOUNG, WILLIAM, Berwickshire, in Jamaica 1773. (SRO.RS18.16.222)

YOUNG, WILLIAM, born in Galloway 1799, settled in Charleston, South Carolina, naturalised in South Carolina 6.10.1830. (US.NA.M1183.1)

YULE, ARCHIBALD, late of the Dumfries Militia, resident in Path, Longtown, Cumberland, applied to settle in Canada 2.1827. (PRO.CO384.16.1E)

EMIGRANTS AND ADVENTURERS
from
Glasgow and the West of Scotland

INTRODUCTION

For nearly 400 years there has been a constant stream of emigrants leaving Glasgow and other ports in the west of Scotland for destinations overseas. In the early seventeenth century the majority were headed for the Plantation of Ulster, while a few were sailing to the continent and a handful to Nova Scotia. As transatlantic trade developed, the economic links led to settlement overseas, particularly along the American coast and in the West Indies. The Union of 1707 removed all restrictions on Scottish trade with the English colonies and soon Glasgow virtually monopolised the Tobacco Trade with the Chesapeake, this too led to further settlement in America. Within a generation Glasgow and Greenock became two of the most prominent ports in British intercontinental trade, soon becoming the main exit ports for Scots emigrants. While much of the emigration from the neighbourhood of Glasgow was by individuals or families there is an early example of a relatively large scale planned emigration. Under the auspices of the Scots America Company of Farmers based in Renfrewshire a Scots settlement was formed in Vermont prior to the American Revolution. After 1783 the British Government encouraged settlement in Canada. During the nineteenth century emigration from Scotland to Australasia rivalled that to North America. While the overall picture is well known there is little in print to identify individual emigrants or their specific places of settlement. This booklet, the first in a series, supplies some of the missing details.

David Dobson
St Andrews, 1994

REFERENCES

ARCHIVES
NEHGS   New England Historic Genealogical Society, Boston
          SCS - Scots Charitable Society MSS .B/S.36.v6
NJA   New Jersey Archives, Trenton
PRO   Public Record Office, London
          AO   Audit Office
          HCA   High Court of the Admiralty of England
          PCC   Prerogative Court of Canterbury
SRA   Strathclyde Regional Archives, Glasgow
SRO   Scottish Record Office, Edinburgh
          CS   Court of Session
          RD   Register of Deeds
          RS   Register of Sasines
          SH   Services of Heirs
USNA   United States National Archives, Washington

PUBLICATIONS
ANY   Biographical Register of the St Andrews Society of New York
          [A. McBean, N.Y. 1911]
BA   Officers of the Bengal Army [V.Hodson, London, 1927]
BLG   Burke's Landed Gentry, [Townsend, London, 1939]
Car.   Caribeanna, series [London, 1910]
CCNE   Colonial Clergy of New England, 1620-1776
          [F.L.Weis, Baltimore, 1977]
Col.Fams. Colonial Families of the United States,
          [G.N.MacKenzie, Baltimore, 1966]
EEC   Edinburgh Evening Courant
F   Fasti Ecclesiae Scoticanae [H.Scott, Edinburgh, 1920s]
HBRS   Hudson Bay Record Society publications, [London]
Laing   The Laing Charters, 854-1837 [Edinburgh 18
MAGU   The Matriculation Albums of Glasgow University, 1727-1858
          [W.I.Addison, Glasgow, 1913]
RGS   The Register of the Great Seal of Scotland, series, [Edinburgh]
SSA   Scots and Scots descendants in America [N.Y., 1917]

ABBREVIATIONS
cnf   confirmation of testament
g/s   gravestone inscription
pro   probate

EMIGRANTS AND ADVENTURERS FROM GLASGOW AND THE WEST OF SCOTLAND.
(PART ONE)

AIKEN, JOHN, Ayr, member of the Scots Charitable Society of Boston 1745. (NEHGS)

AIKMAN, WILLIAM, Glasgow, member of the Scots Charitable Society of Boston 1718. (NEHGS)

AINSLIE, HEW, born in Bargeny Mains, Ayrshire, to America 1822, author, died in Louisville, Kentucky, 1878. (SSA85)

AITKEN, JOHN, born in Cumbernauld 1806, merchant in New York, died there 6.1.1879. (ANY.2.272)

ALEXANDER, JOHN, Lanarkshire, married Margaret Glassen, emigrated via Ireland to Pennsylvania 1736. (VG35)

ALEXANDER, WILLIAM, Greenock, member of the Scots Charitable Society of Boston 1750. (NEHGS)

ALEXANDER, WILLIAM, Glasgow, member of the Scots Charitable Society of Boston 1758. (NEHGS)

ANDERSON, GILBERT, Crawfordjohn, member of the Scots Charitable Society of Boston 1767. (NEHGS)

ANDERSON, JAMES, Greenock, member of the Scots Charitable Society of Boston 1757. (NEHGS)

ANDERSON, JOHN, Glasgow, member of the Scots Charitable Society of Boston 1759. (NEHGS)

ARMOUR, SAMUEL, divinity student 1808, licenced by Glasgow Presbytry 3.12.1811, minister in Dunfermline, later in Doune and Dunblane 1813-1820, settled in Canada as an Episcopal minister. (OSC)

ARTHUR, ROBERT, Crawfordsdyke, member of the Scots Charitable Society of Boston 1731. (NEHGS)

AUCHINCLOSS, THOMAS, Glasgow, member of the Scots Charitable Society of Boston 1769. (NEHGS)

BAIN, ROBERT, born 1759 son of Archibald Bain farmer in Rhu and Jane Taylor, merchant in Norfolk, Virginia. (Gourock g/s)

BAIRD, HUGH, merchant in Rio de Janeiro, son of Thomas Baird, merchant in Kilmarnock. (SRO.SH.1845)

BAIRD, JOHN, born in Ayrshire 1730, army officer in Pennsylvania 1758-1760, married Catherine McLean 1755, died 1760. (Col.Fams.6.58)

BALLANTINE, JOHN, Ayr, member of the Scots Charitable Society of Boston 1687. (NEHGS)

BAN, JAMES, born in Glasgow 1812, planter in Charleston District, South Carolina, naturalised in South Carolina 3.2.1842. (US.NA.M1183.1)

BANNATYNE, FRANCIS, Glasgow, merchant in New Providence, Bahamas, pro 13.8.1760 New Providence

BAREY, JAMES, Glasgow, member of the Scots Charitable Society of Boston 1729. (NEHGS)

BARNHILL, JAMES, Crawfordykes, member of the Scots Charitable Society of Boston 1759. (NEHGS)

BARR, ALEXANDER, born in Glasgow, died in Georgia 1801. (Colonial Museum and Savanna Advertiser 11.12.1801)

BARR, JAMES, born in Kilbarchan 12.12.1752, settled in Ipswich, New Hampshire, 1773, married Molly Cummings (1764-1845) in 1783, died 7.3.1829. (Imm.NE.9)

BARR, ROBERT, merchant in Demerara, son of James Barr, merchant in Port Glasgow, 1803. (SRO.S/H)

BAXTER, ARCHIBALD, born in Greenock 1823, emigrated to New York 1856, died in Brooklyn 3.8.1886. (ANY.2.287)

BEGGS, THOMAS, born in Ayrshire 1770, merchant, died in Savanna, Georgia, 11.9.1806. (Savanna Death Register)

BELL, JAMES, Lanark, member of the Scots Charitable Society of Boston 1767. (NEHGS)

BELL, PATRICK, Glasgow, member of the Scots Charitable Society of Boston 1718. (NEHGS)

BELL, ROBERT, Glasgow, member of the Scots Charitable Society of Boston 1770. (NEHGS)

BELL, WILLIAM, born in Paisley, settled in Chester, New Hampshire, pre 1780, married Beatrice Barr from Glasgow, died 1817. (Imm.NE.12)

BIGGAR, WILLIAM, Glasgow, member of the Scots Charitable Society of Boston 1748. (NEHGS)

BIGGS, ARCHIBALD, Lesmahagow, Lanarkshire, settled in Elizabeth, Essex County, New Jersey, pro 9.4.1816. (NJA.10961 G)

BLACK, JOHN, born in Greenock 1810, carpenter in Charleston, South Carolina, naturalised in South Carolina 31.8.1832. (US.NA.M1183.1)

BLAIR, ROBERT, Kilbarchan, member of the Scots Charitable Society of Boston 1766. (NEHGS)

BLUE, JOHN, Glasgow, married Magdalene Claes in Delft, Netherlands, 7.5.1610. (Leiden Marriage Register, G.95)

BLYTH, ROBERT, Walhalla, Victoria, son of James Blyth, pit oversman in Dalry, Ayrshire, who died 29.4.1864. (SRO.SH.1881)

2

BOGLE, THOMAS, Glasgow, member of the Scots Charitable Society of
    Boston 1747. (NEHGS)
BORLAND, JOHN, merchant in Boston, New England, presently in London,
    1699. (SRO.RS42.XI.67)
BOUCHER, JAMES, Greenock, member of the Scots Charitable Society of
    Boston 1735. (NEHGS)
BOWMAN, SAMUEL, Glasgow, member of the Scots Charitable Society of
    Boston 1738. (NEHGS)
BOYD, ALEXANDER, educated at Glasgow University, minister, settled in
    Georgetown, Maine, 1748-1753, in Newcastle, Maine, 1754-1758.
    (CCNE)
BOYD, JAMES, Kilbride, Ayrshire, member of the Scots Charitable Society
    of Boston 1741. (NEHGS)
BOYD, JOHN, Ayrshire, member of the Scots Charitable Society of Boston
    1751. (NEHGS)
BOYD, JOHN, Ayrshire, then in Lisbon, Portugal. pro 1774 Edinburgh
BRASH, Reverend JOHN, born in Glasgow 26.6.1824, son of Reverend
    William Brash, educated at Glasgow University 1844, settled in New
    York 1854, died in South Amboy, New Jersey, 21.3.1881. (ANY.2.288)
BRENTON, THOMAS, goldsmith from Clydesdale, married Leonora Janszon
    from Antwerp in Rotterdam 9.9.1590.   (Rotterdam Marriage Register)
BRICE, NINIAN, Glasgow, member of the Scots Charitable Society of Boston
    1731. (NEHGS)
BROCK, WILLIAM, settled in Australia prior to 1856, son of Christina Brock
    in Dunoon. (SRO.SH.1856)
BROWN, ARCHIBALD, born in Paisley 1787, son of Robert Brown, farmer,
    educated at Glasgow University, to Demerara 1818, minister there
    1818-1824, died in Edinburgh 1826. (F.7.674)
BROWN, DUNCAN, Rothesay, arrived at Port Adelaide 1863.
    (SRO.NRAS.2365.DRI.36.6)
BROWN, HUGH, Glasgow, member of the Scots Charitable Society of Boston
    1746. (NEHGS)
BROWN, JOHN, Glasgow, member of the Scots Charitable Society of Boston
    1726. (NEHGS)
BROWN, JOHN, Glasgow, member of the Scots Charitable Society of Boston
    1738. (NEHGS)
BROWN, WILLIAM, Glasgow, member of the Scots Charitable Society of
    Boston 1763. (NEHGS)
BROWN, WILLIAM, born in Kilmaurs, Ayrshire, 1790, employee of the Hudson
    Bay Company, later Chief Trader, 1811-1827, died 19.3.1827.
    [(HBRS.1.431)(London, 1938)]
BRYCE, PATRICK, merchant in Glasgow, member of the Scots Charitable
    Society of Boston 1684. (NEHGS)

BUCHANAN, DAVID WILLIAM RAMSAY, in Pau, France, son of Andrew
Buchanan, Greenfield House, Shettleston, who died 12.8.1879.
(SRO.SH.1881)
BUCHANAN, JAMES, Glasgow, member of the Scots Charitable Society of
Boston 1729. (NEHGS)
BUCHANAN, WILLIAM, settled in Melbourne, Australia, prior to 1852, son of
Janet Black or Buchanan in Paisley then in Rutherglen. (SRO.SH.1852)
BUNTEN, ROBERT, settled in Australia before 1854, son of Robert Bunten,
iron merchant in Glasgow. (SRO.SH.1854)
BURNS, ALAN, born in Glasgow 18.9.1781, son of Reverend John Burns,
physician to the Russian Imperial Court, died 24.6.1813. (F.3.394)
CALDWELL, JAMES, born in Kilmarnock 1822, merchant in New York 1856,
died there 16.2.1862. (ANY.2.264)
CALDWELL, JOHN, manufacturer in Paisley, absconded to New York pre
1825. (SRO.CS236.Sed.Bk.1/7)
CAMERON, WILLIAM, Greenock, member of the Scots Charitable Society of
Boston 1731. (NEHGS)
CAMPBELL, CHARLES, Glasgow, HEICS surgeon, died in Sumatra 19.1.1808.
(EEC.3.9.1808)
CAMPBELL, JAMES, born in Glasgow 1776, cooper, died in Savanna, Georgia,
13.6.1810. (Savanna Death Register)
CAMPBELL, JOHN, merchant in Glasgow, member of the Scots Charitable
Society of Boston 1684. (NEHGS)
CAMPBELL, Captain ROBERT, born in Greenock 1776, died in Georgia 1818.
(Colonial Museum and Savanna Advertiser 1.4.1818)
CARENS, JOHN, Glasgow, indentured as a servant to William Moore in
Southwark 24.11.1772. (Records of Indentures in Philadelphia)
CARLILE, ALEXANDER, Glasgow, member of the Scots Charitable Society of
Boston 1744. (NEHGS)
CARMICHAEL, ROBERT, emigrated from Ayrshire to Pennsylvania 1800.
(BLG2603)
CARNEGIE, PATRICK, Glasgow, member of the Scots Charitable Society of
Boston 1750. (NEHGS)
CARRICK, JAMES, Glasgow, member of the Scots Charitable Society of
Boston 1747. (NEHGS)
CASWELL, MARGARET, born in Glasgow 1695, married Gowen Fulton,
settled in Topsham, Maine, died 1791. (Imm.NE)
CHALMERS, JAMES, Greenock, member of the Scots Charitable Society of
Boston 1757. (NEHGS)
CHAPMAN, DAVID, son of Daniel Chapman, manufacturer in Kirkintilloch,
educated at Glasgow University, minister of Girvan South 1860
-1872, died in Virginia 1893. (F.3.43)

CHARITY, JAMES, Glasgow, member of the Scots Charitable Society of
Boston 1762. (NEHGS)
CHRISTOWAL, EDWARD, soldier from Glasgow, married Catelincken de
Clerck near Middelburg, Netherlands, 14.2.1615. (Arnemuiden
Marriage Register)
CLARK, JOHN, Greenock, member of the Scots Charitable Society of Boston
1731. (NEHGS)
CLARK, JOHN, Greenock, member of the Scots Charitable Society of Boston
1737. (NEHGS)
CLARK, WILLIAM, Glasgow, member of the Scots Charitable Society of
Boston 1753. (NEHGS)
CLAYTON, THOMAS, Potterhill, Paisley, died 1.10.1793 at Poplar Grove,
Wilmington, South Carolina. [Gentleman's Magazine:63.1214]
CLYDE, DANIEL, born in Clydesdale 1683, via Ireland to New England 1730,
joiner, settled in Boston 9.9.1730, married Esther Rankin, died
6.1753. (Imm.N.E.35)
COCHRANE, WILLIAM, soldier from Glasgow, married Jakelijne Van Camme
from Bomene in Arnemuiden, Netherlands, 9.3.1614. (Arnemuiden
Marriage Register)
COCHRANE, WILLIAM, son of Captain Cochrane in Greenock, died in Quebec
1803. (Gentleman's Magazine.73.1254)
COLLINS, GRACE, seamstress in Paisley, arrived in Hobart, Tasmania, on
the Conway 14.10.1855. (SRA.TD292)
COLLINS, JOHN, born 1820, labourer in Paisley, arrived in Hobart,
Tasmania, on the Conway 14.10.1855. (SRA.TD292)
COLQUHOUN, JAMES, Glasgow, member of the Scots Charitable Society of
Boston 1759. (NEHGS)
COLVILLE, CHARLES, Ayrshire, member of the Scots Charitable Society of
Boston 1747. (NEHGS)
CORBETT, WILLIAM, Glasgow, member of the Scots Charitable Society of
Boston 1756. (NEHGS)
COULTER, HUGH, Glasgow, member of the Scots Charitable Society of
Boston 1747. (NEHGS)
CRAGG, THOMAS, Glasgow, pro 11.7.1718 Barbados. (RB6.4.342)
CRAIGE, ROBERT, Irvine, member of the Scots Charitable Society of Boston
1748. (NEHGS)
CRAWFORD, DAVID, Greenock, member of the Scots Charitable Society of
Boston 1735. (NEHGS)
CRAWFORD, JAMES, Glasgow, member of the Scots Charitable Society of
Boston 1733. (NEHGS)
CRAWFORD, JAMES, Glasgow, member of the Scots Charitable Society of
Boston 1750. (NEHGS)

CRAWFORD, JOHN, merchant in Ayr, member of the Scots Charitable
Society of Boston 1684. (NEHGS)
CRAWFORD, JOHN, son of John Crawford merchant in Ayr, member of the
Scots Charitable Society of Boston 1684. (NEHGS)
CRAWFORD, JOHN, Glasgow, member of the Scots Charitable Society of
Boston 1757. (NEHGS)
CRAWFORD, JOHN, farmer in Bullanto, Victoria, greatgrandson of John
Crawford in Paisley, and his wife Jean Whyte who died 15.1.1829.
(SRO.SH.1881)
CRAWFORD, MATTHEW, Glasgow, member of the Scots Charitable Society
of Boston 1700. (NEHGS)
CRAWFORD, ROBERT, Glasgow, member of the Scots Charitable Society of
Boston 1750. (NEHGS)
CUMMING, MATTHEW, ba.20.12.1693, son of Mathew Cumming and Mary Muir
in Glasgow, member of the Scots Charitable Society of Boston 1719.
(NEHGS)
CUMMING, ROBERT, Port Glasgow, member of the Scots Charitable Society
of Boston 1689. (NEHGS)
CUNNINGHAM, ALEXANDER, of Blook, scholar, son of Reverend John
Cunningham of Blook and Elizabeth Cunningham, died at The Hague
12.1730. (F.3.25)
CUNNINGHAM, JOHN, Glasgow, member of the Scots Charitable Society of
Boston 1734. (NEHGS)
CUNNINGHAM, THOMAS, Kilmarnock, member of the Scots Charitable
Society of Boston 1732. (NEHGS)
CUNNINGHAM, WILLIAM, Glasgow, member of the Scots Charitable Society
of Boston 1747. (NEHGS)
CURRIE, GILBERT E., born in Glasgow 31.12.1818, to USA 1853, publisher in
New York, died in Brooklyn 22.11.1882. (ANY.2.295)
CURRIE, WALTER, Glasgow, member of the Scots Charitable Society of
Boston 1756. (NEHGS)
DANIELS, WILLIAM, soldier from Glasgow, married ... Willetson (?) from
Perth, in Delft, Netherlands, 9.11.1605. (Delft Marriage Register)
DAVIDSON, WILLIAM, born in Kilmarnock, died in Georgia 14.12.1801.
(Colonial Museum and Savanna Advertiser 18.12.1801)
DEWAR, JOHN, merchant in Glasgow, emigrated to America ca. 1827.
(SRO.CS44.1827.Johnstone)
DICKSON, JOHN, born 1830, blacksmith in Lanarkshire, arrived in Hobart,
Tasmania, on the Donald McKay 6.9.1855. (SRA.TD292)
DICKY, JOHN, Ayrshire, member of the Scots Charitable Society of Boston
1751. (NEHGS)

DONALDSON, JOHN, born near Glasgow 1801, emigrated to America 1820, settled in Rochester, New York, 1837, married Jeanette Brownlee from Edinburgh. (NCSA.2.64)

DOUGALL, JOHN, born in Paisley 18.5.1786, fourth child of Duncan Dougall and Janet Gemmell, married Margaret Yool in Paisley 1812, manufacturer and merchant in Paisley, father of John and James, emigrated to Canada 1828, died in Montreal 28.8.1836. ["James Dougall of Glasgow and his descendents" (Ann Arbor, 1973)]

DOUGALL, MARY, born in Paisley 17.12.1781, third daughter of Duncan Dougall and Janet Gemmell, married Archibald Young in Paisley 1803, mother of Janet, Archibald, Margaret, James, Duncan, Mary, Bertram, and Jane, emigrated to Ontario 1820, died in Phimpton, Lambton County, Ontario, 24.9.1870. [("James Dougall of Glasgow and his Descendents" (Ann Arbor, 1973)]

DRAFFIN, Mrs MARY, born 1813, housekeeper in Ayrshire, arrived in Hobart, Tasmania, on the Conway 14.10.1855. (SRA.TD292)

DRAFFIN, SAMUEL, born 1839, labourer in Ayrshire, arrived in Hobart, Tasmania, on the Conway 14.10.1855. (SRA.TD292)

DUNCAN, ANDREW, Glasgow, merchant in Worcester, Massachusetts, 1768, Loyalist, died 1787. (PRO.AO13.24.72)

DUNCAN, DONALD, son of James Duncan (died 1823) merchant in Greenock, died in St Louis on the Mississippi. (Greenock g/s)

DUNCAN, ROBERT, Glasgow, member of the Scots Charitable Society of Boston 1759. (NEHGS)

DUNCAN, GEORGE, emigrated from Glasgow to New York, married Catherine Wetmore 11.9.1802, merchant in New York, died there 30.1.1812. [ANY.I.392]

DUNDAS, ALEXANDER, Greenock, member of the Scots Charitable Society of Boston 1747. (NEHGS)

DUNLOP, JAMES, Irvine, member of the Scots Charitable Society of Boston 1738. (NEHGS)

DUNLOP, WILLIAM, Glasgow, member of the Scots Charitable Society of Boston 1744. (NEHGS)

DUNLOP, WILLIAM, Glasgow, member of the Scots Charitable Society of Boston 1751. (NEHGS)

EDMISTON, JOHN, born in Glasgow 2.3.1828, merchant in New York, died in Bloomfield, New Jersey, 28.1.1895. (ANY.2.284)

EDMONDS, JAMES, born in Govan 1794, died in Georgia 2.11.1821. (Augusta Herald 6.11.1821)

ELLIS, AGNES, born 1828, servant in Glasgow, arrived in Hobart, Tasmania, on the Conway 14.10.1855. (SRA.TD292)

ELLIS, GEORGE, born 1840, farm labourer in Lanarkshire, arrived in Hobart, Tasmania, on the Wellington 26.11.1855. (SRA.TD292)

ELLIS, JANE, born 1819, servant in Lanarkshire, arrived in Hobart, Tasmania, on the Wellington 26.11.1855. (SRA.TD292)

ELLIS, JOHN, born 1819, farm labourer in Lanarkshire, arrived in Hobart, Tasmania, on the Wellington 26.11.1855. (SRA.TD292)

ERSKINE, EBENEZER, Glasgow, settled in New Jersey, pro 19.8.1785 New Jersey. (NJA.Lib 27.55)

ESSON, ROBERT, Greenock, member of the Scots Charitable Society of Boston 1766. (NEHGS)

EWING, JAMES, Glasgow, member of the Scots Charitable Society of Boston 1748. (NEHGS)

EWING, ROBERT, born in Glasgow 1796, died in Georgia 18.7.1824. (Georgia Republican 27.7.1824)

EWING, WILLIAM, born in the Vale of Leven 1785, educated at Glasgow University, tutor in Virginia - 50 years in USA, died in Glasgow 27.4.1865. (Bonhill g/s)

FACHRIE, JAMES, born in Greenock 1773, ship's captain, died in Savanna, Georgia, 17.7.1809. (Savanna Death Register)

FARQUHAR, JAMES, born 1742, son of Dr William Farquhar in Gilmilnescroft, Ayr, emigrated to New York by 1757, merchant and shipmaster there, married Elizabeth Curson 15.9.1774, died in New York 21.10.1831. [ANY.I.232]

FARQUHAR, WILLIAM, son of James Gilmilnescroft, Ayrshire, and Jean Portersfield, to America as an army surgeon, married (2) Jane Colden 1759, physician in New York and New Jersey, Loyalist, died 2.5.1787. [ANY.I.10]

FARLEY, EDWARD, Glasgow, settled in America 1826. (BLG2679)

FERGUSON, MARTIN PATERSON, born 16.6.1826, son of John Ferguson, merchant in Kilmarnock, and Elizabeth Muir, minister in Argentina 1862-, died 2.9.1906. (F.7.681)

FERRY, JOHN, Irvine, member of the Scots Charitable Society of Boston 1748. (NEHGS)

FERSEY, JOHN, Glasgow, soldier, married Aechtgen Touprounne in Schiedam, Netherlands, 22.10.1639. (Schiedam Marriage Register)

FINNEY, ANDREW, Greenock, member of the Scots Charitable Society of Boston, 1732. (NEHGS)

FISHER, ARCHIBALD, Glasgow, member of the Scots Charitable Society of Boston 1758. (NEHGS)

FLEMING, JOHN STUART, in New Zealand, grandson of Andrew Fleming, weaver in Flemington, Strathaven, who died 1816. (SRO.SH.1881)

FLEMING, JOHN STUART, in Nelson, New Zealand, son of Andrew Fleming, weaving agent in Strathaven who died 14.2.1850. (SRO.SH.1880)

FLEMING, JOHN STUART, in Nelson, NewZealand, nephew of Jean Fleming
(widow of Thomas Reid, manufacturer in Glasgow) who died
16.10.1880. (SRO.SH.1880)
FRASER, JAMES, born in Greenock 1759, died in Darien, Georgia,
18.12.1828. (Georgia Republican 29.12.1828)
FULLERTON, G., Ayrshire, merchant in Charleston, South Carolina, pro
3.1.1709 South Carolina.
FULLERTON, ALEXANDER, born 1825, sawyer in Ayrshire, arrived in Hobart,
Tasmania, on the Conway 14.10.1855. (SRA.TD292)
GALBRAITH, ARCHIBALD, Glasgow, member of the Scots Charitable Society
of Boston 1758. (NEHGS)
GAMBLE, WILLIAM, Glasgow, emigrated via Ireland to America 1800,
settled in Ohio. (BLG2698)
GARDNER, ARCHIBALD, Glasgow, member of the Scots Charitable Society of
Boston 1743. (NEHGS)
GARDNER, ROBERT, Irvine, member of the Scots Charitable Society of
Boston 1719. (NEHGS)
GARDNER, ROBERT, wigmaker in Glasgow, settled in Boston, Massachusetts
by 1729. (Imm.NE.67)
GEBBIE, FRANCIS, born in Galston, Ayrshire, 3.5.1831, son of James Gebbie,
farmer, and Ellen Smith, educated at Glasgow University, minister in
Argentina 1857-1883, died in Edinburgh 1918. (F.7.681)
GIBSON, JAMES, born 1753 in Paisley, son of William Gibson a shoemaker,
emigrated to America by 1790, an accountant and merchant in New
York, married Jean Morrison, Orange County, New York, died
20.9.1816. [ANY.I.276]
GIBSON, JOHN CAMPBELL, born in Kingston, Glasgow, son of Reverend
James Gibson, missionary in Swatow, China, died in Glasgow
25.11.1919. (F.3.419)
GILLIES, ROBERT MACLAURIN, born in Glasgow 1.4.1750, son of Reverend
John Gillies, merchant in Jamaica, died 3.1.1778. (F.3.399)
GLAISTER, ROBERT, born in Greenock 1771, ship's captain, died in Savanna,
Georgia, 8.10.1806. (Savanna Death Register)
GLASSFORD, JAMES, Glasgow, member of the Scots Charitable Society of
Boston 1763. (NEHGS)
GLENN, DAVID, Ayrshire, married Ann Boyle 1795, to America 1819,
settled in Vevay, Switzerland County, Indiana, died 1822. (BLG2707)
GLEN, JOHN FRANCIS GARDNER, in Port Elizabeth, Cape of Good Hope, son of
John Glen, engraver in Alexandria, who died 24.7.1852.
(SRO.SH.1880)
GOULD, JOHN, Renfrewshire, member of the Scots Charitable Society of
Boston 1769. (NEHGS)

9

GOURLIE, WILLIAM, Old Monklands, Lanarkshire, member of the Scots
    Charitable Society of Boston 1766. (NEHGS)
GOVAN, DONALD, merchant in Glasgow, admitted as a burgess and
    guildsbrother of Glasgow 25.9.1673 by right of father Donald Govan
    merchant burgess, member of the Scots Charitable Society of
    Boston 1684. (NEHGS)
GOW, ANDREW, Glasgow, merchant in Charleston, South Carolina, 1798.
    (Virginia Magazine of History and Biography: 6.135)
GRAHAME, ALEXANDER, Glasgow, member of the Scots Charitable Society
    of Boston 1747. (NEHGS)
GRAHAM, ALEXANDER, born 1769, M.D. in Glasgow, emigrated via Ireland to
    New York on the Eagle, master Andrew Riker, 27.8.1803.
GRAHAM, NIGEL CARLYLE, born in Glasgow 15.6.1881, son of Reverend
    Henry Graham, died in Egypt 12.11.1909. (F.3.417)
GRAHAM, WILLIAM, born in Lochmaben 14.5.1859, son of John Graham and
    Mary White, educated at Edinburgh University, minister in
    Newfoundland 1887-1895, in Jamaica 1896-, died 1922. (F.7.669)
GRANT, Mrs ANNE MCVICAR, born in Glasgow 1755, American author, died
    1838. (SSA84)
GRANT, JOHN, born 1834, boilersmith in Lanarkshire, arrived in Hobart,
    Tasmania, on the Donald McKay 6.9.1855. (SRA.TD292)
GRAY, ANDREW, Glasgow, member of the Scots Charitable Society of
    Boston 1758. (NEHGS)
GRAY, WILLIAM, Glasgow, member of the Scots Charitable Society of
    Glasgow 1747. (NEHGS)
GREENLAW, JOHN, Calder near Glasgow, member of the Scots Charitable
    Society of Boston 1762. (NEHGS)
GREGG, JAMES, born 1690 in Ayrshire, via County Antrim to New England
    1718, settled in Londonderry, New Hampshire, married Janet Cargill.
    (Imm.N.E.78)
GUTHRIE, JOHN, possibly from Kilmarnock, Ensign of the East India
    Company in Bengal 1774. (SRO.S/H)
GUY, ROBERT CUNNINGHAM, born in Johnstone 24.4.1862, son of John Guy,
    educated at Glasgow University, minister in Kingston, Jamaica, 1886
    1888, journalist and teacher in Kingston, Jamaica, died in Glasgow
    1916. (F.7.669)
HAMILTON, ARCHIBALD, probably from Avondale, Lanarkshire, a merchant
    in Russia 1655. (RGS.X.374)
HAMILTON, ARCHIBALD, Glasgow, member of the Scots Charitable Society
    of Boston 1748. (NEHGS)
HAMILTON, BERBEL, from Clydesdale, married Adam Peters born in
    "Edendij" Scotland, in Arnemuiden, Netherlands, 11.5.1630.
    (Arnemuiden Marriage Register)

10

HAMILTON, JAMES, Glasgow, member of the Scots Charitable Society of
Boston 1699. (NEHGS)
HAMILTON, JAMES, Glasgow, member of the Scots Charitable Society of
Boston 1755. (NEHGS)
HAMILTON, JOHN, possibly the son of Alexander Hamilton in Ayrshire, and
brother of James Hamilton in the West Indies, emigrated to New
England 1717, settled in Pelham, Massachusetts, then in Shutesbury,
Connecticut. (Imm.NE.81)
HAMILTON, PATRICK, born in Glasgow 6.9.1757, son of Reverend John
Hamilton and Mary Bogle, died in Jamaica 15.1.1788. (F.3.458)
HAMILTON, ROBERT, Glasgow, member of the Scots Charitable Society of
Boston 1742. (NEHGS)
HARVEY, WILLIAM, Glasgow, member of the Scots Charitable Society of
Boston 1751. (NEHGS)
HASTIE, JAMES, Greenock, member of the Scots Charitable Society of
Boston 1743. (NEHGS)
HENDERSON, WILLIAM, emigrated from Glasgow to Dover, New Hampshire,
1650, ship's carpenter and builder. (Anc.H-NE)
HENIE, Mrs JANE, born in Ayrshire 1777, died in Georgia 5.10.1815.
(Georgia g/s)
HENIE, WILLIAM, born in Glasgow 1784, mariner, died in Savanna, Georgia,
11.7.1808. (Savanna Death Register)
HENRY, WILLIAM, Greenock, member of the Scots Charitable Society of
Boston 1735. (NEHGS)
HODGES, JAMES, Greenock, member of the Scots Charitable Society of
Boston 1732. (NEHGS)
HOUSTOUN, PATRICK, Glasgow, member of the Scots Charitable Society of
Boston 1750. (NEHGS)
HUME, JAMES, Glasgow, member of the Scots Charitable Society of Boston
1741. (NEHGS)
HUNTER, ANDREW, born in Glasgow 1777, cotton machine maker, died in
Savanna, Georgia, 16.8.1807. (Savanna Death Register)
HUNTER, DAVID, Ayrshire, member of the Scots Charitable Society of
Boston 1742. (NEHGS)
HUNTER, JAMES, Greenock, member of the Scots Charitable Society of
Boston 1738. (NEHGS)
HUNTER, NATHANIEL, Irvine, member of the Scots Charitable Society of
Boston 1762. (NEHGS)
HYNDMAN, JOHN, Greenock, member of the Scots Charitable Society of
Boston 1730. (NEHGS)
IMBRIE, JAMES, born in Paisley 1780, son of Reverend James Imbrie,
settled in Philadelphia 1805, died 30.5.1835. (BLG2761)

ISAAC, ROBERT, born in Glasgow 1780, died in Georgia 16.10.1827. (Georgia g/s)(Georgia Republican 16.10.1827)

JACOBSON, STEVEN, soldier from Clydesdale, married Leentgen Jansdaughter in Leiden, Netherlands, 1.9.1576. (Leiden Marriage Register, A.38)

JAMIESON, ALEXANDER, son of Reverend Alexander Jamieson in Govan, died in the West Indies pre 1706. (F.3.412)

JAMIESON, ROBERT, Gourock, member of the Scottish Charitable Society of Boston 1759. (NEHGS)

JAMIESON, ROBERT, born in Glasgow 20.1.1851, son of Reverend Robert Jamieson and Eliza Jamieson, died in Canada 7.5.1891. (F.3.464)

JOHNSTON, DAVID, manufacturer in Glasgow, emigrated to America 1816. (SRO.CS36.17.88)

JOHNSTON, JOHN YUILL, in Pietermaritzburg, Natal, son of John Johnston, farmer in Cambusnethan, who died 9.4.1863. (SRO.SH.1881)

KELSO, ROBERT, Greenock, member of the Scots Charitable Society of Boston 1732. (NEHGS)

KENNEDY, HUGH, ba.1.11.1768, son of Daniel Kennedy and Mary Brodie in Glasgow, died in Philadelphia 1803. [Gentleman's Magazine:73.86]

KILLOCH, WILLIAM, Crawforddyke, Renfrewshire, member of the Scots Charitable Society of Boston 1762. (NEHGS)

KINLOCH, CHRISTINA, born 1842, daughter of John Kinloch and Ann David, died in Patterson, New Jersey, 17.2.1881. (Alexandria g/s)

KNOX, ALEXANDER, born in Paisley 1807, manufacturer in New York 1827, died there 29.10.1892. (ANY.2.24)

KNOX, MARY, born 1769 in Paisley, emigrated via Greenock to USA, naturalised 22.12.1830 in New York.

KNOX, THOMAS, Saltcoats, member of the Scots Charitable Society of Boston 1756. (NEHGS)

LAING, JAMES, Paisley, settled in Sydney pre 1881. (SRO.SH.1881)

LAMONT, DUNCAN, born in Greenock 31.10.1792, merchant in New York by 1851, died in Brooklyn 13.2.1865. (ANY.2.259)

LANG, JOHN, born in Glasgow 9.1.1808, son of Gilbert Lang and Elizabeth McFie, Colonel of the 36th Bengal Native Infantry, died in London 10.3.1882. (BA.3.14)

LANG, WILLIAM, Glasgow, member of the Scots Charitable Society of Boston 1759. (NEHGS)

LAURIE, JOHN, son of Reverend James Laurie (died 1764) and Ann Ord in Kirkmichael, Ayrshire, Governor of the Mosquito Shore. (F.3.45)

LEE, ALLEN, born in Paisley 1777, emigrated via Grenock to USA, gardener, naturalised 18.2.1817 in New York.

LEES, ROBERT, Glasgow, member of the Scots Charitable Society of Boston 1740. (NEHGS)

LEIPER, THOMAS, born in Strathaven, Lanarkshire, 1745, merchant in
Philadelphia, died 1825. (SSA40)
LEITCH, THOMAS, born 1836, cutler in Renfrew, arrived in Hobart,
Tasmania, on the Conway 14.10.1855. (SRA.TD292)
LENNIE, DUNCAN, born 1814, son of Robert Lennie merchant in Glasgow,
educated at Glasgow University, minister in Tobago 1837-1844, died
in Northumberland 12.12.1858. (F.7.671)
LENNOX, JAMES, born 1790, son of Alexander Lennox and Helen Wilson in
Helensburgh, surgeon in Jamaica, died 15.9.1814. (Rhus g/s)
LOCKHART, RICHARD DICKSON, born in Glasgow 31.3.1807, son of Reverend
John Lockhart and Elizabeth Gibson, Ensign of the 68th Bengal Native
Infantry, drowned at Sandoway, Arakan, 27.12.1826. (BA.3.72)
LOCKHART, WILLIAM, born in Cambusnethan 28.9.1787, son of Reverend
John Lockhart and Elizabeth Dinwiddie, Brevet Captain of the 17th
Bengal Native Infantry, died in Milton Lockhart 25.11.1856.
(BA.3.72)
LOGAN, WALTER, New Kilpatrick, near Glasgow, member of the Scots
Charitable Society of Boston 1762. (NEHGS)
LORIMER, ALEXANDER GORDON, born 1843, son of Reverend John Gordon
Lorimer and Jane Campbell, missionary at Gordon Memorial, Natal,
died 19.1.1900. (F.3.440)
LORIMER, DAVID, Glasgow, member of the Scots Charitable Society of
Boston 1749. (NEHGS)
LOWRIE, JAMES, Irvine, member of the Scots Charitable Society of
Boston 1771. (NEHGS)
LYON, JOHN, Greenock, member of the Scots Charitable Society of
Boston 1740. (NEHGS)
MACADAM, JAMES, born in Maybole 20.4.1809, son of John MacAdam and
Janet Blane, Lieutenant Colonel 33rd Native Infantry, Bengal, died in
England 13.3.1888. (BA.3.104)
MACALESTER, Reverend JOHN, Arran, member of the Scots Charitable
Society of Boston 1737. (NEHGS)
MCALPIN, ARCHIBALD, born in Glasgow 1772, settled in South Carolina and
then Georgia, died in Savanna, Georgia, 1822. ("Georgia for the
Country, Savanna" 28.9.1822)
MCALPIN, WALTER, Glasgow, member of the Scots Charitable Society of
Boston 1744. (NEHGS)
MCALPINE, WILLIAM, Greenock, printer in Boston 1753, member of the
Scots Charitable Society of Boston 1755, died in Glasgow 1788.
(NEHGS)(Imm.NE.118)
MCARTHUR, JOHN, Dunoon, member of the Scots Charitable Society of
Boston 1743. (NEHGS)

MCAUSLINE, DUNCAN, Greenock, member of the Scots Charitable Society
of Boston 1748. (NEHGS)
MACBETH, JAMES, born in Dalrymple 1810, son of James MacBeth surgeon
in Newton on Ayr, to America 1850. (F.3.422)
MCCAUL, JOHN, son of John McCaul merchant in Glasgow, educated at
Glasgow University 1799 and at Oxford 1810, merchant in St Croix,
died in Cane Valley, St Croix, 16.3.1860. (Car.4.79)
MCCLINTOCK, WILLIAM, Glasgow, member of the Scots Charitable
Society of Boston 1758. (NEHGS)
MCCLURE, WILLIAM, born in St Quivox, Ayrshire, 1800, son of William
McClure schoolmaster, educated at Glasgow University, minister in
Nassau, Bahamas, 1837-1863, died 10.3.1863. (F.7.666)
MCCREDIE, ANDREW, born in Ayrshire 1757, son of William McCredie of
Pierceton and Barbara Wilson, shipmaster and merchant in Savanna,
Georgia, died in Savanna 17.4.1807. (Savanna Death Register)
(ANY.I.338)(Colonial Museum and Savanna Advertiser 24.4.1807)
MCCULLOCH, ALEXANDER, Ayr, member of the Scots Charitable Society
of Boston 1691. (NEHGS)
MCCULLOCH, JOHN, Glasgow, member of the Scots Charitable Society of
Boston 1727. (NEHGS)
MCCULLOCH, THOMAS, Ayr, member of the Scots Charitable Society of
Boston 1691. (NEHGS)
MCCUN, ARCHIBALD, Greenock, member of the Scots Charitable Society
of Boston 1748. (NEHGS)
MCCUN, JOHN, Greenock, member of the Scots Charitable Society of
Boston 1747. (NEHGS)
MCCUNN, WILLIAM, Glasgow, member of the Scots Charitable Society of
Boston 1743. (NEHGS)
MCDONALD, CATHERINE, Port Glasgow, indentured with Francis Lee in
Philadelphia 9.10.1772. (Records of Indentures in Philadelphia)
MACDONALD, FRANCIS, born in Helensburgh 1825, settled in New York
1848, shipping agent, died on Staten Island 7.11.1878. (ANY.2.279)
MCDONALD, JOHN, Port Glasgow, indentured with Alexander Bartram in
Philadelphia 9.10.1772. (Records of Indentures in Philadelphia)
MCDOWALL, JAMES, son of William McDowall of Castle Semple, educated at
Glasgow University 1764, died in St Lucia 30.5.1808. (Car.4.15)
MCDOWAL, WILLIAM, Greenock, member of the Scots Charitable Society
of Boston 1767. (NEHGS)
MCEWEN, ALEXANDER ROY, born in Glasgow 16.1.1828, son of James
McEwen, educated at Glasgow University 1844, settled in New York
1853, died in Brooklyn 12.11.1860. (ANY.2.300)
MACFARLANE, JAMES, born in Arrochar 1820, tannery manager in La Porte,
Pennsylvania, died there 10.9.1914. (ANY.2.284)

MACFARLANE, PARLAN, son of Thomas MacFarlane in Pollockshaws, to America 1820s, Indian trader in St Paul, Minnesota, died 1874. [The History of the Clan MacFarlane; D.J.Clark, Glasgow, 1922)

MCGILCHRIST, WILLIAM, born in Inchinnan 1707, son of James McGilchrist, educated at Balliol College, Oxford, 1735, clergyman in Charleston, South Carolina, 1741-1745, Salem, New England, 1747-1780, died 19.4.1780. (CCNE)

MACGOMERY, PETER, Glasgow, member of the Scots Charitable Society of Boston 1748. (NEHGS)

MCHENRY, ROBERT, born in Glasgow, died in Darien, Georgia, 7.9.1822. ("Georgia for the Country, Savanna" 10.9.1822)

MCHUTCHESON, WILLIAM, born in Renfrew 1827, son of James McHutcheson a merchant, educated at Glasgow University, minister of Banton, emigrated to New Zealand 1857, died in Arrowtown, New Zealand, 2.2.1904. (F.3.371)

MCILVAINE, WILLIAM, born in Ayrshire 1722, married Anne Emerson, to America 1745, died 1770. (BLG2869)

MCILWRAITH, MARGARET, daughter of John McIlwraith and Susanna Boag, wife of Duncan McGown, died in Alma Township, Peel, Canada West, 30.6.1871. (Greenock g/s)

MCILWRAITH, ROBERT, born 1756, Greenock, merchant, died in Tobago 1.1798. (Inverkip g/s)

MACINTOSH, GEORGE MORRIS, clerk in Rangoon, son of Thomas MacIntosh, cashier in Glasgow, who died 18.6.1881. (SRO.SH.1881)

MCIVER, JOHN, Greenock, settled in Columbia, South Carolina, ca1820, died in Alabama 25.5.1833. ("Telescope" 18.6.1833)

MCKAY, AGNES, Glasgow, indentured with David Evans in Philadelphia 9.10.1772. (Records of Indentures in Philadelphia)

MCKAY, ALEXANDER, Glasgow, indentured with William Richmond in Philadelphia 9.10.1772. (Records of Indentures in Philadelphia)

MCKAY, ANGUS, Port Glasgow, indentured with Patrick Ewing in Little Britain township, Lancaster County, Pennsylvania, 8.10.1772. (Records of Indentures in Philadelphia)

MCKAY, ANN, indentured with Samuel Preston Moore in Philadelphia 23.10.1772. (Records of Indentures in Philadelphia)

MCKAY, ANNA, Glasgow, indentured with William Falconer in Philadelphia 12.10.1772. (Records of Indentures in Philadelphia)

MCKAY, CATHERINE, Glasgow, indentured with Isaac Eyre in Chester, Chester County, Pennsylvania, 9.10.1772. (Records of Indentures in Philadelphia)

MCKAY, CATHERINE, Glasgow, indentured with John Murray in Philadelphia 10.10.1772. (Records of Indentures in Philadelphia)

MCKAY, DONALD, Port Glasgow, indentured with Patrick Ewing in Little
Britain township, Lancaster County, Pennsylvania, 8.10.1772.
(Records of Indentures in Philadelphia)
MCKAY, ISABELLA, Glasgow, indentured with Elizabeth Sharpe in
Pittsgrove, Salem County, West New Jersey, 21.10.1772. (Records of
Indentures in Philadelphia)
MCKAY, JAMES, Port Glasgow, indentured with Patrick Ewing in Little
Britain township, Lancaster County, Pennsylvania, 8.10.1772.
(Records of Indentures in Philadelphia)
MCKAY, JEAN, Port Glasgow, indentured with Patrick Ewing in Little
Britain township, Lancaster County, Pennsylvania, 8.10.1772.
(Records of Indentures in Philadelphia)
MACKAY, JOHN, Kilmarnock, member of the Scots Charitable Society of
Boston 1774. (NEHGS)
MCKAY, JOHN, Glasgow, indentured with John Grant in Burlington, West
New Jersey, 9.10.1772. (Records of Indentures in Philadelphia)
MCKAY, MARGARET, Glasgow, indentured with John Elmsley in Philadelphia
9.10.1772. (Records of Indentures in Philadelphia)
MCKAY, SANDIE, Port Glasgow, indentured with Patrick Ewing in Little
Britain township, Lancaster County, Pennsylvania, 8.10.1772.
(Records of Indentures in Philadelphia)
MCKAY, WILLIAM, Port Glasgow, indented as a servant to Patrick Ewing,
Little Britain Township, Lancaster County, Pennsylvania, 8.10.1772.
(Records of Indentures in Philadelphia)
MCKEAN, WILLIAM, Glasgow, tobacconist, Charles Wharf, North End, Boston,
Massachusetts, 1764. (ImmNE.134); admitted to the Scots
Charitable Society of Boston 1767. (NEHGS)
MACKENZIE, ALEXANDER, Glasgow, mercantile agent in Charleston, South
Carolina, Nassau and New York, ca 1802. (SRO.CS238.L655)
MCKENZIE, ANDREW, Glasgow, member of the Scots Charitable Society
of Boston 1748. (NEHGS)
MCKENZIE, ANDREW, merchant in Dominica then in Glasgow 1792.
(SRO.RD3.274.826)
MCLACHLAN, HUGH, of Cameron, merchant in Kingston, Jamaica, then
Glasgow, 1756. (SRO.S/H)
MCLEAN, JOHN, Irvine, member of the Scots Charitable Society of
Boston 1748. (NEHGS)
MCLEAN, JOHN, son of John McLean merchant in Glasgow, educated at
Glasgow University 1794, died at the Bay of Honduras 14.3.1806.
(MAGU176)
MCLEAN, PATRICK, born in Gorbals 25.4.1807, son of Reverend James
McLean, merchant in Buenos Ayres, died 3.2.1855. (F.3.1855)

MCLEAN, ROBERT CRAWFORD, born in Gorbals 21.8.1811, son of Reverend James McLean, merchant in Monte Video and in Manchester, died 29.4.1870. (F.3.409)

MCLEISH, JOHN, Irvine, member of the Scots Charitable Society of Boston 1726. (NEHGS)

MACLEOD, NORMAN, born in Barony parish, Glasgow, 3.10.1853, son of Reverend Norman MacLeod, journalist, emigrated to USA, died in Chicago 4.1897. (F.3.394)

MCLURE, WILLIAM, born in Ayr 1763, settled in Philadelphia 1796, merchant and geologist, died 1840. (SSA78)

MCMICHAEL, JAMES, born in Muirkirk 1772, son of George McMichael, emigrated to Pennsylvania 1793, settled in Townsend, Norfolk County, Ontario, 1820, died 9.9.1821. (BLG2748)

MACNAIR, THOMAS MAXWELL, born in Glasgow 13.1.1827, son of Mathew MacNair and Mary Wallace, to USA 1849, merchant in New York, died in Brooklyn 26.6.1911. (ANY.2.300)

MACNAUGHTON, WILLIAM, born in Paisley 8.11.1820, fur trader in New York, died in Brooklyn 6.2.1879. (ANY.2.279)

MCNEIL, JOHN, Bute, member of the Scots Charitable Society of Boston 1733. (NEHGS)

MCTAGGART, JOHN, Irvine, member of the Scots Charitable Society of Boston 1734. (NEHGS)

MCWHORTER, JOHN, Strathyre, Ayrshire, member of the Scots Charitable Society of Boston 1770. (NEHGS)

MAIN, JAMES, Glasgow, member of the Scots Charitable Society of Boston 1747. (NEHGS)

MAIN, WILLIAM, Glasgow, indentured servant, emigrated from Glasgow to New York on the Commerce, Captain Nicholls, absconded 22.6.1774. (New York Gazette and Weekly Mercury 27.6.1774)

MALCOLM, ANDREW, Ayr, member of the Scots Charitable Society of Boston 1691. (NEHGS)

MATTHEWSON, NEIL, Glasgow, indentured with Francis Gurney in Philadelphia 9.10.1772. (Records of Indentures in Philadelphia)

MAXWELL, JAMES, Glasgow, member of the Scots Charitable Society of Boston 1726. (NEHGS)

MAXWELL, JAMES, Glasgow, member of the Scots Charitable Society of Boston 1733. (NEHGS)

MAXWELL, WILLIAM, born in Glasgow 1700, educated at Glasgow University 1723, minister in Charleston, South Carolina, 1724-1730, died in Scotland 1780. (F.3.488)

MILLEN, QUENTIN, Glasgow, emigrated to Edenton, North Carolina, Loyalist -settled in Nova Scotia, later a merchant in New York, died there 30.8.1817. [ANY.I.292]

MILLER, JOHN, Lanark, member of the Scots Charitable Society of
Boston 1733. (NEHGS)
MILLER, JOSEPH, Glasgow, member of the Scots Charitable Society of
Boston 1739. (NEHGS)
MILLAR, WILLIAM, Glasgow, member of the Scots Charitable Society of
Boston 1758. (NEHGS)
MILLER, WILLIAM, Glasgow, member of the Scots Charitable Society of
Boston 1765. (NEHGS)
MITCHELL, ALEXANDER, M.D., son of John Mitchell, exciseman in Ayr, died in
Bladensburg, America, 29.9.1804. [Gentleman's Magazine.75.183]
MITCHELL, JAMES, born in Kilmarnock 1800, carpet weaver, emigrated
from Greenock to USA, naturalised 18.3.1822 New York.
MITCHELL, THOMAS, Irvine, member of the Scots Charitable Society of
Boston 1750. (NEHGS)
MITCHELL, WILLIAM, born in Glasgow1703, son of John Mitchell and Janet
McLauchlan, married Agnes Buchanan, father of William 1735, to
New England 1755, settled in Chester, Connecticut. (NNQ.VII.89)
MOFFAT, SAMUEL, Ayrshire, Covenanter at Battle of Bothwell Bridge 1679,
via Ireland to America 1708, settled in Woodbridge, New Jersey.
(BLG2829)
MONTEATH, WILLIAM, born in Houstoun 5.11.1769, son of Reverend John
Monteath and Ann Fullerton, surgeon, died in St Vincent 16.8.1793.
(Car.4.17) (F.3.140)
MONTGOMERY, JAMES, Glasgow, member of the Scots Charitable Society
of Boston 1733. (NEHGS)
MONTGOMERY, JAMES, Saltcoats, member of the Scots Charitable
Society of Boston 1748. (NEHGS)
MONTGOMERY, JOHN, Glasgow, member of the Scots Charitable Society
of Boston 1758. (NEHGS)
MONTGOMERY, ROBERT, West Kirkbride, member of the Scots Charitable
Society of Boston 1734. (NEHGS)
MONTGOMERY, ROBERT, Irvine, merchant in St Croix, West Indies, pre 1829.
(SRO.CS239.S49.9)
MONTGOMERY, WILLIAM, Irvine, member of the Scots Charitable Society of
Boston 1738. (NEHGS)
MONTGOMERY, WILLIAM, born at Blantyre Mills, 3.3.1820, son of James
Montgomery, settled in Maine 1837, died in Wakefield,
Massachusetts, 15.9.1905. (ANY.2.302)
MONTER, JAMES, Glasgow, member of the Scots Charitable Society of
Boston 1739. (NEHGS)
MOODY, HUGH, Glasgow, member of the Scots Charitable Society of Boston
1758. (NEHGS)

MOODY, HUGH, Greenock, member of the Scots Charitable Society of Boston 1764. (NEHGS)

MOODIE, ROBERT, Lanark, member of the Scots Charitable Society of Boston 1766. (NEHGS)

MORRISON, JAMES, born in Glasgow 1789, educated at Glasgow University, minister in Nova Scotia 1829-1833, minister in Bermuda 1839 -1849, died 16.8.1849. (F.7.661)

MORRISON, JOHN, merchant in Antigua, later in Dumfries, cnf 1770 Dumfries

MORRISON, ROBERT, Inverkip, Renfrewshire, member of the Scots Charitable Society of Boston 1766. (NEHGS)

MORRISON, WILLIAM, Kilwinning, member of the Scots Charitable Society of Boston 1748. (NEHGS)

MORRISON, WILLIAM, Greenock, member of the Scots Charitable Society of Boston 1757. (NEHGS)

MUIR, JAMES, born in Cumnock 12.4.1757, son of Reverend George Muir, educated at Glasgow University 1776, minister in Bermuda 1782 -1787, minister in Virginia 1789-1820, died in Alexandria, Virginia, 8.8.1820. (F.7.661)

MURRAY, ARCHIBALD DOUGLAS, born in Ayrshire 1826, son of James Murray, farmer, educated in Glasgow University, minister in British Guiana 1852-1863, died 3.12.1863. (F.7.674)

MURRAY, HELEN, Glasgow, indentured with Benjamin Swett in Burlington, West New Jersey, 9.10.1772. (Records of Indentures in Philadelphia)

MURRAY, JOHN, Glasgow, indentured with Jacob Lewis in Philadelphia 17.10.1772. (Records of Indentures in Philadelphia)

MURRAY, ROBERT, Glasgow, indentured with Benjamin Swett in Gadsbury township, Lancaster County, Pennsylvania, 9.10.1772. (Records of Indentures in Philadelphia)

MYLNE, WILLIAM CRAIG, born in Glasgow 13.11.1805, merchant in New York 1828, died in Liverpool 22.10.1855. (ANY.2.25)

NICHOLLS, JAMES, Glasgow, member of the Scots Charitable Society of Boston 1733. (NEHGS)

NICOL, JAMES, born in Paisley 1798, weaver, emigrated from Greenock to USA, naturalised 27.11.1822 New York.

NICOLLS, JOHN, Glasgow, member of the Scots Charitable Society of Boston 1748. (NEHGS)

NOBLE, WILLIAM, Dumbarton, member of the Scots Charitable Society of Boston 1757. (NEHGS)

NORVAL, JAMES, born in Glasgow 1823, surgeon - educated at Glasgow University, settled in New York 1850, died there 21.5.1874. (ANY.2.302)

ORR, GEORGE, born 1823, gardener in Ayrshire, arrived in Hobart, Tasmania, on the Sultana 12.1.1856. (SRA.TD292)

ORR, JOHN, born 1830, clerk in Ayrshire, arrived in Hobart, Tasmania, on the Conway 14.10.1855. (SRA.TD292)

ORR, JAMES, Greenock, member of the Scots Charitable Society of Boston 1761. (NEHGS)

PARK, ALEXANDER, merchant in Amsterdam, son of Andrew Park, writer in Kilwinning, 1747. (SRO.S/H)

PARK, JAMES, Kilwinning, member of the Scots Charitable Society of Boston 1747. (NEHGS)

PARK, ROBERT, Ayr, member of the Scots Charitable Society of Boston 1771. (NEHGS)

PARK, WILLIAM, born in Glasgow 7.10.1704, son of James Park and Lilias Liddle, married Anna Law in Glasgow 6.5.1730, emigrated to Boston 1756, father of Margaret and Janet, died in Groton, Massachusetts, 17.6.1788. (Imm.NE.151)

PARKER, WILLIAM, born in Kilmarnock 11.1.1804, son of William Parker and Agnes Paterson, Lieutenant of the Bengal Army, died in Cawnpore, India, 10.4.1831. (BA.3.459)

PATERSON, HUGH, Irvine, member of the Scots Charitable Society of Boston 1745. (NEHGS)

PATON, ROBERT, in New Zealand, son of Robert Paton in Glasgow, and of Jean Miller who died 6.12.1869. (SRO.SH.1880)

PEADY, JOHN, Glasgow, member of the Scots Charitable Society of Boston 1699. (NEHGS)

PEASLY, ROBERT, Glasgow, member of the Scots Charitable Society of Boston 1737. (NEHGS)

PEDIE, JAMES, Glasgow, member of the Scots Charitable Society of Boston 1743. (NEHGS)

PETERS, THOMAS, GIAsgow, member of the Scots Charitable Society of Boston 1700. (NEHGS)

PETTIGREW, JOHN, Glasgow, settled in Sunbury, St Joseph's parish, Georgia, pro.8.10.1775 Georgia

PETTIGREW, WILLIAM, physician, Crawforddyke, Renfrewshire, member of the Scots Charitable Sociey of Boston 1766. (NEHGS)

PICKEN, ANDREW, born in Stewarton, Ayrshire, married Mary Wyndham Burdett in Inveraray 1.2.1782, emigrated to New York on the New York 3.10.1785, died 1796. (ANY.I.216)

POLLOCK, GEORGE, in Boston, USA, son of Thomas Pollock merchant in Paisley who died pre 11.1838. pro 11.1838 PCC

POLLOCK, ROBERT, Mearns, Renfrewshire, emigrated to America 1726. (American Weekly Mercury 7.12.1732)

POLLOCK, THOMAS, in Boston, USA, son of Thomas Pollock merchant in Paisley who died pre 11.1838. pro. 11.1838 PCC

POTT, GIDEON, born in Glasgow 2.1786, merchant in New York by 1807, died in New York 20.3.1843. (ANY.2i.5)

PURDIE, HUGH, Glasgow, member of the Scots Charitable Society of Boston 1750. (NEHGS)

QUIG, MICHAEL, born in Glasgow ca1796, bleacher, emigrated from Londonderry to USA, naturalised 16.4.1821 New York.

RAE, JOHN, Glasgow, member of the Scots Charitable Society of Boston 1747. (NEHGS)

RAMSAY, THOMAS KENNEDY, born in Kirkmichael, Ayrshire, 7.1.1788, son of Reverend John Ramsay and Margaret McFadzean, Lieutenant of the 11th Bengal Native Infantry, died at Komona 30.10.1807. (BA.3.606)

RANKINE, GEORGE, Kirkbride, member of the Scots Charitable Society of Boston 1734. (NEHGS)

RANKINE, JOHN, emigrated from Glasgow to New England pre 1719, married Sarah Clark in Boston 1719. (Imm.NE)

REDDIE, GEORGE BURD, born in Glasgow 21.4.1809, son of James Reddie and Charlotte Marion Campbell, Major General of the 29th Bengal Native Infantry, died in Bath 17.3.1880. (BA.3.621)

REID, DAVID, born in Greenock 28.8.1813, son of James Reid and Helena ..., Major General of the Bengal Army, died 29.2.1876. (BA.3.626)

REID, Reverend WILLIAM, born in Paisley 27.3.1811, son of Robert Reid merchant, minister in Gretna, died in Huntly, Mandeville, Jamaica, 25.10.1866. (F.2.397)

REID, WILLIAM, Ayr, member of the Scots Charitable Society of Boston 1734. (NEHGS)

REID, WILLIAM, born in Paisley 1726, ship's mate - mutineer, escaped from jail in St Thomas, West Indies, and fled to Puerto Rico 1753. (New York Mercury 25.6.1753)

RENNISON, LEWIS WILLIAMS, born in Glasgow 4.4.1845, son of Reverend Alexander Rennison, educated at Glasgow University, minister in Suva, Fiji, 1884-1887, died in Australia. (F.7.602)

RENWICK, JAMES, born in Lochmaben 1744, married Catherine Mee 1768, emigrated from England to New York 1783, merchant in New York, died 25.9.1803. (ANY.I.181)

RILLEY, HUGH, Irvine, member of the Scots Charitable Society of Boston 1772. (NEHGS)

RITCHIE, JOHN, Glasgow, member of the Scots Charitable Society of Boston 1732. (NEHGS)

RITCHIE, JOHN, Irvine, member of the Scots Charitable Society of Boston 1766. (NEHGS)

RITCHIE, ROBERT, Glasgow, member of the Scots Charitable Society of
Boston 1758. (NEHGS)
RITCHIE, JOHN, in Sydney, New South Wales, son of Robert Ritchie, carrier
in Crosshill, Ayrshire, who died 13.6.1880. (SRO.SH.1881)
ROBERTON, JOHN, born in Lanarkshire 1819, son of James Roberton, whisky
importer in New York until 1872, died in Oban 18.12.1882.
(ANY.2.281)
ROBERTSON, CHARLES LACHLAN, born in Greenock 29.7.1861, son of
Reverend Frederick Robertson, settled in Canada and USA. (F.3.435)
ROBERTSON, JAMES, born in Arran, married Anneken Jans in Schiedam
7.9.1640. (Schiedam Marriage Register)
ROBERTSON, WILLIAM, born 1834, son of William Robertson merchant in
Glasgow, educated at Glasgow University, missionary in Demerara
1872-1876, minister in Kemmingford, Quebec, 1877-, died there
4.1.1894. (F.3.371)
RODGERS, MENEVITH, Greenock, member of the Scots Charitable Society of
Boston 1748. (NEHGS)
ROGERS, JAMES, physician in St Petersburg, son of James Rogers, wright
in Hamilton, who died 8.1851. (SRO.SH.1859)
ROGERS, JOSEPH, born in Paisley ca1794, stonecutter, emigrated from
Greenock to New York, naturalised 19.2.1823 New York.
RONALDS, JAMES, born in Paisley 1752, settled in America ca1776,
carpenter and builder in New York, died 17.5.1812. (ANY.I.248)
ROSS, ANDREW, Glasgow, indentured with James McCutcheon in
Philadelphia 19.10.1772. (Records of Indentures in Philadelphia)
RUSSELL, ALEXANDER, auctioneer and builder in Glasgow, emigrated to
North America 1826. (SRO.CS238.C18.37)
RUSSELL, JOHN, Glasgow, member of the Scots Charitable Society of
Boston 1755. (NEHGS)
SAVAGE, EDWARD, born in Loudoun, emigrated from Ireland to New England
pre 1727. (Imm.NE.173)
SCOTT, GAVIN, Glasgow, hairdresser in Chatham County, Georgia, pro
3.2.1812 Chatham County, Georgia
SCOTT, HUGH, Glasgow, member of the Scots Charitable Society of Boston
1731. (NEHGS)
SCOTT, JAMES, Greenock, member of the Scots Charitable Society of
Boston 1731. (NEHGS)
SCOTT, JAMES, Greenock, member of the Scots Charitable Society of
Boston 1748. (NEHGS)
SCOTT, JAMES, jr, Glasgow, member of the Scots Charitable Society of
Boston 1758. (NEHGS)
SCOTT, JOHN, Renfrew, member of the Scots Charitable Society of Boston
1747. (NEHGS)

SCOTT, MATHEW, Glasgow, member of the Scots Charitable Society of Boston 1756. (NEHGS)

SCOTT, WILLIAM, Glasgow, member of the Scots Charitable Society of Boston 1757. (NEHGS)

SCOULLER, JOHN, merchant and factor in Rouen, France, son of William Scouller, merchant in Glasgow, 1675. (SRO.RD4.36.448)

SHAW, JOHN, born in Greenock 1811, to America 1827, settled in Rockingham, New Hampshire, naturalised 2.1839 in Rockingham, New Hampshire.

SHEDDEN, WILLIAM RALSTON, Roughwood, Ayr, died in New York. pro 7.1852 PCC

SHERROT, HELEN, born in Ayr 1800, died in White Bluff, Georgia, 21.10.1814. (Savanna Republican 27.10.1814)

SELKRIGG, JAMES, Shottstown, Lanarkshire, member of the Scots Charitable Society of Boston 1766. (NEHGS)

SEMPLE, JOHN, Renfrew, member of the Scots Charitable Society of Boston 1773. (NEHGS)

SERVICE, ROBERT, Saltcoats, member of the Scots Charitable Society of Boston 1765. (NEHGS)

SERVICE of SARVISS, SAMUEL, member of the Scots Charitable Society of Boston 1735. (NEHGS)

SERVICE, THOMAS, born in Irvine 1767, merchant in New York, married Sarah Tinney 1796, died 21.11.1806. (ANY.I.350)

SIM, JAMES, soldier from Ayr, married Henneken Derex in Nijmegen 2.2.1644. (Nijmegen Marriage Register)

SINCLAIR, ROBERT, Greenock, member of the Scots Charitable Society of Boston 1752. (NEHGS)

SLOOPER, JAMES, Alloway, member of the Scots Charitable Society of Boston 1733. (NEHGS)

SMITH, ADAM FREER, born in Galston, Ayrshire, 1.6.1791, son of Reverend George Smith and Marion Freer, a merchant in Calcutta. (F.3.40)

SMITH, ANDREW, son of Deacon Smith tailor in Ayr, mercantile agent in New York ca. 1800. (SRO.CS229.Mc8.42)

SMITH, JOHN, born in Dunbarton 1649, mariner, settled in Boston, Massachusetts, 1682. (PRO.HCA.Vol.81.Lopez v. Anthony 1698)

SMITH, JOHN, in the East Indies, son of John Smith, surgeon in Greenock, and Ursilla Hamilton, 1783. (SRO.S/H)

SMITH, MARGARET, born in Irvine ca1736, runaway indentured servant of Gilbert Shearer 22.6.1762. (New York Mercury 5.7.1762)

SMITH, PATRICK, merchant, son of Patrick Smith, merchant in Glasgow, and Janet Manwell, emigrated to Jamaica 1763. (SRO.B10.15.7085)

SMITH, ROBERT, Glasgow, member of the Scots Charitable Society of Boston 1730. (NEHGS)

SMITH, WALTER, born in Ayrshire 1784, died in Georgia 13.5.1840. (Georgia g/s)

SMOLLETT, BENJAMIN, surgeon, emigrated from Dunbarton to Plymouth, Massachusetts, 1687, settled in Connecticut. (Anc.H.NE)

SOMERVILLE, JOHN, Glasgow, member of the Scots Charitable Society of Boston 1743. (NEHGS)

SOMERVILLE, WILLIAM H., born in Glasgow ca1795, butcher, emigrated from Liverpool to USA, naturalised 30.9.1819 New York.

STARK, ARCHIBALD, born in Glasgow 2.1687, son of James Stark and Katherine Hamilton, educated at Glasgow University, emigrated from Londonderry to New England 1720, married Elizabeth Nicholas, settled in Londonderry, New Hampshire, and Derryfield, New Hampshire, died 25.6.1758. (Imm.NE.187)

STEEL, ARCHIBALD, Saltcoats, member of the Scots Charitable Society of Boston 1748. (NEHGS)

STEEL, ROBERT MEGGAT, born in Ayrshire, shipmaster in New York, married Isabella White 9.2.1804, father of Eliza, Emily, Isabella, and Caroline, drowned 1813. (ANY.I.372)

STEPHENSON, ALLEN, Glasgow, member of the Scots Charitable Society of Boston 1758. (NEHGS)

STEPHENSON, JAMES, Glasgow, member of the Scots Charitable Society of Boston 1733. (NEHGS)

STEVENSON, GABRIEL, merchant in Hamburg, son of Mary Fleming or Stevenson in Kilmarnock who died 27.4.1842. (SRO.SH.1850)

STEVENSON, JOHN, Neilston, Renfrewshire, member of the Scots Charitable Society of Boston 1762. (NEHGS)

STEVENSON, THOMAS, Renfrewshire, to New England 1763, settled in Boston, Massachusetts, member of the Scots Charitable Society of Boston 1765. (NEHGS)(Imm.NE.189)

STEVENSON, WILLIAM, Glasgow, member of the Scots Charitable Society of Boston 1747. (NEHGS)

STEWART, ALEXANDER, Glasgow, soldier, married Elizabeth Dempster from Brechin in Schiedam, Netherlands, 3.3.1635. (Schiedam Marriage Register)

STEWART, HELENA, daughter of John Stewart in Ayr, married George Chisholm Mitchelson (?) from Edinburgh in Dordrecht 18.3.1593. (Dordrecht Marriage Register)

STEWART, JAMES, merchant in Paisley, emigrated from Greenock to Bristol, Rhode Island, settled in New York by 1812. (SRO.CS230.Misc.24.1)

STEWART, JAMES, born in Kilmarnock, settled in Darien, Georgia, 1818, died at Lower Bluff, Georgia, 20.8.18??. (Darien Gazette 24.8.18??)

STEWART, JAMES, born 13.11.1785, merchant in Greenock and
Newfoundland, died 11.11.1837. (Greenock g/s)
STEWART, JAMES, born in Greenock 1811, emigrated to New York 1830,
builder, died in New York 22.9.1876. (ANY.2.272)
STEWART, ROBERT, Glasgow, emigrated from Ireland to New England 1718,
settled in Andover, Massachusetts. (Imm.NE.192)
STIRLING, JOHN, Glasgow, member of the Scots Charitable Society 1756.
(NEHGS)
STIRLING, MICHAEL FINLAYSON, merchant in Belize, Honduras, son of John
Stirling, surgeon in Glasgow, and Helen Rose. (SRO.SH.1853)
STORRY, ANDREW, third son of Andrew Storry, farmer in Shotts,
Lanarkshire, educated at Glasgow University ca. 1780, merchant in
New York, died in Kingston, New York, 20.1.1820. (ANY.I.351)
STRUTHERS, JOHN, born in Glasgow 1.1764, son of John Struthers, maltman
burgess, and Hanna Stiven, brewer, died in Savanna, Georgia,
24.2.1790. (Savanna g/s)
STUART, ROBERT, Emigrated from Glasgow to New England pre 1719,
settled in Amherst, New Hampshire. (Imm.NE.)
SUMMER, JOHN, Glasgow, member of the Scots Charitable Society of Boston
1731. (NEHGS)
SUTHERLAND, CHRISTIAN, Glasgow, indentured with James Inglis in
Philadelphia 9.10.1772. (Records of Indentures in Philadelphia)
SUTHERLAND, CHRISTIAN, Glasgow, indentured with Peter Howard in
Philadelphia 9.10.1772. (Records of Indentures in Philadelphia)
SYM, ANDREW, Glasgow, member of the Scots Charitable Society of Boston
1741. (NEHGS)
TAIT, GEORGE, son of James Tait, exciseman in Glasgow, died on Sullivan's
Island, near Charleston, South Carolina, 30.8.1801. [Gentleman's
Magazine.71.1053]
TARBOT, HUGH, Glasgow, member of the Scots Charitable Society of
Boston 1756. (NEHGS)
TARBOTT, JAMES, Carnwoth, member of the Scots Charitable Society of
Boston 1741. (NEHGS)
TAYLOR, WILLIAM, born in Glasgow 2.12.1790, son of Reverend William
Taylor, Lieutenant General HEICS, died in New Zealand 27.6.1868.
(F.3.441)
TAYLOR, ..., Irvine, settled in Cape Breton pre 1819. (SRO.CS38.1819)
TELFORD, FRANCIS, born in Dunbarton 1740, shipmaster in New York,
married Rebecca ...., father of Rebecca, died in New York 22.8.1836.
(ANY.I.250)
TEMPLETON, GILBERT. born 1825, shepherd in Ayrshire, arrived in Hobart,
Tasmania, on the White Star 1855. (SRA.TD292)

25

THOM, JOHN ALFRED, clerk in Brazil, grandson of William Ferguson, coalmerchant in Greenock, who died 24.3.1841. (SRO.SH.1858)

THOMAS, WILLIAM, from Ayr, married Grietge Liendsdr from Flanders in Gouda 17.2.1590. (Gouda Marriage Register)

THOMPSON, JAMES, gardener in Hamilton, member of the Scots Charitable Society of Boston 1767. (NEHGS)

THOMSON, ANDREW, Strathaven, naturalised 31.12.1803 in New York.

THOMSON, RALPH WARDLAW, Bellary, East Indies, son of Janet Crawford Wardlaw or Thomson there once in Garthamlock, Glasgow. (SRO.SH.1854)

THOMSON, ROBERT, Clydebank, Gipp's Land, New South Wales, brother of James Thomson, Lauriston, Glasgow. (SRO.SH.1851)

THOMSON, THOMAS, physician in Calcutta, son of Dr Thomas Thomson, Professor of Chemistry in Glasgow. (SRO.SH.1859)

THOMSON, WILLIAM GREGORY, born in Kilmarnock 1825, son of Robert Thomson and Mary Gregory, carpet agent in New York, died in Kilmarnock 17.2.1900. (ANY.2.282)

TORBET, ROBERT, Melbourne, brother of John Torbet, surgeon in Paisley. (SRO.SH.1854)

TRAN, ALEXANDER, Glasgow, member of the Scots Charitable Society of Boston 1735. (NEHGS)

TURNER, ANDREW, Greenock, member of the Scots Charitable Society of Boston 1764. (NEHGS)

TURNER, DOUGALD, Australia, son of Robert Turner, weaver in Glasgow. (SRO.SH.1858)

TURNER, ROBERT, Greenock, member of the Scots Charitable Society of Boston 1733. (NEHGS)

TYRIE, JAMES, born in Greenock (?) 1758, shipmaster in New York, ships chandler in New York 1801-1806, died 16.12.1806. (ANY.I.252)

VINIAN, HENRY, Largs, member of the Scots Charitable Society of Boston 1766. (NEHGS)

WADDEL, ROBERT, Lanark, tailor, admitted as a citizen of Leiden, Netherlands, 23.5.1608. (Leiden Citizenship Book, II.33)

WALKER, JOHN, Glasgow, member of the Scots Charitable Society of Boston 1755. (NEHGS)

WALKER, ROBERT, born in Govan 2.6.1795, son of William Walker and Janet Walker, married Christian ..... born in Glasgow 1795, father of Mary born in Glasgow 1818, emigrated from Greenock to USA, naturalised 19.3.1827 New York.

WALKINGSHAW, WILLIAM, Glasgow, member of the Scots Charitable Society of Boston 1731. (NEHGS)

WALLACE, HUGH, Greenock, planter and merchant in Biscany, Jamaica, 1820s. (SRO.CS239.W36.1)

WALLACE, JOHN, Glasgow, member of the Scots Charitable Society of
Boston 1700. (NEHGS)
WALLACE, JOHN, Ayr, member of the Scots Charitable Society of Boston
1700. (NEHGS)
WALLACE, JOHN, Ayr, member of the Scots Charitable Society of Boston
1728. (NEHGS)
WALLACE, JOHN, Saltcoats, member of the Scots Charitable Society of
Boston 1771. (NEHGS)
WALLACE, JOHN, born in Pollockshaws 6.11.1827, son of John Wallace and
Agnes McGhie, educated at Glasgow University, minister at North
Shore, New Zealand, 1866-1880, died in Glenbuck 3.12.1895. (F.3.44)
WALLACE, PETER, born 1730, emigrated from Glasgow to New England on
the Apollo, died in Newbury, Maine, 1748. (Imm.NE)
WALLACE, SAMUEL, son of John Wallace in Ayrshire, merchant in Veere,
Zealand, 1646. (RGS.IX.1676)
WARDEN, JAMES, Greenock, member of the Scots Charitable Society of
Boston 1748. (NEHGS)
WARDEN, WILLIAM, Greenock, member of the Scots Charitable Society of
Boston 1736. (NEHGS)
WARDEN, WILLIAM, Greenock, member of the Scots Charitable Society of
Boston 1758. (NEHGS)
WARNOCK, JOHN, Australia, son of Andrew Warnock, manufacturer in
Paisley, who died 28.5.1853. (SRO.SH.1854)
WATSON, HUGH, born in parish of Mearns 1778, carpet weaver, married
Elizabeth ... born in Kilwinning 1785, father of Robert, Janet,
Matthew, George, and William all born in Paisley between 1805 and
1811, emigrated from Greenock to USA, naturalised 18.3.1822 in
New York.
WATSON, WILLIAM, Glasgow, member of the Scots Charitable Society of
Boston 1726. (NEHGS)
WATT, JOHN, Mearns, member of the Scots Charitable Society of Boston
1740. (NEHGS)
WEIR, ALEXANDER, Paisley, bookseller, husband of Sarah Collins,
pro. 26.10.1790 New York
WEIR, JAMES, Glasgow, member of the Scots Charitable Society of Boston
1747. (NEHGS)
WEIR, ROBERT, born in Paisley 1770, son of Walter Weir merchant, settled
in New York as a shipmaster and merchant, married Maria Brunkley
there 27.8.1802, father of Robert, James, William, Charles, John, and
Mary, died in New York 5.2.1825. (ANY.I.365)
WHITE, JOHN, born in Glasgow 1672, emigrated from Ireland to New
England, died in Lunenburg, Massachusetts, 1739. (Imm.NE.212)

WHITE, SAMUEL, Glasgow, member of the Scots Charitable Society of Boston 1759. (NEHGS)

WHITEFOORD, GEORGE, Lieutenant HEICS Cawnpore, son of Sir John Whitefoord of Whitefoord, Ayrshire, 1788. (Laing 3272)

WHYTLAW, JOHN, merchant in Glasgow then in Bay Island, New Zealand. (SRO.SH.1853)

WILSON, ANDREW, from Ayr, married Jelles Ritgers from Rotterdam, in Rotterdam 13.10.1630. (Rotterdam Marriage Register)

WILSON, ARCHIBALD, Inverkip, Renfrewshire, member of the Scots Charitable Society of Boston 1769. (NEHGS)

WILSON, THOMAS, soldier from Glasgow, married Maritghe Willems in Delft, Netherlands, 26.1.1592. (Delft Marriage Register)

WINNING, WILLIAM, born in Lanarkshire 1790, pocketbookmaker, emigrated from London to New York, naturalised 29.5.1821 New York.

WOOD, GEORGE, born in Port Glasgow 30.11.1794, son of Andrew Wood and Janet Johnston, merchant, naturalised in New York 3.5.1817.

WOOD, WILLIAM, born in Glasgow 21.10.1808, banker in New York 1828, died there 1.10.1894. (ANY.2ı.25)

WOODRUP, ALEXANDER, Glasgow, member of the Scots Charitable Society of Boston 1739. (NEHGS)

WYSE, JOHN, mariner in Australia, son of David Wyse, steamboat master in Glasgow, who died 17.3.1851. (SRO.SH.1854)

YOUNG, JOHN, Greenock, member of the Scots Charitable Society of Boston 1748. (NEHGS)

YOUNG, JOHN, born 6.11.1732 in Glasgow, son of John Young and Marion Anderson, saddler, emigrated to Philadelphia 1762, settled in New York 1784, married Margaret Bassett 1786, died in New York 16.9.1798. (ANY.I.193)

YOUNG, JOHN, Old Kirk, Greenock, member of the Scots Charitable Society of Boston 1772. (NEHGS)

YOUNG, MATHEW, Glasgow, member of the Scots Charitable Society of Boston 1732. (NEHGS)

YOUNG, WILLIAM, born in Irvine 1775, publisher and printer in Philadelphia, died 1829. (SSA86)

YUIL, ARCHIBALD, Glasgow, member of the Scots Charitable Society of Boston 1750. (NEHGS)

YUILE, GEORGE, Glasgow, member of the Scots Charitable Society of Boston 1746. (NEHGS)

YUILE, JAMES, Glasgow, member of the Scots Charitable Society of Boston 1753. (NEHGS)

YUILE, JOHN, Glasgow, member of the Scots Charitable Society of Boston 1759. (NEHGS)

EMIGRANTS AND ADVENTURERS
from
Orkney and Shetland

INTRODUCTION

Emigration is a long established feature of Scottish demography for many centuries. The degree and destination of emigration has changed from being relatively small scale and directed towards continental Europe in the sixteenth and seventeenth centuries to being substantial and predominently to North America during the eighteenth century and worldwide but mainly Australasia and North America thereafter. The Northern Isles, far from being isolated, were abreast one of the main sea routes from North West Europe to Canada and the eastern seaboard of the United States, with Stromness acting as the last port of call for vessels crossing the Atlantic. This book, the first of a series, attempts to identify individual emigrants from Orkney and Shetland to destinations worldwide and is based on research in Scotland and elsewhere into primary and secondary sources.

David Dobson
St Andrews, 1995

REFERENCES

Archives

NEHGS	New England Historic Genealogical Society, Boston
	SCS	Scottish Charitable Society MSS B S 36x6
SAB	Stats Arkivet i Bergen
SRO	Scottish Record Office, Edinburgh
	GD	Gifts and Deposits
	NRAS	National Register of Archives, Scotland
	RS	Register of Sasines
	SH	Services of Heirs
PRO	Public Record Office, London
	AO	Audit Office
	HCA	High Court of the Admiralty of England
	PCC	Prerogative Court of Canterbury

Publications

ANY	Biographical Register of the St Andrews Society of New York [N.Y., 1922]
BA	List of Officers of the Bengal Army [London, 1945]
BLG	Burke's Landed Gentry [London, 1937]
BPP	British Parliamentary Papers
F	Fasti Ecclesiae Scoticanae [Edinburgh, 1928]
HBRS	Hudson Bay Record Society publications, series
Imm.NE	Immigrants to New England [Salem, 1931]
POAS	Proceedings of the Orkney Antiquarian Society, series
SG	The Scottish Genealogist, series

Abbreviations

g/s	gravestone inscription
OPR	Old Parish Register
pro	probate

EMIGRANTS AND ADVENTURERS

FROM ORKNEY AND SHETLAND

[Part One]

ADAMSON, JOHN, cooper in Orkney, citizen of Bergen, Norway,
1642. [SAB]
ADAMSON, WILLIAM, born in Tingwall, Shetland, Hudson Bay
Company employee 1842-1850, labourer, middleman and
slooper. [HBRS.16.352]
AIM, WILLIAM, Orkney, settled in Saltcoats, North West
Territory, 15.7.1888. [BPP.9.484]
AITKEN, WILLIAM, in Bergen, Norway, son of David Aitken
merchant in Kirkwall, 1630. (SRO.RS43.4.121)
ALBERTSON, ALBERT, Orkney, citizen of Bergen, Norway, 1614.
[SAB]
ALBERTSON, GILBERT, Orkney, burgess of Bergen, Norway, 1617.
(POAS.XIII.39)[SAB]
ALBERTSON, PETER, Orkney, burgess of Bergen, Norway, 1621.
(POAS.XIII.39)
ALBERTSON, PETER, Orkney, citizen of Bergen, Norway, 1621.
[SAB]
ALBERTSON, PETER, weaver in Orkney, citizen of Bergen, Norway,
1644.[SAB]
ALLAN, ALEXANDER, Orkney, citizen of Bergen, Norway, 1625.
[SAB]
ANDERSON, ADAM, Orkney, burgess of Bergen, Norway, 1614.
(POAS.XIII.39)

ANDERSON, ADAM, Orkney, citizen of Bergen, Norway, 1623. [SAB]

ANDERSON, ALBERT, Orkney, burgess of Bergen, 1614. (POAS.XIII.39)

ANDERSON, ANDREW, Orkeny, citizen of Bergen, Norway, 1643. [SAB]

ANDERSON, DAVINA LUCY MURRAY, born in Walls and Flotta 19.7.1850, daughter of Reverend William Anderson and Lucy Hay Murray, married Gerard Affleck Scott, physician in Australia. (F.7.256)

ANDERSON, JOHN, born 1800, son of Reverend John Anderson and Margaret Izatt, Stronsay, settled in Jamaica, New York, and Mexico, father of William Wemyss Anderson, died 1867. ['The Andersons in Phingask" Aberdeen, 1910]

ANDERSON, OLIVER, Orkney, citizen of Bergen, Norway, 1636. [SAB]

ANDERSON, ROBERT, leather worker in Orkney, citizen of Bergen, Norway, 1659. [SAB]

ANDERSON, WILLIAM, Orkney, citizen of Bergen, Norway, 1647. [SAB]

BALLENDEN, JOHN, born in Stromness 1810, Hudson Bay Company employee 189-1856, died 7.12.1856. (HBRS.3.427)

BEATTIE, JOHN, born in Evie and Rendall parish, Orkney, 24.3.1844, son of Reverend William Beattie and Isabella Rankin, a merchant in Montreal. (F.7.216)

BEGG, THOMAS, merchant in Bergen, Norway, son of Magnus Begg and Margaret Mowat in Gossigar, Orkney, 1625. (SRO.RS43.3.140)

BIRSAY, JAMES, burgess of Bergen, son of William Birsay udaller in Greeny, 1625. [SRO.RS43(Orkney) III.3]

BOAG, JOHN, ba.13.3.1690 Kirkwall St Magnus, son of Thomas Boag and Marion Linklatter, emigrated to New England, married Elizabeth Preston 24.12.1724, settled in Portsmouth, New Hampshire. (Imm.NE.17)

BODELSON, GEORGE, Shetland, burgess of Bergen, Norway, 1621. (POAS.XIII.39)

BRACE, DAVID, ba. 28.3.1733 Sandwick, Orkney,son of Alexander Brass and Marion Butron, member of the Scots Charitable Society of Boston, 1758. (NEHGS)

BROOK, JAMES, Kirkwall, indentured servant of Thomas Brown, Richmond County, Georgia, ca.1783. [PRO.AO13.34]

BROWN, MAGNUS, seaman, indentured for fours years service at "the Bottom of the Bay" by the Hudson Bay Company 13.4.1683. [HBRS.IX.95]

BRUCE, ALEXANDER. Orkney, member of the Scots Charitable Society of Boston 1761. (NEHGS)

BRUCE, JAMES, Carsten, Orkney, member of the Scots Charitable Society of Boston 1744. (NEHGS)

CARRIGEL, JOHN, Aukland, Orkney, indentured servant of Thomas Brown, Richmond County, Georgia, ca.1783. [PRO.AO13.34]

CHRISTIANSON, THOMAS, Germiston, Orkney, burgess of Bergen, 1615. (POAS.XIII.39)

CLEWSTON, JAMES, ba.15.6.1734, son of Henry Clewston and Anna Robertson in Stenness, Orkney, member of the Scots Charitable Society of Boston 1751. (NEHGS)

CLEWSTON, WILLIAM, Orkney, member of the Scots Charitable Society of Boston 1756. (NEHGS)

CLOUSTON, EDWARD, born in parish of Cross and Burness 27.9.1787, son of Reverend William Clouston of Kingshouse and Isabella Traill, planter in Jamaica, died 1866. (F.7.253); Edward Clouston of Kingshouse, late of Jamaica, 1834. [SRO.R.S.Orkney, 173]

CLOUSTON, JAMES, Stromness, Hudson Bay Company employee 1842-185, labourer. [HBRS.16.354]

CLOUSTON, THOMAS, a shipmaster in Newberry, New England, son of Robert Clouston, carpenter and sailor in Stromness, 17.6.1776. [SRO.RS.Orkney.133]

CLOUSTOUN, WILLIAM, born in Orkney 1794, Hudson Bay Company employee 1812-1843. [HBRS.3.431]

CLOUSTON, WILLIAM, born in Sandwick and Stromness 22.12.1839, son of Reverend Charles Clouston and Margaret Clouston, died in India 9.5.1869. (F.7.249)

3

COPELAND, GEORGE, born in Shetland, settled in New York pre
1785, grocer, died 25.12.1820 New York. (ANY.I.377)
CORGILL, JOHN, Harra, Orkney, servant of Thomas Brown in
Richmond County, Georgia, 1783. (PRO.AO13.34)
CORRIGAL, JOHN, Orphir, Hudson Bay Company employee 1837-
1848, labourer, settled at Red River 1848, married Eliza
Firth 25.5.1848, father of Eliza and William Charles.
[HBRS.16.355]
CORRIGALL, JOHN, in New Zealand, nephew of Mary Corrigall,
(daughter of John Corrigall in Redland) who died 27.4.1879.
(SRO.SH.1881)
COVIE, PATRICK, son of Patrick Covie, merchant in Kirkwall, and
Elizabeth Drevar, lost off the Cape of Good Hope 9.1864.
[St Magnus, Kirkwall, g/s]
CROMARTY, JAMES, [possibly] ba.4.2.1728 son of James
Cromarty and Christian Spence in Holm & Paplay, Orkney,
member of the Scots Charitable Society of Boston 1750.
(NEHGS)
CROMARTY, THOMAS, merchant in Bergen, Norway, formerly in
Walls, Orkney, 1639. (SRO.RS43.6.67)
CROMARTY, WILLIAM, in Bergen, Norway, son of Thomas
Cromarty in Kirkbister, Orkney, 1631. (SRO.RS43.4.277)
CUMLAQUOY, JAMES, Orkney, in Norway, 1632, (SRO.RS43.4.292)
CURSITER or QUOYBANKS, THOMAS, Orkney, cooper in Bergen,
Norway, 1634. (SRO.RS43.5.39)
DANIELSON, JOHN, Orkney, citizen of Bergen, Norway, 1626.
[SAB]
DAVIDSON, ANDREW, Orkney, burgess of Bergen, Norway, 1619.
(POAS.XIII.39)[SAB]
DAVIDSON, FRANCIS, Orkney, citizen of Bergen, Norway, 1630.
[SAB]
DAVIDSON, WILLIAM, Orkney, burgess of Bergen, Norway, 1619.
(POAS.XIII.39)
DAVIDSON, WILLIAM, cooper in Orkney, citizen of Bergen,
Norway, 1628.[SAB]

DENNISON, ROBERT SCARTH, son of James Dennison {1806-1875} and Margaret Wallace {1798-1874}, settled in Winsted, Connecticut. [Lady g/s, Stronsay][St Magnus, Kirkwall, g/s]

DICKEY, CHARLES COOPER LESLIE, born in Holm, Orkney, 25.12.1886, son of Reverend William Dickey and Elizabeth Ferguson, a financial secretary in USA. (F.7.242)

DICKEY, JOSIAH LESLIE PORTER, born in Holm, Orkney, 13.1.1885, son of Reverend William Dickey and Elizabeth Ferguson, a marine engineer in USA. (F.7.242)

DICKSON, JOHN, Orkney, citizen of Bergen, Norway, 1642. [SAB]

DUNCANSON, BERNT, Orkney, citizen of Bergen, Norway, 1635. [SAB]

EFUERTSON, ALBERT, Orkney, citizen of Bergen, Norway, 1614. [SAB][POAS.XIII.39]

EFFUERTSON, MAGNUS, Orkney, citizen of Bergen, Norway, 1644. [SAB]

EFFUERTSON, THOMAS, Orkney, citizen of Bergen, Norway, 1632. [SAB]

EWARTSON, JOHN, Orkney, burgess of Bergen, Norway, 1621. (POAS.XIII.39)[SAB]

EWARTSON, MAGNUS, Orkney, burgess of Bergen, Norway, 1621. (POAS.XIII.39)[SAB]

FALCONER, PATRICK or PETER, born in Sandwick and Stromness 16.7.1779, son of Reverend John Falconer and Clementina Gordon, Captain of the Indian Army. (F.7.253)

FEA, ISABELLA J.Y., born 1873, wife of J.M.Yorston, died 20.10.1898, buried in Lilluet Cemetery, British Columbia. [Lady g/s, Stronsay]

FEA, MARCUS, cooper in Orkney, citizen of Bergen, Norway, 1642. [SAB]

FIRTH, JOHN, Harra, Orkney, servant of Thomas Brown in Richmond County, Georgia, 1783. (PRO.AO.13.34)

FLETT, GEORGE, born in Firth 1775, emigrated from Stromness to York Factory 1796, Hudson Bay Company employee 1796 -1823, died at Red River 10.6.1850. (HBRS.2.213)(Orkney Library MS21.5)

FLETTE, GEORGE, born in Birsay 1803, Hudson Bay Company
employee 1833-1849, sailor, drowned near York Factory
15.10.1849. [HBRS.16.357]

FLETT, JAMES, tablemaker in Orkney, citizen of Bergen, Norway,
1672.[SAB]

FLETT, JOHN, born 1737 in Gentha, Orkney, settled in Portland,
Maine, died 23.3.1760. [Imm.NE.59]

FLETT, THOMAS, in Severn, Hudson Bay, husband of Margaret
Sinclair,   28.12.1789. [SRO.RS.Orkney.199]

FLETT, WILLIAM, Orkney, Hudson Bay Company employee 1784-.
[Orkney Library MS21.5]

FOLSTAR, JOHN, Firth, Orkney, Hudson Bay Company employee
1838-1847, labourer, married (1) Flora McDonald in Red
River Colony 22.2.1844, (2) Isabella Brown 8.3.1849 in Red
River Colony. [HBRS.16.357]

FOTHERINGHAM, ANNE TRAILL, wife of Thomas Traill of Westove,
died 13.3.1828, buried at St Martin's Church, Vevey,
Switzerland.   [SRO.NRAS.0110.43]

GABRIELSON, WILLIAM, Orkeny, citizen of Bergen, Norway, 1645.
[SAB]

GARSON, DAVID, Orkney, steersman employed by the Hudson
Bay Company ca.1817. (Orkney Library MS21.5)

GARSON, GEORGE, son of Reverend John Garson and Elizabeth
Main in Birsay, a water commissioner in Victoria, Australia.
(F.7.242)

GEORGESON, ADAM, Orkney, burgess of Bergen, Norway, 1619.
[SAB]

GEORGESON, JOHN, Orkney, citizen of Bergen, Norway, 1643.
[SAB]

GIFFORD, JOHN, soldier from Orkney, married Janneken le
Beston in Cadzand, Netherlands, 16.7.1629. (Cadzand
Marriage Register)

GILBERTSON, LAURENCE, Orkney, citizen of Bergen, Norway,
1640. [SAB]

GILLIES, JAMES, born ca1800 in Stromness, emigrated to
Bonadventure County, Quebec, 1825. [SG.32.2/61]

GOWRIE, ALEXANDER, Orkney, member of the Scots Charitable
Society of Boston 1765. (NEHGS)

GRAHAM, JAMES, Kirkwall, member of the Scots Charitable
Society of Boston 1754. (NEHGS)

GRAHAM, JAMES, chairmaker, Island of Rosey, Orkney, member
of the Scots Charitable Society of Boston 1767. (NEHGS)

GRAHAME, JAMES, son of Reverend Andrew Grahame (1688
-1746), and Christian Flett in Orkney, housewright in
Boston, New England. (F.7.236); member of the Scots
Charitable Society of Boston 1754.(NEHGS)

GRANT, JAMES, born in Cross and Burness parish 28.8.1804, son
of Reverend William Grant and Isabella Haggart, died in
Jamaica. (F.7.259)

GRANT, ROBERT LAING, born in Cross and Burness parish
29.4.1794, son of Reverend William Grant and Isabella
Haggart, died in St Anne's, Jamaica, 17.7.1824. (F.7.259)

GRANT, WILLIAM, born in Cross and Burness parish 21.12.1797,
son of Reverend William Grant and Isabella Haggart, died in
Jamaica 1819. (F.7.259)

GRIMSTON, THOMAS CHRISTIANSON, Orkney, citizen of Bergen,
Orkney, 1615. [SAB]

GUNN, ISOBEL, Orkney, Hudson Bay Company employee ca1806.
[Orkney Library, MS21.1]

HALCRO, JOSHUA, ba. 8.8.1787 son of William Halcro and Janet
Flett in Orphir, Orkney, Hudson Bay Company employee
1810-, clerk and trader. [Orkney Library.MS21.5]

HALCROW, UMPHRA, born in Burra, Shetland, Hudson Bay Company
employee 1842-1850, settled in Canada. [HBRS.16.360]

HAMILTON, JOHN MACAULAY, born in Orkney 28.11.1799, son of
Reverend Gavin Hamilton and Penelope MacAulay,
physician, emigrated to Canada. (F.7.244)

HARRISON, CHARLES, Northmavine, Shetland, Hudson Bay
Company employee 1852-1856, slooper. [HBRS.16.357]

HARVEY, ANDREW, son of Andrew Harvey in Birsay, Hudson Bay
Company employee at York Fort, probate 23..1786 PCC.
[PRO.PCC.Admonitions 1786]

HAY, JAMES, born in Lerwick 22.5.1791, son of James Hay of
Laxfirth (1750-1830), merchant in New York by 1817, died
in Pelhamville, New York, 5.5.1854. (ANY.II.69)
HEDDLE, ALEXANDER, Lieutenant of the African Corps,
Grahamstown, Cape of Good Hope, 1843.
[SRO.NRAS.0110.51]
HENDERSON, ANDREW, smith in Orkney, citizen of Bergen,
Norway, 1646.[SAB]
HENDERSON, JOHN, Orkney, citizen of Bergen, Norway, 1625.
[SAB]
HENDERSON, THOMAS, Orkney, citizen of Bergen, Norway, 1643.
[SAB]
HENDRY, HENDRY, soldier from Orkney, married Grietge Williams
from Ireland, in Rotterdam 26.3.1606. (Rotterdam Marriage
Register)
HENRY, Captain ARCHIBALD, born 1793, son of Thomas Henry of
Buraston, and Lillias Henry, died on the River Mississippi
3.1837, [Walls g/s]
HEPBURN, WILLIAM, born in Orphir, Hudson Bay Company
employee 1845-1851. able seaman, died in London 1851.
[HBRS.16.359]
HUTCHISON, EDWARD, born in Papa Westray, Hudson Bay Company
employee 1843-1847. [HBRS.16.360]
INGSTER, PETER, weaver in Orkney, citizen of Bergen, Norway,
1638. [SAB]
IRVING, EDWARD, son of John Irving in Borwick Orkney, settled
in Lubeck, Germany, by 1636. (SRO.RS43.5.230)
IRVING, HENRY, Orkney, member of the Scots Charitable Society
of Boston 1750. (NEHGS)
IRVING, JOHN, Orkney, member of the Scots Charitable Society
of Boston 1748. (NEHGS)
IRVING, WILLIAM, born in Shapinsay, Orkney, 31.8.1731, married
Sarah Sanders 18.5.1761, settled in New York 1763, father
of Ebenezer and Washington, died 1807. (BLG2762)
ISBISTER, JAMES, fisherman in Orkney, Hudson Bay Company
employee 1803-. [Orkney Library, MS21.5]

ISBISTER, JAMES, fisherman in Orkney, Hudson Bay Company
employee at Fort Wedderburn 1803-1821, at Fort
Wedderburn 1818-1821. [Orkney Library, MS21.5]
[HBRS.I.443]
ISBISTER, THOMAS, fisherman in Orkney, Hudson Bay Company
1809-1821, at Fort Wedderburn 1818-1821.
[Orkney Library, MS21.5][HBRS.I.443]
JAMIESON, GILBERT, Orkney, citizen of Bergen, Norway, 1615.
[SAB]
JAMIESON, JAMES, Orkney, citizen of Bergen, Norway, 1623.
[SAB]
JAMIESON, MAGNUS, Orkney, citizen of Bergen, Norway, 1621.
[SAB]
JAMIESON, THOMAS, Orkney, citizen of Bergen, Norway, 1637.
[SAB]
JAMIESON, THOMAS, cooper in Orkney, citizen of Bergen,
Norway, 1647.[SAB]
JOHNSON, ANDREW, Orkney, citizen of Bergen, Norway, 1636.
[SAB]
JOHNSON, HENRY, Orkney, citizen of Bergen, Norway, 1616. [SAB]
JOHNSON, JAMES, cooper in Orkney, citizen of Bergen, Norway,
1626. [SAB]
JOHNSON, JOHN, Orkney, citizen of Bergen, Norway, 1615. [SAB]
JOHNSON, JOHN, weaver in Orkney, citizen of Bergen, Norway,
1619. [SAB]
JOHNSON, JOHN, Orkney, citizen of Bergen, Norway, 1626. [SAB]
JOHNSON, MICHAEL, Orkney, citizen of Bergen, Norway, 1653.
[SAB]
JOHNSON, THOMAS, cooper in Quebanks, Orkney, burgess of
Bergen, Norway, 1618. [SAB]
JOHNSON, STEVEN, Orkney, citizen of Bergen, Norway, 1615.
[SAB]
JOHNSTON, HARRY, planter in St Kitts, 1791.
[SRO.R.S.Orkney, 250]

JOHNSTON, JAMES, born 1769, in Outbrecks, Stenness, a former carpenter in Hudson Bay Company Service, died 17.4.1842, [Stenness g/s]

KENNEDY, ALEXANDER, born in South Ronaldsay 1781, Hudson Bay Company employee 1798-1830, emigrated from Stromness to York Factory on the King George, died in London 1832. (HBRS.2.225)

KENNEDY, ALEXANDER, son of Alexander Kennedy of Braehead Hope and Agatha Isbister, born 2.2.1808, at Mouse Lake, North America, baptised 26.5.1822 in South Ronaldsay. [South Ronaldsay OPR]

KINCH, THOMAS, Kirkwall, citizen of Bergen, Norway, 1639. [SAB]

KIRKNESS, GEORGE, Sandwick, Shetland, Hudson Bay Company employee 1845-1851, boatbuilder. [HBRS.16.361]

LAKERSON, DAVID, Orkney, burgess of Bergen, Norway, 1617. [SAB]

LEITH, WILLIAM, boatman at Firth, Orkney, Hudson Bay Company employee at Peace River ca1802. [Orkney Library, MS21.5]

LENNEY, WILLIAM, Orkney, member of the Scots Charitable Society of Boston 1750. (NEHGS)

LESLIE, ERNEST ELPHINSTONE, born in Evie and Rendall parish, Orkney, 11.3.1885, son of Reverend Alexander Leslie and Catherine Scott, to Bengal. (F.7.217)

LESLIE, WILLIAM, born 1847, son of James Leslie and Isabel Shearer, died in New South Wales 21.1.1881. [St Peter's, Stronsay, g/s]

LESLIE, WILLIAM, born 1849, son of James Leslie and Isabel Shearer, died at Lake Michigan 7.11.1872. [St Peter's. Stronsay, g/s]

LIDDLE, PETER, born 1824, died at the Gilbert River goldfield, Northern Queensland, 23.9.1869. [Lady g/s, Stronsay] [St Magnus, Kirkwall, g/s]

LINKLATER, ANDREW, Orkney, Hudson Bay Company employee ca 1818, middleman. [Orkney Library, MS21.5]

LINKLETTER, THOMAS, husband of Maria Willcocks, probate 1750 St Croix, Danish West Indies. [Rigsarkivet, Kobenhavn]

LINKLETTER, WILLIAM, Hudson Bay Company, 6.8.1798.
[SRO.RS.Orkney.426]
LISK, JOHN, Orkney, member of the Scots Charitable Society of
Boston 1755. (NEHGS)
LOCHORE, WILLIAM BRODIE, born in St Andrews parish, Orkney,
2.4.1851, son of Reverend Gavin Lochore and Sarah Wilkin,
settled in Melbourne. (F.7.212)
LOGIE, MARGARET LENDRUM, born in Kirkwall 1815, daughter of
Reverend William Logie, married Reverend George Smellie
19.6.1843, emigrated to Fergus, Ontario, died 11.3.1904.
(F.7.265)
LOGIN, JOHN SPENCE, M.D., son of John Login and Margaret Moar
Spence in Stromness, settled in Bengal before 1841.
[SRO.S/H]
LOUTTIT, JOHN, Hudson Bay Company, grandson of William
Louttit in Lyking, Stromness, 13.7.1808.
[SRO.RS.Orkney.755]
LOUTIT, WILLIAM, Orkney, settled in Saltcoats, North West
Territory,10.9.1888. [BPP.9.484]
MAIN, JOHN THOMASON, cooper in Orkney, citizen of Bergen,
Norway, 1630. [SAB]
MANSON, ALEXANDER, weaver in Orkney, citizen of Bergen,
Norway, 1626.[SAB]
MANSON, ANDREW, Orkney, citizen of Bergen, Norway, 1614.
[SAB]
MANSON, DAVID, Orkney, citizen of Bergen, Norway, 1630. [SAB]
MANSON, EDWARD, Kirkwall, citizen of Bergen, Norway, 1634.
[SAB]
MANSON, HENRY, Orkney, burgess of Bergen, Norway, 1618. [SAB]
MANSON, JOHN, baker in Orkney, citizen of Bergen, Norway,
1641. [SAB]
MANSON, MAGNUS, Orkney, citizen of Bergen, Norway, 1640.
[SAB]
MANSON, MICHAEL, Orkney, citizen of Bergen, Norway, 1628.
[SAB]

MANSON, WILLIAM, a skipper in Philadelphia 1773, later a
merchant in Augusta, Georgia, 1780.
[SRO.NRAS.0627, box9, bundle2; box 18, bundle 12]
MARCUSON, JAMES, Orkney, citizen of Bergen, Norway, 1671.
[SAB]
MAXWELL, GILBERT, ba.13.8.1736 son of Edward Maxwell and
Margaret Allan, Holm & Paplay, Orkney, member of the
Scots Charitable Society of Boston 1764. (NEHGS)
MEIL, HENRY, born 1820, a farmer in Orkney, settled in Saltcoats,
Assiniboia, North West Territory 15.4.1889. [BPP.9.484]
MEIL, HENRY, jr., born 1851, a farmer in Orkney, settled in
Saltcoats, Assiniboia, North West Territories 15.4.1888.
[BPP.9.484]
MEIL, JOHN, born 1854, a farmer in Orkney, settled in Saltcoats,
Assiniboia, North West Territories, 15.4.1888. [BPP.9.484]
MELLORD, DAVID, Roa (Rousay?) servant to Thomas Brown in
Richmond County, Georgia, 1783. (PRO.AO.13.34)
MELLORD, ISABELLA, Roa (Rousay?) servant to Thomas Brown in
Richmond County, Georgia, 1783. (PRO.AO13.34)
MILL, JAMES, son of Reverend James Mill (died 1718) and Isabel
Bruce (1688-1771) in Lerwick, died in the East Indies.
(F.7.285)
MILL, LAURENCE, son of Reverend James Mill (died 1718) and
Isabel Bruce (1688-1771) in Lerwick, died in the West
Indies. (F.7.285)
MILLAR, JAMES, Orkney, member of the Scots Charitable Society
of Boston 1758. (NEHGS)
MILLS, GEORGE, Kirkwall, member of the Scots Charitable
Society of Boston 1739. (NEHGS)
MOAT, JOHN, Kirkwall, in Jamaica 1764. [SRO.GD31.300]
MOODIE, THOMAS, born in Walls and Flotta 1.6.1790, son of James
Moodie of Melsetter and Elizabeth Dunbar, Lieutenant of the
34th Bengal Native Infantry, died in Kalpi, India, 27.4.1824,
buried at Kalpi, pro 12.6.1824. (BA.3.317)
MOWAT, GEORGE, Orkney, member of the Scots Charitable
Society of Boston 1744. (NEHGS)

MOWAT, JOHN, Island of Burrow, Orkney, member of the Scots
Charitable Society of Boston 1770. (NEHGS)
MOWAT, JOHN, son of Reverend Hugh Mowat and Elizabeth Baikie
in Orkney, planter at Orkney Hall, Jamaica, died 1800.
(F.7.216)
MOWATT, MAGNUS, ba.11.1.1733 son of George Mowat, Evie and
Rendall, Stromness, Orkney, settled in New England pre
1767, married Anna Pickman in Salem 22.3.1767.
(Imm.NE.143)
MUDIE, JOHN JAMIESON, weaver in Kirkwall, citizen of Bergen,
Norway, 1654. [SAB]
NEWGAR, PETER, Orkney, member of the Scots Charitable
Society of Boston 1749. (NEHGS)
NICHOLSON, ROBERT, Island of Weetra, Orkney, member of the
Scots Charitable Society of Boston 1767. (NEHGS)
NICOLSON, JAMES, born in Kirkwall 16.6.1788, son of Robert
Nicolson and Elizabeth Balfour, Captain of the Bengal Native
Infantry, died in Mussoorie, India, 19.2.1835, pro 31.7.1835.
(BA.3.393)
NIELSON, GABRIEL, Orkney, citizen of Bergen, Norway, 1623.
[SAB]
NIELSON, THOMAS, Orkney, citizen of Bergen, Norway, 1613.
[SAB]
NISBET, WILLIAM, born in Shapinsay 1721, son of Reverend
Alexander Nisbet, educated at Edinburgh University,
minister of Firth and Stenness 1747-1766, prisoner in
Inverness Tolbooth, adulterer, banished to the American
Plantations 1765, possibly settled in Jamaica. (F.7.236)
OLLASON, JOHN, shoemaker in Orkney, citizen of Bergen,
Norway, 1647. [SAB]
OMAND, HENRY, Orkney, member of the Scots Charitable Society
of Boston 1766. (NEHGS)
OMAND, MARGARET, Stromness, relict of Charles Gregory,
skipper in Prince George County, Virginia, 1792.
[SRO.R.S.Orkney, 288, 289]

13

PAPLAY, STEPHEN, Orkney, settled in Flushing, Walcheren, Netherlands, by 1631. (SRO.RS43.4.270)

PEACE, EDWARD, born 1859, son of John Pollexfen Peace and Margaret Bell, died in Kalgoorlie, Western Australia, 22.5.1924. [St Magnus, Kirkwall, g/s]

PEACE, WILLIAMINA BELL, born 1859, daughter of John P. Peace and Margaret Bell, died in Perth, Western Australia, 4.9.1897. [Lady g/s, Stronsay][St Magnus, Kirkwall, g/s]

RAMSAY, JOHN, born in Whalsay, Shetland Islands, 1780, Captain of the 21st Bengal Native Infantry, died at Brijetolla, Calcutta, 20.8.1818. (BA.3.602)

RANNIE, JOHN, born in Walls, Orkney, 1829, son of John Rannie schoolmaster, educated at King's College, Aberdeen, minister in Ontario 1859-1876, minister in British Guiana 1876-1904, died in Essex 1910. (F.7.673)

RAE, WILLIAM GLEN, born in Stromness 1809 son of John Rae, Hudson Bay Company employee 1827-1845, died in San Francisco 19.1.1845. [HBRS.4.355]

RIAMERS, JAMES, Orkney, citizen of Bergen, Norway, 1624. [SAB]

RICH, THOMAS, Orkney, member of the Scots Charitable Society of Boston 1756. (NEHGS)

RIDLON, MAGNUS, born Orkney 1674, settled in York, Saco, Maine, married (1) Susannah Young (2) Maisie Townsend, father of Matthias, died 1771. (Imm.NE.165)

RITCHIE, CHARLES, born 1848, a farm manager in Orkney, with his wife, four sons and four daughters, settled in Saltcoats, North West Territory, Canada, 15.4.1888. [BPP.9.484]

ROBERTSON, EDWARD, Kirkwall, citizen of Bergen, Norway, 1660. [SAB]

ROBERTSON, JAMES, Hudson Bay Company, 7.10.1807. [SRO.RS.Orkney.730]

ROBERTSON, JOHN, Kirkwall, citizen of Bergen, Norway, 1650. [SAB]

ROBERTSON, JOHN, born in Orkney, Hudson Bay Company employee 1805-1830, settled in Canada. (HBRS.2.239)

ROBERTSON, JOHN, born in Evie, Hudson Bay Company employee 1805-1828, died Berens River, Winnipeg,1828. (HBRS.2.240)

ROBERTSON, MAGNUS, Orkney, burgess of Bergen, Norway, 1617. [SAB]

ROBERTSON, WILLIAM, Orkney, citizen of Bergen, Norway, 1613. [SAB]

ROSIE, EDWARD JAMES, in Norfolk, Virginia, grandson of Edward Rosie of Sucquoy, Sandwick, South Ronaldsay, 23.4.1803. [SRO.RS.Orkney.511]

ROSS, ALEXANDER, born in Stroma 19.10.1717, married Elizabeth in Portland, Maine, died in Falmouth, Maine, 24.11.1768. (Imm.NE.169)

ROSS, Mrs ELIZABETH, born 1.1.1721 in South Ronaldsay, married Alexander Ross, died in Gorham, Maine, 1.3.1798. (Imm.NE.169)

ROSS, JAMES, Burray, Orkney, boatman of the Hudson Bay Company at Peace River 1802. (Orkney Library MS21.5)

RUDDACH, THOMAS, merchant in Tobago 1791, son of Reverend Alexander Ruddach in Kirkwall. [SRO.R.S.Orkney, 252]

RUSSELL, JOSEPH, born in Shetland 7.10.1842, son of Walter Russell and Ann Booth in Bressay, died in Yokohama 30.4.1879. (Banchory Ternan g/s)

SANDERSON, ALEXANDER, Walls, Orkney, citizen of Bergen, Norway, 1622. [SAB]

SANDERSON, EDWARD, Orkney, citizen of Bergen, Norway, 1638. [SAB]

SANDERSON, THOMAS, Orkney, citizen of Bergen, Norway, 1635. [SAB]

SANDERSON, WILLIAM, Orkney, citizen of Bergen, Norway, 1626. [SAB]

SANGSTER, PATRICK, eldest son of John Sangster, Widewall, Orkney, died in Grenada 1817. [Scotsman.32.17]

SCOLLAY, JOHN, merchant in Jamaica 1788. [SRO.NRAS.0630.box10,bundle14]

SCOTT, JOHN, born in Ronaldsay 1781, Hudson Bay Company employee 1800-1825, returned to Scotland on the Prince of Wales, 1825. [HBRS.3.453]; John Scott, late in Hudson Bay Company Service, then in Stromness, 1834. [SRO.R.S.Orkney, 167]

SELLAR, THOMAS, born in Mowick, Shetland, 12.1.1820, a merchant in New York 1840 to 1846, died in Cannes, France, 22.10.1885. [ANY.2.239]

SHEARER, JAMES, Orkney, settled in Saltcoats, North West Territory, Canada,11.9.1888. [BPP.9.484]

SINCLAIR, ARTHUR, surgeon in Masulipatam, East Indies, 1785. [SRO.GD31.410]

SINCLAIR, JAMES, at York Fort, Hudson Bay, 2.8.1797. [SRO.RS.Orkney.407]

SINCLAIR, THOMAS, Orkney, mariner in Hudson Bay Company service 1824-1834, sailed to England on the bark Ganymede 2.1834. [HBRS.3.456]

SINCLAIR, ROBERT, born in Kirkwall 1660, mariner, settled in New York 1680. (PRO.HCA.Vol.81,Phillips v. Mauritz 1692)

SLATER, JAMES, Hudson Bay Company, 6.7.1810. [SRO.RS.Orkney.805]

SLATER, ROBERT ROBERTSON, Orkney, citizen of Bergen, Norway, 1643, died 1683. [SAB]

SLATER, PETER, (?) ba. 8.4.1722 son of Alexander Slater and Janet Groundwater in Orphir, Orkney, member of the Scots Charitable Society of Boston, Massachusetts, 1750. (NEHGS)

SMELLIE, GEORGE, born in parish of St Andrew and Deerness 14.6.1811, son of Reverend James Smellie, educated at Glasgow University, minister of Lady parish 1839-1843, married Margaret Lendrum Logie 1843, emigrated to Canada, minister of Fergus, Ontario, father of James and Elizabeth, died 22.11.1896. (F.7.265)

SMELLIE, JAMES, son of Reverend James Smellie and Margaret Spence in St Andrews parish, Orkney, died in Demerara 1883. (F.7.212)

SMITH, JOHN, Birsay, Orkney, member of the Scots Charitable Society of Boston, Massachusetts, 1755. (NEHGS)

SMITH, MALCOLM LAING, son of Allan Smith (died 1800) in Turmiston, Orkney, settled in Seaford, Van Diemen's Land before 1845. [SRO.S/H]

SMYTH, PATRICK, son of Patrick Smyth of Braco, Orkney, servant to Alexander Johnston, a cloth merchant in Danzig, 1647. [SRO.GD190.2.186]

SNODIE, ADAM, born in Orphir 1783, Hudson Bay Company employee 1801-1822, died in Stromness after 1832. (HBRS.2.242)

SPENCE, DAVID, Kirkwall, settled in Bergen, Norway, died before 1630.[SRO.GD31.37]

SPENCE, PETER, Orkney, member of the Scots Charitable Society of Boston, Massachusetts, 1764. (NEHGS)

SPENCE, THOMAS, Orkney, member of the Scots Charitable Society of Boston, Massachusetts, 1760. (NEHGS)

STEVENS, JOHN, Orkney, member of the Scots Charitable Society of Boston, Massachusetts,1750. (NEHGS)

STEWART, ARCHIBALD, ba. 27.9.1738 son of Archibald Stewart in Westray, Orkney, member of the Scots Charitable Society of Boston, Massachusetts, 1765. (NEHGS)

STEWART, CHARLES, ba. 26.5.1725 son of Charles Stewart and Marjory Traill, Kirkwall, member of the Scots Charitable Society of Boston, Massachusetts, 1747. (NEHGS)

STEWART, JAMES, son of Reverend Walter Stewart and Helen Sinclair in South Ronaldsay, died abroad 1661. (F.7.230)

STEWART, JAMES, Orkney, citizen of Bergen, Norway, 1640. [SAB]

STOBBS, JOHN GARROW, born in Stromness 1.7.1840, son of William Stobbs, educated at Glasgow University 1864, minister in Melbourne 1875-, died 10.8.1882. (F.7.598)

STRANG, WILLIAM, South Ronaldsay, member of the Scots Charitable Society of Boston, Massachusetts, 1739. (NEHGS)

TAIT, JAMES, St Olla, Orkney, seaman on HMS Captain, died in Boston, Massachusetts, pro. 1799 PCC

TAIT, WILLIAM, late of of the Hudson Bay Company, then at the Red River Colony 1834. [SRO.R.S.Orkney 167]

TATE, JOHN, Orkney, settled at Fort Vancouver, Oregon, pro 1.1855 PCC

TAYLOR, BENJAMIN, born 1830, died in Christchurch, New Zealand, 18.8.1877. [South Walls g/s]

TAYLOR, HUGH, Orkney, member of the Scots Charitable Society of Boston, Massachusetts,1757. (NEHGS)

TAYLOR, PETER, ba. 29.12.1728 son of Peter Taylor and Isobel Smith, Stromness, Orkney, member of the Scots Charitable Society of Boston, Massachusetts, 1762. (NEHGS)

THOMSON, ALEXANDER, born 1841, a farmer in Orkney, with his wife, seven sons, and two daughters, settled in Saltcoats, North West Territory, Canada, 18.5.1888. [BPP.9.484]

THOMSON, DAVID, ba. 16.12.1734 son of David Thomson and Isobel Miller, Stromness, Orkney, member of the Scots Charitable Society of Boston, Massachusetts, 1763. (NEHGS)

THOMSON, JAMES, Orkney, member of the Scots Charitable Society of Boston, Massachusetts, 1756. (NEHGS)

THOMSON, JOHN, shoemaker in Orkney, citizen of Bergen, Norway, 1625. [SAB]

THOMSON, MAGNUS, Orkney, citizen of Bergen, Norway, 1623. [SAB]

THOMSON, MAGNUS, weaver in Orkney, citizen of Bergen, Norway, 1641. [SAB]

THOMSON, PETER, Orkney, citizen of Bergen, Norway, 1640. [SAB]

THOMSON, THOMAS, Orkney, citizen of Bergen, Norway, 1624. [SAB]

THOMASON, JOHN, weaver in Orkney, citizen of Bergen, Norway, 1671.[SAB]

TILLOCK, MAGNUS, Orkney, member of the Scots Charitable Society of Boston, Massachusetts, 1749. (NEHGS)

TOMISON, WILLIAM, chief factor at York Fort, Hudson Bay, 1.7.1805.[SRO.RS.Orkney.632]

TRAILL, GEORGE, Kirkwall, member of the Scots Charitable Society of Boston 1746. (NEHGS)

TRAILL, GEORGE, born in Lady parish 25.4.1746, son of Reverend Thomas Traill of Hobbister and Sibella Grant, died in Grenada 1774. (F.7.264)

TRAILL, HENRY, Orkney, (possibly ba. 3.9.1720 son of Patrick Traill and Isabel Kaa), member of the Scots Charitable Society of Boston, Massachusetts, 1751. (NEHGS)

TRAILL, HENRY WILLIAM, Public Land Office, Kangaroo Point, Brisbane, Australia, 1848, son of John Heddle Traill.[SRO.NRAS.0110.53]

TRAILL, ISOBEL, born in Lady Parish 2.1.1736, daughter of Reverend Thomas Traill of Hobbister and Sibella Grant, married William Tate in Boston, USA, died 17.5.1792. (F7.264)

TRAILL, ISABELLA, relict of Christopher Thuring in Helsingfors, Sweden, 1839. [SRO.GD31.513, 514]

TRAILL, JAMES, born 23.4.1797, son of Reverend Walter Traill and Margaret McBeath, surgeon in the service of the Honourable East India Company, died in Mysore 1829. (F.7.264)

TRAILL, JOHN, Kirkwall, a merchant in Boston, Massachusetts, died before 1750. (Imm.N.E.200)

TRAILL, ROBERT, Orkney, (nephew of John Traill), a merchant in Boston, Massachusetts, pre 1756. (Imm.N.E.200)

TRAILL, ROBERT, born in Lady parish 29.4.1744, son of Reverend Thomas Traill of Hobbister and Sibella Grant, settled in Philadelphia, died 31.7.1816. (F.7.264)

TRAILL, THOMAS, born in Lady parish 16.4.1749, son of Reverend Thomas Traill of Hobbister and Sibella Grant, settled in St Vincent. (F.7.264)

TULLOCH, JOHN, Kirkwall, wife Janet Seatter, children Janet, Samuel, Magnus, Mary and Elizabeth, servants to Thomas Brown in Richmond County, Georgia, 1783. (PRO.AO13.34)

TWATT, MAGNUS, at York Fort, Hudson Bay, 13.12.1806 and 5.6.1807.[SRO.RS.Orkney.695.715]

UMPHRAY, WILLIAM, son of Reverend William Umphray (died 1668) and Janet Umphray in parish of Bressay, Burra and Quarff, "went abroad". (F.7.280)

VELLZON, ANDREW, ba. 22.12.1725 son of William Vellzon in Birsay, Orkney, member of the Scots Charitable Society of Boston 1750. (NEHGS)

WALLACE, JAMES, born in Kirkwall 1673, son of Reverend James Wallace and Elizabeth Cuthbert, physician at Darien, later with the East India Company, died 1724. (F.7.222)

WALTERSON, ALBERT, Orkney, citizen of Bergen, Norway, 1631. [SAB]

WATERS, JAMES, born 1840, died in Boston, Massachusetts, 26.11.1912. [Lady g/s, Stronsay]

WATT, R., Kirkwall, a planter in St George's parish, Jamaica, 1778.[SRO.GD31.390]

WILDRAGE, Mrs ISABELLA, born 1740 in South Ronaldsay, wife of Captain James Wildrage, died 23.9.1780, buried East Cemetery, Portland, Maine. (Imm.N.E.212)

WILLIAMSON, ALEXANDER, Orkney, citizen of Bergen, Norway. 1648. [SAB]

WILLIAMSON, EDWARD, Kirkwall, citizen of Bergen, Norway, 1648. [SAB]

WILLIAMSON, JEREMY, Orkney, burgess of Bergen, Norway, 1617. [SAB]

WILLIAMSON, JOHN, cooper in Orkney, citizen of Bergen, Norway, 1616.[SAB]

WILLIAMSON, JOHN, Orkney, citizen of Bergen, Norway, 1639. [SAB]

WILLIAMSON, MAGNUS, Orkney, citizen of Bergen, Norway, 1622. [SAB]

WILLIAMSON, ROBERT, Orkney, citizen of Bergen, Norway, 1638. [SAB]

WILLIAMSON, THOMAS, Kirkwall, citizen of Bergen, Norway, 1613.[SAB]

WILLIAMSON, WILLIAM, wright in Orkney, citizen of Bergen, Norway, 1620.[SAB]

WILLIAMSON, WILLIAM, Orkney, citizen of Bergen, Norway, 1628. [SAB]

WILLIS, JAMES, Shetland, member of the Scots Charitable Society of Boston 1733. (NEHGS)

WILSON, ANDREW, born in Orphir 1787, Hudson Bay Company employee 1806-1835, drowned in Lake Winnipeg 1835. [HBRS.3.461]

WILSON, DANIEL, born in Stennes, Shetland, 1820, Hudson Bay Company employee 1842-1857, settled at Red River. [HBRS.16.378]

YORSTON, ROBERT, at York Factory, Hudson Bay, son of Robert Yorston, a farmer in Harray, 29.1.1810. [SRO.RS.Orkney.789]

EMIGRANTS AND ADVENTURERS
from
The Lothians

INTRODUCTION

Emigration has been for several centuries a feature of Scottish demography. The degree and destination of emigration has changed over the centuries from being relatively small scale and directed towards continental Europe in the sixteenth and seventeenth centuries to being substantial and predominantly to North America in the eighteenth and nineteenth centuries and Australasia in the nineteenth century. For centuries Leith was the main port of Scotland and its trade links provided routes for many of the early emigrants but by the late eighteenth century the rise of intercontinental trade led to the Clyde ports being the main emigration ports. This book, the first in a series, attempts to identify those who emigrated from Edinburgh and the Lothians to destinations worldwide and is based on research in Scotland and elsewhere into primary and secondary sources.

David Dobson
St Andrews, 1995

REFERENCES

ARCHIVES

NEHGS   New England Historic Genealogical Society,
         Boston
         Scots Charitable Society Papers
NJA   New Jersey State Archives, Trenton
PRO   Public Record Office, London
         PCC Prerogative Court of Canterbury
SAB   Stats Arkivet, Bergen
SRA   Strathclyde Regional Archives, Glasgow
SRO   Scottish Record Office, Edinburgh
         CS   Court of Session
         NRAS National Register of Archives
         RD   Register of Deeds
         RS   Register of Sasines
         SH   Services of Heirs

PUBLICATIONS

AJ   Aberdeen Journal {series}
ANY   Biographical Register of the St Andrews Society
         of New York [New York, 1922]
AP   Historical Catalogue of the St Andrews Society of
         Philadelphia, 1749-1907 [Philadelphia 1907]
AUR   Aberdeen University Review {series}
BA   List of Officers of the Bengal Army [London 1945]
BLG   Burke's Landed Gentry [London 1937]
CCMC   Colonial Clergy of the Middle Colonies[Baltimore1978]
CCNE   Colonial Clergy of New England [Baltimore 1977]
DAB   Directory of American Biography {series}
EBR   Edinburgh Burgh Records {series}
EEC   Edinburgh Evening Courant {series}
ETR   Edinburgh Tolbooth Records [Edinburgh 1923]
F   Fasti Ecclesiae Scoticanae [Edinburgh 1928]
HBRS   Hudson Bay Record Society {series}
NS   Northern Scotland {series}
RGS   Register of the Great Seal of Scotland {series}
RPC   Register of the Privy Council of Scotland {series}
S   The Scotsman {series}
SIP   The Scots in Poland [Edinburgh 1910]

ABBREVIATIONS

         cnf.= confirmation of testament; g/s=gravestone;
         OPR=Old Parish Register; pro=probate

EMIGRANTS AND ADVENTURERS FROM

THE LOTHIANS

[Part One]

ABERCROMBIE, ROBERT, born in Edinburgh 1712, minister in Pelham, New
England, 1744-1755, died in Pelham 3.3.1780. (Immigrants to New
England, p.1, Salem, Mass., 1931)

ADAM, CATHERINE, from Leith, married Andrew Mill, soldier from
Caithness, in Schiedam 26.4.1635. (Schiedam Marriage Register)

ADAM, JAMES, born 1814, a civil engineer, died in New Zealand 23.11.1841.
[St Cuthbert's g/s]

ADAM, ELIZABETH, born 1820, wife of Rowart Ronald, died in Sydney
23.10.1847. [St Cuthbert's g/s]

ADAM, JOHN SHEDDEN, born 1823, died in Wahroonga, Sydney, 5.12.1906.
[St Cuthbert's g/s]

AIKEN, ROBERT, born in Dalkeith 1734, publisher in Pennsylvania, died
1802. (SSA86)

AITKEN, THOMAS, born in Bo'ness 1799, son of James Aitken a merchant,
educated at Glasgow University 1818, Rector of Halifax Academy,
Nova Scotia, 1828-. (F.7.613)

AIKMAN, PETER, born 1819, second son of George Aikman, engraver, and
Alison Mackay, died in New York 15.9.1883. [St Cuthbert's g/s]

ALBERTSON, THOMAS, Leith, burgess of Bergen, Norway, 1641. [SAB]

ALEXANDER, THOMAS, Edinburgh, member of the Scots Charitable Society
of Boston 1772. (NEHGS)

ALLAN, JOHN, Queensferry, citizen of Bergen, Norway, 1692. [SAB]

ANDERSON, HUGH, born in Edinburgh, secretary of the New York Insurance
Company 1804-1810, died in New York 24.12.1812. (ANY.I.374)

ANDERSON, JAMES, Leith, a merchant in Virginia, 1791.
[SRO.R.S.Caithness, 211]

ANDERSON, JAMES, saddler in Paris, son of William Anderson, saddler in
Haddington, 1830. (SRO.SH.1830)

ANDERSON, JAMES, physician in Melbourne, son of James Anderson, teacher
in Edinburgh, 1856. (SRO.SH.1856)

ANDERSON, ROBERT, Edinburgh, factor in Veere. cnf Edinburgh 1674.

ANDERSON, ROBERT, son of Henry Anderson cordiner burgess of Edinburgh,
merchant in Antigua, burgess of Edinburgh 1812. (EBR)

ANNAND, THOMAS, in Edinburgh, formerly a King's Guardsman in France, cnf
1664 Edinburgh

EMIGRANTS FROM THE LOTHIANS

ASTLEY, CHARLES JOSEPH, merchant in Pernambuco, Brazil, brother of
Thomas Astley, chemist in Musselburgh, 1851. (SRO.SH.1851)
AULD, THOMAS, merchant in Edinburgh, son of David Auld, merchant in
Poland, 1688. (SRO.NRAS0364.2/2)
AULD, WILLIAM, born 1770, surgeon in Edinburgh, to Hudson Bay 1790 on
the Seahorse, Hudson Bay Company employee 1790-1815, died in
Edinburgh after 1830. (HBRS.2.204)
BAIRD, FRANK, merchant in Melbourne, brother of Sophia Isabella Baird
who died 20.6.1857. (SRO.SH.1858)
BAIRD, JOHN, in Sydney, New South Wales, son of Thomas Baird, surgeon in
Linlithgow, who died 1.12.1825. (SRO.SH.1881)
BAIRD, Captain WILLIAM, son of Sir James Baird of Saughtonhall, died in
Boulogne sur Mer 20.5.1823. (SM.86.776)
BALLANTINE, GEORGE, confectioner from Edinburgh, admitted as a citizen
of Leiden, Holland, 18.5.1618. (Leiden Citizenship Book II.112)
BARNSTON, GEORGE, born 1800 in Edinburgh, a North West Company
employee 1820-1821, a Hudson Bay Company employee 1821-1863.
[HBRS.3.427]
BARTHOLEMEW, WILLIAM, soldier from Linlithgow, married Lizbeth Bowens
from Oudewater, in Schiedam 27.4.1635. (Schiedam Marriage
Register)
BELL, GEORGE COATES, Indian Army physician, son of Dandeson C. Bell and
Jane Smytton who died in Edinburgh 1.6.1859. (SRO.SH.1859)
BELL, Captain Jack, soldier from Linlithgow, married Margriete
Engelbrechs, from Deventer, in Schiedam 28.11.1637. (Schiedam
Marriage Register)
BELL, PETER, Bo'ness, citizen of Bergen, Norway, 1675. [SAB]
BELL, WILLIAM, late merchant in Charleston, South Carolina, now in
St Andrew's Church parish, married Isabella Dempster 27.7.1815.
[Edinburgh OPR]
BENNIE, JOHN, born 1796, son of James Bennie, merchant in Haddington,
educated at Glasgow University, missionary in South Africa 1824-,
died 9.2.1869. (F.7.561)
BINNEY, ARCHIBALD, born in Portobello 1763, typefounder in Philadelphia
1796, died 1838. (SSA86)
BINNING, JOHN, Edinburgh, member of the Scots Charitable Society of
Boston 1762. (NEHGS)
BLACK, GEORGE, sailmaker in Sydney, son of James Black, ropemaker in
Leith, and Margaret Scott, 1856. (SRO.SH.1856)
BLACKADDER, CHRISTOPHER, Cockenzie, member of the Scots Charitable
Society of Boston 1739. (NEHGS)
BORTHWICK, PETER, Abercorn, married Jannitge Dircx Bled from Delft, in
Schiedam 26.12.1637. (Schiedam Marriage Register)

2

EMIGRANTS FROM THE LOTHIANS

BORTHWICK, WILLIAM, cashier of the East Lothian Banking Company, absconded to America ca.1835. (SRO.CS231,Sed.Bk.2/1)

BOTHWELL, ELIZABETH, from Edinburgh, married James Bruce, soldier, in Utrecht 5.2.1643. (Utrecht Marriage Register)

BOUDEN, JAMES, Edinburgh, member of the Scots Charitable Society of Boston 1697. (NEHGS)

BOWIE, JOHN, prisoner in Edinburgh Tolbooth, to Holland as a soldier under Captain William Douglas 6.3.1683. (Edinburgh Tolbooth Records)

BOWIE, JOHN, born in Dalhousie, carpenter, died in Georgia 17.9.1801. (Georgia Gazette 24.9.1801)

BREMNER, JAMES, Edinburgh, musician, to Philadelphia 1763. ("Scotland and America in the Age of Enlightenment", p259, R. Scher: Edinburgh 1990)

BROWN, GEORGE, born in Edinburgh 1780, died in Georgia 23.12.1833. (Georgia g/s)

BROWN, WILLIAM, carpenter in Leith thereafter in Leghorn, Italy, cnf 1774 Edinburgh

BRUCE, CHRISTINA, Leith, married Thomas Mauritsz, a pedlar, in Leiden, Netherlands, 13.9.1635. (Leiden Marriage Register, L.11)

BRUCE, DAVID, born in Edinburgh, Moravian missionary in Pennsylvania, New York, New Jersey, 1740-1749, died in Sharon, Connecticut, 9.7.1749. (CCMC)

BRUCE, GEORGE, born in Edinburgh 26.6.1781, son of John Bruce, emigrated to Philadelphia 1795, printer and typefounder in New York, married (1) Margaret Watson 1803, (2) Catherine Wolfe, father of David,died 1866. (ANY.I.383)

BRUNTON, WILLIAM, born in Newbattle 1766, to Canada 1820, minister in Quebec 1820-1839, died 12.8.1839. (F.7.628)

BRYCE, DAVID, Jamaica, died in Musselburgh 18.2.1798. [AJ2618]

BUCKHAM, ANDREW, born in Edinburgh 1780, physician in New York, died there 21.4.1844. (ANY.2.144)

BUNCLE, GEORGE, servant to Joseph Wardrope carpenter in Edinburgh, emigrated via Leith to Savanna, Georgia, 3.1734. (ESG65)

BURTON, WILLIAM, North Berwick, member of the Scots Charitable Society of Boston 1765. (NEHGS)

BUTLER, WILLIAM, shoemaker in Edinburgh, possibly emigrated to America in 1812. (SRO.CS233.Seqn.B1.34)

CALDERWOOD, OLIVER, son of John Calderwood a baillie of Musselburgh, a student, died in Paris, pro. 1680 PCC

CALLENDAR, JAMES, born in Leith 4.6.1829, to New York 1850, merchant in New York, died in Brooklyn 23.4.1903. (ANY.2.264)

EMIGRANTS FROM THE LOTHIANS

CAMPBELL, COLIN, born in Edinburgh 1686, son of John Campbell and
Margaret Stewart, founder of the Swedish East India Company 1731,
married Elizabet Clarges, died in Gothenburg 9.5.1757.
(NS.7.1.145)(AUR.42.38)

CAMPBELL COLIN, the younger of Smiddygreen, Lieutenant of the 74th Foot,
husband of Leititia, daughter of Robert Campbell, merchant in
Halifax, Nova Scotia, parents of Robert campbell born 13.3.1781 in
Fort George, Penobscott, Lincoln County, North America, baptised in
St Cuthbert's, Edinburgh, 14.2.1782. [St Cuthbert's OPR]

CAMPBELL, JOHN, son of Patrick Campbell in Edinburgh, died in Berbice
10.12.1805. (EEC.1806)

CAMPBELL, Dr PATRICK, late of Jamaica, then at Liberton Kirk, Edinburgh,
cnf 1787 Edinburgh

CAMPBELL, ROBERT, born in Edinburgh 28.4.1767, son of Samuel Campbell,
bookseller, stationer and publisher in Philade'phia, died in
Frankford, Philadelphia, 14.8.1800. (ANY.I.254)

CAMPBELL, SAMUEL, born Edinburgh 18.7.1765, son of Samuel Campbell,
bookbinder, and Catherine Taylor, bookseller in New York, married
(1) Eliza Duyckinck 1786, (2) Euphemia Duyckinck 1799, died in New
York 26.6.1836. (ANY.I.198)

CAMPBELL, SAMUEL, born 1738, Edinburgh, died in New York 17.4.1813.
(SM.75.639)(EEC.1813)

CAMPBELL, THOMAS RONALD, born 1803, son of John Campbell of Riccarton,
died 14.2.1821. [South Park g/s, Calcutta]

CANDLISH, JOHN BOGLE, born 2.11.1837, son of Reverend Robert Smith and
Jessie Brock in Edinburgh, insurance agent in Australia. (F.1.106)

CARMICHAEL, HENRY, in New South Wales, brother of Mary Carmichael in
Edinburgh, 1857. (SRO.SH.1857)

CARRUTHERS, JAMES, Edinburgh, member of the Scots Charitable Society
of Boston 1733. [NEHGS]

CATTENACH, JOHN ALVA, fourth son of Peter Lorimer Cattenach and Jane
Bladworth Hardie, died in Johannesburg 10.1.1910.[St Cuthbert's g/s]

CHARTERS, ALEXANDER, merchant in Edinburgh, citizen of Bergen, Norway,
1739. [SAB]

CHARTERS, HEW, burgess of Edinburgh, merchant in Gothenburg, cnf
Edinburgh 1644.

CHISHOLM, GEORGE, born in Leith 1754, died in Calcutta 20.2.1833.
[Scotch Burial Ground g/s. Calcutta]

CHRISTIE, JAMES, born in Edinburgh 13.1.1750, son of John Christie and
Janet Clarkson, emigrated to Philadelphia 1775, American Army
officer 1776-1783, merchant in New York, married Mary Weygandt,
died 31.3.1793. (ANY.I.160) (Matthew's American Armoury and
Bluebook, London, 1903)

4

EMIGRANTS FROM THE LOTHIANS

CHRISTIE, ROBERT, Edinburgh, admitted as a citizen of Cracow, Poland, 14.7.1702. (SIP43)
CLARK, JOHN, merchant in Calcutta, cnf 1778 Edinburgh
CLEGHORN, JAMES, merchant in Gothenburg, 1766. [SRO.RS27.{Edinburgh}.173.132/186.154]
CLELAND, DANIEL, of the Canadian Rifles, son of James Cleland and Janet Douglas in Whitburn, 1856. (SRO.SH.1856)
CLERIHUE, JAMES, Captain Lieutenant of Artillery in Bengal, son of John Clerihue, vintner in Edinburgh, cnf 1792 Edinburgh
COCHRAN, ALEXANDER, born 18.8.1790, son of Reverend John Cochran and Catherine Miller in Oldhamstocks, merchant, died in the Canary Islands. (F.1.413)
COCKBURN, HENRY, born in Haddington 1801, educated at Edinburgh University, minister in Grenada 1838-, died 19.7.1854. (F.7.667)
COLVILLE, WILLIAM, Liberton, member of the Scots Charitable Society of Boston 1774. (NEHGS)
COULT, OLIVER, MD, in Bantargu-sur-Mer, France, 1764. [SRO.RS27{Edinburgh}.165.43]
COUPAR, JOHN, Edinburgh, apothecary in Rotterdam 1686. (RPC.12.358)
COWAN, WILLIAM, brassfounder in St Petersburg, Russia, son of Thomas Cowan in Edinburgh. (SRO.SH.1832)
CRAIG, JOHN, Lothian, in Greipswald, Germany, 1628. (SRO.RS24.13.267)
CRAWFORD, ALEXANDER, Edinburgh, member of the Scots Charitable Society of Boston 1740. (NEHGS)
CRAWFORD, JOHN, born 15.1.1842 in Crichton, son of Reverend John Crawford and Ann Thomson, chaplain at Meerut, India. (F.1.213)
CROSBIE, ROBERT, in Kew, Melbourne, son of Jane Rae or Crosbie or Stuart in Edinburgh who died 26.10.1877. (SRO.SH.1880)
CUMMING, GEORGE, Midlothian, member of the Scots Charitable Society of Boston 1769. (NEHGS)
CUNNINGHAM, ARCHIBALD, Haddington, member of the Scots Charitable Society of Boston 1765. (NEHGS)
CUNNINGHAM, ARCHIBALD, born in Linlithgow 1795, to America 1818, died 1875. (BLG2643)
CUNNINGHAM, DAVID, prisoner in Edinburgh Tolbooth, sent to Holland as a soldier under Colonel James Douglas, 14.11.1682. (ETR)
CUNNINGHAM, HENRY, Edinburgh, physician in St Augustine, East Florida, pro 10.4.1771 Georgia.
DALRYMPLE, Colonel CAMPBELL, former Governor of Guadaloupe, 1764. [SRO.RS27{Edinburgh}166.335]
DANIELS, ELIZABETH, from Edinburgh, married James White, a Scots soldier, in Utrecht 24.10.1613. (Utrecht Marriage Register)

5

EMIGRANTS FROM THE LOTHIANS

DAVIDSON, HENRY, in Hobart Town, son of Thomas Davidson, tenant in Pleasance of Cockairney, 1835. (SRO.SH.1835)

DAWSON, Reverend WILLIAM, born 1718 in East Lothian, minister in St John's, Colleton County, South Carolina, died 1767, pro 13.10.1768 South Carolina

DE THORAIS, ELIZA, in Moscow, grand-daughter of Thomas Purdie, merchant in Edinburgh, 1855. (SRO.SH.1855)

DEVENER, JAMES, prisoner in Edinburgh Tolbooth, to Holland as a soldier under Captain William Douglas 6.3.1683. (ETR)

DEWAR, ANDREW, Leith, member of the Scots Charitable Society of Boston 1746. (NEHGS)

DEWAR, ROBERT, merchant in Antigua, 1768. [SRO.RS27{Edinburgh}.180.276]

DEWAR, THOMAS, educated at Edinburgh University, minister of St Andrew's, Nassau, Bahamas, 1827-1830, died 1830. [F.7.671]

DICK, ARCHIBALD, born in Edinburgh 1715, son of Thomas Dick, settled in Pennsylvania pre 1771, died 1782. (BLG2997)

DICKSON, JOHN, in Jamaica, 1762. [SRO.RS27{Edinburgh}159.164]

DISTANT, WILLIAM, Leith, member of the Scots Charitable Society of Boston 1693. (NEHGS)

DIXON, WILLIAM, Haddington, member of the Scots Charitable Society of Boston 1769. (NEHGS)

DOBIE, RICHARD, born in Libberton, Edinburgh, 1730, merchant in Montreal, died there 23.3.1805. (Gentleman's Magazine.75.773)

DON, JOHN, born in Edinburgh 1771, died in Augusta, Georgia, 10.8.1810. (Augusta Chronicle 11.8.1810)

DOUGLAS, CORNELIUS, Gifford, Midlothian, member of the Scots Charitable Society of Boston 1753. (NEHGS)

DOUGLAS, JAMES, in Stanhouend, Germany, 1625. (SRO.RS24.10.225)

DOUGLAS, ROBERT, General of the Swedish Army in Germany, son of Patrick Douglas of Standingstone, Lothian, and Christina Lesels, 1648. (RGS.IX.1995)

DREDDAN, JAMES, skipper in Fisherrow, citizen of Bergen, Norway, 1692. [SAB]

DRUMMOND, ALEXANDER, HM Consul in Aleppo, Syria, 1765. [SRO.RS27{Edinburgh}167.323]

DRUMMOND, JOHN, in Edinburgh, Ensign of a regiment in Swedish service, shipped from Leith via Cromarty to Stralsund, Germany, 1638. (RPC.7.84)

DRYSDALE, ROBERT,son of Margaret Thomson or Drysdale, a widow in Leith, a sailor in Schiedam, Holland, 1627. (SRO.RS25.12.323)

DUFFIE, DUNCAN, born in Edinburgh, married Mary Thomson, emigrated to New York pre 1763. (ANY.I.298)

EMIGRANTS FROM THE LOTHIANS

DUN, WILLIAM, in New South Wales, son of Reverend W. Dun in the
Canongate and grandson of A. Campbell, excise collector.
(SRO.SH.1836)

DUNCAN CHRISTINA, born in Linlithgow, married John Hill, from Falkirk but
resident in Rotterdam, in Schiedam 11.7.1643. (Schiedam Marriage
Register)

DUNCAN, DAVID, born in Edinburgh 1819, son of John Duncan, to America
1830, importer in New York, died in New Jersey 15.6.1891.
(ANY.2.297)

DUNCAN, JAMES, Leith, member of the Scots Charitable Society of Boston
1734. (NEHGS)

DUNCAN, JOHN, Edinburgh, emigrated to America 1830, merchant in New
York. (ANY.II.297)

DUNCAN, WILLIAM BUTLER, born 17.3.1830 in Edinburgh, son of Alexander
Duncan, educated at Edinburgh University and Brown University,
Rhode Island, banker and entrepreneur in America, died in New York
20.6.1912. (ANY.2.274)

DUNDAS, JOHN, HEICS Bencoola, son of Patrick Dundas, surgeon in
Linlithgow, cnf 1788 Edinburgh

EDWARDS, ALEXANDER, born in Edinburgh 11.4.1814, granite importer in
New York, died in Brooklyn 6.6.1871. (ANY.2.298)

EDWARDS, THOMAS JEOFFREYS, engineer in Java, son of Marion Edwards in
Edinburgh, 1854. (SRO.SH.1854)

EECKE, WILLIAM from Edinburgh married Anna Gerrits in Utrecht 6.12.1642.
(Utrecht Marriage Register)

EMO, JOHN, soldier from Edinburgh, married Catherine Ford from London
18.5.1618 in Leiden, Netherlands, 16.5,1618. (Leiden Marriage
Register, H.22)

ERSKINE, JOHN, Edinburgh, member of the Scots Charitable Society of
Boston 1740. (NEHGS)

EWING, Reverend ALEXANDER, son of Alexander Ewing, mathematician in
Edinburgh, died in Bermuda 15.10.1822. (SM.86.255)

FARLEY, SARAH, formerly in Edinburgh, then in Savannah, Georgia, pro.
10.1814 PCC

FERGUSON, THOMAS, Dunbar, merchant in the East Indies 1783. (SRO.S/H)

FERRIER, WILLIAM, in Oamamu, New Zealand, son of Catherine Leith Lowe,
wife of David Ferrier, in Edinburgh who died 15.3.1866.
(SRO.SH.1880)

FINLAYSON, DAVID, late of Savannh-la-Mar, Jamaica, Member of the
Assembly for Westmoreland, Jamaica, died in Edinburgh 3.2.1799.
[AJ2666]

FLEMING, JOHN, Edinburgh, member of the Scots Charitable Society of
Boston 1764. (NEHGS)

EMIGRANTS FROM THE LOTHIANS

FLETCHER, GEORGE, son of Andrew Fletcher merchant in Dalkeith and Margaret Stevenson, merchant burgess of Gothenburg 1774, died in Dalkeith 9.6.1775. (NS.7.1.146)

FORBES, ALEXANDER, printer in Edinburgh, member of the Scots Charitable Society of Boston 1767. (NEHGS)

FORBES, CHARLES WILLIAM, in Ceylon, son of George Forbes, banker in Edinburgh, who died 26.9.1857. (SRO.SH.1858)

FORBES, SARAH HORN, third daughter of Alexander Forbes, wife of James Grant, died in Montreal 20.11.1858. [St Cuthbert's g/s]

FORDYCE, CHARLES, Edinburgh, Captain of the 14th Regiment of Foot, died in Virginia, pro. 1777 PCC

FOREST, ARTHUR, Edinburgh, member of the Scots Charitable Society of Boston 1739. (NEHGS)

FORREST, Reverend JOHN, born in Edinburgh 1799, minister in Charleston, South Carolina, naturalised in South Carolina 14.12.1840. (US.NA.M1183.1)

FORREST, ROBERT, born in Dunbar, minister - ordained in Saltcoats 27.2.1798, emigrated from Greenock to New York on the Recovery 8.10.1802, settled in Stafford, Delaware County, New York, 1810 -1846, died 17.3.1846. (ANY.I.385)

FORTUNE, ALEXANDER, Haddington, Captain HEICS, died in Lucknow, India, 1823. (SRO.CS239.Misc.26/4)

FRASER, ALEXANDER, Edinburgh, member of the Scots Charitable Society of Boston 1746. (NEHGS)

FRASER, JAMES, born in Edinburgh 25.1.1826, son of Andrew Fraser and Isabella Smith, settled in New York 1842, leather merchant, died 15.12.1897. (ANY.2.237)

FRASER, THOMAS, born in Musselburgh, son of Andrew Fraser, leather merchant in New York, died 1.2.1863. (ANY.2.195)

GAIRDNER, JAMES, born in Edinburgh 1761, married Mary Gordon, to Charleston, South Carolina, 1780, cotton planter in Georgia, died 1830. (BLG2696)

GAIRDNER, MEREDITH, son of Dr Ebenezer Gairdner and Harriet Gairdner in Edinburgh, medical student at Glasgow University, from London to Hudson Bay on the Ganymede 9.1832, a Hudson Bay Company physician 1832-1837, died in Hawaii 26.3.1837. [HBRS.4.344]

GALBRAITH, JOHN, East Barns, East Lothian, member of the Scots Charitable Society of Boston 1817. (NEHGS)

GEDDES, CHARLES, Edinburgh, member of the Scots Charitable Society of Boston 1774. (NEHGS)

GEORGE, NICOLAS, from Edinburgh, married Gertge Jans in Utrecht 26.12.1604. (Utrecht Marriage register)

8

EMIGRANTS FROM THE LOTHIANS

GIBSON, JAMES, Edinburgh, member of the Scots Charitable Society of
Boston 1734. (NEHGS)

GIBSON, WILLIAM, son of John Gibson a ropemaker in Edinburgh, settled in
Australia before 1848. [SRO.S/H]

GIFFORD, ANDREW, born in Loanhead 1761, cabinetmaker, to New York
1784, furniture manufacturer and timber merchant in New York, died
28.11.1846. (ANY.II.299)

GILLESPIE, ANDREW, Linlithgow, via London to New England pre 1759,
tobacconist at North End, Boston, member of the Scots Charitable
Society of Boston 1761. (NEHGS)(Imm.N.E.69)

GILMORE, DAVID, born 1740, late a ropemaker in St Petersburg, died
12.1.1805. (St Cuthbert's g/s)

GLASSELL, WILLIAM, possibly from Haddington,settled in Fredericksburg,
Virginia, by 1792. [Spotsylvania Deed Book N, 3.4.1792]

GLEDSTANES, JOHN, prisoner in Edinburgh Tolbooth, shipped to Holland to
serve as a soldier under Captain Bruce 8.5.1685. (ETR)

GOLDIE, ALEXANDER, born in Midlothian 1804, educated at Edinburgh
University, to Jamaica 1846, minister there, died in Jamaica
22.7.1847. (F.7.669)

GOODSIR, JAMES, in Melbourne, son of James Tod Goodsir in Edinburgh,
1859. (SRO.SH.1859)

GRAHAM, JOHN, born in Edinburgh 1694, educated at Glasgow University
1714, to Londonderry, New Hampshire 1718, minister and physician
in Connecticut 1723-1774, died in Southbury, Connecticut
11.12.1774. (CCNE)

GRAHAM, MUNGO, Captain in Dutch Service, 1769.
[SRO.RS27{Edinburgh}185.210]

GRAHAM, WILLIAM, prisoner in Edinburgh Tolbooth, shipped to Holland to
serve as a soldier under Captain Bruce 8.5.1685. (ETR)

GRANT, DUNCAN, merchant in Antigua, burgess of Edinburgh 1760. (EBR)

GRANT, GEORGE MORISON, born 30.12.1815, assistant surgeon HEICS, killed
at Kabul 13.11.1841. [St Cuthbert's g/s]

GRANT, PATRICK, born 25.7.1777, 5th son of John Grant, merchant in Leith,
settled in Boston, Massachusetts, 1802, married Anna Powell 1807,
died 20.11.1812. (BLG2719)

GRAY, ANDREW, born in Edinburgh 1801, gardener in Charleston, South
Carolina, naturalised in South Carolina 21.4.1845. (US.NA.M1183.1)

GRAY, Dr GEORGE, late of Calcutta, 1761. [SRO.RS27{Edinburgh}157.164]

GRAY, JAMES, prisoner in Edinburgh Tolbooth, recruited for service in
Holland as a soldier 12.4.1681. (ETR)

GRAY, WILLIAM, prisoner in Edinburgh Tolbooth, shipped to Holland to serve
as a soldier under Captain Bruce 8.5.1685. (ETR)

9

EMIGRANTS FROM THE LOTHIANS

GREENSHIELDS, GEORGE, in Melbourne, ex Edinburgh (?), 1856.
(SRO.SH.1856)

GREIG, JAMES, born in Edinburgh 1767, baker and confectioner in New York
1796-, died there 20.12.1804. (ANY.I.362)

GUTHRIE, JOHN, Edinburgh, settled in Litchfield County, Connecticut, died
1730. (DAB.8.62)

HALDANE, ROBERT, possibly from Edinburgh, settled in Bogata before 1840.
[SRO.S/H]

HALL, DAVID, born in Edinburgh 1714, printer, settled in Philadelphia
1743, died 24.12.1772. (DAB.8.123)

HALL, ROBERT, gardener in Haddington, member of the Scots Charitable
Society of Boston 1767. (NEHGS)

HALL, ROBERT, born 13.7.1826 in Edinburgh (?), merchant in New York, died
28.3.1889. (ANY.2.245)

HALYBURTON, ANDREW, Edinburgh, member of the Scots Charitable Society
of Boston 1722. (NEHGS)

HAMILTON, ALEXANDER, Edinburgh, member of the Scots Charitable Society
of Boston 1744. (NEHGS)

HAMILTON, ALEXANDER, born 9.7.1751, son of Reverend John Hamilton and
Jean Wight in Bolton, East Lothian, HEICS, died 7.8.1777. (F.1.357)

HAMILTON, ANDREW, brother of Archibald Hamilton - merchant burgess of
Edinburgh, merchant in Prussia, dead by 1655. (RGS.10.374) {cf
Andrew Hamilton, merchant in Prussia and Poland 1664.
(SRO.RD2.11.538)}

HAMILTON, ARCHIBALD, Edinburgh, merchant in Prussia, 1655. (RGS.X.374)

HAMILTON, CLAUD, of the Bank of Bengal at Mirzapore, brother of Marion
Hamilton in Portobello, 1853. (SRO.SH.1853)

HAMILTON, MARY ANN, late of Edinburgh, married Edward Marshall alias
Peter Fisher in the Cathedral of St John the Baptist, St John,
Newfoundland, 23.2.1815. (Gentleman's Magazine.85)

HAMILTON, OTTO, East Lothian, member of the Scots Charitable Society of
Boston 1737. (NEHGS)

HAMILTON, ROBERT, born 14.9.1753, son of Reverend John Hamilton and
Jean Wight in Bolton, East Lothian, Member of the Legislature of
Ontario, died 1811. (F.1.357)

HARDY, WILLIAM, born 23.5.1785, son of Reverend Thomas Hardy and Agnes
Young in Edinburgh, Captain HEICS, died 1824. (F.1.147)

HART, SAMUEL, Edinburgh, member of the Scots Charitable Society of
Boston 1743. (NEHGS)

HASTINGS, JOHN, Prestonpans, master of the James, died in Virginia,
pro.1707 PCC

HAY, ROBERT, Bo'ness, member of the Scots Charitable Society of Boston
1729. (NEHGS)

EMIGRANTS FROM THE LOTHIANS

HENDERSON, CHARLES MURRAY, born 2.4.1815, son of Reverend John
Henderson and Grace Bell in Tranent, surgeon HEICS. (F.1.397)
HENDERSON, FRANCIS CHARTERIS, born 24.7.1808, son of Reverend John
Henderson and Grace Bell in Tranent, surgeon HEICS. (F.1.397)
HENDERSON, GEORGE, New South Wales, son of Alison Johnston or
Henderson in Portobello, 1850. (SRO.SH.1850)
HENDERSON, PATRICK, New South Wales, son of Alison Johnston or
Henderson in Edinburgh, 1850. (SRO.SH.1850)
HENDERSON, ROBERT, second son of John Henderson in Bo'ness, died in
Barbados 29.5.1798. [AJ2640]
HENDERSON, WILLIAM, merchant in Edinburgh, son of James Henderson and
Hielos Brun, admitted as a citizen of Cracow, Poland, 1600. (SIP47)
HODGE, ROBERT, born in Edinburgh 1746, emigrated from London to
Philadelphia 1770, bookseller in New York, died 23.8.1813.
(ANY.I.170)
HOGG, ROBERT, born in East Lothian, emigrated to North Carolina 1756,
merchant in Wilmington, North Carolina, Loyalist, died in New York
1779. (James Hogg pp; Southern Historical Collection, University of
North Carolina)
HOG, THOMAS, soldier, husband of Elizabeth Armour in Leith, killed in
Tangiers ca1681. (South Leith KSR 8.9.1681)
HOPE, JAMES, Geelong, Port Phillip, New South Wales, grandson of James
Hope, mason in Morebattle, 1851. (SRO.SH.1851)
HORNE, SOPHIA, Edinburgh, settled in New Jersey pre 1747. (East Jersey
Deeds, Liber E, fo.101)
HUME, ALEXANDER, born 23.6.1819, fifth son of James Hume the Granton
pilot, died 6.7.1847. [St Stephen's g/s, Dum Dum, Bengal]
HUTCHISON, Mr JOHN, prisoner in Edinburgh Tolbooth, exiled to Holland
8.7.1682, died at Sandy Hook, (New Jersey?), 1684. (ETR)
HYSLOP, WILLIAM, born 1714, Humley, Haddington, pedlar, member of the
Scots Charitable Society of Boston 1746, died 1796.
(NEHGS)(Imm.N.E.95)
IMRIE, ELIZABETH, wife of Robert Waterston in Sydney, New South Wales,
and daughter of James Imrie, writer in Edinburgh, and Elizabeth
Bruce. (SRO.SH.1856)
INGLIS, ALEXANDER, Dunbar, member of the Scots Charitable Society of
Boston 1746. (NEHGS)
INGLIS, ANN, born 1834, housekeeper in Leith, arrived in Hobart, Tasmania,
on the Duke of Lancaster 14.2.1855. (SRA.TD292)
INGLIS, JOHN, merchant burgess of Edinburgh, sometime in Bordeaux, 1652.
(RGS.X.20)
IRELAND, GEORGE, HEICS, son of Reverend Dr Walter Foggo Ireland in North
Leith who died 2.1828. (SRO.SH.1831)

11

EMIGRANTS FROM THE LOTHIANS

JACK, ARCHIBALD HAY, eldest son of Andrew Jack, a printer in Edinburgh, died in Melbourne, 21.11.1879. [S.11386]

JACKSON, ROBERT, Dunbar, member of the Scots Charitable Society of Bos on 1746. (NEHGS)

JACKSON, PETER, Musselburgh (?), staple factor in Veere, 1791.(SRO.S/H)

JACKSON, ROBERT WINCHESTER, born in Leith 28.12.1847, son of Robert Jackson and Agnes Todd, educated at Edinburgh University, minister in New Zealand 1900-1921. (F.7.603)

JACOBS, DAVID, Edinburgh, carpenter in Leiden, married Aaltgen Jacobsdaughter in Leiden, Netherlands, 26.9.1630. (Leiden Marriage Register, K.207)

JAMIESON, COLIN, son of Reverend Dr Jamieson in Edinburgh, Ensign of the 56th regiment, died at Bellary, Madras, 2.1.1813. (SM.75.959)

JAMIESON, JAMES WARDROPE, Genoa, son of William Jamieson and Elizabeth Jane Turnbull in Portobello, 1851. (SRO.SH.1851)

JAMIESON, THOMAS, surgeon in Guayaguil, South America, son of William Jamieson and Elizabeth Jane Turnbull in Portobello, 1851. (SRO.SH.1851)

JEFFREY, JAMES, born 1837, son of John Jeffrey and Euphemia Hart, died in Shanghai 17.10.1870. (St Cuthbert's g/s)

JOHNSDAUGHTER, BARBARA, from Leith, married Evert Thomasz from Woerden, South-Holland, in Leiden, Netherlands, 1.6.1625. (Leiden Marriage Register, L.96)

JOHNSON, CHARLES, merchant in Berwick, citizen of Bergen, Norway, 1695. [SAB]

JOHNSON, DANIEL, from Edinburgh, married Beertge Adriaens from Nieuwenoort, in Utrecht 7.2.1604. (Utrecht Marriage Register)

JOHNSON, PETER, Edinburgh, tailor, married Neeltgen Naertensdaughter from South-Holland in Leiden 5.9.1609. (Leiden Marriage Register, G.64); admitted as a citizen of Leiden 9.2.1610. (Leiden Citizenship Book, II.46)

JOHNSON, SAMUEL, born in Edinburgh 1787, died in Georgia 13.9.1820. (Colonial Museum and Savanna Advertiser 16.9.1820)

JOHNSON, THOMAS, from Edinburgh, married Elsken Daniels from Schalwijck in Utrecht 8.2.1624. (Utrecht Marriage Register)

JOHNSTON, ARCHIBALD, in Musselburgh, to Barbados 21.7.1682. (PRO.C6.3228.15)

JOHNSTON, Lady GEORGINA COCHRANE, third daughter of the Earl of Hopetoun, wife of Hon. Cochrane Johnstone, Governor of Dominica, died in Dominica 17.9.1797. [AJ2608]

JOHNSTON, JOHN R., New Zealand, son of Reverend John Johnston in Edinburgh, 1857. (SRO.SH.1857)

EMIGRANTS FROM THE LOTHIANS

JOHNSTON, JOHN, M.D., born 1812, eldest son of Alexander Johnston, died in Asuncion, South America, 9.10.1857. (St Cuthbert's g/s)

JOHNSTON, WILLIAM, Australia, son of James Johnston, mealdealer in Edinburgh, and Isabella Scott, 1855. (SRO.SH.1855)

JOLLIE, MARTIN, son of James Jollie tailor burgess of Edinburgh and Mary McNaught, land agent in East Florida, Member of HM Council in East Florida 1767-1776. ("East Florida as a British Province 1763-1784" p43, C.L.Mowat, Gainesville 1964)

JONES, WILLIAM, born in Leith 1793, mariner, died in Savanna, Georgia, 21.7.1809. (Savanna Death Register)

KEDDIE, ROBERT, son of John Keddie a candlemaker in Edinburgh, settled in New South Wales before 1840. [SRO.S/H]

KEIR, ADAM, a brewer in Edinburgh, son of Margaret Gray or Keir, settled in New Zealand before 1848. [SRO.S/H]

KEMP, HENRY, born in Musselburgh, 10.12.1814, settled in New York 1840s, died 16.5.1898. (ANY.2.232)

KERR, ALEXANDER, merchant in Bordeaux, 1763. [SRO.RS27{Edinburgh}173.139]

KIDD, ROBERT, soldier from Edinburgh, married Trijntge Pieters from Hamburgh in Schiedam 25.1.1634. (Schiedam Marriage Register)

KILGOUR, PETER MARTIN, Calcutta, son of William Kilgour, merchant in Edinburgh, 1855. (SRO.SH.1855)

KINLOCH, FRANCIS, merchant in Edinburgh and later in Paris, died pre 1685, wife Margaret Aldistoun. (SRO.RD22.1.895)

KINNEAR, WILLIAM, merchant in Edinburgh, citizen of Bergen, Norway, 1708. [SAB]

KIRKWOOD, ALEXANDER, Dunbar, member of the Scots Charitable Society of Boston 1750. (NEHGS)

KIRKWOOD, ALEXANDER, born in Edinburgh 1818, died on the William Nicol of Glasgow 17.4.1839. [Scotch Burial Ground g/s, Calcutta]

KIRKWOOD, JAMES, Dunbar, member of the Scots Charitable Society of Boston 1751. (NEHGS)

KIRKWOOD, MARGARET, from Edinburgh, married Andrew Thilger, soldier from Aberdeen, in Schiedam 29.12.1641. (Schiedam Marriage Register)

KNOX, JAMES, born in Edinburgh1690s, son of Reverend Henry Knox once in Bowden, minister in St Kitts. (F.2.172)

KNOX, JOHN, born in Edinburgh, merchant in New York, died there 18.7.1810. (ANY.I.305)

KNOX, PATRICK, son of Reverend William Knox (1569-1623) minister of Cockpen, factor for the States of Zealand for their possessions in India. (F.1.307)

EMIGRANTS FROM THE LOTHIANS

LAURIE, JAMES, born 1832, blacksmith in Edinburgh, arrived in Hobart, Tasmania, on the Donald McKay 6.9.1855. (SRA.TD292)

LAURIE, ROBERT JOSEPH, born 1870, son of William Muir Laurie, drowned at Selkirk's Drift, Kromme River, South Africa, 8.6.1891. (St Cuthbert's g/s)

LAW, JOSEPH, Edinburgh, to America 1674, settled in Liberty County, Georgia. (BLG2782)

LEARMONTH, JOHN, son of Alexander Learmonth in Edinburgh, formerly a pilot in Philadelphia, requested to contact Dr William Moore, Wall Street, New York, 1781. (New York Gazette and Weekly Mercury 8.1.1781)

LEARMONTH, WILLIAM, Edinburgh, citizen of Bergen, Norway, 1672. [SAB]

LECKIE, GEORGE, Edinburgh, settled in New York pre 1841. (ANY.2.181)

LECKIE, JOHN, educated at Edinburgh University, teacher at New York University Grammar School, died 22.8.1841. (ANY.2.181)

LEISHMAN, WALTER, factor in Veere, Netherlands, son of Thomas Leishman, merchant in Edinburgh, 1664. (SRO.RD4.1.358)

LEWIS, JOHN, Edinburgh, member of the Scots Charitable Society of Boston 1762. (NEHGS)

LIDDLE, JOHN, soldier from Edinburgh, married Grietken Hendricx from Diepenheim, in Dordrecht 7.5.1595. (Dordrecht Marriage Register)

LINDSAY, GEORGE, North Leith, member of the Scots Charitable Society of Boston 1762. (NEHGS)

LINDSAY, Captain, born Edinburgh, settled in New York city 1758, sought 1782. (New York Gazette and Weekly Mercury 18.3.1782)

LITTLEJOHN, DAVID, Edinburgh, member of the Scots Charitable Society of Boston 1748. (NEHGS)

LIZARS, WILLIAM, in Georgetown, British Guina, son of William Lizars, shoemaker in Leith, 1833. (SRO.SH.1833)

LORIMER, JOHN, M.D., born 21.8.1837, son of John Lorimer, builder, and Christian Mathieson, died in Batavia 8.1.1872. [St Cuthbert's g/s]

LYELL, GEORGE SIMPSON, New South Wales, son of George Lyell in Portobello who died 10.5.1832. (SRO.SH.1859)

LYALL JOHN, Dunbar, member of the Scots Charitable Society of Boston 1766. (NEHGS)

MCCRAE, JOHN MORISON, born in Edinburgh 8.5.1804, son of William Gordon McCrae and Margaret Morison, Ensign of the 17th Bengal Native Infantry, died in Ludhiana 15.6.1822. (BA.3.113)

MCCULLOCH, WILLIAM, born in St Cuthbert's 28.2.1816, son of John Ramsay McCulloch and Isabella Stewart, Lieutenant Colonel of the 13th Bengal Native Infantry, died in Shillong, Assam, 4.4.1885. (BA.3.115)

EMIGRANTS FROM THE LOTHIANS

MCDERMOD, HUGH, drummer in New York, husband of Grizel Colvill in New Greyfriars parish, Edinburgh, father of Peter born 14.1.1768. [Edinburgh OPR]

MACDONALD, Reverend JOHN, born in Edinburgh 17.2.1807, arrived in Calcutta 4.2.1838, died 1.9.1847. [Scotch Burial Ground g/s, Calcutta]

MCDONALD, WILLIAM, planter in Jamaica, husband of Ann Campbell, 1768. [SRO.RS27{Edinburgh}179.206/211]

MCFARLANE JOHN, Leith, member of the Scots Charitable Society of Boston 1758. (NEHGS)

MCHENRY, Mrs MARION, born in Edinburgh 1795, married James McHenry in Savanna, Georgia, died in Lexington, Oglethorpe County, Georgia, 22.10.1822. (Georgia Journal 5.11.1822)

MCIVOR, EDWARD, Edinburgh, member of the Scots Charitable Society of Boston 1734. (NEHGS)

MCKENZIE, GEORGE, son of John Mackenzie in Edinburgh, merchant in Bridgetown, Barbados, pro 28.8.1711 Barbados.

MCKENZIE, WILLIAM, Edinburgh, naturalised Charleston, South Carolina, 5.10.1831.(US.NA.M1183, roll 1)

MACLEISH, ROBERT, skipper in Dunbar, citizen of Bergen, Norway, 1737. [SAB]

MACLELLAND, SAMUEL, skipper in Edinburgh, citizen of Bergen, Norway, 1702. [SAB]

MCMATH, JOHN, land major in Tangiers, burgess of Edinburgh 1679. (EBR) cnf 1695 Edinburgh

MACNEAL, HECTOR, born 22.10.1746 in Rosebank, Roslin, later in St Kitts, Guadaloupe, St George's Grenada, and Kingston, Jamaica. [SRO.NRAS.0052]

MCPHERSON, JOHN, born in Edinburgh 1726, son of William MacPherson, writer, and Jean Adamson, skipper and privateer in Philadelphia pre 1751, died in Philadelphia 6.9.1792. ("Colonial Families" Vol.5, p364)(AP259)

MCWHIRTER, JOHN PEACH, son of Dr J McWhirter in Edinburgh, settled in Bengal before 1849. [SRO.S/H]

MABON, ALEXANDER, Edinburgh, sword burnisher in Gorkum, South Holland, married Maycken van Haelemis from Flanders, in Leiden, Netherlands, 28.1.1605. (Leiden Marriage Register, F.17)

MACK, Reverend JOHN, born in Edinburgh 12.3.1797, died in Serampore, Bengal, 30.4.1845. [Serampore g/s]

MANSON, GEORGE WRIGHT, born in Edinburgh 16.6.1845, son of George Manson and Janet Steele Reid, educated at Edinburgh University 1869, Indian chaplain 1870-1893, died in Edinburgh 9.10.1915. (F.7.577)

15

MARTIN, ROBERT, born 12.1.1842, son of Reverend Samuel Martin and Janet Weir in Bathgate, died in Natal 1862. (F.1.194)

MATHESON, DONALD, son of Duncan Matheson an advocate in Edinburgh, settled in Macao before 1842. [SRO.S/H]

MAULE, JOHN, a merchant in Demerara, son of Charles Maule in Leith, died in Demerara 17.10.1798. [AJ2664]

MEIN, JOHN, son of John Mein slater burgess of Edinburgh, bookseller in Boston, member of the Scots Charitable Society of Boston 1765. (NEHGS)

MELVILL, ROBERT, Governor General of Grenada, 1765. [SRO.RS27{Edinburgh}167.347]

MILL, JAMES, in St Michael's, Barbados, son of Robert Mill of Belfray, father of David. 1761. [SRO.RS27{Edinburgh}151.437]

MILL, ROBERT, Musselburgh, burgess of Bergen, Norway, 1655. [SAB]

MILLER, EBENEZER, Edinburgh, died in Calcutta 4.12.1797. [AJ2629]

MILLER, WILLIAM, son of Reverend William Miller (1649-1716) in Kirkliston, minister in Barbados. (F.1.213)

MILLER, WILLIAM, Edinburgh, member of the Scots Charitable Society of Boston 1762. (NEHGS)

MITCHELL, JAMES, prisoner in Edinburgh Tolbooth, sent to Holland as a soldier under Colonel James Douglas, 14.11.1682. (ETR)

MITCHELL, ROBERT, Bo'ness, member of the Scots Charitable Society of Boston 1731. (NEHGS)

MITCHELLHILL, CHRISTINA, eldest daughter of Peter Mitchellhill, late in Edinburgh, The Grange, Mathoura, New South Wales, married Philip Bull, Melbourne, at Tweedside, Eddonden, near Melbourne, 20.11.1873. [S.11395]

MOFFATT, DAVID, born in Musselburgh 1810, to New York 1827, currier, died 24.7.1887 at Cold Spring on the Hudson. (ANY.2.268)

MOIR, JAMES, born 15.3.1817 in Edinburgh, son of James Moir and Margaret Stenhouse, merchant in New York, died there 7.12.1899. (ANY.2.247)

MORRISON, WALTER, Edinburgh, married Geesken Roemersens in Zwolle, Netherlands, 22.7.1590. (Zwolle Marriage Register)

MOWBRAY, ROBERT C., son of W. Mowbray merchant in Leith, died in Rome 2.3.1823. (SM.86.648)

MUNRO, JAMES, son of late John Munro merchant in Edinburgh, died in China 1.1799. [AJ2652]

MURRAY, JAMES, Edinburgh, member of the Scots Charitable Society of Boston 1754. (NEHGS)

MURRAY, WILLIAM R., born 1820, eldest son of John Murray and Anne Jane Borland, assistant surgeon HEICS, died in Dhoolia, India, 16.1.1850. [St Cuthbert's g/s]

EMIGRANTS FROM THE LOTHIANS

NAYSMYTH, CHARLES JAMES, merchant in Calcutta, son of James Nasmyth, goldsmith in Edinburgh, who died 17.3.1855. (SRO.SH.1856)

NEILSON, JAMES, Dunbar, member of the Scots Charitable Society of Boston 1738. (NEHGS)

NEILSON, JAMES, Haddington, member of the Scots Charitable Society of Boston 1817. (NEHGS)

NEWLAND, ALEXANDER, son of John Newland in Edinburgh, pro 4.12.1809 New Jersey. (NJA.10593G)

NEWLAND, ANTHONY, born in Edinburgh 1769, merchant in New York 1808, died in Newark, New Jersey, 29.11.1809. (ANY.I.394)

NICHOLSON, FRANCIS MAXWELL, born 24.12.1855 in Pencaitland, son of Reverend Maxwell Nicholson and Frances Oliphant, merchant in Buenos Ayres. (F.1.116)

NICHOLSON, GEORGE, born in Leith 1746, apprentice ship's carpenter, ran away from George McAlin, ship's carpenter in Philadelphia 19.7.1765. (New York Mercury 12.8.1765)

NICHOLSON, STUART OLIPHANT, born 29.1.1849 in Pencaitland, son of Reverend Maxwell Nicholson and Frances Oliphant, cotton merchant in New Orleans. (F.1.116)

NIVEN, SAMUEL A., son of Robert Niven in Edinburgh, died in Ontario 14.11.1876. [AJ6728]

NOTMAN, PETER, born in Edinburgh 14.8.1820, to America 1833, underwriter in New York, died in Brooklyn 26.10.1893. (AP300)

OGILVIE, JAMES, Leith, died in Georgia 1790. (Georgia Gazette 19.8.1790)

OGILVIE, JOHN, in Holland, son of Robert Ogilvie, merchant in Leith. (SRO.SH.1859)

ORR, Captain SAMUEL, son of James Orr merchant in Leith, died in Kingston, Jamaica, 9.7.1813. (SM.75.959)

OWEN, THOMAS, born 1774, surgeon, died in Madras 14.1.1833. [St Cuthbert's g/s]

PARK, THOMAS CRAIGIE, Springfield, Haddington, married Maggie, daughter of Reverend Dr A. Tupp in Knox Church. Toronto, 11.6.1874. [AJ6597]

PARKER, WILLIAM, soldier from Edinburgh, married Annitgen Everts from Rotterdam in Schiedam 30.6.1635. (Schiedam Marriage Register)

PATERSON, GEORGE, Edinburgh, member of the Scots Charitable Society of Boston 1736. (NEHGS)

PATERSON, WILLIAM GILBERT SPENCE, born 30.8.1854 in Cockburnspath, son of Reverend William Paterson and Jessie Hay Spence, British Consul in Reykyajik, died 28.3.1898. (F.1.405)

PATON, ANDREW ARCHIBALD, in Brussels, son of Andrew Paton, saddler in Edinburgh, who died 13.10.1852. (SRO.SH.1855)

PATON, JAMES, born 13.9.1798, son of Reverend John Paton and Margaret Main in Lasswade, Captain of the Bengal Artillery, died 1848. (F.1.330)

PATON, THOMAS, born 4.1806, son of Reverend John Paton and Margaret Main in Lasswade, banker in Canada and New Zealand. (F.1.330)

PATON, WILLIAM, born in Edinburgh 1818, settled in New York 1832, merchant, died 25.9.1890. (ANY.2.179)

PATTULLO, JAMES LEBURN, born in Edinburgh 12.11.1853, son of James Pattullo and Jane Morrison Leburn, educated at Edinburgh University, minister in New Zealand 1883-. (F.7.605)

PEARSON, ADAM, born in Cockenzie 1817, son of Adam Pearson and Jane Stewart, merchant in New York, died in Edinburgh 29.7.1889. (ANY.2.240)

PEARSON, DAVID, born in Cockenzie 10.12.1821, son of Adam Pearson and Jane Stewart, bookkeeper in New York, died 18.3.1886. (ANY.2.270)

PETERS, JOHN, Haddington, married Marritgen Peters from Gouda 4.1576. (Gouda Marriage Register)

PETTIGREW, ROBERT, born in East Lothian 1783, labourer, wife Eleanor - born in East Lothian 1782, children John 1805, Margaret 1807, Jane 1808, Ann 1815, and Ellen 1812, emigrated from Leith to America, naturalised in New York 1.11.1826.

PITCAIRN, JOHN, M.D., born 1800, son of William Pitcairn, died in Java 8.1840. (St Cuthbert's g/s)

POWRIE, WILLIAM in Barbados, pro 4.4.1649 Barbados. (EBR.25.1086)

PRESTON, WILLIAM, born in Edinburgh 1718, son of George Preston, educated at Balliol College, Oxford, 1735-1739, Episcopal minister in New Jersey 1767-1777, died in Shrewsbury, New Jersey, 7.3.1781. (CCMC)

PRINGLE, ANDREW, Edinburgh, member of the Scots Charitable Society of Boston 1734. (NEHGS)

PROVAN, JOHN, Aberlady, East Lothian, member of the Scots Charitable Society of Boston 1746. (NEHGS)

RAE, ELLIS, merchant in Poland, son of John Rae writer in Edinburgh, 1729. (SRO.S/H)

RAIT, ROBERT, born in Edinburgh 1806, jeweller in New York 1833-1866, died 1.2.1869. (ANY.2.182)

RAMAGE, ALEXANDER, Linlithgow, member of the Scots Charitable Society of Boston 1765. (NEHGS)

RAMSAY, ARCHIBALD, M.D., Linlithgow, member of the Scots Charitable Society of Boston 1736. (NEHGS)

RANKINE, ROBERT, Lothian, member of the Scots Charitable Society of Boston 1744. (NEHGS)

EMIGRANTS FROM THE LOTHIANS

RANKIN, ROBERT, merchant and grocer in Edinburgh 1821-1834, absconded to New York, later in Savannah and possibly Virginia. (SRO.CS46.1835)

RANNIE, DAVID, late of Calcutta, 1761. [SRO.RS27{Edinburgh}157.98]

REID, ALEXANDER, born 1777 in Edinburgh, watchmaker, naturalised in Charleston, South Carolina, 27.9.1813. (US.NA.M1183, roll 1)

REID, JOHN, Edinburgh, member of the Scots Charitable Society of Boston 1734. (NEHGS)

RENTON, JOHN, Prestonpans, member of the Scots Charitable Society of Boston 1754. (NEHGS)

RICHARDSON, WILLIAM BROWN, born 1840, youngest son of FRancis and Christian Richardson, died in Venezuela 18.2.1880.[St Cuthbert's g/s]

RITCHIE, EUPHAN, born 1772 in Edinburgh, naturalised in Charleston, South Carolina, 26.6.1832. (US.NA.M1183, roll1)

RITCHIE, JAMES, born 20.2.1833, son of Reverend William Ritchie and Isabella Brown in Athelstaneford, died in Switzerland. (F.1.355)

ROBERTSON, ADAM SWANSTON, son of James Robertson in Edinburgh, a farmer in Port Philip, Austrlia, before 1845. [SRO.S/H]

ROBERTSON, ALEXANDER, born in Edinburgh 1775, emigrated to New Brunswick 1798, married Margaret Stuart in St John, New Brunswick, 1804, died 1842. (BLG2892)

ROBERTSON, JAMES, printer and bookseller in Edinburgh, newspaper publisher in Charleston, South Carolina, printer in Boston and New York, settled in Nova Scotia 1783. (SRO.CS236.R12/3)

ROBERTSON, JAMES, born in Edinburgh 1777, confectioner,. wife Margaret, born in Edinburgh 1781, children Margaret 1804, Jean 1813, James 1816, and John 1819, emigrated from Greenock to America after 1819, naturalised in New York 31.5.1823.

ROBERTSON, JAMES, born in Edinburgh 10.1.1833, son of John Robertson, book distributor in New York, died London 30.4.1920. (ANY.2.304)

ROBERTSON, JOHN, cooper in Leith, burgess of Bergen, Norway, 1616. [SAB]

ROBERTSON, JOHN THOMAS, born 1562 in Edinburgh, soldier, married Elizabeth Peters Tenneson, born 1576 in Dundee, in Breda 14.3.1598. (Breda Marriage Register)

ROBERTSON, JOHN, born in Edinburgh 1787, carpenter, died in Savanna, Georgia, 6.9.1809. (Savanna Death Register)

ROBERTSON, ROBERT, Edmonstone, Midlothian, member of the Scots Charitable Society of Boston 1767. (NEHGS)

ROBERTSON, ROBERT, born in Edinburgh 6.4.1740, freeman of New York 7.2.1769, merchant in New York, died 6.11.1805, buried in Trinity Churchyard. (ANY.I.218)

ROBERTSON, WILLIAM, Queensferry, citizen of Bergen, Norway, 1693. [SAB]

ROBERTSON, WILLIAM FINDLAY, born 31.12.1786 in Dalmeny, son of Reverend Thomas Robertson and Jane Jackson, Lieutenant HEICS. (F.1.202)

ROCHEAD, JAMES, Edinburgh, merchant in New York, pro 26.1.1740 Monmouth, New Jersey. (Monmouth Wills lib.C. fo.378)

ROGERS, JOHN, in St Petersburg, grand-nephew of Thomas Rogers, merchant in Edinburgh. (SRO.SH.1841)

ROLLO, WILLIAM, Edinburgh, member of the Scots Charitable Society of Boston 1766. (NEHGS)

RONALDSON, JAMES, born in Gorgie, Edinburgh, 1768, son of William Ronaldson and Marion Cleghorn, settled in Philadelphia 1794, printer, died 29.3.1841. (AP305)

ROSS, ALEXANDER, Edinburgh, settled in Savannah, Georgia, 28.12.1734. (ESG94)

ROSS, D.M., former Captain of the 34th Regiment of Foot, resident at Poltonbank, Lasswade, applied to settle in Canada 26.5.1819. (PRO.CO.384)

RUDDIMAN, WALTER, son of Thomas Ruddiman printer in Edinburgh, midshipman on the frigate Venus, died in the West Indies 10.5.1813. (SM.75.478)

RUNCIMAN, ELIZABETH ISABELLA, born in Edinburgh 14.12.1855, daughter of Reverend David Runciman and Margaret Aitchison, wife of George O'Connell, died in Venado, Tuerto, Argentina, 4.8.1918. (F.3.435)

RUNCIMAN, JOHN AITCHISON, born in Edinburgh 6.6.1842, son of Reverend David Runciman and Margaret Aitchison, banker in Pietermaritzburg, South Africa, died 1902. (F.3.435)

RUNCIMAN, ROBERT INGLIS, born in Edinburgh 9.4.1848, son of Reverend David Runciman and Margaret Aitchison, merchant in Buenos Ayres. (F.3.435)

RUSSELL, JAMES, Edinburgh, member of the Scots Charitable Society of Boston 1745. (NEHGS)

RUTHVEN, JAMES, born in Edinburgh 1783, son of John Ruthven and Elizabeth Irvin, horner in New York and Bridgeport, Connecticut, died in New York 25.11.1855. (ANY.2.111)

SAMUEL, JOHN, eldest son of John Samuel and Margaret Hutcheson, died in Kimberley, South Africa, 5.9.1890. [St Cuthbert's g/s]

SANDERSON, PATRICK, Captain HEICS, son of Patrick Sanderson and Mary McQueen in Edinburgh, 1833. (SRO.SH.1833)

SCOTT, ARCHIBALD, son of John Scott of Malleny and Susan Hay, to India 1776, Lieutenant of the 35th Native Infantry, Bengal Army, died 16.8.1781 Benares. (BA.4.29)

EMIGRANTS FROM THE LOTHIANS

SCOTT, DAVID, born 23.12.1779 in Haddington, son of Reverend Robert
Scott and Margaret Sheriff, HEICS surgeon, died in India 4.6.1816.
(F.1.373)

SCOTT, DONALD, farmer in Kiata, Victoria, son of Adam Bisset Scott,
tailor in Leith, who died 15.11.1872. (SRO.SH.1880)

SCOTT, GEORGE ROBERTSON, born in Edinburgh 3.5.1793, son of George
Robertson Scott, advocate, and Isabella Pattison, Captain of
Artillery, Bengal Army, died 19.8.1854. (BA.4.34)

SCOTT, JAMES CORSE, born in Edinburgh 2.6.1810, son of John Corse Scott
and Catherine ..., to India 1826, Major General of the Bengal Army,
died in Edinburgh 7.3.1890. (BA.4.44)

SCOTT, WILLIAM, born 8.4.1783 in Haddington, son of Reverend Robert
Scott and Margaret Sheriff, surgeon in Madras, died 14.3.1866.
(F.1.373)

SCRYMGEOUR, JOHN, bap. in Edinburgh 30.11.1746, son of David Scrymgeour
of Birkhill and Katherine Wedderburn, Captain of the Bengal Army,
died in Mysore 3.3.1791. (BA.4.45)

SETON, ROBERT, born 1.6.177 in Edinburgh, son of Daniel Seton of
Powderhall, lace merchant in Edinburgh, and Rebecca Meggat, to India
1794 on the <u>Pitt</u>, Lieutenant of the Bengal Army, died 29.12.1797 at
Masulipatam. (BA.4.53)

SHAIRP, CHARLES MORDAUNT, born in Bathgate 3.8.1810, son of William
Shairp of Kirkton, customs collector, and Eustatia David, to India
1829, Lieutenant General of the Bengal Army, died 24.10.1841 at
Etawah. (BA.4.57)

SHAIRP, NORMAN, born 20.10.1779, son of Thomas Shairp of Houston, West
Lothian, and Mary McLeod, to India 1800, Captain of the 12th Native
Infantry, Bengal Army, died 7.4.1864. (BA.4.58)

SHEPPARD, JOHN, born 1833, son of John Sheppard and Alison Darey, died
on his estancia near Monte Video 1.11.1868. (St Cuthbert's g/s)

SHERIFF, ANDREW, Prestonpans, member of the Scots Charitable Society of
Boston 1740. (NEHGS)

SHERIFF, ARTHUR MCEWEN, born 15.4.1822 in Edinburgh, son of Reverend
Thomas Sheriff and Janet McEwen, minister in Australia 1849-, died
in New South Wales 8.11.1864. (F.1.319)

SHERIFF, JANE CHRISTIE, born 29.12.1831 in Fala, son of Reverend Thomas
Sheriff and Janet McEwen, died in Australia 10.1880. (F.1.319)

SHERIFF, JOHN LIDDLE, born 19.11.1829 in Fala, son of Reverend Thomas
Sheriff and Janet McEwen, bookseller, died in Sydney, New South
Wales 5.1882. (F.1.319)

SIBBALD, JOHN, merchant in Gothenburg, 1768.
[SRO.RS27{Edinburgh}181.101]

EMIGRANTS FROM THE LOTHIANS

SIMPSON, Captain ANDREW, shipmaster of Leith, Commander of the Czar of
Moscow's ships 1706. (SRO.RD3.109.311)
SIMPSON, JOHN, Colonel HEICS, son of Edward Simpson in Edinburgh, 1835.
(SRO.SH.1835)
SLOZER, CHARLES, Edinburgh, member of the Scots Charitable Society of
Boston 1762. (NEHGS)
SMITH, JOHN, Edinburgh, sayworker in Leiden, married Rembrecht van
Thoornburch in Leiden, Netherlands, 10.11.1618. (Leiden Marriage
Register, H.71)
SMITH, ROBERT, born in Lugton, Dalkeith, 14.1.1722, son of John Smith, a
baker, and Martha Lawrie, to America 1748, builder and architect in
Philadelphia, died 1777, ("Scotland and America in the Age of
Enlightenment" pp275/276, R. Scher, Edinburgh 1990)
SPENCE, MARGARET, daughter of James Spence in Queensferry and widcw
of John Vernor of Dalvick, pro 11.8.1689 New Jersey. (East Jersey
Deeds, Liber B, fo..475-522)
STEDMAN, HUNTER, born in Edinburgh 20.12.1812, to West Indies 1839,
settled in Philadelphia 1849, winemerchant, returned to West Indies
1890, died in Rosseau, Dominica, 2.9.1900. (AP333)
STEEL, ROBERT, Edinburgh, member of the Scots Charitable Society of
Boston 1756. (NEHGS)
STEEL, THOMAS, born in Edinburgh 1740, educated at King's College,
Aberdeen, 1759, minister of Dordrecht, Netherlands, 1770, died
1771. (F.7.544)
STENHOUSE, REBECCA, daughter of John Stenhouse baker in Edinburgh,
settled in Zante by 1841. [SRO.S/H]
STEPHENS, ..., son of David Stephens trunkmaker in Edinburgh, died in New
York 1799. (SRO.CS233.Seqn.S1/19)
STEUART, JAMES, born 1795, seventh son of David Steuart in Edinburgh,
Lieutenant of HMS Hebrus, died 11.4.1820. [South Park g/s, Calcutta]
STEVENSON, HUGH, merchant in Peru, nephew of Margaret Maule in
Edinburgh. (SRO.SH.1853)
STEWART, ALEXANDER, Edinburgh, member of the Scots Charitable Society
of Boston 1819. (NEHGS)
STEWART, ARCHIBALD, prisoner in Edinburgh Tolbooth, to Holland as a
soldier under Captain William Douglas 6.3.1683. (ETR)
STEWART, JAMES, Edinburgh, member of the Scots Charitable Society of
Boston 1740. (NEHGS)
STEWART, KENNETH, Edinburgh, Captain in the late North Carolina
Highlanders, pro 7.1815 PCC
STEWART, ROBERT, merchant in Bordeaux, France, son of Provost James
Stewart of Edinburgh, 1674. (SRO.RD3.36.287)

22

EMIGRANTS FROM THE LOTHIANS

STEWART, ROBERT, a stationer, son of John Stewart of 24 Leith Street, Edinburgh, died in Sydney, Australia, 16.10.1876. [AJ6727]

STRUTHERS, JAMES, born in Edinburgh 1800, son of Reverend James Struthers, educated at St Andrews University 1819, minister in British Guiana 1826-1857, died in Edinburgh 4.8.1858. (F.7.675)

SUTHERLAND, JOHN MACKAY, born 1852, died in Ailsa, Paterson, New Jersey, 14.11.1879. [St Cuthbert's g/s]

SUTHERLAND, WILLIAM, born 1847, died in Ailsa, Paterson, New Jersey, 28.6.1895. [St Cuthbert's g/s]

SWANSTON, WILLIAM, a surgeon in St Kitts 1802, son of John Swanston in Haddington. [SRO.RS.Shetland, 452]

SWINTON, GEORGE STEEL, son of H. Swinton a merchant in Grangemouth and Jean Steel, settled in the Sandwich Islands before 1847. [SRO.S/H]

TAIT, GEORGE, born in Leith 1815, merchant in New York, died in New Jersey 5.8.1886. (ANY.2.241)

TAIT, JAMES HILL, born 31.8.1835, son of Reverend Adam Duncan Tait in Kirkliston, educated at Edinburgh University, ordained in Linlithgow 1861, Church of England chaplain in France and Italy, died in Rome 18.4.1900. (F.1.353)

TAYLOR, JAMES, Leith, member of the Scots Charitable Society of Boston 1711. (NEHGS)

TAYLOR, ROBERT, Edinburgh, member of the Scots Charitable Society of Boston 1731. (NEHGS)

TENNANT, S......, merchant in Veere, 1765. [SRO.RS27{Edinburgh}171.71]

THOMSON, EDWARD, born 19.4.1821 in Duddingston, son of Reverend John Thomson and Frances Ingram Spence, died in Australia. (F.1.20)

THOMSON, GEORGE, Edinburgh, burgess of Bergen, Norway, 1641. [SAB]

THOMSON, HENRY FRANCIS, born 3.8.1819 in Duddingston, son of Reverend John Thomson and Frances Ingram Spence, coffee planter, died in Ceylon. (F.1.20)

THOMSON, JOHN, skipper in Prestonpans, citizen of Bergen, Norway, 1695. [SAB]

TOWER, ALEXANDER, born 1801, died in Paris 3.8.1866, buried in Montmartre. (St Cuthbert's g/s)

TREMBLE, JAMES, Dunbar, member of the Scots Charitable Society of Boston 1694. (NEHGS)

TROTTER, THOMAS, Lieutenant in the Royal Artillery, son of William Trotter in Edinburgh, died at Idanho Novo, Portugal, 30.12.1812. (SM.75.238)

TULLIDEPH, WALTER, in Antigua, burgess of Edinburgh 1757. (EBR)

TURNBULL, GEORGE MATHESON, banker in Mount Gambier, South Australia, son of Christian Thomson, widow of Alexander Turnbull, in Leith who died 19.1.1880. (SRO.SH.1880)

EMIGRANTS FROM THE LOTHIANS

VANS, ELIZABETH, Edinburgh, resident in Leiden, married William Barrett from Colchester, England, in Leiden 25.3.1644. (Leiden Marriage Register, N.92)

WALKER, EMILIA, daughter of Alexander Walker, Queen Street, Edinburgh, wife of Edward Maxwell of the Bengal Civil Service, died on the East Indiaman Balcarres 26.7.1822. (SM.86.383)

WALKER, JAMES, merchant in Leith, later Collector of Customs in the Bahamas, father of Agnes Elizabeth Walker and John Geddes Walker. (SRO.SH.1853)

WALLACE, JOHN, from Edinburgh, married Sara Wright from Edinburgh, in Dordrecht 27.8.1595. (Dordrecht Marriage Register)

WALTERS, CATHERINE, born in Edinburgh 1764, died in Savanna, Georgia, 22.9.1808. (Savanna Death Register)

WEBSTER, GEORGE, born 15.10.1744 in Edinburgh, son of Reverend Alexander Webster and Mary Erskine, civil paymaster HEICS, died in Bengal 7.1794. (F.1.120)

WEIR, WILLIAM, merchant in Hamburg, formerly in Edinburgh, 1772. (SRO.RS38.XIII.178)

WHITE, GEORGE, born 1807 in Edinburgh, naturalised in Charleston, South Carolina, 3.8.1831. (US.NA.M1183, roll 1)

WILLIAMSON, ABRAHAM, from Leith, shoemaker in Leiden, Netherlands, married Maertgen Jansdaughter in Leiden 17.2.1628. (Leiden Marriage Register, M.85)

WILLIAMSON, CHARLES, born in Edinburgh, British Army officer, founded Bath, New York, 1793, militia officer and public official, died 1808. (Scots and Scots descendants in America p38 (NY1917)

WILLIAMSON, JAMES, born in Edinburgh 13.3.1810, metal broker in New York 1837-1872, died 23.1.1872. (ANY.2.180)

WILLOX, ALEXANDER, Leith, applied to emigrate to Canada 1819. (PRO.384.5.327)

WILSON, JOHN, born in Leith 1767, cartman, emigrated via Portsmouth to USA, naturalised in New York 31.3.1821.

WILSON, JOHN, in Tours, France, nephew of William Wilson, ironmaster in Kinneil, who died 24.9.1862. (SRO.SH.1880)

WILSON, PETER, surgeon in New Zealand, brother of Margaret Wilson in Belhaven. (SRO.SH.1859)

WILSON, THOMAS, born in Edinburgh 1758, gentleman, married Matilda ..., emigrated from Greenock to New York, naturalised in New York 16.11.1818.

WINGRAVE, WILLIAM MEARNS, in Bonn, Germany, son of Matthew Wingrave in Kirkbank, Edinburgh, who died 23.11.1848. (SRO.SH.1850)

24

EMIGRANTS FROM THE LOTHIANS

WOOD, JAMES, born 14.3.1840, son of Reverend James Julius Wood and
Christian Inglis in New Greyfriars, Edinburgh, banker in Sydney,
Australia. (F.1.35)

YOUNG, JOHN LAWSON, in Melbourne, son of David Young, excise officer in
Edinburgh, who died 10.12.1872. (SRO.SH.1881)

YOUNG, THOMAS, second son of James Young a brewer in Leith, died in
Jamaica 24.10.1798. [AJ2661]

YOUNG, THOMAS, born 1734, Dalmeny, Queensferry, settled Savannah,
Georgia, planter, died 7.11.1808, pro 14.11.1808 Chatham County,
Georgia. (Savanna Death Register)(Georgia g/s)

YOUNG, THOMAS, solicitor in Hobart Town, nephew of Annabella Fullerton
Young in Edinburgh, 1835. (SRO.SH.1835)

YOUNG, WILLIAM, born in Edinburgh, British Army surgeon, married
Elizabeth Clauson in Annapolis Royal, Nova Scotia, 5.1.1785, settled
on Staten Island, New York. (ANY.II.43)

YOUNG, WILLIAM, born in Uphall, West Lothian, died in Trelawney,
Cornwall, Jamaica, 1815. (SRO.RH1.2.804/1)

EMIGRANTS AND ADVENTURERS
from
Argyll and the Northern Highlands

INTRODUCTION

For nearly three hundred years emigrants have been leaving Argyll and the Northern Highlands for destinations worldwide. Although the main places of settlement and the reasons for the movement are reasonably well known very little information exists in print to identify these emigrants. This booklet, the first in a series, attempts to redress this imbalance.

During the seventeenth century there was relatively little emigration from the region and that which did occur was mainly of soldiers recruited to fight on the continent especially in Scandinavia, Poland, Germany, the Netherlands and France. Some of the earliest Scots (including some Highlanders) to be found in the Americas arrived as prisoners of war exiled by Cromwell around 1650, while many of the soldiers who participated in the Darien Expedition had formerly fought in Argylls Regiment in Flanders. Highland emigration direct to the mainland American colonies, especially North Carolina, Georgia and New York, began in the 1730s and expanded rapidly after the end of the French and Indian Wars in 1763 when Highland troops were demobilised there. After the American War of Independence the emphasis of settlement was in Canada though soon Australasia became a major destination. By the end of the nineteenth century emigrants from Argyll and the Northern Highlands could be found in virtually every corner of the then British Empire as this book attests.

David Dobson
St Andrews, 1993

Càirdean nan Gàidheal le fonn

Tha nis air am bonn 's gach àit;

Cothrom gu fhaotainn do'n t-sloagh

An deas agus tuath gun dàil

REFERENCES

ARCHIVES

PRO	Public Record Office, London
SRO	Scottish Record Office, Edinburgh
NEHGS	New England Historic and Genealogical Society, Boston: Scots Charitable Society MS
DFpp	Montgomery County Archives, New York: Duncan Fraser Papers
GSA	Georgia State Archives
US.NA	United States, National Archives, Washington, D.C.

PUBLICATIONS etc

ANY	Biographical Register of the St Andrew Society of New York, A. McBean, (New York, 1922)
BA	List of the Officers of the Bengal Army, 1758-1834, V.C.P.Hodson, (London, 1946)
BLG	Burke's Landed Gentry, (London, 1939)
CCMC	Colonial Clergy of the Middle Colonies, F.L.Weis, (Baltimore,1978)
CCNE	Colonial Clery of New England, F.L.Weis, (Baltimore, 1979)
CGS	The Campbells and other Glengarry Stormont and Harrington Pioneers, R.B.Campbell, (Ottawa, 1983)
CMN	The Clan McNeill, (New York, 1923)
ESG	A List of the Early Settlers of Georgia, E.M.Coulter & A.B.Saye, (Baltimore, 1983)
F	Fasti Ecclesiae Scoticanae, H.Scott, (Edinburgh 1928)
HBRS	Hudson Bay Record Society publications, (London)
ImmNE	Immigrants to New England, 1700-1775, (Salem, 1931)
JRA	The Justiciary Records of Argyll and the Isles, 1705-1742, J.Imrie, (Edinburgh, 1969)

KCA	Officers and Graduates of the University and King's College, Aberdeen, P.J.Anderson, (Aberdeen, 1893)
NCSA	North Carolina Scottish Ancestry, S.Buie, (Fort Worth, 1992)
SHA	Scotch Highlanders in America, J.P.MacLean, (Baltimore, 1968)
SPI	The Skye Pioneers and the Island, (Charlottetown, 1930)
SSA	Scots and Scots Descendants in America, (New York, 1917)
TML	The MacLeods - The genealogy of a Clan, D.Mackinnon & A.Morrison, (Edinburgh, 1969)

ABBREVIATIONS	cnf	confirmation
	g/s	gravestone
	pro	probate

EMIGRANTS AND ADVENTURERS FROM ARGYLL AND THE NORTHERN HIGHLANDS (PART ONE)

ALLAN, DONALD, born in Ross-shire 1812, educated at King's College, Aberdeen, 1829, minister in Ontario 1838-1874, died in Goderich 12.1884. (F.7.624)

ANDERSON, ALEXANDER ROSE MUNRO, son of John Anderson (1789-1840) and Mary Ross (1806-1871), died in Broken Hill, Australia. (Kincardine, Ardgay g/s)

ANDERSON, JAMES, born in Cromarty 1797, son of James Anderson a farmer, educated at Marischal College, Aberdeen, 1829, minister in Ontario 1835-, died in Ormstown 6.4.1864. (F.7.625)

ANDERSON, MALCOLM, born in Sleat 1788, to North Carolina 1799, settled in Savanna, Georgia, 1811, died in Savanna 11.10.1814. (Savanna Republican 27.10.1814)

ANDERSON, ROBERT MUNRO, son of John Anderson (1789-1840) and Mary Ross (1806-1871), died in New York. (Kincardine, Ardgay, g/s)

ARMSTRONG, DONALD, born 1866, son of Thomas Armstrong, died in Blackall, Queensland, 14.6.1899. (Kildonan g/s)

ARMSTRONG, WILLIAM, born 1853, son of Thomas Armstrong, died in Waikawa, New Zealand, 8.12.1898. (Kildonan g/s)

ARTHUR, JAMES INNES, born in Resolis 22.7.1785, son of Reverend Robert Arthur and Anne Munro, settled in Demerara, died 20.8.1816. (F.7.19)

BELL, ANGUS, Islay, settled in Megantic County, Quebec, 1850. (NCSA.2.94)

BETHUNE, DAVID, born in Dingwall 1771, emigrated to Tobago, settled in New York 1792, merchant in New York, married Joanna Graham 1795, died in New York 18.9.1824. (ANY.I.318)

BETHUNE, JOHN, born in Alness 2.10.1774, son of Reverend Angus Bethune and Catherine Munro, settled in Berbice, died 18.4.1819. (F.7.27)

BOLIN, JAMES, born in Kintyre 1767, died in Cumberland County, North Carolina, 1.4.1843. (NCSA.2.23)

BRACKENRIDGE, HUGH HENRY, born in Campbelltown 1748, settled in Pittsburgh 1782, author and judge, died 1816. (SSA84)

BROOMFIELD, ELIZABETH, born 1825, daughter of George Broomfield and Ann Brander, married James Armstrong, died in Australia 30.3.1858. (Clyne Kirkton g/s)

1

BRUCE, WILLIAM, born 1828, son of Robert Bruce and Betsy Mackay, died at Donald, Victoria, 17.4.1894. (Clyne Kirkton g/s)

BUDGE, WILLIAM, Caithness, member of the Scots Charitable Society of Boston 1732. (NEHGS)

BULLOCH, ANN GRAHAM, Inverness, widow of James Bulloch, Mulberry Grove, Georgia, pro 26.6.1764 Georgia.

BURGESS, JOSEPH, wife Margaret, emigrated from Inverness to Georgia on the Prince of Wales, Captain William Dunbar, 20.10.1735, settled in Darien, killed at the Siege of St Augustine 6.1740. (ESG66)

CAMERON, ALEXANDER, born in Glenmoriston 1727, to America 1773, settled on the Kingsborough Patent, New York, soldier of the Royal Regiment of New York 1780-1783, settled in Cornwall, Ontario, died 1.1823. (DFpp)

CAMERON, DONALD, son of John Cameron, emigrated to America, settled on the Kingsborough Patent, New York, Loyalist 1776, settled in Cornwall, Ontario. (DFpp)

CAMERON, EWEN, son of Alexander Cameron (1767-1857) and Anne ....(1777-1853), Munerrigie, Glengarry, settled in Australia before 1854. (Gairlochy g/s)

CAMERON, EWEN, son of Donald Cameron (died 1877) tacksman of Guisachan, Lochshielside, and Margaret McLean (died 1850), settled in Australia. (St Finnan's Isle g/s)

CAMERON, HUGH, to America 1774, settled on the Kingsborough Patent, New York, soldier of the Royal Regiment of New York, settled in Cornwall, Ontario. (DFpp)

CAMERON, JANET KNEATH, born 1855, daughter of Angus Cameron (1816-1878) and Elizabeth McDonald (1817-1878), died in Townsville, Australia, 1897. (Glen Nevis g/s)

CAMERON JOHN, born 1732, deserter from Captain John de Garmo's Company in New York 1764. (New York Mercury 12.3.1764)

CAMERON, JOHN, Inverness, member of the Scots Charitable Society of Boston 1733. (NEHGS)

CAMERON, JOHN, born in Glen Moriston, to America 1773, settled on the Kingsborough Patent, New York, Loyalist, settled in Cornwall, Ontario, 1785. (DFpp)

CAMERON, JOHN, son of Dugald Cameron in Camghail and Catherine McMaillan (1804-1843), settled at Portland Bay, Australia. (Kilmallie g/s)

CAMERON, MARTIN, son of Doandl Cameron (died 1877), tacksman of Guisachan, Lochshielside, and Margaret McLean (died 1850), died in Australia. (St Finnan's Isle g/s)

CAMERON, MURDOCH, son of Alexander Cameron, (1784-1872), farmer in Achlonachan, and Margaret Ross (1787-1843), settled in Victoria, Australia. (Lochbroom g/s)

CAMERON, WILLIAM, to America 1774, settled on the Kingsborough Patent, New York, soldier of the Royal Regiment of New York 1776-1783, settled in Charlottenburg, Ontario. (DFpp)

CAMPBELL, AENEAS, born 1839, son of Donald Campbell and Christine Campbell, died in Benin 10.9.1863. (Dornoch g/s)

CAMPBELL, ALEXANDER, born in Glenelg, emigrated to Canada 1817, settled in Harrington, Quebec. (CGS82)

CAMPBELL. COLIN, born in Glassary 4.7.1777, son of Reverend Peter Campbell and Margaret Scott, physician, died in Jamaica 8.5.1824. (F.4.7)

CAMPBELL, DONALD, born 1754, Loyalist, British Army officer 1776-1783, married Margaret E. Campbell in New York 2.8.1815, died 18.8.1825, pro 31.8.1825 New York. (Loyalists of New Jersey in the Revolution, p39)

CAMPBELL, DONALD, born 1847, son of Charles Campbell and Ann ..., died in America 1874. (Balnakeil, Durness, g/s)

CAMPBELL, DUGALD WILLIAM, born in Glassary 6.6.1779, son of Reverend Peter Campbell and Margaret Scott, died in Bahia 11.7.1823. (F.4.7)

CAMPBELL, DUNCAN, Glenelg, emigrated to Canada, settled at Cote St George, Quebec, 1817. (CGS79)

CAMPBELL, DUNCAN, born in Ardchattan 24.1.1812, son of Reverend George Campbell and Jane McDiarmid, physician in Toronto. (F.4.82)

CAMPBELL, EDWARD, born in Kintyre 1757, married Mary McLellan (died South Carolina 1816), emigrated from Greenock to South Carolina 1788, settled in Florida 1819, died Escambia County, Florida, 2.1837. (NCSA.2.70)

CAMPBELL, FINLAY, born in Glenelg 1795, emigrated to Canada 1817, settled at Cote St George, Quebec, died 1872, buried at Maxville, Ontario. (CGS82)

CAMPBELL, GEORGE JAMES, born in Ardchattan 12.10.1814, son of Reverend George Campbell and Jane McDiarmid, HEICS and later US Vice Consul in Jamaica, died 3.6.1841. (F.4.82)

CAMPBELL, HUGH, Glenelg, emigrated to Canada 1817, settled in Quebec. (CGS82)

CAMPBELL, JAMES, Argyll, emigrated to Canada 1801, settled in Martintown North, Ontario. (CGS506)

CAMPBELL, or MCIVER, JOHN, in Auchinshelloch, Argyll, son of Charles Dow Campbell or McIver in Upper Rudill, Argyll, thief, banished from Great Britain for life at Inveraray 28.4.1729. (JRA.2.403)

3

CAMPBELL, JOHN, born in Glenelg 1774, emigrated from Fort William to Montreal 7.1802, settled in Locheil, Ontario, died 11.1.1836, buried in Kirkhill, Ontario. (CGS452)

CAMPBELL, JOHN, Glengarry, married Margaret McPhee, emigrated to Canada pre 1802, settled at Loch Garry, Glengarry, Ontario. (CGS24)

CAMPBELL, JOHN, born in Kilmelford 18.2.1768, son of Reverend Patrick Campbell and Ann Campbell, died in India 1794. (F.4.97)

CAMPBELL, JOHN, born in Glassary 23.4.1766, son of Reverend Peter Campbell and Margaret Scott, merchant in Virginia, died 12.1796. (F.4.7)

CAMPBELL,KENNETH, son of John Campbell (1720-1805) and Margaret McLeod, died in the East Indies. (Dunvegan g/s)

CAMPBELL, MALCOLM, born in Glenelg 1796, emigrated to Canada 1817, settled at Cote St George, Quebec, died 1864, buried Maxville, Ontario. (CGS82)

CAMPBELL, MURDOCH, born in Glenelg 1797, emigrated to Canada 1817, settled at Cote St George, Quebec, married Catherine McNaughton (1811-1875), died 1873. (CGS82)

CAMPBELL, MURDOCH, son of John Campbell (1720-1805) and Margaret McLeod, died in America. (Dunvegan g/s)

CAMPBELL, PETER, born in Glassary 15.9.1775, son of Reverend Peter Campbell and Margaret Scott, died in Jamaica 6.11.1795. (F.4.7)

CAMPBELL, RODERICK, son of John Campbell (1720-1805) and Margaret McLeod, died in Jamaica. (Dunvegan g/s)

CAMPBELL, WILLIAM, born in Cowal, Argyll, 1741, to Massachusetts 1768, merchant in Worcester, Massachusetts, Loyalist, settled in Halifax, Nova Scotia, and then in St John, New Brunswick, died there 1823. ("The Loyalists of Massachusetts" p76)(PRO.AO13.24.72.4)

CAMPBELL, WILLIAM, born in Glenelg 1786, settled at Cote St George, Quebec, 1817, then at Harrington, Argenteuil County, Quebec, died 1866, buried at Lost River, Quebec. (CGS82)

CAMPBELL, WILLIAM, born 1883, son of Charles Campbell and Ann ..., died in Canada 2.11.1906. (Balnakeil, Durness, g/s)

CARMICHAEL, DANIEL, born 1750, emigrated from Lismore to North Carolina 1792. (NCSA.2.47)

CARMICHAEL, JOHN, born in Tarbert, Argyll, 17.10.1728, son of Donald Carmichael and Elizabeth Alexander, to America 1737, minister - educated at Princeton University, settled in Pennsylvanai, died at the Forks of Brandywine 15.11.1785. (CCMC)

CHISHOLM, ALEXANDER, born in Inverness 1738, to South Carolina 1746, married Christian Chisholm in Charleston 1766, died 10.12.1810. (BLG2615)

4

CHISHOLM, ALEXANDER, emigrated to America 1773, settled on the
Kingsborough Patent, New York, soldier of the Royal Regiment of New
York 1777-1783, settled in Charlottenburg, Ontario. (DFpp)
CHISHOLM, WILLIAM, emigrated to America 1773, settled on the
Kingsborough Patent, New York, soldier of the Royal Regiment of New
York, settled in Charlottenburg, Ontario. (DFpp)
CHISHOLM, WILLIAM, born 1843, died in Boston, USA, 26.1.1911.
(Creich g/s)
CLARK, DANIEL, from Castle Stewart, Petty parish, Inverness, Indian
trader in Augusta, Georgia, pro 13.5.1757 Georgia
CLARK, JOHN, born in Jura 1705, emigrated to Wilmington, North Carolina,
1735, settled in Duplin County, North Carolina, died 1767.
(NCSA.2.52)
COLQUHOUN, ANGUS, born in Argyll 1782, settled in Montgomery County,
Georgia, pre 1812. (NCSA.2.71)
COLQUHOUN, KATHERINE, born in Skye 1785, daughter of Malcolm Colquhoun
and Christian McCorqudale, emigrated to Virginia later settling in
Cumberland County, North Carolina. (NCSA.2.83)
CRAMOND, JAMES, son of Jane Cramond in Tain, merchant in Philadelphia
and New York, died in New York 29.9.1799. (ANY.I.200)
CRAMOND, WILLIAM, son of Jane Cramond in Tain, Ross-shire, emigrated to
America pre 1779, merchant in Philadelphia 1785, died 26.10.1843.
(ANY.I.200)
CRAWFORD, DUGALD, born in Kilmorie 15.5.1752, son of David Crawford,
farmer in Sisgan, educated at Glasgow University, deputy chaplain to
a regiment in Dutch Service in America 1781-, died in Scotland
22.3.1821. (F.4.63)
CULBERTSON, ROBERT, Laggan, Kintyre, emigrated to America, died 1766.
(BLG2642)
CUTHBERT, JAMES, Castlehill, Inverness, wife Anne, son George, settled
Drakies, Christchurch parish, Georgia, pro 20.10.1770 Georgia
DAETES, HENRY, Cantre, near Inverness, glover in Briel, Netherlands,
married Hester Wills from Sandwich, England, in Leiden,
Netherlands, 27.4.1605. (Leiden Marriage Register, F.34)
DARROCH, ALEXANDER, of Ardfernal, born 1806 in Jura, married Janet
Shaw in 1828, settled in Cumberland County, North Carolina, 1847.
(NCSA.2.57)
DINGWALL, JAMES, born 1821, son of Murdow Dingwall, (1783-1861) and
Charlotte Sutherland, (1778-1866), died in Dunedin, New Zealand,
28.2.1914. (Clyne Kirkton g/s)
DOUGLAS, ROBERT, born in Bowmore 1794, emigrated from Belfast to
America, cartman, naturalised in New York 31.3.1821.

5

DUNBAR, WILLIAM, son of Sir George Dunbar of Mochrum, army officer 1757-1763, settled in Canada, married Josette D'Eschambault by 1770, officer of the 84th (Royal Highland Emigrants) Regiment, died in Montreal 16.10.1788. (ANY.I.112)

DUNLOP, JOHN, Campbelltown, to America 1775, settled in Chambersburg, Pennsylvania, married Nancy Colvin, father of Robert. (BLG2667)

FERGUSON, DUNCAN, born in Dalmally, Glen Orchy, 1767, settled in North Carolina 1793, married Isabella Macnabb, died 1808. (BLG2681)

FRASER, COLIN ALEXANDER, born in Ardchattan 11.12.1833, son of Reverend Hugh Fraser and Maria Campbell, Legislature Assemblyman in New South Wales. (F.4.83)

FRASER, DONALD, born in Inverness-shire 1781, died 1827, buried in Midway Cemetery, Georgia. (Midway g/s)

FRASER, DONALD, born in Invergordon 3.2.1864, son of Alexander Fraser and Isabel McDougall, educated at Aberdeen University 1886, minister in New South Wales 1893-. (F.7.588)

FRASER, DUNCAN ALEXANDER, born in Ardchattan 27.12.1831, son of Reverend Hugh Fraser and Maria Campbell, surgeon general in Malta, died 28.8.1912. (F.4.83)

FRASER, JAMES, born in Inverness 1739, labourer, deserted from the 22nd Regiment of Foot in New York 4.1761. (New York Mercury 11.5.1761)

FRASER, JAMES, born in Foddarty, Ross, 1800, educated at King's College, Aberdeen, 1822, missionary in Cape Breton 1837-, died there 8.4.1874. (F.7.607)

FRASER, JOHN, Ross-shire, member of the Scots Charitable Society of Boston 1734. (NEHGS)

FRASER, JOHN, Inverness, member of the Scots Charitable Society of Boston 1758. (NEHGS)

FRASER, JOHN, born 1723, son of Captain Andrew Fraser, Captain of the 82nd Regiment 1776-1783, settled at Fraser's Point, Pictou, Nova Scotia, 1783, later at Inverlochy, Inverness-shire, died pre 1801. ("The Macleans of Sweden" p 37, J.N.M.MacLean, Edinburgh 1971)

FRASER, WILLIAM, born in Petty, Inverness, 26.3.1775, son of Donald Fraser and Mary Ann Smith, emigrated to Caledonia, New York, 1804, married Janet Christie (1785-1807) in 1807, died 16.7.1843. ("Genealogy of Miller and Tillotson" {Scotsville, New York, 1951})

FRASER, WILLIAM WILBERFORCE, born in Ardchattan 24.8.1830, son of Reverend Hugh Fraser and Maria Campbell, died in Australia 1918. (F.4.83)

FRASER, WILLIAM, born 1860, son of Alexander Fraser (1825-1904) and Janet Gordon (1825-1891), blacksmith, died in Ipswich, Queensland, 30.10.1890. (Dornoch g/s)

6

FYFFE, GABRIEL, born at Loch Fannich, Ross and Cromarty, to America 1783, settled in Albany, New York. (BLG2865)

GARDNER, GORDON ANDERSON, in Brisbane, Queensland, grandson of Colonel Sir Alexander Anderson of Campbelltown who died 26.7.1842. (SRO.SH.1880)

GEAR, JOHN, Inverness, member of the Scots Charitable Society of Boston 1745. (NEHGS)

GILCHRIST, GEORGE, born 1854, son of William Gilchrist and Annie Polson, died in Indiana 30.9.1896. (Loth, Brora, g/s)

GILCHRIST, WILLIAM, born 1847, son of William Gilchrist and Annie Polson, drowned off Sydney 26.10.1881. (Loth, Brora, g/s)

GILLAN, JAMES, Inverness, planter in St John's parish, Antigua, died pre 1797. (ANY.I.148)

GILLANDERS, ALEXANDER, son of Lachlan Gillanders, (1769-1844), farmer in Kishorn, and Margaret Mackenzie, (1783-1832), settled in Canada West. (Kishorn g/s)

GILLESPIE, JOHN, born in Port Charlotte, Islay, 1778, married Catherine Bell from Kilchoman parish, settled in Harriston, Wellington County, Ontario. (NCSA.2.68)

GILLESPIE, JOHN, Islay, settled in Eldon township, Victoria County, Ontario, 1828. (NCSA.2.94)

GILLIS, DANIEL, born 1770, emigrated to Wilmington, North Carolina, 1788, married (1) Nancy Paterson 1793 (2) Katherine Paterson, settled in Wayne County, Tennessee, before 1824. (NCSA.2.67)

GILLIS, DONALD, born in Inverness 1760, married Catherine McLeod, emigrated to America 1803, tailor and farmer in North Carolina. (NCSA.2.75)

GORDON, Mr, "a young gentleman from the Scottish Highlands", to New York on the Pearl, Captain Tucker, died in New York city 27.10.1773. (New York Gazette and Weekly Mercury 1.11.1773)

GRAHAM, ARCHIBALD, born in Argyll 1735, married Mary Baxter,settled in Cumberland County, North Carolina, 1766. (NCSA.2.8)

GRAHAM, JOHN, born 1710, wife Elizabeth Smylie, in North Knapdale, died in Cumberland County, North Carolina. (NCSA.2.36)

GRANT, ANGUS, emigrated to America 1774, settled on the Kingsborough Patent, New York, soldier in the Royal Regiment of New York, settled in Charlottenburg, Ontario. (DFpp)

GRANT, ARCHIBALD, emigrated to America 1774, settled on the Kingsborough Patent, New York, soldier of the Royal Regiment of New York 1776-1783, settled in Charlottenburg, Ontario. (DFpp)

GRANT, DONALD, Inverness-shire, emigrated to New England 1760, settled in Newtown, Connecticut. (Imm.NE)

7

GRANT, DONALD, emigrated to America 1773, settled on the Kingsborough
Patent, New York, soldier of the Royal Regiment of New York 1776
-1783, settled in Charlottenburg, Ontario. (DFpp)
GRANT, DONALD, weaver in Croskey, emigrated to America 1773, settled
on the Kingsborough Patent, New York, soldier of the Royal Regiment
of New York 1776-1783, settled in Charlottenburg, Ontario. (DFpp)
GRANT, DONALD, Grantown, settled in America 1814. (BLG2719)
GRANT, DUNCAN, emigrated to America 1773, settled on the Kingsborough
Patent, New York, soldier of the Royal Regiment of New York 1776
-1783, settled in Charlottenburg, Ontario. (DFpp)
GRANT, FINLEY, emigrated to America 1773, settled on the Kingsborough
Patent, New York, soldier of the Royal Regiment of New York, settled
in Charlottenburg, Ontario. (DFpp)
GRANT, JOHN, emigrated to America 1773, settled on the Kingsborough
Patent, New York, soldier of the Royal Regiment of New York, died in
Canada 1777. (DFpp)
GRANT, JOHN, born in Inverness 1788, emigrated to America 1800, settled
in Portsmouth, New Hampshire, naturalised 3.1839 Rockingham
County, New Hampshire.
GRANT, JOSHUA, son of Duncan Grant, merchant in Inverness, and Anne
Grant, settled in Bassterre, St Kitts, by 1766. (SRO.SC29.55.11.33)
GRANT, PETER, emigrated to America 1774, settled on the Kingsborough
Patent, New York, soldier of the Royal Regiment of New York 1776
-1783, settled in Charlottenburg, Ontario. (DFpp)
GUNN, JOHN, born in Farr 1806, educated at King's College, Aberdeen, 1830,
missionary in Cape Breton 1838-, died at Broad Cove, Cape Breton,
2.11.1870. (F.7.607)
GUNN, PETER, born in Caithness 1816, son of John Gunn, educated at
Marischal College, Aberdeen, minister in Australia 1842-1864, died
5.6.1864. (F.7.589)
HENDERSON, GEORGE, born in Halkirk, Caithness, 1797, to Canada 1817,
settled in Boston, Massachusetts, 1819, naturalised in Rockingham
County, New Hampshire, 10.1840.
HERD, WILLIAM, born 1860, son of James Herd and Marion Ross, died in
Brisbane, Queensland, 18.8.1910. (Dornoch g/s)
HORNE, GEORGE ALEXANDER, born 1872, son of George Horne, died in Barkly
West, Cape Colony, 25.7.1917. (Tongue g/s)
HOSACK, SIMON, born in Avoch, Ross-shire, minister, educated at Aberdeen
University 1779, emigrated to New York, married Catherine Carr
(1767-1795) in Goshen, New York, settled in Johnstown, New York,
1790. ("Some Pioneer Women of Johnstown" {Johnstown 1937})

8

INGLIS, ALEXANDER, Inverness, member of the Scots Charitable Society of Boston 1747. (NEHGS)

KELSO, ELIZABETH, in Kilmure, Arran, married Patrick Murphy, emigrated to America 1774, settled on the Black River, North Carolina. (BLG2839)

LAMBIE, WILLIAM, born in Argyll 28.12.1758, son of Reverend Archibald Lambie and Catherine McLachlan, educated at Glasgow University, died in Jamaica 29.7.1794. (F.4.14)

LAMONT, ANGUS, Cowal,Argyll, pro 5.4.1652 Barbados. (RB6.11498)

LAMONT, DUGALD, born in Kilfinan 17.3.1762, son of Reverend Alexander Lamont and Margaret Campbell, Captain of the 8th Regiment, killed at Seringapatam 1799. (F.4.29)

LESLIE, HUGH, born in Inverness 1793, Hudson Bay Company employee 1813 1825. (HBRS.2.230)

LIVINGSTON, ALEXANDER born in Argyll 1815, emigrated from Liverpool via New York to Charleston, South Carolina, 1835, settled in South Carolina, petitioned for naturalisation 14.10.1850. (Marlboro County Records)

LOTHIAN, JOHN, born in Campbelltown 3.5.1842, son of James Lothian, minister, to New Zealand 1877, died 1925. (F.7.604)

MACALISTER, DONALD, born in Clachaig, Argyll, 16.2.1790, son of Alexander MacAlister of Strathaird and Janet McLeod, Captain of Artillery in Bengal, died 1828. (BA.3.104)

MCALLISTER, HUGH, Argyll, settled in Lancaster County, Pennsylvania, 1732, died 1769. (BLG2800)

MCALISTER, NORMAN, born Skerrinish, Skye, son of Ranald MacAlister and Anne McDonald, Brevet Major of Artillery in Bengal, died 1810. (BA.3.105)

MCALLISTER, THOMAS, Castle Kilcohee, Inverness, resident in St Lucy's parish, Barbados, pro 24.3.1684 Barbados. (RB6.10.337)

MCARTHUR, JAMES, born in Bute 15.8.1832, son of Reverend John McArthur, educated at Glasgow University, minister in Kilmodan 1869-1877, Episcopal minister in Victoria and New South Wales. (F.4.32)

MACASKILL, DONALD, St John's parish, Barbados, pro 15.3.1710 Barbados. (RB6.5.450)

MCASKILL, HECTOR, born in Skye 1790, married Christian Chisholm, settled in North Carolina. (NCSA.2.77)

MCASKEL, JOHN, born in the Highlands 1757, runaway indentured servant of James McLure in Cumberland, York County, Pennsylvania, 1775. (Pennsylvania Gazette 10.5.1775)

MACAULAY, ALEXANDER, Garlock, Ross-shire, member of the Scots Charitable Society of Boston 1740. (NEHGS)

9

MACAULAY, Reverend JOHN, born 1737, son of John MacAulay, tacksman of Baleloch, educated at King's College, Aberdeen, 1754-1758, minister in South Uist, emigrated to America 1772, died 29.7.1776. (F.7.195)

MACBARNET, JAMES WILLIAM, born in Kingussie 23.5.1814, son of Donald MacBarnet of Chiry and Helen McPherson, Cadet of the Bengal Infantry, died Rangamati, Berhampore, 16.5.1832. (BA.3.109)

MCBEAN, JOHN, born in Nairn 1.4.1811, son of John McBean, educated at King's College, Aberdeen, 1832, minister in New Brunswick 1841 -1847, minister in Columbo, Ceylon, 1854-1862, minister in Australia 1850-1854 & 1862-1884, died in North Adelaide 13.8.1897. (F.7.593)

MCBEAN, JOHN GORDON, born in Inverness 20.11.1797, son of Robert MacBean of Nairnside and Margaret MacIntosh, Captain of the 52nd Bengal Native Infantry, died in Chittagong 14.6.1828. (BA.3.110)

MCBEATH, ADAM, son of Neil MacBeath and Margaret Rose in Doll, died in Toronto 1880. (Clyne Kirkton g/s)

MCBEATH, JOHN, son of Neil MacBeath and Margaret Rose in Doll, died in Toronto 1888. (Clyne Kirkton g/s)

MCCALLUM, PETER, born in the Highlands 1753, stole the sloop Betsy, master Philip Lacey, at Cape Henlopen 1775. (Pennsylvania Gazette 27.12.1775)

MCCOY, DANIEL, born in the Highlands 1738, tailor, absconded from James Richey in Kingston, Ulster County, New York, 1768. (New York Gazette and Weekly Mercury 20.11.1768)

MCCULLOCH, HUGH, son of Kenneth McCulloch and Barbara Ross, settled in Calloa, South America, by 1857. (Balnakeil, Durness, g/s)

MCDONALD, ALEXANDER, emigrated from Skye to North Carolina in 1800, settled in Moore County, North Carolina. (NCSA.2.24)

MCDONALD, ALEXANDER, 50, former crofter in Ulva, evicted, resident in Tobermory, wife Flora, children Coll 18, Lachlan 16, Donald 14, Mary 9, Christy 7, Marion 5, and Julian 1, emigrated from Liverpool to Van Dieman's Land on the Panama 8.1.1853. (SRO.HD4/5)

MCDONALD, JAMES, born Culloden 1766, died in Savanna, Georgia, 10.9.1811. (Savanna Republican 12.9.1811)

MCDONALD, JOHN, emigrated from Skye to Cumberland County, North Carolina, 1802. (NCSA.2.65)

MACDONALD, JOHN, born in Borrodale, Ardnamurchan, 8.6.1808, son of John MacDonald of Borrodale and Jane McNab, Lieutenant Colonel of the 66th Bengal Native Infantry, died in Aberdeen 16.2.1892. (BA.3.125)

MCDONALD, JOHN, born 1874, son of Alexander McDonald and Jessie Anderson, died at Botany Bay, Australia, 1.5.1889. (Golspie g/s)

10

MACDONALD, JOHN, bon 1848, son of Thomas MacDonald and Margaret
Cameron, died in Melbourne 9.3.1908. Golspie g/s)
MACDONALD, RODERICK, born in Snizort, Skye, 12.4.1804, son of Alexander
MacDonald and Christian MacLeod, Brevet Captain of the 69th Bengal
Native Infantry, died in Edinburgh 3.3.1837. (BA.3.127)
MACDONALD, SOIRLE, settled in North Carolina, farmer, Loyalist Captain,
settled in Shelbourne, Nova Scotia, 1783. ("The Loyalists in Nova
Scotia", p.153, D. Wetmore, Hantsport, 1983)
MACDONALD, WILLIAM, born 1830, son of Murdo MacDonald and Catherine
MacDonald, settled Westland, Otago, New Zealand, died 24.12.1916.
(Annat, Loch Torridon, g/s)
MCDONELL, ALEXANDER, born in Boleskine, Stratherrick, to America 1773,
settled on the Kingsborough Patent, New York, Loyalist, soldier in
the 1st Battalion of the Royal Regiment of New York 1776-1783,
settled at River Raison, Ontario. (DFpp)
MCDONELL, ALEXANDER, born in Knoydart, to America 1773, settled on the
Kingsborough Patent, New York, Loyalist, soldier in the 84th
Regiment, settled in Cornwall, Ontario. (DFpp)
MCDONELL, ALEXANDER, born in Aberchalder, Jacobite 1745, emigrated
from Fort William to New York on the Pearl 1773, Loyalist, Captain
of the 84th regiment and of the Royal Regiment of New York, married
...Macdonell, settled in Glengarry, Ontario. (DFpp)
MCDONELL, ALEXANDER, born in Fort Augustus 1762, son of Allan McDonell
and Helen Chisholm, to America on the Pearl 1773, soldier in the
84th Regiment and Butler's Rangers, Loyalist, settled in Canada, died
in Toronto 1842. (DFpp)
MCDONELL, ALLAN, born 1712 in Collachie, Loch Oich, Jacobite in 1745,
emigrated from Fort William to America on the Pearl 1773, settled
on the Kingsborough Patent, New York, Captain of the 84th Regiment,
Loyalist, settled in Quebec 1779, married Helen McNab, died Cap
Rouge, Quebec, 1792. (DFpp)
MCDONELL, ALLEN, to America 1773, settled on the Kingsborough Patent,
New York, Loyalist, soldier of the 1st Battalion of the Royal
Regiment of New York, settled Charlottenburg, Ontario. (DFpp)
MCDONELL, ANGUS, to America 1773, settled on the Kingsborough Patent,
New York, Loyalist, soldier of the 84th Regiment, settled in
Cornwall, Ontario. (DFpp)
MCDONELL, ARCHIBALD, settled on the Kingsborough Patent, New York, pre
1780, Loyalist, Lieutenant of the 84th Regiment. (DFpp)
MCDONELL, DONALD, born in Kilmorack, to America 1773, corporal of the
84th Regiment, settled in Charlottenburg, Ontario. (DFpp)

11

MCDONELL, DUNCAN, born in Glen Moriston, settled on the Kingsborough Patent, New York, Loyalist, soldier of the 2nd Battalion of the Royal Regiment of New York 1780-1783, settled in Cornwall, Ontario. (DFpp)

MACDONELL, GEORGE, born in Glenelg 20.3.1787, son of John MacDonell of Finiskaig, Lieutenant of the 23rd Bengal Native Infantry, died in Calcutta 8.9.1818. (BA.3.128)

MCDONELL, JOHN, born in Inveroucht, Inverness, to America 1773, settled on the Kingsborough Patent, New York, soldier of the 2nd Battalion of the Royal Regiment of New York 1780-1783, settled at River Raison, Ontario. (DFpp)

MCDONELL, JOHN, born in Dalechreggan, Inverness, to America 1774, settled on the Kingsborough Patent, New York, soldier of the 1st Battalion of the Royal Regiment of New York, settled in Canada. (DFpp)

MCDONELL, JOHN, born in Collachie, to America 1773, settled on the Kingsborough Patent, New York, soldier in the 84th Regiment 1776 -1783, settled in the Eastern District, Ontario. (DFpp)

MCDONELL, JOHN, born Leek, Loch Oich, 1707, Jacobite 1745, Officer in the 78th Regiment during the French and Indian Wars, emigrated from Fort William to America on the Pearl 1773, farmer on the Kingsborough Patent, New York, married Jean Magdalene Chisholm, Loyalist, Captain of the 84th Regiment, settled in Canada, died in Montreal 11.11.1782. (DFpp)

MCDONELL, JOHN, born in Baldron, Inverness-shire, emigrated to America 1774, settled on the Kingsborough Patent, New York, soldier of the Royal Regiment of New York 1782, settled in Charlottenburg, Ontario. (DFpp)

MCDONELL, JOHN, born in Fort Augustus, to America 1773, settled on the Kingsborough Patent, New York, soldier of the 1st Battalion of the Royal Regiment of New York, died 1786. (DFpp)

MCDONELL, JOHN, born in Auchengleeen, Invernessshire, to America 1773, settled on the Kingsborough Patent, New York, soldier of the 84th Regiment 1776-1783, settled in New Johnstown, Cornwall, Ontario. (DFpp)

MCDONELL, JOHN ROY, to America 1773, settled on the Kingsborough Patent, New York, soldier of the 84th Regiment 1776-1783, settled in Glengarry, Canada. (DFpp)

MCDONELL, KENNETH, to America 1773, settled on the Kingsborough Patent, New York, soldier of the 84th Regiment 1776-1783, settled in Cornwall, Ontario. (DFpp)

MCDONELL, MILES, born in Inverness 1767, settled in Tryon County, New
York, Loyalist, officer of the Royal Canadian Volunteers, in Hudson
Bay Company Service 1811-1820 died at Port Fortune, Ottawa River,
28.6.1828. (HBRS.2.232)
MCDONELL of ARDNABEE, RANOLD, soldier in the French and Indian War,
emigrated to America on the Pearl 1773, settled on the Kingsborough
Patent, New York, Loyalist, settled in Cornwall, Ontario, 1783.
(DFpp)
MCDONELL, RODERICK, born in Glen Moriston, to America 1774, settled on
the Kingsborough Patent, New York, soldier of the Royal Regiment of
New York 1776-1783, settled in Charlottenburg, Ontario. (DFpp)
MCDOUGALL, PETER, born in Inveraray, merchant in New York 1782-,
married Helen Robertson 1791, died 19.9.1798. (ANY.I.175)
MCFARLANE, DUGALD, 40, crofter and fisherman in Tobermory, wife Effy
35, children Lachlan 14, Donald 12, Mary 10, Ann 8, Neil 6, Kate 4,
and Sally 4 months, emigrated from Liverpool to Victoria on the
British Queen 8.1.1853. (SRO.HD4/5)
MCFARLANE, HUGH FALCONER, born in Inverness 15 January 1788, son of
Andrew MacFarlane, Bishop of Moray, and Magdalen Duff, Lieutenant
of the 3rd Bengal Native Infantry, died at Serampore 13.2.1817.
(BA.3.131)
MCFARLANE, WALTER, son of Andrew McFarlane in Glenfruin, advertised for
in New York during 1773. (New York Gazette and Weekly Mercury
16.8.1773)
MCFIE, FRANCIS NICOLSON, born in Portnahaven 17.2.1850, son of Reverend
Daniel McFie and Janet McFie, settled in Canada. (F.4.79)
MCGEACHY, ALEXANDER, born in Knockmoran, Campbelltown, 18.2.1758,
died in Robeson County, North Carolina. (NCSA.2.72)
MCGILLIS, DONALD, born in Muneraghie, Invernessshire, to America 1773,
settled on the Kingsborough Patent, New York, sergeant of the Royal
Regiment of New York 1777-1783, settled in Williamstown,
Charlottenburg, Ontario. (DFpp)
MCGILLIVRAY, ALEXANDER, born in Croy, son of Alexander McGillivray,
educated at King's College, Aberdeen, 1827, minister in Nova Scotia
1833-, died 16.2.1862. (F.7.615)
MCGILLIVRAY, CHARLES CALDER, born in Berriedale 26.5.1818, son of
Reverend Donald MacGillivray and Ann Allan, settled in Grenada.
(F.4.135); died there 6.4.1845. (Kilmallie g/s)
MCGRIGOR, DAVID, born 1799, son of Alexander McGrigor and Ann Mackay,
house carpenter in La Belle Alliance, Demerara, died 15.9.1839.
(Croick g/s)

13

MCGRUER, DONALD, to America 1773, farmer at Johnson's Bush, Kingsborough Patent, New York, soldier of the 84th Regiment, died at Sorel. (DFpp)

MCGRUER, JOHN, born in Boleskine, Abertarff, to America 1773, settled on the Kingsborough Patent, New York, 1775, corporal of the Royal Regiment of New York, settled in Charlottenburg, Ontario. (DFpp)

MCINTAYLOR, JOHN, born 1717, tailor, settled in New York 1738, runaway indentured servant of Lieutenant Governor Georg Clark in 1739. (New York Gazette 29.10.1739)

MCINTOSH, DONALD, born in Inverness 1726, to America on the Prince of Wales, master George Dunbar, 1736, settled on the Sepelo River, Georgia, 1746, died there 1801. (Colonial Museum and Savanna Advertiser 3.7.1801)

MCINTOSH, GEORGE, labourer, killed in New York 1764. (New York Mercury 21.5.1764)

MCINTOSH, JAMES, born in Strathdearn 1754, son of William Roy McIntosh of Dell and Marjory McIntosh, to New York 1776, merchant in New York, died in New York 4.11.1811. (ANY.I.176)

MCINTOSH, JAMES, born in Ross-shire, educated at King's College, Aberdeen, 1818, minister in Charlottetown, Prince Edward Island, 1830-1836. (F.7.621)

MCINTOSH, JOHN, born in Inverness 1737, silversmith, deserted from the 17th Regiment of Foot at Ticonderoga, New York, 1760. (New York Mercury 3.3.1760)

MCINTOSH, JOHN, to America 1773, settled on the Kingsborough Patent, New York, soldier of the 84th Regiment 1776-1783, settled at River aux Raisins, Ontario. (DFpp)

MCINTOSH, of BORLUM, LACHLAN, settled in Bristol, Rhode Island, pre 1721, married Elizabeth McIntosh, father of Elizabeth and Mary, died 6.1723. ("Genealogical Gleanings in England" p1288, Baltimore 1969)

MCINTOSH, WILLIAM, son of Alexander MacIntosh (1769-1802), merchant in Inverness, settled in Surinam before 1843. (Kilmallie g/s)

MACINTYRE, ALEXANDER CAMPBELL, born in Shieldaig 17.12.1864, son of Reverend Alexander Campbell MacIntyre and Mary Ralston, died in Toowoomba, Australia. (F.4.90)

McINTYRE, ALLAN, born in Kilmonivaig, son of Duncan McIntyre a farmer, educated at Glasgow University, minister in New South Wales 1854 -1870, died in Sydney 28.5.1870. (F.7.593)

MCINTYRE, ARCHIBALD, born in Glenorchy 16.8.1774, son of Reverend Joseph McIntyre and Christian McVean, settled in Jamaica. (F.4.87)

14

MCINTYRE, DONALD, born in Glenorchy 8.11.1778, son of Reverend Joseph McIntyre and Christian McVean, died in Jamaica. (F.4.87)

MACINTYRE, ISABELLA, born in Kilmonivaig 17.6.1837, daughter of Reverend John MacIntyre and Eliza Clark, married Duncan MacIntyre in Glenoe, Tasmania, 1859, died 11.9.1919. (F.4.137)

MCINTYRE, JOHN, born in Glenorchy 12.8.1766, son of Reverend Joseph McIntyre and Christian McVean, army officer, died in Bengal 2.1793. (F.4.87)

MCINTYRE, NICOL, 44, Torosay, wife Janet 33, children Angus 14, Peter 10, and Mary 6, emigrated from Liverpool to Van Dieman's Land on the Panama 8.1.1853. (SRO.HD4/5)

MCINTIRE, PETER, born 1744, labourer, deserted from Captain Richard Rea's New York troops at Schenectady 1764. (New York Mercury 5.4.1764)

MACINTYRE, THOMAS, born in Kilmonivaig 29.1.1834, son of Reverend John MacIntyre and Eliza Clark, died in Glenoe, New South Wales, 1.10.1911. (F.4.137)

McINTYRE, WILLIAM, born in Kilmonivaig, son of Duncan McIntyre a farmer, educated at Glasgow University 1829, minister in New South Wales 1837-1870, died 12.6.1870. (F.7.594)

MCIVER, DONALD, born at Lochalsh 1.11.1778, son of Reverend Murdoch MacIver and Mary Mackenzie, merchant in New York, died in Bermuda. (F.7.155)

MCIVOR, KENNETH, Stornaway, emigrated to America 1772, settled in North Carolina. (BLG2809)

MCIVER, MURDO, born 1852, son of Evander McIver and Mary MacDonald, died in South Africa 1891. (Scourie g/s)

MCKAY, AENEAS, Inverness, member of the Scots Charitable Society of Boston 1745. (NEHGS)

MCKAY, ANGUS, emigrated to America 1772, settled on the Kingsborough Patent 25.9.1773, moved to Canada 1776, soldier of the Royal Regiment of New York, settled in Lancaster, Glengarry County, Ontario. (DFpp)

MACKAY, DAVID SCOTT, born 1847, son of Hugh Mackay, died in New Zealand 27.12.1874. (Lochinver g/s)

MCKAY, DONALD, emigrated to America 1773, settled on the Kingsborough Patent, New York, soldier of the 1st Battalion, the Royal Regiment of New York, married Elspeth Kennedy, settled at River Raisons, Ontario. (DFpp)

MCKAY, HUGH, Inverness, member of the Scots Charitable Society of Boston 1750. (NEHGS)

15

MACKAY, HUGH, son of George Mackay of Bighouse and Louisa Campbell, died in Antigua 1818. (BM332)

MCKAY, JAMES, Durness, member of the Scots Charitable Society of Boston 1817. (NEHGS)

MACKAY, JOHN, son of John Mackay in Lower Brora, settled in the East Indies before 1852. (Clyne Kirkton g/s)

MACKAY, JOHN, son of John Mackay in Oldtown (1774-1856) and Chirsty MacLeod 1784-1851), settled in Horseshoebush, New Zealand, before 1865. (Clyne Kirkton g/s)

MACKAY, NEIL, born 1842, son of Neil Mackay (1807-1882), died in Texas 17.6.1879. (Kildonan g/s)

MACKAY, ROBERT, son of Donald Mackay of Bighouse and Mary McInnes, died in Antigua 29.9.1816. (BM332)

MACKAY, ROBERT, born 1818, son of John Mackay and Ann Alexander, died in Whampoa, China, 6.7.1843. (Auchness g/s)

MCKENZIE, ALEXANDER, born 1749, settled in Prince Edward Island, died there 28.2.1824, buried in Belfast churchyard. (SPI.40)

MCKENZIE, ANGUS, emigrated from Loch Broom to Pictou, Nova Scotia, on the Hector 1773, settled in Windsor and later Green Hill, Nova Scotia. (SHA244)

MCKENZIE, ANGUS, born in Kylestrome, Sutherland, banker in St John, New Brunswick, 1820s, settled in New York 1836. (ANY.II.253)

MCKENZIE, DONALD HUGH, born 1862, son of George McKenzie, died in Chifwoo, China, 11.10.1903. (Lochinver g/s)

MACKENZIE, GEORGE, son of .... Mackenzie and Isabella Cameron (1789-1871), settled in Canada West. (Dornoch g/s)

MACKENZIE, HENRY, born 1886, son of George MacKenzie and Anne MacRae, died in Battleford, Canada, 21.8.1906. (Stoer g/s)

MCKENZIE, HUGH, born 1821, son of Reverend David McKenzie, died in Demerara 1844. (Farr g/s)

MCKENZIE, JOHN, born in Inverness-shire 1793, cabinetmaker in Charleston, South Carolina, naturalised in South Carolina 6.8.1847. (US.NA.M1183.1)

MCKENZIE, JOHN, son of Donald Mackenzie, (1758-1846), farmer in Balnagra, and Ann MacKenzie (1773-1854), settled in California. (Lochcarron g/s)

MCKENZIE, KENNETH, born in Ross-shire, painter and glazier in New York 1797, died in Bloomingdale, New York, 10.1803. (ANY.I.363)

MCKENZIE, NORMAN, born 1848, son of Alexander McKenzie and Jane MacRae, died in Kenona, Canada, 12.1910. (Stoer g/s)

MCKENZIE, PETER, Cromarty, member of the Scots Charitable Society of Boston 1739. (NEHGS)

MCKENZIE, RODERICK, son of Alexander McKenzie (died 1802), chief factor of the Hudson Bay Company. (Lochinver g/s)

MCKENZIE, RODERICK, son of John MacKenzie, (1778-1825), farmer in Balnacra, merchant in Cape Breton. (Lochcarron g/s)

MCKENZIE, WILLIAM, Stornaway, member of the Scots Charitable Society of Boston 1749. (NEHGS)

MCKENZIE, WILLIAM JOHN, son of Reverend David McKenzie (1783-1868), died in Otago, New Zealand, aged 44. (Farr g/s)

MCKINNON, ALASTAIR DOWNIE, born 1827, son of A.K.MacKinnon in Corry and Flora Downie, died in Mocofferpore, East Indies, 1860. (Cill Chriosd g/s)

MCKINNON, CHARLES FARQUHAR, born in Sleat 1820, son of Reverend John MacKinnon and Anne MacKinnon, settled in Melbourne. (F.7.183)

MCKINNON, DANIEL, born 1658, physician, settled in Antigua, married Elizabeth Thomas, pro 20.3.1720 Antigua

MCKINNON, DONALD LEWIS, born in Strath, Skye, 3.3.1863, son of Reverend Donald MacKinnon and Emma McLeod, died in Calcutta 12.2.1888. (F.7.183)

MCKINNON, DONALD, 26, Mull (?), emigrated from Liverpool to Victoria on the British Queen 8.1.1853. (SRO.HD4/5)

MCKINNON, GODFREY BOSVILLE, born in Strath, Skye, 1834, son of Reverend John MacKinnon and Anne MacKinnon, settled in Melbourne. (F.7.183)

MACKINNON, JOHN, born 1857, son of Reverend John MacKinnon, died in India 11.1907. (Cill Chriosd g/s)

MCKINNON, NEIL, 44, Tobermory, wife Christiana 39, children Jane 21, Mary 19, Hugh 17, John 15, Christiana 10, Juliet 8, and Dugald 13, emigrated from Liverpool to Van Dieman's Land on the Panama 8.1.1853. (SRO.HD4/5)

MACKINNON, WILLIAM MACLEAN, born 1859, son of Reverend John MacKinnon, died in Kalgurlie, Australia, 10.1.1901. (Cill Chriosd g/s)

MACKINTOSH, JAMES GRANT, born in Cawdor 1823, educated at King's College, Aberdeen, 1848, minister in Hobart, Tasmania, 1858-1861, died in Scotland 1895. (F.7.601)

MCLACHLAN, NEIL, born 1753, maried Sarah Leitch (1763-1851) in Kilmichael, Glassary, Argyll, 1785, settled in Cumberland County, North Carolina, 1804, died there 1833. (NCSA.2.8)

MCLARTY, EDWARD, born in Argyll 1814, mariner in Charleston, South Carolina, naturalised in South Carolina 2.10.1847. (US.NA.M1183.1)

MCLEAN, ALLAN, born in Skye, educated at King's College, Aberdeen, 1762, physician and minister in Bristol, Maine, 1773-1795, died there 1805. (CCNE)(KCA)

MACLEAN, ANDREW O'HARA, born in Mull 1755, son of Dr Alexander MacLean and Janet Fraser, Russian Army officer 1773-, killed in St Petersburg 6.12.1812. ("The Macleans of Sweden" p39, J N M MacLean, Edinburgh, 1971)

MCLEAN, ARCHIBALD, from Mull, wife Ann MacKenzie or Matheson from Coll, emigrated to North Carolina pre 1798, died before 1822. (NCSA.2.7)

MACLEAN, ALEXANDER, born in Tiree 30.6.1820, son of Reverend Neil MacLean and Isabella MacDonald, emigrated to Australia. (F.4.121)

MACLEAN, CHARLES, born in Kiltearn 29.1.1846, son of Reverend Alexander MacLean and Margaret Davidson, settled in British Columbia. (F.7.44)

MCLEAN, DONALD, son of Charles McLean of Drimnin, Morvern, and Isobel Cameron, surgeon of the 77th(Montgomery Highlanders) Regiment in America 1757-1763, settled in Cairo, Greene County, New York, by 1768, married Henrietta McDonald 1780, druggist in New York City, Loyalist, died in New York 10.1.1782. (ANY.I.106)(New York Gazette & Weekly Mercury 14.1.1782)

MCLEAN, DUNCAN, emigrated to America 1773, settled on the Kingsborough Patent, New York, 25.9.1773, soldier of the Royal Regiment of New York, settled in Charlottenburg, Canada. (DFpp)

MCLEAN, JESSIE, born in Uist 19.6.1822, daughter of Reverend Roderick McLean and Elizabeth McLeod, married Norman MacDonald, died in Broadmeadow, New South Wales. (F.7.196)

MCLEAN, MARY, born 1734, runaway indentured servant of Jacob Eage, Campbell Hall, Ulster County, New York, 1759. (New York Mercury 17.12.1759)

MCLEAN, MURDOCH, emigrated to America 1773, settled on the Kingsborough Patent, New York, sergeant of the Royal Regiment of New York 1776-1783, settled in Charlottenburg, Ontario. (DFpp)

MCLEAN, MURDOCH, born in Salen 31.1.1829, son of Reverend Duncan McLean and Flora McLeod, died in New Zealand 16.6.1865. (F.4.87)

MCLEAN, NORMAN, born in Uist 11.10.1814, son of Reverend Roderick McLean and Elizabeth McLeod, died in Australia. (F.7.196)

MCLEAN, PETER, born in Uig. Lewis, 1800, educated at King's College, Aberdeen, missionary in Cape Breton 1837-, died 20.3.1868. (F.7.607)

MACLEAY, WILLIAM, born 1811, son of Alexander MacLeay in Invershin and Esther Grant, died in Geelong, New South Wales, 17.7.1852. (Kincardine, Ardgay, g/s)

MCLENNAN, EWAN, born Killilan 1802, son of John McLennan and Catherine McRae, planter in Jamaica, died Skye 1850. (Kiel Duich g/s)

MCLENNAN, JOHN, born in Ross-shire 1800, educated at King's College, Aberdeen, minister in Prince Edward Island 1823-1849. (F.7.622)

MCLEOD, ALEXANDER, born in Skye 1730, wife Nancy Ann McDonald, settled in Cumberland County, North Carolina, 1783, died 30.5.1815. (NCSA.2.64)

MCLEOD, ALEXANDER, born in Kilfinichen 12.6.1774, son of Reverend Neil McLeod and Margaret McLean, minister in New York. (F.4.113)

MCLEOD, ALEXANDER, son of Reverend Lauchlan McLeod (1762-1832) and Marion McLean, died in San Domingo. (F.7.194)

MACLEOD, ALEXANDER, Raasay, emigrated to Prince Edward Island 1821. (SPI.162)

MCLEOD, ARCHIBALD, born in Kilfinichen 17.3.1772, son of Reverend Neil McLeod and Margaret McLean, settled in Montreal. (F.4.113)

MCLEOD, ARCHIBALD, son of Captain Norman McLeod, (died 1804), tacksman of Bernisdale, and Ann McLeod, (died 1830), settled in Marywate, New South Wales. (Dunvegan g/s)

MCLEOD, Dr DONALD, born in Skye 1754, settled in Georgia 1779, died in Savanna, Georgia, 20.6.1802. (Colonial Museum and Savanna Advertiser 22.6.1802)

MCLEOD, DONALD, son of Magnus McLeod and Margaret Isabella MacDonald in Talisker, emigrated from Skye to Van Diemen's Land on the Skelton 1820, settled in Sydney, New South Wales, 1837, died there 11.4.1838. (TML.2.11)

MACLEOD, DONALD BAN OIG, Valtos, Skye, wife Mary Martin, children Donald, John, Malcolm, Roderick, Samuel, Nancy, Margaret and Catherine, emigrated to Prince Edward Island 1829. (SPI.141)

MACLEOD, DONALD, born 1778, MD, Inspector General of Hospitals in India, died 12.11.1840, buried in Calcutta. (Dunvegan g/s)

MCLEOD, HUGH NORMAN, born in Coll Castle, Isle of Coll, 30.11.1818, son of Donald McLeod and Catherine MacLean, emigrated from Skye to Van Diemen's Land on the Skelton 1820, settled at Geelong, Victoria, died 9.3.1892. (TML.2.12)

MCLEOD, JOHN, son of Alexander McLeod, settled in North Carolina, Loyalist, settled in Shelburne, Nova Scotia, 1783. ("The Loyalists in Nova Scotia" p153, D. Wetmore, Hantsport, 1983)

MCLEOD, JOHN, born 1805, son of James McLeod and Anne MacDonald, died in America 12.1861, (Creich g/s)

MCLEOD, JOHN, son of Donald McLeod and Jane McDonald, died in Sydney 15.2.1865. (Golspie g/s)

MCLEOD, MAGNUS, born in Talisker, Skye, 30.11.1808, son of Donald McLeod and Catherine MacLean, emigrated from Skye to Van Diemen's Land on the Skelton 1820, died there 1886. (TML.2.17)

19

MCLEOD, MALCOLM, soldier in the French and Indian Wars, settled on the Kingsborough Patent, New York, by 1778, Loyalist, died 1778, wife Isobel and six children moved to Cornwall, Ontario, 1783. (DFpp)

MCLEOD, MURDOCH, born in Skye 1815, son of Norman McLeod and Margaret McPhee, emigrated to Prince Edward Island 1829, married Margaret Gunn in Miramachi, New Brunswick, 6.10.1837, died 29.7.1889. (SPI.160)

MCLEOD, NORMAN, born in Skye 1762, son of Neil McLeod and Sophia Nicholson, married Margaret McPhee, emigrated to Prince Edward Island, settled in Uigg, died 1837. (SPI.159)

MCLEOD, NORMAN, son of Donald Mcleod of Talisker and Christina ..., British Army officer in North America 1756-1763, settled in Nova Scotia 1770. (ANY.I.61)

MCLEOD, PHILIP, Christ Church parish, Barbados, pro 4.8.1687 Barbados.

MCLEOD, RODERICK, born in Skye 1803, son of Norman McLeod and Margaret MacPhee, emigrated to Prince Edward Island 1829, married Catherine ..., died 2.12.1882. (SPI.160)

MCLEOD, SAMUEL, born in Skye 1796, son of Norman McLeod and Margaret MacPhee, emigrated to Prince Edward Island 1829, married Margaret Currie, Baptist minister in Uigg and Belfast, Prince Edward Island, 1840-1870, died 23.8.1881. (SPI.159)

MCLEOD, WILLIAM, emigrated to America 1773, settled on the Kingsborough Patent, New York, Lieutenant of the Royal Regiment of New York, settled in Charlottenburg, Ontario. (DFpp)

MCLEOD, WILLIAM, born 1882, son of William McLeod and W.J. Mackay, died at Sawdon Station, Burke's Pass, Canterbury, New Zealand, 11.9.1908. (Farr g/s)

MCMARTIN, DUNCAN, emigrated to America, settled on the Kingsborough Patent, New York, pre 1780. (DFpp)

MCMILLAN, DUNCAN BAIN, Lochaber, settled in Finch, Stormont County, Quebec, pre 1810. (BLG2813)

MCMULLEN, DONALD, emigrated to America 1773, settled on the Kingsborough Patent, New York, Loyalist, settled at River Aux Raisins, Ontario, 1783. (DFpp)

MCNAUGHTON, DONALD, son of Donald McNaughton and Margaret Cameron in Fort William, died in Woodside, Auckland, New Zealand, 1860. (Inverlochy g/s)

MCNEELAGE, DONALD, born in Argyll 1736, housecarpenter, deserted from the 1st Highland Regiment in America 1759. (New York Mercury 4.6.1759)

MACNEIL, HECTOR, son of Hector Og MacNeil of Orsary, Barra, emigrated to Pictou, Nova Scotia, 1802. (CMN)

MCNEILL, ISABELLA, 12, in Tobermory, emigrated from Liverpool to Van
Dieman's Land on the Panama 8.1.1853. (SRO.HD4/5)

MACNEIL, JOHN, emigrated from Barra to Cape Breton Island 1817. (CMN)

MACNEIL, JOHN, Barra, settled at Grand Narrows, Cape Breton Island 1804.
(CMN)

MCNEILL, JOHN, 28, in Tobermory, emigrated from Liverpool to Van
Dieman's Land on the Panama 8.1.1853. (SRO.HD4/5)

MCNEILL, LACHLAN, 20, in Tobermory, emigrated from Liverpool to Van
Dieman's Land on the Panama 8.1.1853. (SRO.HD4/5)

MCNEILL, LACHLAN, born 22.4.1834, son of Lachlan McNeill, farmer in
Kilmun, and Jane Black, educated at Glasgow University, missionary
in Uruguay 1866-1877, minister in Argentina 1883-, died in England
18.12.1917. (F.7.683)

MCPHERSON, ALEXANDER, emigrated to America 1773, settled on the
Kingsborough Patent, New York, soldier of the Royal Regiment of New
York 1776-1783, settled in Edwardsburgh, Grenville County, Ontario.
(DFpp)

MCPHERSON, DUNCAN, son of John MacPherson (died 1873) and Mary Russell
(died 1847) settled in New York. (Kilmore g/s)

MCPHERSON, JOHN, Strathspey, member of the Scots Charitable Society of
Boston 1758. (NEHGS)

MCPHERSON, LAUCHLAN, emigrated to America, settled on the
Kingsborough Patent, New York, by 1778, soldier of the Royal
Regiment of New York. (DFpp)

MCPHERSON, MURDOCH, emigrated to America on the Pearl 1773, soldier of
the 22nd Regiment, settled on the Kingsborough Patent, New York,
sergeant of the Royal Regiment of New York, settled in
Charlottenburg, Ontario. (DFpp)

MCPHERSON, WILLIAM, emigrated to America 1773, settled on the
Kingsborough Patent, New York. (DFpp)

MCQUARRIE, ALLAN, 49, Tobermory, wife Catherine 40, children Flora 9,
Lachlan 7, and Hugh 5, emigrated from Liverpool to Van Dieman's
Land on the Panama 8.1.1853. (SRO.HD4/5)

MCQUARRIE, HECTOR, 45, boatbuilder and crofter in Tobermory, wife Mary
35, children Christy 13, Hugh 10, Kate 8, and Donald 3, emigrated
from Liverpool to Van Dieman's Land on the Panama 8.1.1853.
(SRO.HD4/5)

MCQUEEN, DONALD, born in Barra 3.1.1794, son of Reverend Edmond
MacQueen and Mary McLean, surgeon in Jamaica. (F.7.186)

MACRAE, DONALD, born in Poolewe 3.10.1839, son of Reverend Donald
MacRae and Jessie Russell, physician in Iowa. (F.7.163)

21

MACRAE, DUNCAN, born in North Uist 16.11.1829, son of Reverend Finlay
MacRae and Isabella MacDonald, emigrated to Australia, died 1866.
(F.7.192)
MACRAE, JAMES RUSSELL, born in Poolewe 1840s, son of Reverend Donald
MacRae and Jessie Russell, farmer at Council Bluffs, USA. (F.7.163)
MACRAE, JOHN, born in Lewis 27.10.1834, son of Reverend John MacRae and
Penelope Mackenzie, emigrated to Australia. (F.7.16)
MACRAE, JOHN FARQUHAR, born in Poolewe1852, son of Reverend Donald
MacRae and Jessie Russell, settled in Toorak, Melbourne. (F.7.163)
MCTAVISH, DUNCAN, born 1864, son of John McTavish and Helen
McGillivray, died 10.1904, buried Gallag, Peru. (Golspie g/s)
MCVICAR, ARCHIBALD, born 1752, sailor, absconded from the transport
Christie in North River, New York, 1777. (New York Gazette and
Mercury 26.5.1777)
MARTIN, DONALD ARCHIBALD, born in Snizort and Uig 3.8.1855, son of
Reverend Angus Martin and Margaret Nicolson, settled in British
Columbia. (F.7.180)
MARTIN, JOHN LACHLAN, born in Snizort and Uig 10.3.1847, son of Reverend
Angus Martin and Margaret Nicolson, died in India. (F.7.180)
MARTIN, JOHN, wife Catherine McDonald, Skye, emigrated to Prince Edward
Island 1829, settled in Uigg. (SPI.149)
MARTIN, MARTIN, born in Snizort and Uig 3.9.1853, son of Reverend Angus
Martin and margaret Nicolson, died in India. (F.7.180)
MARTIN, SAMUEL MCDONALD, born in Snizort and Uig 11.11.1850, son of
Reverend Angus Martin and Margaret Nicolson, emigrated to
Australia. (F.7.180)
MATHESON, DUNCAN, born in Ross-shire 1784, died in Georgia 30.9.1812,
buried in St Paul's, Augusta, Georgia. (Augusta g/s)
MATHESON, JOHN, died at Santa Barbara 6.1.1895. (Lochinver g/s)
MILL, ANDREW, soldier from Caithness, married Catherine Adam from
Leith, in Schiedam 26.4.1635. (Schiedam Marriage Register)
MILLER, JAMES, bap. 27.5.1714 in Inverness, son of William Miller,
shoemaker, and Elspet Geddes, a squarewright in Georgia,
(GSA.Georgia Miscellaneous Bonds Y-2.321)
MILLAR, ROBERT, born in Thurso 1768, merchant, died in Georgia
26.3.1808. (Savanna Death Register)(Colonial Museum and Savanna
Advertiser 29.3.1808)
MITCHELL, JOHN GUNN, born 1877, died in Argentina 27.10.1907.
(Tongue g/s)
MITCHELL, MARCUS GUNN, born 1875, died in New South Wales 26.2.1920.
(Tongue g/s)

MITCHELL, PETER JAMES, born 1878, died in Wyoming 1.11.1920.
   (Tongue g/s)
MITCHELL, WILLIAM, born 1875, died in Riverton, Wyoming, 19.2.1941.
   (Tongue g/s)
MORRISON, ALEXANDER, Sutherland, member of the Scots Charitable
   Society of Boston 1805. (NEHGS)
MORRISON, HECTOR, Sutherland, member of the Scots Charitable Society of
   Boston 1805. (NEHGS)
MORRISON, RODERICK, Sutherland, member of the Scots Charitable Society
   of Boston 1805. (NEHGS)
MORRISON, WILLIAM, born 1792, son of Reverend Roderick Morrison and
   Jane Fraser in Kintail, died in Demerara 15.5.1814. (Kiel Duich g/s)
MORRISON, WILLIAM, born 1875, son of Hector Morrison (1850-1926) and
   Christian MacLean (died 1940), died in Winnipeg 19.7.1908.
   (Scourie g/s)
MUNRO, ALEXANDER ROSE, born in Invernald 20.5.1835, died in Montreal
   9.8.1869. (Creich g/s)
MUNRO, DAVID, born 1835, son of William and Margaret Munro in Bettyhill,
   died in Kimberley, South Africa, 29.6.1903. (Farr g/s)
MUNRO, DONALD, born 1869, son of Thomas Munro and Betsy Mackay, died in
   Johannesburg 19.6.1901. (Dornoch g/s)
MUNRO, DONALD, son of David Munro and Margaret McDonald, died in Helena,
   Montana, 12.11.1886. (Kincardine, Ardgay, g/s)
MUNRO, EBENEZER, born 1848, son of John Munro and Janet Sutherland, died
   in Vancouver 10.1896. (Auchness g/s)
MUNRO, HECTOR, born 1819, teacher, died in Australia 7.10.1890.
   (Dornoch g/s)
MUNROE, HUGH, emigrated to America 1774, settled on the Kingsborough
   Patent, New York, soldier of the Royal Regiment of New York
   1776 -1783, settled River aux Raisons, Ontario. (DFpp)
MUNRO, JAMES, born in Cromarty 1.7.1772, son of Reverend James Munro
   and Mary Stark, cabinetmaker, emigrated to Pictou, Nova Scotia.
   (F.7.5)
MUNRO, JOHN, born 1831, son of William and Margaret Munro in Bettyhill,
   died in Kimberley, South Africa, 8.4.1913. (Farr g/s)
MURCHISON, DONALD, born in Bochearron, Ross-shire, emigrated to
   America 1816, merchant in Fort Clairborne, Mobile, and Wilmington,
   North Carolina, died at Line Creek, Alabama, 13.11.1819. (Camden
   Gazette 30.12.1819)
MURCHISON, DUNCAN, emigrated to America 1773, settled on the
   Kingsborough Patent, New York, soldier of the Royal Regiment of New
   York, settled in Canada. (DFpp)

MURCHISON, JOHN, emigrated to Amewrica 1773, settled on the
   Kingsborough Patent, New York, soldier of the Royal Regiment of New
   York, settled in Charlottenburg, Ontario, 1783. (DFpp)
MURDOFF, GEORGE, emigrated to America 1773, settled on the
   Kingsborough Patent, New York, soldier of the Royal Regiment of New
   York, settled in Fredericksburgh, Ontario. (DFpp)
MURPHY, MURDOCH, born in Kintyre, died in Robeson County, North Carolina,
   1814. (NCSA.2.36)
MURRAY, ANGUS, son of William Murray, farmer in East Brora, and Maria
   Murray, settled in Dunrobin Plains, Van Dieman's Land, before 1841.
   (Clyne g/s)
MURRAY, ANGUS, born 1828, son of Robert Murray and Margaret Gray, died
   in India 19.11.1860. (Dornoch g/s)
MURRAY, DONALD, born 1849, son of Donald Murray and Jane Munro, died in
   Quilchena, British Columbia, 22.8.1897. (Dornoch g/s)
MURRAY, HUGH, son of David Murray, 1788-1844), and Janet MacDonald,
   (1789-1873), settled in Ontario. (Loth, Brora, g/s)
MURRAY, JOHN, born in Sutherland 1797, carpenter, emigrated from
   Greenock to USA, naturalised in New York 29.3.1827.
MURRAY, PETER, born 1826, son of Robert Murray and Jane Munro, died in
   Pictou, Nova Scotia, 16.11.1861. (Dornoch g/s)
MURRAY, ROBERT, born in Sutherland 1785, tailor in Charleston, South
   Carolina, naturalised in South Carolina 15.7.1831. (US.NA.M1183.1)
MURRAY, WILLIAM, son of Robert Murray and Jane Munro, merchant in
   Halifax, Nova Scotia, drowned in the City of Boston off Halifax
   28.1.1870. (Dornoch g/s)
NICHOLSON, DONALD, born in Stenschuill, Skye, 1780, son of John and Jane
   Nicholson, married Isabella Nicholson, emigrated to Prince Edward
   Island on the Polly 1803, miller at Orwell, Prince Edward Island.
   (SPI.153)
NICOLSON, JAMES, Skye, member of the Scots Charitable Society of Boston
   1733. (NEHGS)
NIVEN, DANIEL, born in Islay 1742, son of Duncan Niven, emigrated to New
   York 1765, engineer and architect, died in Newburgh, New York,
   20.11.1809. (ANY.I.180)
OLIVER, GEORGE, born 1836, son of George Oliver and Elizabeth Turner,
   died in Australia 8.12.1870. (Clyne Kirkton g/s)
OLIVER, JOHN, son of Thomas Oliver (1797-1865) and Hannah Charleton
   (1790-1866), settled in New Zealand. (Tongue g/s)
PATERSON, COLIN ARCHIBALD, coffee planter in Ootacamund, India, son of
   Colin Paterson, MD, (ex Argyllshire?), died 24.2.1863. (SRO.SH.1880)

PATERSON, ISAAC, born in Inverness-shire 1798, wife Anne ..., born in Ross-shire 1805, emigrated from Liverpool to America, naturalised in New York 30.10.1823.

PATERSON, JAMES, son of James Paterson physician in Glasgow, minister in Kirn, Argyll, 1859-1862, later a minister in Queensland and New South Wales. (F.4.36)

ROBERTSON, ALEXANDER, born at Lochbroom 19.12.1754, son of Reverend James Robertson and Anne Mackenzie, died in Nova Scotia. (F.7.157)

ROBERTSON, HARRY, born in Kiltearn 19.7.1776, son of Reverend Harry Robertson and Anne Forbes, died in Demerara 1795. (F.7.43)

ROBERTSON, HUGH, Slateville, Dunoon, to America 1790. (BLG2891)

ROBERTSON, RODERICK, son of Donald Robertson (1841-1882) and Christine Fraser (1843-1879), settled in Chicago. (Dornoch g/s)

ROSE, MARGARET BAILLIE, born in Nigg 18.7.1833, daughter of Reverend Lewis Rose and Katherine Simpson, married Donald Archibald McLeod, died in Australia. (F.7.73)

ROSS, ALEXANDER, Caithness, member of the Scots Charitable Society of Boston 1748. (NEHGS)

ROSS, ALEXANDER, Caithness, member of the Scots Charitable Society of Boston 1765. (NEHGS)

ROSS, ALEXANDER, born in Golspie, Sutherland, 1792, died at The Thicket, McIntosh County, Georgia, 1819. (Darien Gazette 24.5.1819)

ROSS, ANN, born 1807, son of William Ross and Margaret Cameron in Clyne, died in Quebec 1868. (Loth, Brora, g/s)

ROSS, DONALD, emigrated to America, soldier during French and Indian Wars, settled on Kingsborough Patent, New York, 1763, soldier of the Royal Regiment of New York 1776-1777, died 1787. (DFpp)

ROSS, DONALD, son of Reverend Thomas Ross and Jane Mackenzie at Lochbroom, died in New York 8.1.1853. (F.7.159)

ROSS, DUNCAN, born in Contin, Ross-shire 5.2.1831, son of Henry Ross and Anne McKay, educated at King's College, Aberdeen, 1851, to New South Wales 1856, minister, died 10.1.1901. (F.7.597)

ROSS, FINLAY, born 1740, emigrated to America, settled on the Kingsborough Patent, New York, soldier of the Royal Regiment of New York, settled in Charlottenburg, Ontario, died 1830. (DFpp)

ROSS, HUGH, born in Inverness-shire 1797, to Nova Scotia 1813, minister in Cape Breton and Nova Scotia 1827-, died 1.12.1858. (F.7.622)

ROSS, JAMES, son of John Ross (1810-1867), carpenter in Brora, and Ann Ross, (1817-1898), died in New Zealand. (Invershin g/s)

ROSS, JOHN, born in Cromarty 1807, son of Simon Ross a shoemaker, educated at Marischal College, Aberdeen, 1825, minister in Nova Scotia and New Brunswick 1836-1867, died 9.4.1871. (F.7.611)

ROSS, JOHN, born in Tain 29.1.1729, son of Murdoch Ross and Catherine Simson, merchant in Perth later also in New York 1762 and Philadelphia 1763, died in Philadelphia 8.4.1800. (ANY.I.400)

ROSS, MARGARET, daughter of Donald Ross, (died 1841), and Jane Munro, (died 1843), emigrated to Australia. (Invershin g/s)

ROSS, MARJORY, born in Logie Easter 11.10.1782, daughter of Reverend John Ross and Margaret Smith, died in Gibralter 1813. (F.7.69)

ROSS, THOMAS, tailor, emigrated to America 1772, settled on the Kingsborough Patent, New York, by 9.1773, soldier in the Royal Regiment of New York, settled in Lancaster, Glengarry County, Ontario. (DFpp)

ROSS, THOMAS, born in Drumvaich, emigrated to America 1773, settled on the Kingsborough Patent, New York, soldier in the Royal Regiment of New York 1776-1783, settled in Cornwall, Ontario. (DFpp)

ROSS, THOMAS BANE, born in Greigh, Sutherland, 1729, soldier at Quebec 1763, settled on the Kingsborough Patent, New York, pre 1778, soldier in the Royal Regiment of New York 1779-1783, settled in Lancaster, Ontario, buried South Lancaster Cemetery 10.8.1806. (DFpp)

ROSS, THOMAS, born 1853, son of John Ross and Christian Mackay, died in Townsville, Australia, 21.6.1886. (Lochinver g/s)

ROSS, WILLIAM, Ross-shire, member of the Scots Charitable Society of Boston 1748. (NEHGS)

ROSS, WILLIAM, born 1861, son of Hugh Ross and Mary Forbes, died in Hawaii 1.4.1895. (Kincardine, Ardgay, g/s)

SINCLAIR, ALEXANDER, born 1748, labourer, deserted the 1st Battalion, the Royal American Regiment, in 1772. (New York Gazette & Weekly Mercury 12.10.1772)

SINCLAIR, ALEXANDER, born in Caithness 1789, died in Savanna, Georgia, 30.10.1813. (Savanna Republican 2.11.1813)

SINCLAIR, JOHN, Caithness, member of the Scots Charitable Society of Boston 1739. (NEHGS)

SINCLAIR, PATRICK, pro 12.12.1674 Barbados. (RB6.9209)

SINCLAIR, WILLIAM JAMES, born in Forsnain, Reay, Caithness, 1753, emigrated to North Carolina on the Bachelor of Leith 1774, settled in Anson County, North Carolina, before 1820, pro 4.1824. (NCSA.2.13)

SMITH, HECTOR, wife Mary Campbell, emigrated from Argyll to North Carolina 1803, settled in Moore County, North Carolina. (NCSA.2.47)

SMITH, JOHN PATRICK, born in Argyll 1838, son of Reverend Colin Smith and Ann Campbell, died in Australia 1905. (F.4.10)

SMITH, PATRICK DUGALD, born in Argyll 1851, son of Reverend Colin Smith and Ann Campbell, died in Australia (?) (F.4.10)

SMYLIE, JAMES, wife Jane Watson, in Upper Barr, Killean and Kilkenzie
    parish, Kintyre, emigrated to North Carolina 1776, settled in
    Scotland County, North Carolina, later in Amite County, Mississippi,
    1810. (NCSA.2.26)
STEWART, ANN, daughter of Daniel Stewart, shipmaster in Inverness,
    married Hugh Ross, shopkeeper in Savanna, son John, pro 27.4.1775
    Chatham County, Georgia
STEWART, JAMES, born in Appin 1775, married Margaret McEachin, settled
    in North Carolina, died 29.12.1821, buried Stewartville Cemetery,
    Laurinburg, North Carolina. (NCSA.2.82)
STEWART, MURDOCH, born in Contin, Ross-shire, 1809, educated at
    Marischal College, Aberdeen, 1834, minister in Cape Breton 1843-,
    died in Pictou, Nova Scotia, 30.7.1884. (F.7.608)
STEWART, ROBERT, born in Rothesay 22.6.1713, son of Reverend Dugald
    Stewart and Janet Bannatyne, surgeon on the Isle of Providence.
    (F.4.41)
STUART, PATRICK, soldier from the Highlands, married Lijsbeth Davids
    from Dordt, in Dordrecht 30.1.1647. (Dordrecht Marriage Register)
SUTHERLAND, ALEXANDER, son of Donald Sutherland in Kelfederbeg, (1786-
    1841), settled in Ontario. (Sciberscross, Strathbrora, g/s)
SUTHERLAND, CATHERINE, daughter of Donald Sutherland in Kelfederbeg,
    (1786-1841), settled in Ontario. (Sciberscoss g/s)
SUTHERLAND, CHRISTINE, daughter of John Sutherland (1790-1875) and
    Christine Mann (1820-1868), settled in Embro, Canada.
    (Dornoch g/s)
SUTHERLAND, DONALD, son of Donald Sutherland in Kelfederbeg, (1786-
    1841), settled in Ontario. (Sciberscross g/s)
SUTHERLAND, DONALD, son of John Sutherland (1790-1875) and Christine
    Mann (1820-1868), died in Melbourne, Australia. (Dornoch g/s)
SUTHERLAND, JOHN, son of Elizabeth Sutherland (1792-1821), settled in
    New South Wales. (Clyne Kirkton g/s)
SUTHERLAND, JOHN, born 1834, son of John Sutherland and Margaret
    McPherson, died in Kinloch, Ontario, 6.5.1914. (Navidale g/s)
SUTHERLAND, ROBERT, born in Reay 1817, son of John Sutherland and
    Margaret McLeod, educated at Marischal College, Aberdeen, 1838,
    minister in Australia 1854-1876, died in Reay 31.8.1880. (F.7.599)
SUTHERLAND, ROBERT, son of John Sutherland (1790-1875) and Christine
    Mann (1820-1868), settled in Melbourne, Australia. (Dornoch g/s)
SUTHERLAND, WILLIAM, son of Donald Sutherland (1764-1858) and Rose
    Gordon (1769-1849), settled in Australia. (Kildonan g/s)

TAYLOR, DANIEL, born 1721, "lately from the Highlands of Scotland", runaway indentured servant of John O'Brian, Eastchester, Westchester County, New York, 1739. (New York Gazette 29.10.1739)

TOLMIE, ALLAN, born 4.1842, son of John Tolmie, tacksman of Uiginish, and Margaret Hope MacAskill, died in New Zealand 10.1917. (Dunvegan g/s)

TOLMIE, DONALD ALLAN, born 5.1828, son of John Tolmie, tacksman of Uiginish, and Margaret Hope MacAskill, died in New Zealand 2.1900. (Dunvegan g/s)

TOLMIE, MALCOLM, born 9.1836, son of John Tolmie, tacksman of Uiginish, and Margaret Hope MacAskill, died in Australia 1904. (Dunvegan g/s)

TOLMIE, NORMAND, born in Skye, merchant skipper and ship's chandler in New York 1756-1776, Loyalist, died in New York 1788. (ANY.I.70)

TOLMIE, WILLIAM ALEXANDER, born 3.1833, son of John Tolmie, tacksman of Uiginish, and Margaret Hope MacAskill, died in New Zealand 8.1875. (Dunvegan g/s)

TULLOCH, JAMES, born 1836, son of Reverend George Tulloch and Mary McIntosh Clark, assistant surgeon of the Black Watch, died at Murree, Punjab, 16.7.1867. (Scourie g/s)

URQUHART, GORDON, born in Rosskeen 23.2.1788, son of Reverend Thomas Urquhart and Johanna Clunes, Lieutenant of the 96th Regiment, died in St Croix 5.9.1808. (F.7.68)

URQUHART, JAMES, born in Rosskeen 18.8.1794, son of Reverend Thomas Urquhart and Johanna Clunes, settled in Grenada, died 8.4.1823. (F.7.68)

URQUHART, JOHN, son of Reverend John Urquhart, emigrated from Liverpool to New York on the William 1815, merchant in New York, master of the Mobile packet ship Extio 1832. (ANY.II.42)

URQUHART, WILLIAM, emigrated to America 1773, settled on the Kingsborough Patent, New York, soldier of the Royal Regiment of New York 1776-1783, settled at River aux Raison, Charlottenburg, Ontario, (DFpp)

WALKER, THOMAS, born 1852, son of John Walker and Mary Williamson, died in Jackson, USA, 24.5.1893. (Clyne g/s)

WATSON, JOHN, born in Dalranick, Invernessshire, 1738, labourer, deserted from the 55th Regiment of Foot in America 1759. (New York Mercury 12.3.1759)

WILLIAMSON, JAMES, born in Caithness 1816, settled in Greenvale, Australia, died in London 10.8.1854. (Dornoch g/s)

WOOD, JOSEPH, born in Rosemarkie 29.7.1770, son of Reverend John Wood and Sophia Irvine, emigrated to Jamaica, died 21.2.1811. (F.7.23)

www.ingramcontent.com/pod-product-compliance
Lightning Source LLC
Chambersburg PA
CBHW050509270326
41927CB00009B/1967